The Old Testament

Amy-Jill Levine, Ph.D.

THE
GREAT
COURSES

PUBLISHED BY:

THE GREAT COURSES
Corporate Headquarters
4840 Westfields Boulevard, Suite 500
Chantilly, Virginia 20151-2299
Phone: 1-800-832-2412
Fax: 703-378-3819
www.thegreatcourses.com

Amy-Jill Levine, Ph.D.

E. Rhodes and Leona B. Carpenter Professor
Vanderbilt University Divinity School/
Graduate Department of Religion

Professor Amy-Jill Levine earned her B.A. with high honors in English and Religion at Smith College, where she graduated *magna cum laude* and was a member of Phi Beta Kappa. Her M.A. and Ph.D. in Religion are from Duke University, where she was a Gurney Harris Kearns Fellow and held the W. D. Davies Instructorship in Biblical Studies. Before moving to Vanderbilt, she was Sara Lawrence Lightfoot Associate Professor and chair of the Department of Religion at Swarthmore College.

Professor Levine's numerous books, articles, and essays address such topics as Second-Temple Judaism, Christian origins, and biblical women's roles and representations; she has written commentaries on Ruth, Esther, and Daniel, as well as on the Gospels of Matthew and Mark. She is currently completing a manuscript for Harvard University Press on Jewish narratives from the Hellenistic period and a major commentary on the Book of Esther for Walter de Gruyter Press (Berlin). Professor Levine has served on the editorial boards of the *Journal of Biblical Literature* and the *Catholic Biblical Quarterly*, among other publications, and has held office in the Society of Biblical Literature and the Association for Jewish Studies. Among her awards are grants from the Mellon Foundation, the National Endowment for the Humanities, and the American Council of Learned Societies.

A widely sought speaker, Levine has given lectures and workshops throughout the United States and Canada for universities, biblical associations, synagogues, temples, churches, and interfaith and civic groups, as well as two series of lectures at Chautauqua in the Hall of Philosophy.

As a graduate student at Duke, Levine was initially prevented from teaching New Testament in the Divinity School by an administrator who did not think it appropriate that a Jew would teach this material. "You can teach Old Testament," he told her. "I don't do Old Testament," she said; "You do now," was his response. Thus began her ever-growing fascination with the subject of these lectures. Within a semester, the administrator was no longer at Duke and Levine's teaching opportunities broadened, but she chose to continue in the Old Testament classroom while adding courses in the New Testament. Completing coursework in both Old Testament/*Tanakh* and Christian origins, Levine has been studying and teaching both topics ever since.

Levine and her husband, Jay Geller, Ph.D. (who also teaches religion at Vanderbilt), live with their children, Sarah Elizabeth and Alexander David, in Nashville, Tennessee. ■

Table of Contents

Table of Contents

Table of Contents

SUPPLEMENTAL MATERIAL

The Old Testament

Scope:

The Bible has been labeled, correctly, as the foundation document of Western thought. It is read in synagogues, temples, and churches; it is cited on the floor of the Senate and from the bench in the courtroom. Contemporary politics is inextricably intertwined with it, from conflict in the Middle East to the claim by many in the United States that a return to "biblical values" is warranted. The Bible influenced the Pilgrims to leave England in the 17th century; it inspired the founders of the new republic in the eighteenth; it roused both slave and abolitionist to seek a new Moses and sponsor a new Exodus in the nineteenth and the Jews to establish a homeland in the twentieth. Missionaries, with Bible in hand, journeyed to Asia, Africa, and South America, and among the indigenous populations they met, the Bible galvanized attempts to throw off the yoke of colonialism. Its influence permeates Western literature, from medieval plays to modern novels, art, music, theatre, film and dance; its prophetic calls for social justice challenge all readers to reevaluate their own behavior even as its Wisdom literature challenges our views of God. Replete with genres ranging from myth and saga to law and proverb, containing dry political history and erotic love poetry, informed by a world view much different than our own, these texts are a compendium of a people's sacred story. And that story is the foundation document of Judaism and the first part of the canon of the church.

These twenty-four lectures offer an introduction to the history, literature, and religion of ancient Israel and early Judaism as it is presented in the collection of texts called the Old Testament, the Hebrew Bible, and the *Tanakh*. Not all books will, or even could, be covered; the content of certain books, such as Genesis, could easily fill twenty-four lectures alone, as could the stories of certain figures, such as the Patriarchs and Matriarchs, Moses, and David. Attention is given not only to the content of the biblical books but also to the debates over their meaning and the critical methods through which they have been interpreted. Often, a book will be examined by means of an analysis of a representative text or figure in it.

The lectures presuppose only a very general familiarity with the Bible's major figures and themes (e.g., Adam and Eve, Moses, the Ten Commandments, David and Bathsheba); biblical literacy, as sociologists have noted, is on the wane in the West. Although students do not need to follow the lectures with an open Bible, reading the texts listed at the top of each of the outlines will enhance appreciation for the material.

Oriented toward historical context and literary import, the lectures do not avoid raising issues of religious concern. The goal of an academic course in biblical studies should not be to undermine religious faith. Rather, it should provide members of faith communities with richer insights into the literature that forms their bedrock. Even were one to argue that the text is divinely inspired or dictated by God, one might still want to know as much as possible about the particulars: Why these words? Why this order? Why this social context? Why this translation? ∎

N.B. Many scriptural quotations in the lectures are translated by Dr. Levine directly from the Hebrew and thus may vary slightly with the text of standard printed editions in English. In other cases she draws from the New Revised Standard Version (NRSV), the King James Version (KJV) and the New English Bible (NEB).

In the Beginning
(Genesis 1)
Lecture 1

By the very fact we've got two different definitions and two different communities of faith, already we can see that there are a variety of matters that we can express, controversial issues, method of approach.

This opening lecture introduces not only the content of the Old Testament/*Tanakh* but also a number of issues—historical, theological, and aesthetic—involved in its interpretation. Following a brief description of biblical materials and the means by which they may be appreciated, we turn to several critical tools that are useful for gaining a deeper appreciation of Scripture and some of the technical terms used in its academic study. The general discussion concludes by noting a few biblical contributions to Western culture. At last entering the text, we begin "in the beginning," with the first chapter of Genesis, examining test cases for the diversity of interpretive approaches.

The biblical story spans time from creation (Gen. 1) to Judaism's encounter with Hellenism in the wake of Alexander the Great (Daniel), and for each setting, it provides a variety of literatures. Its genres include cosmological myths and stories of origin (Gen. 1–11), sagas of culture heroes (Gen. 12–50, Joshua, Judges), law codes (Leviticus, Deuteronomy), prophetic oracles (Amos, Isaiah), court tales (Esther, Dan. 1–6), and apocalyptic visions (Zech. 9–14, Dan. 7–12). Among its authors are storytellers, bureaucrats, prophets, priests, scribes, and visionaries; and it's subjects address such diverse questions as: Who are we? What is our history? What are our standards of morality? How do we relate to those outside our community? How, and whom, shall we worship?

This diversity of genres, authors, audiences, and issues requires a complex approach for achieving a well-rounded cognizance. Greater understanding of the corpus requires recognition that it is an anthology, with texts written in different times and locations to meet different concerns. A deeper familiarity comes with knowledge of the ancient Near East and the understanding that what was normative then—such as animal sacrifice and a geocentric universe—is normative no longer. Appreciation of the biblical story is enhanced by a familiarity with how individual materials fit together, chapter by chapter, book by book. Because the Bible is a foundation document not only for Judaism and Christianity but also for much contemporary culture, we do not come to it untouched. Knowledge of materials adapted by communities of faith, children's books and movies, artists and politicians facilitates consideration of how such adaptations affect our own interpretations. Study provides an opportunity to test not only our assumptions but also our biblically based values. The wider the number of critical tools we use and the consequent range of questions we pose, the more complete our appreciation will be.

Religious considerations inevitably enter biblical discussions. An academic approach to Scripture should be sensitive to religious commitments but neither presuppose them, nor proselytize for them. It should enhance rather than threaten faith; any consideration of the text as divinely inspired should include appreciation for the times, places, and peoples wherein and to whom the inspiration occurred. The academic approach should give believers, agnostics, atheists, and those whose religions fall outside the biblical purview all a deeper understanding of the text.

Among the methods used in the academic study of the Bible, the following have had a substantial impact. Historical-critical approaches seek to situate biblical material in its original context and test the accuracy of its presentation. Archaeology has been used to prove, disprove, and understand biblical content and philological investigation of the language of the text—primarily Hebrew, with some in the cognate, Aramaic—makes translation more precise. There can also be a literary-critical approach, revealing textual artistry and complexity. Recognition of literary conventions ("type scenes"); tracing of themes throughout several narratives; and attention to irony, puns, and multiple interpretations of the same passage increase appreciation of the narrative. Even those who believe that a text recounts a historical event or that "history" is the only approach worth pursing might still consider the

In the Beginning
(Genesis 1)
Lecture 1—Transcript

Welcome to this lecture and to the next 23, which will address what Christians call the Old Testament and what Jews call the *Tanakh*, which I'll explain in a minute. But by the very fact we've got two different definitions and two different communities of faith, already we can see that there are a variety of matters that we can express, controversial issues, method of approach. This is a difficult subject area, a complex subject area. So how do we enter?

Let's begin with just a general description of the contents of the text, the centuries it covers, the genres it represents, and then a word or two on the methods that biblical scholars in both church and synagogue, on the one hand, and the academy/secular institutions on the other, bring to bear on this material to try to figure out both what it meant in its original context and what it means according to contemporary forms of interpretation.

Once this basic information gets out on the table, then we can start where the Bible starts, "in the beginning" as it were, and use the first chapter of the first book, Genesis, as a test case to figure out what questions we might bring to this material, how to ask those questions, and what methods might help us unpack what those biblical authors were trying to convey.

So let's begin in terms of contents. There is a lot of stuff here. The biblical material spans the Creation of the World in Genesis, Chapter 1, up to what happens to the Jewish community in the wake of Alexander the Great. In other words, we're looking at everything from creation on down—a spectacular and staggering amount of material.

Now, although the dating the creation of the world is something that occupies, say, evolutionists and creationists and people interested in what to put in public school textbooks, it's not something that the Bible itself is concerned about. The initial chapters of Genesis are not concerned with history per se, they are not setting out there to say: This is how evolution occurred, this is a particular date on which this happened. Rather, the earliest materials are a myth. In terms of the dating, when were they first written down, some of this material may stem from the early Bronze Age or the middle Bronze Age, some time around 2000 to 1800 B.C. or B.C.E., and we'll come back to those dates in a minute.

In terms of actual written materials, perhaps the first transcription is, when that oral material was actually transcribed into writing, perhaps around, oh, the Iron Age, the year 1000, maybe 900 or so. Some biblical scholars will put this transcription at the Court of King David, about the year 900. Other biblical scholars, and here I count myself among them, are not quite sure whether King David actually existed or not. He may be more like King Arthur, a figure of myth and saga, rather than someone whose historicity can actually be located. I would be more inclined to put the writing of this material, the earliest material, some time maybe around 750 or so, when we can actually trace out an Israelite monarchy. And as we go through these lectures, I'll let you know at what time period we are, who the kings are, what is happening in terms of the culture, and where in the ancient Near East we can match up what the Bible says and what other texts and what archaeological evidence show us.

For each period, this collection, as you can already tell, offers a span of literary considerations, which brings us to the question of genre. Among the genres we will encounter, at the beginning are cosmological myths, which is just a fancy way of saying "myths of origin:" How did the world get started? Why are we here? Who is the God who created the world? And what are we supposed to be doing with our lives? That's the material in what's called the "primeval history" or Genesis, Chapters 1 through 11. Most people are familiar in general with this information. The stories of Adam and Eve, Cain and Abel, Noah's Ark and the universal flood, the Tower of Babel. Again, all mythological materials.

Not only does this mythological information help us understand what ancient Israel thought of itself, this material provides remarkable cross cultural comparison. The myths in the histories of Israel are not written in a vacuum, they're written in dialogue, sometimes in competition with other literatures in the ancient Near East, Babylonian stories, Syrian stories, Egyptian stories, and, later on in the text, Greek stories. So we will do a fair amount of cross-cultural comparison to watch how Israel defines itself in relation to its neighbors.

Once we complete the mythological materials, we'll move into stories of some of the culture heroes that we find in Genesis. People such as Abraham, and in Exodus, for example, Moses, and we'll move up into the period of the Judges, where we find heroes such as Samson.

But we now have more historical problems. With myth, we can make tentative guesses on when those myths were written. But when we get up to more historical figures like Abraham or Joshua or Moses or Samson, we then have to ask more specific historical questions. Are these real people? Does the Bible record what actually happened? Did the walls really fall down when Joshua blew the trumpets at Jericho? Did Moses really stand up on a mountain and get a law of some sort? Were there really Israelites enslaved in Egypt? And we have to do history very cautiously here because the vast majority of this early material has no ancient Near Eastern literary or archaeological support. So who then is telling these stories and to what effect? Are they real stories? Are they legends? Are they a combination? And why would ancient Israel tell these particular stories?

When we think about some of these characters, Samson is frankly stupid. Why would they tell a story about a hero who is plain dumb? Abraham is a trickster, and as we'll see in the next couple of lectures he does things like pass his wife off as his sister and place her in harems of foreign kings, which is frankly not nice. But he's the father of this people, the father of the Hebrews. Why tell these stories about him?

The genres continue past these culture heroes into laws. In the Books of Exodus, Leviticus, Numbers, and Deuteronomy, which, together with the Book of Genesis, comprise the Pentateuch (pentateuch is simply a Greek term for five, *penta*, and *teuchos* means scrolls), the five scrolls, sometimes call the Book of Moses. The Pentateuch is replete with legal material.

We might think of the Ten Commandments, those are fairly familiar to most people, these days touchstones for politicians. But beyond questions like: honor your father and mother, which I think is a great idea, and don't commit adultery and don't murder, the Bible is replete with other law codes, which require much more investigation. Dietary regulations. Laws about how to plant your crops. Tort law. Laws about how to run a cult. Why are they there? What effect did they have?

And how do those laws, in general, show how ancient Israel considered itself to be a community in covenant? And covenant is simply a legal contract between itself and God. How are these laws the terms of that contract? The genres continue.

We then move up into the prophetic literature. Normally today when we think about prophets, we think about people who predict the future—people like Nostradamus or Edgar Casey or Jean Dixon, or whoever writes those horoscope columns in the newspaper. But the biblical prophets are not predictors of the far-flung future. To the contrary, they are actually astute political and social critics who tell the people, and often the king or the head of the cult, the priests, if you continue to behave in the way that you are behaving, bad things will happen. That's not necessarily divine intuition. One can normally tell if society continues on a certain road disaster will happen.

The prophets are interested in social justice, and that's much of what they're known for. But the prophets are also interested in political policy. They advise kings when to make foreign alliances and when to remain isolationists. They are interested in the cult—how to run the cult; how to offer sacrifices; how personal interior thought and repentance relates to exterior action. Is it sufficient simply to offer up a bull as a sacrifice without being in a right relationship with your neighbor?

So prophets are much more than predictors, and more than social critics, and more than political analysts. They're fantastic poets who use arresting images and exquisite phrasing in order to get their message across. Because if one is a prophet, one cannot simply get up on a soapbox, which they didn't have back then, but bear with me on that.

You just can't get up on a soapbox and say, "Behave yourselves," because nobody is going to listen. So you have to do it in a way that's going to gain the attention of the people who are supposed to be listening to you. And you have to do it in such a way that people will remember what you said and write down what you said. Part of the extraordinary aspect of ancient Israel is they wrote down material that criticizes, heavily criticizes what they actually did. This is a community that is very interested in making itself better by recognizing what it did that was wrong to begin with.

The genres continue past the prophets. Whereas the prophets talk about how to conduct business in say the cult or in politics, we also have a genre known as wisdom literature, which explains how to conduct business in the market place or among the upper classes. This is literature like Proverbs, which tells you how to behave. But it's also literature that raises those profound questions that philosophers and theologians have yet to resolve. We have, for example, the Book of Job, which asks, in effect: If God is a righteous God, why is Job suffering? Why do the wicked prosper? Why do the good endure pain and death and exile?

And whether Jonah, excuse me, whether Job actually resolves that problem or not is something scholars continue to debate. I think, in fact, Job provides an answer, but it may not be the answer most people think is there. We'll have to wait.

The later books of the canon move to novella, short stories like Ruth and Jonah, which explore in an extremely entertaining way how Israel is to relate to its neighbors. Ruth, the hero of her book, is Moabite, one of the traditional enemies of Israel, and yet Ruth becomes the great-grandmother of the famous King David.

Jonah, who is probably the only prophet whose audience actually listened to him, which is interesting, is commissioned to go speak to the people of Nineveh in Assyria, Israel's major enemy. Jonah doesn't want to go. He doesn't want the Assyrians to listen to him. But what is this text telling us about Assyrian repentance?

And then we move on, we find court tales, stories of Jews, queens, courtiers, who find themselves in royal courts outside of Israel in the diaspora, which simply means the dispersion. Court tales like the Book of Esther, the great

Jewish queen who manages to save her people from certain genocide. Or the story of Daniel who finds himself in both Babylonian and Persian courts and has to fight to retain his identity, given pressures on him to assimilate, to eat food which is not permitted according to his religious laws, to pray in a manner that is not permitted according to his religious ideals.

So what these court tales do is provide instruction to Jews on how to live in the diaspora, how to live when Greek culture comes in, how to live when cultural pressures come upon them. How do you retain your identity? What do you give in to? What makes you *you*? Which is a problem people in covenant communities have today. For Jews and Christians who want to obey the law, how much do we give in to secular society? And how much do we attempt to retain our independent unique identity? The problems that the Bible raises are problems that will always continue.

We end with apocalyptic visions, the end of the Book of Daniel. Questions like: When does righteousness ever show up? Who was the Messiah, and when can we tell that he's arrived? What happens at the end of time? Is there a resurrection of the dead? Does God make everything good again, and, if so, how and when? And throughout, we encounter storytellers and lawmakers and bureaucrats and priests and prophets and scribes and visionaries, and they all wrote for different audiences in different times using different literary genres. They don't always agree with each other, and we may not agree with them either. That's part of the glory of this text.

But in terms of appreciating it, not only must we appreciate the diversity of all this material, we also have to have a multi-faceted approach. I've always thought that biblical studies or religion, in general, is the perfect undergraduate major, because it requires knowledge, a little bit at least, of everything else one learns, at least in the humanities and social sciences. Literary criticism, anthropology, economics, political science, history, art, anthropology, mythology, cross-cultural studies, it's all there.

For example, deeper evaluation of the biblical materials requires the recognition that what was normative in antiquity—slavery, animal sacrifice, wandering from place to place, a lack of urban environments to begin with, a God who talks to people on a day-to-day basis—what was normative then is not normative now. So one thing we need to do in biblical studies is try to make all that strange material familiar, to try to develop a sympathy for these people who live in a world much different than ours.

But at the same time, there is a good much of this material which is extremely familiar to most people, if not through religious backgrounds, then at least through what they've gained through art, history, or watching movies. Therefore, we also need to make some of that familiar stuff a little bit more strange. What are some of those modern connections? Oh, Steinbeck's *East of Eden*, Tony Morrison's *Song of Solomon*, Faulkner's *Absalom, Absalom*. Did they get it right? And how much do we read into the biblical text what we've heard in our culture? Right?

If you've seen some of those Bible movies, the sword and sandals, Gregory Peck, for example, as King David—the David and Bathsheba movies are actually quite different than what the Bible has to say. So we need to look at the Bible as if it is fresh to us, as if we can bracket all those cultural concerns. And in terms of some of these concerns, we also have religious history, because Jews and Christians, and even Muslims, have been interpreting this material for well over 2,000 years. So we also need to consider, in a sensitive way, how religious confession, religious history impacts this material.

A brief word then on religion and biblical studies. Biblical studies ought not to provide a negative to one's religious faith. If one comes to this material from a faith perspective, ideally the academic study of the Bible should enhance one's faith rather than destroy it. For example, if one wants to believe that the Bible is divinely inspired, then I think it behooves that person to know as much as possible about when it was written, where it was written, and to whom it was written. In other words, if God decided to inspire this text, it makes a difference that it was inspired to ancient Israelites rather than people in, say, contemporary Washington, DC, or Tennessee.

But sometimes the biblical material will provide information which seems counter to at least more traditional views of faith. Because sometimes when we look at this material, particularly in light of ancient Near Eastern evidence, we find that the Bible is not necessarily recording history. Archaeology comes in here, as well. The Promised Land, as it's been called, has yielded numerous archaeological sites. But it turns out that the promise of archaeology often yields material that is controversial. It is doubtful that Jerusalem was David's major capital. Because at the time David ostensibly ruled Jerusalem, so archaeologists tells us, it's just a small little hovel, it's not a major city. It's doubtful that Joshua brought down the walls of Jericho, because at the time Joshua ostensibly got there, Jericho was already a ruined city. So, how then does archaeology help us? And why, if archaeology tells us as best as it can that the stories the Bible records are not always history as it happened, how then do we understand what the biblical writer is doing? Is the biblical writer conveying something other than history?

The ever-growing discoveries of history from the ancient Near East, not only through archaeology, but also through literature, also help us. We have philological investigation to help us interpret the words of the Bible better. The Old Testament is written in Hebrew, with a couple of books and chapters in Aramaic. But the more we know about ancient Near Eastern Hebrew and Aramaic, the better translators we can be.

Finally, there's literary concerns—because as I noted, the Bible is also a work of literature. There is narrative art here and not just with the prophets. We might think of modern works of history or biography. There are good biographies, and there are bad biographies, and they might all have the same amount of information. Good biographies are well written. They carry a plot line. They drag us along so that inexorably we keep reading. And the same thing with good histories.

There were conventions here. And it's the same thing with the Bible. We need to recognize its aesthetic value. The Bible, for example, uses literary conventions all the time. They're called type scenes. They're replays of the same scenes.

Literary conventions are today easy to note. Even my children, who are 14 and 10, know what a convention is, because they know what a situation comedy is, and they know what cartoons are supposed to do, and they actually know what westerns are. The ancient Near East and the biblical writers have conventions, as well. Our problem is we don't live them, obviously. We need to determine what those conventions are to see how a lot of the biblical material would have been extremely familiar to its ancient audiences. It is as if we are eavesdropping on ancient material, and that's part of the fun.

Now, one final comment before we get into the text. The biblical text has been used by different communities of faith for different reasons. As I mentioned in my opening remarks, there were different names for this text. And, in fact, the books fall into different orders. There is the Old Testament, which is a Christian designation. The Old Testament begins with Genesis, and then, if you're Protestant, it ends with the Prophets.

The last book in the Old Testament is the prophet Malachi, who predicts the coming of the prophet, Elijah. Elijah, you may remember, is the prophet who never actually dies, but goes up in a heavenly chariot. This is Swing Low, Sweet Chariot. Well, Elijah is actually the one who got into it and went up to heaven. The idea is he will come back before the great day of the Lord, as the prophet Malachi puts it, to bring about the Kingdom of God. Which is lovely, if you happen to be a Christian, because then you can go in the Protestant canon directly from Malachi's prediction of the return of Elijah and the coming of the Kingdom, right to the Gospels, where, at the beginning of the Gospels, John the Baptist is Elijah come back and Jesus announces the Kingdom.

Now, if you're part of the Catholic or Orthodox community, you still have an Old Testament, but the ending is not quite with Malachi. The Eastern Orthodox and Catholic canons also include a second collection of books called either the Old Testament Apocrypha or Deuterocanonical writings. These are books like the Wisdom of Jesus ben Sirach or the Book of Judith. Most of this material is interspersed among the other books in the Old Testament canon. But at the end of the Orthodox and Catholic canon we have additional histories; for example, First and Second Maccabees. The irony here is First and Second Maccabees provide us the story of Hanukkah celebrated in Judaism, but the books are not part of Judaism's canon.

Judaism's canon is called the *Tanakh*, which is simply an acronym, TNK: Torah, the first five books, the Pentateuch; the Prophets in Hebrew, *Nevi'im*, and the Prophets in the Hebrew Bible include both some historical works, such as Joshua, Samuel, and Kings, as well as the Prophets we normally think of, Isaiah, Jeremiah, the twelve minor prophets like Hosea and Amos. And then the book ends with the K, the *Ketuvim*, the writings—books like Esther and Jonah. The last book in the *Tanakh* is Second Chronicles, and it ends with the edict of King Cyrus of Persia in the fifth century telling the people in exile and Babylon, "God has commissioned me, Cyrus, to send you home and to build you a temple back in Jerusalem. Let anyone who is able go up, make *aliyah*," as they say in Hebrew, go back home.

So the Christian Old Testament ends with the promise of the new, and the Jewish *Tanakh* ends with a call: go back home, start again, get it right this time. Different text.

And, of course, this material can be referred to not only as the Old Testament or the *Tanakh*, it can also be called the Bible or even the Hebrew Scriptures, and I'm going to use all of them.

When we look at this material, we find different chapters and verses. Don't let those throw you. The chapters and verses were put in in the Middle Ages in order to make biblical research easier. But it is often the case that chapters and even verse divisions split a text where perhaps the original author and certainly the literary critic does not think that text should be split.

There is a perfect example of this in the first Book of Genesis. The original creation story ends not at the end of Chapter 1, but in Chapter 2, verse 4a. We might look at that a little bit later.

So here we are, let's move into the text, because it's more fun when we can actually get in there. Let's start. Genesis 1:1 starts, "In the beginning," or perhaps better translated, "when in the beginning." That's closer to what the Hebrew says. If we do a little bit of cross-cultural comparison, we find that Genesis, Chapter 1, is likely a response to the Babylonian creation myth, which is called the *Enumah Elish*. And the *Enumah Elish* begins, "when on high...." So we have "when in the beginning" versus "when on high...."

Moreover, the Hebrew cosmogony, the Hebrew story of origins, ends with God resting on the seventh day. God rested on the seventh day from all his work, hallowed the seventh day. And, therefore, we have a day of rest. From "in the beginning" to "the seventh day," the biblical cosmogony talks about time and makes time sacred. The *Enumah Elish* begins "when on high." There is a specific place. And it ends with the founding of the Babylonian capital—space. What does this mean?

Genesis, Chapter 1, was probably written by Jews in exile in Babylon. The *Enumah Elish* is the myth of the conquering kingdom. So what the authors of Genesis 1 are trying to do is say, wait a minute, we have our own God, our own story, and we will privilege time rather than space, because that's actually what makes sense when you're in exile, when you're apart from your temple, apart from your capital, and apart from your land. At least you can keep the Sabbath. You can mark the days and recognize that each one is good. Genesis, Chapter 1, is more than simply a story of origins, it's a story that shows how people define themselves amid an alien culture.

Moving on in Genesis, it even gets better. Let's go back to the *Enumah Elish* for a minute. In the *Enumah Elish*, we encounter two gods of water— one a male god whose name is Apsu, the god of fresh water, and the more important god, Tiamat, it's actually a goddess, is the goddess of salt water, and they represent primeval chaos. We have that same primeval chaos in Genesis, Chapter 1, where the spirit of God hovers over the face of the deep. And the word for deep in Hebrew was *tehom*, which sounds awfully like Tiamat, except in the *Enumah Elish*, the deep, the watery chaos, they are gods. But in the Bible these are not gods, there's only one, and chaos is simply chaos. As the Bible puts it, *tohu wavohu*, "without form and void."

Well, it turns out in the *Enumah Elish*, the Babylonian creation epic, that there's a younger generation of gods, and they decide to go to war with their parents. Nothing much changes in history. The younger gods are led by the god called Marduk, and Marduk goes to war particularly against Tiamat. She is the most recalcitrant. Eventually, he gets the aid of seven gods of wind, and he basically blows Tiamat up. She becomes this huge wind-filled bag, at which point he kills her and splits her body open and, with the top part of her body, makes a vault, this is the Bible's firmament, and with the bottom part of her body, makes the earth.

Now what do we have in Genesis? Genesis continues: The spirit of God hovered over the face of the deep. But the word "spirit," *ruakh* in Hebrew, can also mean wind. So here we have the seven wind gods in the *Enumah Elish*. And the wind of God hovering over the face of the deep. And what does God do? God decides to separate the waters above from the waters below, make organization out of chaos, and creates a vault of heaven and a vault of the earth. It's the same story. But here, there is no war between the gods. Here is one singular God, not manipulating matter, but creating by word of his mouth saying, "Let it be that." This is great.

In the *Enumah Elish*, Marduk decides to create humanity out of the blood of a dead god, and humanity is created to be slaves to Marduk and all of his buddies. In the Babylonian view, with the exception of the king, everybody worked for the gods, which basically meant, worked for the king. In the biblical tradition, God says, "Let us make man in our own image. In the image of God, he created him. In the image of God, he created them male and female." We are not created to be slaves of the gods. We are created to be in the image of God, and, indeed in the biblical text, we are given dominion over the birds, and the fish, and the creepy, crawly things, and the entire world to be fruitful and multiply and subdue it.

This is an extraordinary text, and not just because it's a comparative myth to the *Enumah Elish*. It tells us that we are creatures to be appreciated. It tells us that God in his royal court—that's why God speaks in the plural, "Let us"—it tells us that God has preplanned us. God takes counsel and creates us. It tells us that male and female are equal, both in the image of God. And it sets us forward to a world that God has said "is good." Because when God finished creating in Genesis 1, God saw that everything was good.

Unfortunately, in Genesis, Chapter 2, things start going downhill, where we get stories of Adam and Eve and that nasty snake and the fall from Eden, fratricide with Cain and Abel, world cruelty with Noah, people trying to build a tower to storm heaven with the Tower of Babel. For some people, this creates a problem. Genesis 1 is good; Genesis 2 and 3 are bad. For some, these are different stories. For some, they flow naturally, one right into the other. But we'll have to look at Lecture 2 to see how that works.

Adam and Eve
(Genesis 2:4b–3:28)
Lecture 2

The Garden of Eden is the perfect garden. You're supposed to work it; you're supposed to till it. But the ground yields its fruit. There's no struggle. There's only joy. It's work, but the best sort of work possible.

The Garden of Eden, like the rest of primeval history (Genesis 1–11) is "myth," a foundational story that undergirds cultural norms and explains communal identity. Many scholars suggest that Genesis 2–3, the "J" cosmogony (it uses the name "YHWH" [German: JHWH, the "Y"= the German "J"] for "Lord,"), was composed during Solomon's reign (c. 900 B.C.E.). Three hundred to four hundred years later, the P (Priestly) writer placed Genesis 1 before the J account, creating a new lens by which Eden may be understood. This lecture follows Gen. 2–3, selectively, episode by episode, to highlight its complexity, the effects of Genesis 1 on its interpretation, its possible ancient Near Eastern connections, and the questions that remain debated.

In the beginning: What to notice? What to ask? The first words spoken, "let there be light," mark the first day, but sun and moon ("greater" and "lesser lights") appear on the fourth. Readers unfamiliar with biblical law frequently consider the Bible as a series of "Thou shalt nots"; the first commandment is, however, a positive one: "Be fruitful ..." Genesis 1 offers one explanation for the Sabbath, the divine rest (cf. Exod. 20:8–11); Deut. 5:15 inscribes another, that is, release from Egyptian slavery, into the Decalogue.

The Priestly writers (more on them later) composed Gen. 1:1–2:4a as an introduction to the earlier story of the Garden of Eden, Adam, Eve, and the snake (Gen. 2–3). For some readers, this juxtaposition creates contradictions, and for others it does not. Whereas Gen. 1 depicts a simultaneous creation, *ex nihilo*, of "male and female," Gen. 2 presents a fashioned, sexually indeterminate being. Gen. 2:7, "Then the Lord God formed man from the dust from the ground ..." reflects a Hebrew pun: "Man" is *ha-adam*, "the adam"; "adam" derives from *adamah*—arable soil or, here, "ground." Better translations would speak of an "earthling from the dust of the earth" or a "human" from the "humus," the loamy soil. The juxtaposed Gen. 1 may be seen to ensure a view of divine power and transcendence. The "earthling" is then planted in the Garden of Eden to "till it and keep it" (2:15). Life in Eden (the name means "pleasure") is one of easy work; it is not, however, "dominion over the earth." The agricultural paradise perhaps reflects the dreams of subsistence farmers or, perhaps, the romantic view of Jerusalem's court for the countryside.

God informs the human, "Of the tree of the knowledge of good and evil you shall not eat, for in the day you eat from it you will surely die" (colloquially: "you'll drop dead" [2:17]). This verse prompts theological questions, Is God tempting the human? Does the Deity know what will happen? Has the Deity planned the "fall"? Was humanity originally mortal or immortal? The tree recollects other myths of forbidden fruits and sacred trees (e.g., Ygdrassil, Jason's tree on which the golden fleece hangs). The specific ways each culture tells its story, then, permits understanding of that culture's values.

God next observes: "It is not good that the earthling should be alone. I will make him an *ezer k'negdo*," "a helper as his partner" (NRSV) or, traditionally, "a helper fit for him" (2:18). Is this "helper" to be equal or a subordinate? The idiom "fit for" indicates something corresponding, appropriate, suitable: *ha-adam* requires someone "like" him. The Hebrew *Ezer*, help or helper, is often a predicate of the Deity. Instead of next creating woman, "out of the ground the Lord God formed every animal of the field and every bird of the air, and brought them to the human to see what it would call them." Adam names the animals but finds no "partner fit for him." What then does the woman do to help? Is she needed to challenge man to reach his potential, to encourage him, or even act for him (as, for example, Rebecca does for Jacob or Bathsheba for the dying David)? Or is the answer more utilitarian: only women can "help" men propagate? Does Genesis 1, "Be fruitful and multiply," lead us to this interpretation? This scene, compared to Gen. 1:26–27, prompted the early Medieval Jewish myth of Lilith, the first woman, who rebelled against God and Adam.

Woman's creation from man's "side" or "rib" stimulates cross-cultural and anthropological observations. Genesis may have been influenced by, or serve as a response to, the Sumerian Dilmun (paradise) myth. This myth recounts how the god Enki is cursed by the goddess Ninhursag, because he ate plants she bore painlessly. Ninhursag then creates the goddess Nin-Ti, "lady of the rib" or "lady who makes live," to heal his broken body. Adam may be seen as "giving birth" to Eve, as Dionysius is born from Zeus's "thigh" and Athena, from his head. Some anthropologists suggest that such stories show a co-optation of women's biology: Although Adam's parturition is clean and painless, women can recreate the event only in a messy, painful manner. The rib has also been read as promoting gender equality. One Midrash (rabbinic story) states that woman was not taken from man's head, lest she lord it over him, nor his feet, lest he walk all over her. She is from his side, and they are partners.

Contrary to popular belief, it is not woman who tempts man, but the snake and the tree itself that tempt woman. God had forbidden the earthling merely to eat from the tree. In her response to the snake, the woman adds: "But God said, 'Neither shall you touch it, lest you die.'" According to Phyllis Trible, this comment makes Eve both a "theologian and a translator." According to one popular conservative biblical commentary: "Sin begins with some distortion of the truth." We might also wonder who told the woman about the tree: the Deity? The man?

The conversation and what happens subsequently are often misconstrued. First, the serpent speaks accurately: "You will not die, for God knows that when you eat of it your eyes will be opened, and you will be like the gods, knowing good and evil." Second, the woman's decision is thoughtful: "When the woman saw that the tree was good for food, and that it was a delight to the eyes, and that the tree was to be desired to make one wise, she took of its fruit and she ate." And third, she does not tempt man: "She also gave some to her husband [or new "man"] and he ate."

The Temptation's numerous interpretations include the following. Socially, the temptation may be read as a warning to men against allowing their wives to speak with a stranger, the proverbial "snake in the grass." Historically,

Adam and Eve driven out of paradise.

it may indicate the dangerous power of women in the royal harem, such as those who tempted Solomon with their foreign practices (1 Kgs. 11). Some forms of gnosticism, an early common-era religious movement, suggested that the woman brings *Gnosis* ("knowledge") to a world kept ignorant by a foolish god. And from the New Testament, 1 Tim. 2:14 reads, "Adam was not deceived, but the woman was deceived and became a transgressor." That is, Adam was not seduced; his choice was one of conscious solidarity with his partner.

As a result of the transgression, the couple experiences not death, but loss of innocence or shame, and this loss is compounded by punishments ("curse" is not used). Most translations render 3:16: "I will greatly multiply your pain in childbearing; in pain you shall give birth to children." Carol Meyers translates instead: "I will greatly increase your work and your pregnancies; along with work you shall give birth to children." The term for "work" is the same used in 3:17d: "In work you shall eat of it all the days of your life." The term translated "childbearing" means "pregnancies." Women's lot is thus to work in two spheres: procreation and production. "Yet your desire shall be for your man [husband] and he shall rule over you" (3:16c). Although the "rule" (*mashal*), is not tyrannical (it is associated with "good kings," such as Solomon and Hezekiah, cf. 1 Kgs. 4:3), it does mean "have dominion over" (cf. Gen. 1:18). "Rule" may also suggest "prevail," as in "be the primary economic support." Does the myth tell women that sexual desire is "natural" even though they may die in childbirth (as does Rachel)?

The man's punishment is prefaced by a rationale that is missing from the other two: "Because you have listened to the voice of your wife ..." The phrase is recollected in the expulsion of Hagar and Ishmael (Gen. 21:12). It also responds to Adam's complaint (3:8): "*The woman whom you gave to be with me*, she gave me the fruit and I ate."

Having become like gods, knowing good and evil, man and woman must leave Eden. And so we come to Cain, the flood, Babel. Given this trajectory, the election of Abraham indicates the final attempt at universal stability. ■

Suggested Reading

Gary Anderson, Michael Stone, and Johannes Tromp (eds.), *Literature on Adam and Eve: Collected Essays*, Studies in Veteris Testamenti Pseudepigrapa.

James Barr, *The Garden of Eden and the Hope of Immortality*.

Kristen Kvam, Linda S. Schearing, and Valarie H. Ziegler, *Eve and Adam: Jewish, Christian and Muslim Readings on Genesis and Gender*.

Carol Meyers, *Discovering Eve: Ancient Israelite Women in Context*.

1. This story of Eden is never mentioned again in the Old Testament/*Tanakh* (its next canonical appearances are the Old Testament Apocrypha/ Deuterocanonical writings). How then, if at all, does the story affect interpretations of later texts (e.g., the man speaks of leaving home to cleave to his wife; do most male characters do this)?

2. How closely do later retellings (Milton's *Paradise Lost*, the film *The Bible*, popular cultural renditions) adhere to the text?

3. Is Eden a desirable place? A return to childhood? A prison?

Adam and Eve
(Genesis 2:4b–3:28)
Lecture 2—Transcript

Welcome back to the Old Testament. In our last lecture, we talked at the end about cross-cultural comparisons—how Genesis, Chapter 1, matches up very neatly with the Babylonian creation epic, the *Enumah Elish*. But one does not need to have intensive knowledge of ancient Near Eastern mythology in order to appreciate the biblical text.

My students frequently tell me that just by looking at this text carefully, they begin to see things that a quick read might quickly skim over. For example, they note that the first words spoken by God in the Bible are, "Let there be light," and then we have, "There was light." And then there was evening, and then there was morning, day one. So the first thing they notice is that the day begins at the evening rather than at the morning. So you might think of things like Christmas Eve or Kol Nidre night in Judaism, the night before Yom Kippur. That's when the holidays actually start.

They also note that the sun and moon, which typically mark off day and night, are actually not created until the fourth day. What the Bible is here doing is telling its readers the sun and moon are not gods, which was commonly believed in antiquity. They are simply heavenly bodies which God has created, but time is, in effect, not dependent upon them.

There are other very interesting things we find here. Oftentimes, people think of the Bible as a series of "Thou shall nots," don't do this, don't do that. It turns out that the first commandment of the Bible is the very, very positive "be fruitful and multiply and fill the earth and subdue it." I take it as very encouraging. Indeed, we might read Genesis, Chapter 3, where Adam and Eve are expelled from the Garden of Eden, in light of that initial commandment. How were they going to get out of Eden and fill the earth and subdue it, Eden being a paradise? Perhaps that's why that tree was planted. But we'll get there.

Genesis, Chapter 1, offers, as we mentioned in the last lecture, an explanation for the Sabbath. This is the day God rested after his work of creation. But we'll see later in Deuteronomy, Chapter 5, that there is another explanation for the Sabbath. Yes, the Sabbath could be an honor of God's rest and creation, but the Sabbath according to Deuteronomy is there because the people were slaves in Egypt, and they knew what it was like to work day after day, month after month with no rest. So for Deuteronomy, the Sabbath is a remembrance of that time of slavery in Egypt and an absolute guarantee that no one ever, not only regular citizens, but their slaves as well, will never have time for themselves, time for rest. Here is the complexity of the Bible.

Even when one just looks at Chapter 1 in Genesis, one sees the depth of biblical literature. And the literature becomes even more complex when we move to Chapter 2. Chapter 2 is another creation story, but a much different one. Instead of being everywhere with the creation of the world, we're now in a particular place, the Garden of Eden. And instead of having an abstract God called Elohim, God, who speaks from the heavens, we now have a different God called YHWH, who walks in the Garden of Eden and fashioned humankind from the mud. This a very, very different story.

In terms of dating, the common view is that Genesis, Chapter 2, is actually an earlier story than Genesis, Chapter 1. Genesis, Chapter 1, as I mentioned in the last lecture, was probably written in the sixth century, when the Jews were in exile in Babylon. Genesis, Chapter 2, is dated much earlier, perhaps 900 B.C.E., which simply means "Before the Common Era." It's a non-confessional term for B.C., before Christ. Perhaps at the time of King David or right after him, sometime 900 to 750.

This means, of course, that the writers of Genesis 1 intended to provide a commentary by which we would read Genesis, Chapter 2. This tells us one more thing about how to read the text. We can read it as a completely flowing narrative, Genesis, Chapter 1, into Chapter 2, into Chapter 3. Or we might decide just to look at Chapters 2 and 3, that self-contained story of the Garden of Eden, as a separate unit with its own literary integrity, theological concerns, and sociological background.

Well, let's begin by looking at some of the characterizations in Genesis, Chapter 2. For this I'll go episode by episode reading selectively, looking both at the text in terms of its narrative art and its linguistic background and, when it becomes helpful, also bringing up some of those ancient Near Eastern parallels we saw in the last lecture.

We begin with the creation of humanity. Already we see a difference from Genesis, Chapter 1. Genesis, Chapter 1, God creates *ex nihilo*, out of nothing, and says, "Let us create humankind," and that's what happens. Genesis, Chapter 2, it's really quite different. The first human to be created in Genesis, Chapter 1, is called "man" in most translations, but I would actually prefer "earthling." In most translations, we find Genesis, Chapter 2, verse 7, reading, "Then the Lord God formed man from the dust of the ground...." As with the term *ruakh*, which we saw in Genesis 1 can mean both spirit and wind, the word for "man", *ha-adam*, also has a different meaning. The Hebrew *ha-adam* actually is masculine form of the world *adama*, which means "ground" or, in fact, arable soil. What the English does is mask a wonderful pun. God has created Adam from the *adama*. Or an "earthling" from the "earth." Or, for those you who garden, a "human" from the "humus," that kind of loamy soil.

What this text does is tell us that human beings are intimately connected with the earth. We are part of this created world, as if we're part of that world body. Moreover, there is a theological point here, as well. The God of Genesis, Chapter 1, is transcendent, above, speaking from afar.

The God of Chapter 2, this YHWH God, called Lord—it's by the way, easy to remember that YHWH matches up with Lord, because they both have four letters, Y h w h, or in Hebrew, *yud hei vuv hei*, and Lord, Elohim, meaning God—this YHWH, this Lord, is like a potter who forms humankind from the clay and molds it. (That's actually an image, by the way, from the prophet Jeremiah.)

This is an immanent God. He's here in the world, he walks around in the Garden of Eden in the cool of the day—a much different view of God for a different community, earlier, not in exile. And here, God even has a different plan for humanity. According to Genesis, Chapter 1, God tells man and woman, fill the earth and subdue it, be fruitful and multiply. That's not what this earth creature, this earthling, gets in Genesis, Chapter 2. Instead the earthling is commanded: Go into the Garden of Eden and till it and keep it.

Some of my students think that the Garden of Eden is like the ancient version of being a couch potato—you just sit there and everything is simply handed to you. There's no work whatsoever. That's not quite true. I think of the Garden of Eden much like gardening, assuming that everything I plant actually comes up. The Garden of Eden is the perfect garden. You're supposed to work it, you're supposed to till it. But the ground yields its fruit. There's no struggle. There's only joy. It's work, but the best sort of work possible. That's what Eden is.

I think to the ancient Israelites that's really good news, because the ancient Israelites, perhaps in the year 900 or so, were often subsistence farmers trying to get that rocky hill country soil to produce something. Eden is what they wished for. Eden is their paradise.

But there may be another explanation, as well. If this material is written in the Israelite court by the Kings, perhaps the Garden of Eden is a romanticized notion of those good old agricultural days before there was urban planning, before there was a monarchy. I'm reminded here of Louis XIV and his courtiers playing shepherds on the grounds of Versailles. To be a shepherd is very difficult. Louis XIV had a romantic notion. To be a farmer in Israel is very difficult. What Genesis 2 may give us is a romantic gloss over something very, very hard.

Now in terms of injunctions and commandments, in the first chapter of Genesis, there's only that positive command, "Be fruitful and multiply." In the second chapter of Genesis, there is a negative command, and it's particularly problematic because it has no explanation. The Lord simply informs the human, you may eat from any tree in the Garden. (Humanity is here, by the way, vegetarian.) You may eat from any tree in the garden, "but of the tree of the knowledge of good and evil, you shall not eat, for the day you eat of it, you will surely die." For those of you interested in grammar, the Hebrew was an absolute construction, which really means "dying you will die" or, more colloquially, "you'll drop dead." Here is the commandment.

Next thing we find out: Why is this there? we ask. What are the theological questions? We often think of the temptation as Eve coming up to Adam and saying, "I've got a piece of fruit for you, honey." But is that tree God planted really the first temptation? Is it like my buying a box of chocolate chip cookies, setting them out on the kitchen table, and telling my kids, "Here is a box of chocolate chip cookies set in the middle of the table. If you touch it, dying you will die." I can bet the minute my back is turned those cookies are gone. Is that what God is doing?

Or does God already know what will happen? Is the succumbing of humanity to the temptation preplanned? Does God know everything? Or has the Bible told us that yet? We might even wonder whether humanity was created originally mortal or immortal; because we also discovered that not only is there a tree of knowledge of good and evil in the center of the garden, there is also a tree of immortality. Why plant a tree of immortality if people are immortal to begin with? I've always wondered about that.

And as one question inevitably leads to another, so we have cross-cultural comparisons, as well, because there are other myths of sacred trees and sacred plants, and forbidden trees and forbidden plants. There's the tree on which hung the Golden Fleece, which, by the way, was guarded by a snake. There's the tree in Norse mythology called the "Ygdrassil," which is the center of the world.

Why trees? Is it because the ancient world had a sense that agriculture is their anchor? The trees gave fruit somehow miraculously. That somehow the tree was the connection between the earth, where the roots were, and the heavens, where the branches grew. It's a cross-cultural symbol. And the specific ways each culture uses that symbol permits understanding of that culture's values.

Well, after God gives the injunction against eating from the tree of knowledge, God next observes, "It is not good that the earthling shall be alone. I will make him an *ezer k'negdo*," the Hebrew says, or in English, "a helper as his partner," sometimes translated, "a helper fit for him." And of course, new questions abound.

Among these we note that helper is usually looked at as a subordinate role. I think of the term "sidekick," which is actually a good word when you think of Eve coming out of Adam's side. But that's not actually what helper means in the Bible. In fact, the term is often predicated of God—God is our helper. This is not necessarily a subordinate term. What this human being needs is a helper like him, someone who can match him.

But the question remains, how? Does he need a helper to provide some sort of emotional support or challenge, in the same way that women challenge men to live up to their potential in the stories of Genesis and Kings? For example, as we'll see later on, Rebecca urges her husband Isaac to do what he needs to do. She helps her son, Jacob, get the birthright and the blessing. Bathsheba, David's wife, actually engineers to get her son, Solomon, on the throne. Does humankind, does this earthling need a woman to prod him a little bit? Or perhaps is this helper needed in order to provide some sort of emotional companionship? Dogs are fine, but women are really better. Or perhaps, if you ask, "What does Eve do to help?", there is only one thing that she can do that the rest of the animals can't, and that is to procreate. Does he need a helper like him because she can make the babies? I think that might actually be the case.

And here's another one of those biblical surprises. This fascinates me. After God says, "It is not good that this earthling shall be alone. I shall make a helper fit for him," we would normally think at that point, God, as you know the story, puts Adam to sleep and takes his rib. But that's not what happened. "I will make a helper fit for him," says God, and then God creates all the animals and parades the animals in front of Adam to see what he will name them. And after all the animals go by, the dog and the sheep and the chicken and the pig, no helper was found fit for Adam. Dogs can provide companionship. A sheep can provide warmth. A mynah bird can talk back to you. But only the woman can help make the babies. And then we wind up creating Eve.

Side note: This is obviously a much different story than Genesis, Chapter 1. In Genesis, Chapter 1, women and men are created at the same time, "Male and female created He them." Here, we have the creation of man, and then all the animals, and then women. We might look at this as two separate stories. And as source critics, those biblical scholars who like to say, this book or this chapter came from this writer, this book or that chapter came from some other writer, source critics will say, of course, these are two separate stories. They need not agree. Except until source criticism came alive in about the 18th century with the Enlightenment, people always read these texts as connected.

There is actually Medieval Jewish legend about Lilith who was supposedly this first woman created equal with man. "Male and female created He them," that's Lilith the first woman. Lilith was not a good girl, according to this legend. She decided she wanted to have equal power with Adam, and God admonishes her, "Yes, you should, you should—well, maybe—have equal power, but really let Adam rule the roost." Lilith doesn't like this, so she packs up her bags, and she moves out of Eden, and she becomes a demon. But that's another story for another time.

Let's move back to Eve for a while. Eve is an absolutely fascinating woman. She begins from Adam's rib or Adam's side, and we find immediately that there are cross-cultural comparisons matching up Eve with the ancient Near East. There is a Sumerian story called the myth of Dilmun. Sumer is an ancient culture that predated Israel by a good thousand years. In the Sumerian paradise story, the myth of Dilmun, there was a God named Enki, and Enki, he's not always a God who obeys the rules. There is a garden he's not supposed to go into, and there are forbidden plants in that garden, but Enki goes in anyway, and he eats some of these plants. It turns out that the plants were created, actually borne, by the goddess Ninhursag, without pain by the way, and they were forbidden. Because Enki eats the forbidden fruit, his entire body becomes ruined—headaches, toothaches, pains in the side, stomachaches, charley horses, you name it, he's got it.

Ninhursag, the mother goddess, then needs to create other gods and goddesses, each one to cure a different part of Enki's broken body. And one of the goddesses she creates is called Nintu. She's the goddess who cures broken ribs, and her name is both, "lady of the rib," but it can also be translated, "lady who makes live," which, as we'll see, is Eve's later name, Eve, "the mother of all living." Again, we have a cross-cultural myth. The

Genesis writer is putting his spin on what is a common mythology from the ancient Near East.

We have another problem here with the creation of Eve, and that is the fact that it's actually a man who gives birth. Adam gives birth to Eve from his side. God puts Adam to sleep, God is like the obstetrician, and the next thing you know, there is Eve. This is actually also common in the ancient world, gods frequently give birth. Zeus gives birth to Athena from his head, he gives birth to Dionysus from his thigh. There are many ancient Near Eastern gods, male gods, who give birth, as well.

Some anthropologists suggest that this is a cultural attempt for men to come to terms with women's ability to give birth. The men simply say in their mythology, we did it first, we did it without pain, we did while we are asleep, and you ladies, you get the messy afterwards. Could be. But on the more positive side, I actually like to read the story of the creation of Eve as creating some sort of equality. Not only the sense of woman as a partner fit for him, but the sense of Eve being created from Adam's side.

There is a Rabbinic story, it's called a midrash—which is simply a development of what's in the Bible—a midrash that says Eve was created from Adam's side. Why? If she had been created from his head, she would have lorded over him. If she had been created from his feet, he would have walked all over her. She is created from his side to be his partner and to walk next to him. I take that as quite positive.

Partners or not, the next chapter shows what happens when men and women start to question their assigned roles in the garden. And so we move to Genesis, Chapter 3, which is the temptation story. Now, most people when they think of the temptation story say, oh, yes, the temptation, that's where Eve convinces Adam to eat the forbidden fruit. That's the temptation. Except we find in the story Eve never tempts Adam, there is no temptation per se. He is, in fact, standing right there. But we need to back up and see what actually happens.

We know from Genesis, Chapter 2, that the Lord had forbidden the man from eating from the tree. The woman, who will not be called Eve until the end of the chapter, clearly knows this interdiction. It's not, however, clear who told her, because she hadn't been created yet. And I do wonder, did she get the word directly from God or did she hear it from Adam who was literally born yesterday? And if she heard it from Adam, would she have believed him? She does know the story, and here we have it in the conversation with the snake.

Now, the snake is one of God's creatures mind you, and we heard in Genesis 1 that everything was good, but I do worry about this snake. The snake comes up to the woman, he says, "What about this tree, lady?" He doesn't quite put it that way, but that's the effect. And Eve says not only that God had forbidden eating from the fruit, but she adds, God said, "Neither shall you touch it, lest you die." In other words, she adds something to the divine command. According to some readers who like Eve, this makes Eve a translator and a theologian, she updates the word of God to fit present circumstances. According to more conservative commentaries, sin always begins with some distortion of the truth, and Eve has distorted what God said.

Now, regardless of where you come down on this, the fact is, Eve said, "You're not supposed to eat it; you're not supposed to touch it." And she winds up doing both. But she doesn't do it automatically. She actually thinks about it. The snake says to her, "Well, it's not that you will die if you eat it or you touch it, for God knows," says the snake, "that when you eat of this fruit, your eyes will be opened and you will be like the gods, knowing good and evil." So then Eve has something to consider. She has little experience with God. God has never said anything to her yet. And she has no reason to trust God over the snake—how could you tell?—so she begins thoughtful inquiry. She thinks, "Well, it's good for food, and it's a delight to the eyes, and the tree was to be desired to make one wise." She carefully considers her options, and once she decides this is a good idea, "she took of its fruit, and she ate." And contrary to all those cultural assumptions, she does not wiggle her hips, flip her hair, and say, "Come here, big boy," to Adam, "eat this fruit." The text simply says, "She also gave some to her man standing with her, and he ate." He was standing there the entire time.

So what's going on then with this first act of human disobedience? On the practical level, the myth is clearly a warning to men, don't let your women go out and talk to other people, particularly other people whose religious views are different than yours, who think of God differently. This is the proverbial "snake in the grass." But there is more than that here. On an historical level, if this story can be dated to the time of the royal court, perhaps it's a warning against those powerful women in the harem, women like Bathsheba or any of those other women, for example, Solomon's 300 wives and 700 concubines who led him astray with their false gods. Watch out for women!

There's a group in the ancient world, first or second century C.E., Common Era—that's simply a non-confessional way of saying, A.D., which is "in the year of our Lord"—first or second century Common Era called Gnostics. It's where we get the term *agnostic*. The Gnostics looked at Eve as a hero who brought knowledge to a world from which knowledge was hidden. Eve here is the good girl; God is the bad god. I don't think at all that's what the Genesis author was saying, but I can understand where the Gnostic writers would have gotten it. "Why," they asked, "would God have prevented humankind from gaining knowledge?" It's a good question.

As for early Christian appropriation of the story, we have in the New Testament a document called First Timothy. And First Timothy, Chapter 2, verse 14, reads as follows: "Adam was not deceived, but the woman was deceived and became a transgressor." That is, Adam was not seduced or deceived, his action was not out of ignorance, he ate the fruit out of solidarity with his wife knowing she was to be damned, she was to be thrown out of Eden and he, what a good guy, decides to go with her.

Well, as noted, at the very least, we can say that the snake was on the literal level correct. The man and woman experienced not death, but loss of innocence, because their eyes are opened, and suddenly they realize that they are naked and they hide themselves. What they get is not death, but loss of innocence. They're no longer comfortable with their bodies. They've become adults. They've lost that childhood ability to be free with their own corporality. They gain shame, and that's the death we all have at infancy's end.

And humanity's loss is then compounded by statements of what will be the so-called curses. Well, there is an etiology, a story of origins, that begins the curses. This describes why the snake crawls on its belly. Obviously, it's been cursed by God. That one's easy.

But then we have the woman being addressed. Until then, the only person who had actually talked to her was the snake. You can understand why she might have been sympathetic. But here, God finally talks to this woman, but it's not a very good talk. He says, "What have you done?" says God. And then he proceeds to give her a curse.

But we have a problem with translation here. Most translations render Genesis 3, verse 16, "I will greatly multiply your pain in childbearing. In pain, you shall give birth to children." Convincingly, in my view, a biblical scholar named Carol Meyers translates instead, "I will greatly increase your work and your pregnancies. Along with work, you shall give birth to children." And she's got very good warrant for this revision.

The term for "work" appears again in Genesis, 3:17, just the next verse, when the Lord God says to Adam, "In work, you shall eat of it [that's the Earth] all the days of your life." Further, the term usually translated to *childbearing* really does mean *pregnancies*.

So the point of Eve's curse is not really pain in childbirth, but it's a much more profound and, indeed, ongoing curse. It says women's lot is not to rest easy. Women are responsible for both child production and to work in the subsistence economy, for both procreation and production. Along with having children, she still has labor in the workforce. This is what contemporary sociologists call "the second shift." And that was, in fact, the case in Israel's early period.

Women did not sit back in some upper tower and talk about how wonderful they were with other women. They worked. They gardened. They farmed. They did weaving. They did baking. They did childcare. They did pretty much everything men do, because most women in antiquity are peasants, and most peasants, be they male or female, do not have the luxury of free time.

But this curse for women comes at a psychological cost. As God says, "Yet your desire shall be for your husband (or "your man"), and he shall rule over you." Now, it's true the term "rule" (Hebrew *mashal*) is not tyrannical; it's associated with good kings like Hezekiah or Solomon. But it does really mean: call the shots, prevail, have dominion, in a benevolent way, yes. I think it might also have a sense that man will prevail over women in terms of how much money he brings in. Men in antiquity, as well as today, brought more into the family household. Why? Because women are busy with that first curse: the pregnancies, the childcare, parturition.

And finally, on this section, the pronouncement on women's desire: "Yet your desire shall be for your husband, and he shall rule over you," finds a tragic example later on. Women in antiquity knew that death in childbirth often happened, was likely to happen. It was a very common way for women to die. This curse says, "Your desire shall be for your husband," you'll want that relationship even though it may bring death. And we find in just a few more chapters of Genesis, Jacob's wife, Rachel, says to Jacob, "Give me children, or I shall die." And it turns out that Rachel's second child, Benjamin, causes her death; she dies in childbirth. That's part of that curse of Eve coming back around.

Moving to the man's punishment, we find a rationale for the descriptions. The Lord God opens by saying, "Because you have listened to the voice of your wife"—it would have been easier if he had just said, "Because you ate the fruit...," thus women received a kind of double share or blame—this phrase, "listened to the voice of your wife," will also echo in later biblical text.

It's repeated in Genesis, Chapter 21, when Abraham, who we'll meet in a lecture or two hence, is enjoined by God to listen to the voice of his wife, and the result of his listening, his other wife, Hagar, and their child, Ishmael, are cast out into the wilderness. Listen to the voice of your wife, and you may find yourself out of Eden.

The Lord God's opening comment to Adam also responds to Adam's complaint. When God says to Adam, "What has happened?" Adam says to God, "The woman whom you gave to be with me, she gave me the fruit, and

I ate it." Adam wants to shift the responsibility back onto God. "God, if you hadn't made this woman we never would have had the problem in the first place." But you can bet Adam is not going to win this debate. Unlike the snake who will henceforth crawl on its belly, and the women condemned to pregnancies along with work, the man receives no curse in his body, rather the ground is cursed because of him. He's not only exiled from the easy care of the garden, he's alienated from the ground, his originary source.

But Genesis 3, does not end on a completely depressing note. It's actually remarkably helpful. In Genesis, Chapter 3, verse 20, Adam calls his wife's name "Eve," and she becomes the "mother of all living." That's actually the name of an ancient Near Eastern mother goddess. The mother goddess is now not some foreign creature; she is the Lady Eve.

And when Adam and Eve are driven out of the garden, God actually makes clothes of fur for them. And when, as first happens when they leave, Eve becomes pregnant and has Cain, she says, "I have gotten a man with the help of the Lord." When they leave Eden, God goes with them. But when Cain is created and then Abel, more bad things happen as we'll see in the next lecture.

Murder, Flood, Dispersion
(Genesis 4:1–11:32)
Lecture 3

God goes with Adam and Eve when they leave Eden. Eve has a child, Cain; it looks like things are going to be okay. But it turns out, as we go through the rest of the primeval history from Genesis 4 through Genesis 11, things get worse and worse. ... We have humankind becoming so cruel, so awful that God decides to wipe out creation with a flood.

Genesis 1–11 depicts the increasing alienation of humanity from one another, the uneasy relationship between animal husbandry and agriculture, the wilderness and the city-state, and the increasing alienation between humanity and God. This lecture investigates these themes through analysis of the stories of Cain and Abel, Noah's flood, and the Tower of Babel. The lecture also observes the tantalizing hints in the primeval history of other myths, likely known to the Bible's early audiences but now lost to history.

The story of Cain and Abel continues the downward spiral of history begun with the expulsion from Eden. Genesis 4 may recreate Israel's early struggles between agriculture and animal husbandry. The account may favor animal sacrifices over harvest offerings. Supporting this view is its insistence on the potency of blood. Was Abel's sacrifice more fitting because he brings "of the *firstlings* of his flock and of their *fat portions*" while Cain brings just "An offering of the fruit of the ground" (4:3–4)? Cain, the founder of the first city and, therefore, of sustainable agricultural produce, prevails, but his pastoral brother remains (nostalgically?) mourned. The notion of primogeniture, followed here, is contradicted by later biblical stories. In the Old Testament/*Tanakh*, birth order is less important than one's merit and divine sponsorship.

Some historians propose that Cain's story is an etiology for the *Kenites*, a group represented by Moses's in-laws (Jdg. 1:16) and, likely, Jael, the tent-peg–wielding heroine of Deborah's Song (Jdg. 4–5). They worship YHWH and settle in Canaan (1 Sam. 30:29) but are not members of Israel. The mark of "Cain" (a cognate to "Kenite") may represent a tribal insignia. The connection may reveal Israel's uneasiness with these neighbors.

The absence of explicit rationale for God's rejection of Cain's sacrifice has also prompted more theological interpretations. One murder equals the death of one-quarter of the world's population. Sacrifice cannot buy divine favor.

Along with the ever-popular queries concerning Cain's wife, in which the Bible displays no interest, the primeval history hints at more complete mythic antecedents. " … all the days of Enoch were 365 years. And Enoch walked with God; and he was not, for God took him" (Gen. 5:21–24). Because Enoch does not appear to have died, messianic speculation will attach to him in the Second Temple period. Enoch may symbolize the sanctity of time; 365 is not an arbitrary number. The Babylonian myths also record that the seventh antediluvian hero was taken by the gods (to be a servant).

Mythic speculation attaches to the *Nephilim*, the "fallen ones," who "were on the earth in those days … when the sons of God came into the daughters of men, and they bore children to them. These were the mighty men of old … giants in the earth" (6:1-4). The relation to the "daughters of men" prompts associations with both ancient Near Eastern and, especially, Greek myths (e.g., Europa, Io, Semele). Num. 13:33 counts among the Canaanite population Nephilim; that Joshua conquers them highlights Israel's ability. Perhaps the Nephilim represent the royal court: the "sons of God" (cf. 2 Sam. 7). Did they seduce women they should have protected (e.g., David and Bathsheba; Amnon and Tamar [2 Sam. 11–13]); did they rebel against God's representative (e.g., Absalom's civil war [2 Sam. 13–20])? Does the story argue against intermarriage, perhaps reflecting the breakdown of the generation of the "sons of God," such as Solomon?

This situation leads to the story of Noah, which is by no means a children's story. Problems begin with Noah's characterization. He is "a righteous man, blameless in his generation; Noah walked with God" (6:9). But the comparison to his generation is hardly complimentary. Nor does Noah, unlike

Abraham for Sodom, Moses for Israel, and several of his counterparts in ancient Near Eastern flood stories, advocate for humanity. Noah's is only one of a flood of ancient Near Eastern and Greek deluge tales; other flood heroes include Atrahasis, Zuisudra, Deucalion and Pyrrha, and—from Tablet XI of the Gilgamesh epic—Utnapishtim. Comparisons between Utnapishtim and Noah indicate a shared mythic structure. Both heroes, warned by gods about the flood, build boats. Utnapishtim's is a cube, but the design is in both cases divinely given. Neither boat seems to have a rudder. Both survive a flood caused by rain descending from the vault of the heavens and subterranean waters coming up (the cosmology promoted by Gen. 1). The earth is being un-created and dissolving into watery chaos. Both arrive on a mountain and offer sacrifices. In the Gilgamesh epic, the gods "Smelled the savor, smelled the sweet savor; the gods crowded like flies about the sacrificer." Gen. 8:21 reads: "When YHWH smelled the pleasing odor, he said in his heart: 'I will never again curse the ground … '"

The comparison also aids in determining cultural values. Informed by the gods/God of the flood, Utnapishtim weeps; Noah does nothing. Unlike Utnapishtim, he is mortal, flawed, and not to be considered divine. Utnapishtim is secretly warned by the god Ea; the gods find humankind too noisy and, therefore, intend destruction. Instructed by Ea to lie about his ark, Utnapishtim tells his neighbors he is attempting to escape from the threats of the god Enlil; ironically, they help him build. The Genesis God regrets the evil—not the noise—of humankind; there is no secrecy, warning, or demand for repentance: humanity's fate is sealed. Utnapishtim takes on board craftspeople; Noah brings only his immediate family. For the primeval history, "culture" is an ambivalent category (e.g., Cain's descendant, the violent Lamech, is the progenitor of musicians and metal workers [Gen. 4:17–24]). Although Utnapishtim attempts to convince Gilgamesh that immortality can never again be achieved, Gilgamesh nevertheless obtains the flower of immortality at the bottom of the sea (i.e., he personally experiences a flood). Falling asleep on reaching land, he awakes to discover a snake has taken the flower. For Genesis, there is no longer the possibility of immortality, of the human becoming divine. Genesis emphasizes justice (the elimination of evil) and mercy, as God establishes a covenant with "as many as came out of the ark" (9:8).

The Noachide Covenant extends, likely through editing by the Priestly (P) writers, motifs from earlier chapters. The sign of the "bow"—a weapon of war—signals peace, just as the mark on Cain signals protection. Other such signs include, notably, circumcision. Gen. 9:1ff. repeat 1:28: "Be fruitful and multiply and fill the earth." Noah and his family receive new dietary regulations: "As I gave you the green plants [the language resembles Gen. 1:29], I give you everything" (9:3); humanity is no longer vegetarian. But, echoing Gen. 1:26–27 and Abel's murder: they "shall not eat flesh with its life, that is, its blood ... whoever sheds the blood of man, by man shall his blood be shed; for God made man in his own image." The notice in Gen. 7:2–3 that the animals boarded seven by seven rather than two by two (Gen. 6:19; 7:9) not only ensures animals for Noah's sacrifice but also anticipates the categories of clean and unclean foods detailed in Lev. 11.

Just as the forbidden fruit brings knowledge as well as shame, so does Noah's viniculture comfort even as it leads to drunkenness. Noah is introduced with the prophecy "Out of the ground which YHWH has cursed, this one shall bring us relief from our work and from the toil of our hands" (Gen. 5:29). That Noah is the first person whose birth is recorded after Adam's death makes this prediction poignant. Noah "drank the wine, and became drunk, and lay uncovered in his tent." Fruit leads him back to the Edenic, but now inappropriate, nakedness.

What happens next is indeterminate; an earlier story appears to have been suppressed. We are told that Ham saw his father uncovered and informed his brothers Shem and Japhet; the brothers, walking backward in order not to witness Noah's shame, cover him. "When Noah awoke from his wine and knew what his youngest son had done to him, he said 'Cursed be Canaan'" (Gen. 9:25). What was "done"? Why curse Canaan? Cross-cultural parallel suggests the something "done" was castration. This is a common mythic motif describing the transfer of powers from father (gods) to sons. ■

Lloyd R. Bailey, *Noah: The Person and the Story in History and Tradition.*

Alan Dundes (ed.), *The Flood Myth.*

1. What are today's equivalents for "sacrifice"—a practice in antiquity as common as we find watching television?

2. Is Noah a hero? Is his story comforting or threatening? Why would ancient Israel so describe its flood story's protagonist and its God?

3. Why does Israel detail, at the beginning of its sacred history, God's disappointments and humanity's continual failures?

Murder, Flood, Dispersion
(Genesis 4:1–11:32)
Lecture 3—Transcript

As we've seen, the Old Testament starts out with the world in very, very good shape. God creates the world, and we have the refrain, "And it was good, and it was very good." And then we saw in Genesis, Chapter 2, how man and woman are put in a Garden of Eden, a garden of earthly delights. They're naked, they're happy, they've got enough to eat. But then in Genesis 3, as we saw in the last lecture, things begin to go downhill. Man and woman eat from the forbidden fruit of the Tree of Knowledge. They're booted out of Eden, and they can't get back, because God places at the entrance to Eden an angel with a flaming sword going this way and that. There is no way back to immortality.

But as we've also seen, God goes with Adam and Eve when they leave Eden. And Eve has a child, Cain. It looks like things are going to be okay. But it turns out, as we go through the rest of the primeval history from Genesis 4 through Genesis 11, things get worse and worse. We have a tale of fratricide in which Cain kills his brother. We have humankind becoming so cruel, so awful that God decides to wipe out creation with a flood, which only Noah and his family and some animals survive.

And then humankind seems to get its act together again, but they decide to build a tower and, in fact, storm heaven and become like the gods. And as we know from Genesis 2 and 3, the Adam and Eve story, humankind is supposed to be human, not supposed to be like the gods. It's a story of alienation from each other, from God, and from the land. Genesis is no bedtime story; it's no children's story.

Let's go look and see what happens with Cain and Abel just to start. Cain's struggle with his younger brother, Abel, is the stuff of legends. It's also a template for stories we will find later.

As Adam, leaving the Garden of Eden, finds that the earth will no longer yield its produce, so we come to the story of the first person besides Adam to engage in farming; this is Cain, who was an agriculturalist. And we also find that Cain has a younger brother named Abel, who was a shepherd; he's involved in animal husbandry. So right at the beginning of the creation story, we have here that age-old rivalry between the shepherds and the agriculturalists. This is like the play, *Oklahoma*, about the herdsmen and the farmers. It's an age-old story. We're never going to lose it.

Here's that competition in Israel between farming and animal husbandry. And it's also a competition between nostalgia for the past life, when the people of Israel were out in the wilderness and what they have now, an urban environment with settled agricultural produce.

So what does happen with Cain and Abel? They both bring sacrifices to the Lord, but while Abel's sacrifice proves acceptable, Cain's does not. And yet again we're left with a list of questions. There are, in fact, maybe too many answers to this problem rather than too few.

The favoring of Abel's sacrifice may represent the ancient community's prioritizing of blood sacrifice over agricultural produce. As I mentioned earlier, the world of antiquity is not our world. Back then, blood sacrifice was exceptionally important. Blood was sacred matter, and we can see this almost immediately when God says to Cain, "The blood of your brother [the blood of your brother] is crying out to me from the ground." We'll see increasingly how important blood becomes when we get to the law codes where blood is forbidden for people to consume.

Well, we might also recollect that perhaps Cain's sacrifice, the sacrifice of agricultural produce, was already set up for us. It was agricultural produce, that Tree of the Knowledge of Good and Evil, that caused all the problems in the first place. Agriculture comes at a price, and that price is not always a good one.

Or perhaps was Abel's sacrifice accepted because, as the text said, he brought from "the *firstlings* of his flock," the best animals he brought, as the text goes on to say, from "their *fat portions*," which is what God wants. He holds back nothing.

Cain, on the other hand, simply brings "an offering of the fruit of the ground." Is that opposed, perhaps, to first fruits or best fruits? In other words, did Abel give the best he had, and Cain gave whatever was there, and is that why Abel's sacrifice was accepted? Again, we don't know.

In fact, all of these explanations can work. The Bible does not necessarily give us mutually exclusive ideas. Many explanations to many of these stories work, and that's typical for myth. A myth can evoke many, many interpretations, all of which are valid.

Indeed, some theologians have suggested, and I think they might be right, that there is no good answer to why Cain's sacrifice was rejected and Abel's accepted. Perhaps God works in arbitrary and mysterious ways. And that would also make sense.

This is not a text in which God is on call; you know, offer sacrifice, push a button, and God simply comes in and does what you want. One offers sacrifices, because that's what God commands, that's what God wants. But whether God chooses to accept that sacrifice or not is God's business, not ours. We cannot use sacrifices to bribe God. We can only do what is required of us, and then hope that God takes care of the rest. There may be no answer for why one was accepted and one not.

And, indeed, if there is no good answer, then Cain is not a lackadaisical guy, who simply couldn't bring the best, and he's not selfish or greedy. He's simply a tragic character, sort of like King Saul, whom we'll see later in the monarchy, for whom God's rejection is not entirely his fault. Looking at Cain as a tragic figure, rather than as an evil fratricide, a guy who kills his brother, may be a different way of understanding him, but it is also a legitimate way for looking at the biblical text.

Now, the struggle that takes place between the brothers in the Garden of Eden is one that, I mentioned, will be replayed throughout Genesis and even into the books of First and Second Samuel.

In the ancient Near East, in antiquity, there was something called the law of primogeniture, which suggested that the oldest son inherited the bulk of the estate—*primo*, first; *genitor*, in terms of generation, who was born first. But what the biblical text does is complicate this idea of primogeniture and sometimes even dismiss it entirely.

In this case with Cain and Abel, yes it is the older son who winds up succeeding, in that the younger son, Abel, is dead. But as we go on, we'll find out Abraham has two sons, an older one named Ishmael, a younger named Isaac, and it will be the younger, Isaac, who inherits the promise. Isaac has two sons, twin boys named Jacob and Esau. Esau, the older, will not inherit; Jacob, the younger, will. And as we go on, we see consistently younger sons wind up succeeding. In fact, David is seven sons down.

The biblical text says it's not necessarily what your birth order is that's important, it's what you do, and it helps enormously if God is on your side. Perhaps this is a way the Bible says, we're going to favor the underdog. Not the person whom society says will inherit, whom society says will rule, but rather the person who deserves it, based on merit, based on ability, and based on divine love.

The narrator is at best, here in Genesis Chapter 4, ambivalent about Cain. Yes, he has committed fratricide. Yes, that was not a good thing. I would have thought at this point Cain should have been struck dead by God. Right? If Adam and Eve, for eating a piece of fruit, get tossed out of Eden, surely killing your brother is worse than eating a piece of fruit. But that's not what happens. Again, God works in very mysterious ways.

Now, it's been said by some people who are trying to find an excuse for Cain and for God, maybe Cain didn't know what murder was. Maybe he didn't realize that when he attacked Abel something bad was going to happen. I don't buy it. Right? If you attack somebody, I think you can pretty much figure that something negative would accrue from that attack. Cain knew that something bad was going to happen. But instead of punishment, Cain actually gets protection, and there are some explanations for this.

Some historians propose that Cain's story is an etiology, a story of origins, for a group of people called the Kenites. These are the people to whom Moses's father-in-law belongs, and there's a Kenite woman or at least a woman married to a Kenite man in the Book of Judges. Her name is Jael, and, as we'll see in the Judges 4 and 5, she's a murderous, treacherous, exciting heroine who winds up dispatching the enemy general after giving him milk, tucking him in, and tiptoeing over to his bed, except with a tent peg instead of a bottle.

The Kenites are members of the covenant community. They move in with Israel, but they retain their own ethnic identity. Is that what Cain is, a stranger in the community, somebody different than everybody else, but protected, somebody to be a little bit wary of, but somehow marked also by God as a special person? That could be. The Bible simply does not tell us.

Mysteries continue in this text, and the mysteries themselves are often accompanied by theological explanations, as well. Could it be with Genesis, Chapter 4, that God is telling us, "If you kill one person, you kill one-quarter of the world's population?" That's what happens with Cain and Abel. There are only four people there.

But the story has to go on. Actually according to the Bible, there had to be more than four people around, because we know that Cain eventually gets married, settles down, and finds a city. This raises the inevitable question, as my students always ask, where did Cain find his wife? The Bible doesn't care. It is totally of no interest to the Bible.

In Hellenistic texts, works produced by Jews during the Greek period after Alexander the Great, this speculation comes back around. And we normally find out that Adam and Eve not only had Cain and Abel, and then after Abel died, his brother Seth, but they also had lots of daughters whom the biblical authors just didn't bother to mention. Whom did Cain marry? According to later tradition, his sister. But again, the Bible doesn't care.

Cain goes on to found a city. He seems to succeed. Here again that ambivalence about cities. Founded by a fratricide. Is Abel's way of life, the shepherd, still what is to be preferred?

The stories go on. For example, in Genesis, Chapter 5, we find the following: When Enoch, who is seven generations down from Adam, has lived 65 years, he became the father of, and yes, Methuselah is the oldest living person in the text, 969 years.... Enoch, as I said, became the father of Methuselah. And then, we're told, Enoch walked with God after the birth of Methuselah, 300 years, and he had other sons and daughters. Thus, all the days of Enoch were 365 years. And Enoch walked with God, and "he was not, for God took him."

Now, this brief notice gives rise to intense mythological speculation in the early Hellenistic and Roman periods by both Jews and later by Christians, because Enoch does not appear to have died. He simply walked with God, which actually in biblical Hebrew is a euphemism for "he died," but it doesn't actually say that in so many words. Because he does not appear to have died, speculation will later attach to him. He becomes a divine judge, sometimes a messianic figure. He is like Elijah, whom we've met before, somebody who exists in heaven, who at the end time might come down and serve as a redeemer figure.

Enoch may also symbolize the sanctity of time. Three hundred sixty-five is not an arbitrary number. Perhaps this is the symbol of royal year or a sacred year. And this brings us back to Genesis, Chapter 1, where it is time, rather than space, that is sanctified. Or, in fact, Enoch may simply be the biblical version of a good old ancient Near Eastern myth, because it turns out actually in the Babylonian mythic corpus there is a hero seven generations before the flood or, in this case, after Adam, who was taken by the gods to be a servant to them. There is something important about that seventh generation. This is simply the Bible's take on it.

To some extent, the story of Enoch may be considered an imported myth. In other words, the ancient Near Eastern readers knew much more about some of these characters than we know. If I were to mention today, Monica Lewinsky, people today would have heard of her. I think maybe 10 years from now many people will never have heard that name, and if you haven't, go look her up. Back then, people would have heard of Enoch. They would have known the story. They would have known another odd mention, someone in Genesis identified as Nimrod, a mighty hunter before the Lord. And the text says, "He was called Nimrod, a mighty hunter before the Lord, because he was a mighty hunter before the Lord." End of story. The original readers would have known the story. We've simply lost it. It's not there anymore. There were, no doubt, additional stories about Enoch. We don't have them.

And as we move on, we find a story, or at least a reference to a group of people called the Nephilim. This is Genesis, Chapter 6, literally the "fallen ones." *Naphal* in Hebrew means to fall. The Nephilim, who Genesis says "were on the earth in those days, when men began to multiply on the face of the ground, and daughters were born to them. The sons of God saw that the daughters of men were fair, and they took to wife such as them as they chose. When the sons of God came in to the daughters of men, they bore children to them. These were the mighty men of old, the Nephilim, giants in the earth." That's it. Surely, there is more to the story than that. And we're not exactly sure what it is.

The Nephilim do show up again. In Numbers, Chapter 13, Joshua, who will succeed Moses as leader of the Israelites, is scouting out the land of Israel. And he and his fellow scouts go into the land trying to figure out how they're going to conquer this place. And they come back, and they say, "There are giants in the land. There are Nephilim. We are like grasshoppers compared to them." What are they saying? They are saying, "The people in Canaan are so big and so strong they are like those mythological heroes." But they are also saying, "Look at how great we are, because we managed to beat them."

The Nephilim are mythological figures everyone would have heard of back then. But something else, as well. There is a connection here between the Nephilim and the "sons of God" and the "daughters of men."

This business about divine beings and human women getting together and producing children is an age-old model from both Greek mythology and the ancient Near East. Many people are familiar with Greek myths, for example, the story of Hercules, whose mother is a human being, and his father is Zeus. And the same thing can be said for Theseus and Perseus and even Dionysus, who becomes a god. Gods and human women get together all the time.

The problem, here in Genesis, is it works out not for good, as the good of Hercules or the good of Perseus. It works out for evil. This becomes a problem, and this is what leads to God's deciding to wipe out the world.

I think perhaps the story of the Nephilim has a couple of practical lessons that the biblical writers might want to tell us, as well. The "sons of God" could also be considered members of the royal court. In Second Samuel, Chapter 7, God adopts David. Kings are "sons of God." That's a standard phrase. And the princes in the court, David's sons or Solomon's children, they're "sons of God," too.

Perhaps the story is saying, hey, people in the royal court, you're supposed to be taking care of the weaker people in the population. You're not supposed to be abusing them.

But we will find out later that one of David's sons, Amnon, will rape a princess in the royal court, and another of David's sons, Absalom, will rape some of David's wives and concubines.

Perhaps the story of the Nephilim, the "fallen ones," says people who are in positions of authority, people appointed by God to rule, need to rule, not to abuse, and not to get involved with women who are inappropriate. That may well be part of the background here.

At the very least, we can be sure that the Nephilim had improper relations, because of the "sons of God" and "daughters of men" business, and that leads to increasing social upheaval. "The Lord saw that the wickedness of humanity was great in the Earth and that every imagination of the thoughts of their hearts was only evil continually." A heavenly response is needed, and we're told that God actually regrets creating humankind. At this point, I look at God in a sort of sympathetic way. He did his best, he blew it, this isn't going to work.

But then I begin to wonder about the solution. God being God you figure a little bit of tinkering might work, but no, God decides to start again and decides to have a universal flood. As we saw at the beginning, the world was watery chaos, and then the waters are separated above and below. What happens with the flood is the subterranean waters come up, the heavenly waters come down, and the world collapses back into chaos into the uncreated realm without form and void.

But there is a distinction here. God decides to save one person, Noah, who was called "a righteous man, blameless in his generation." This is not a compliment. If you consider the generation in which Noah lived, to say blameless in his generation is not saying much.

I actually don't like Noah very much. My students fuss at me for this, because they remembered the Noah of their childhood, of their Sunday school lessons. I don't like this man. He makes me very nervous. Why? He seems somewhat like a robot, like an automaton. God says to Noah, "Build a boat," Noah builds a boat. He doesn't say, "Why?" He doesn't get an answer. God says, "Build a boat." Noah builds a boat. God says, "Find some animals; get them on." Noah finds some animals. He gets them on the boat. God says, "I'm going to send the flood to destroy the entire world." Noah says, "Okay. No problem." God tells him to "enter the boat." Noah gets into the boat. And God actually closes the doors. It's a very nice little touch.

The contrast he provides to somebody like Abraham, our next major character, who will fight over the fate of Sodom and Gomorrah, the wickedest cities there were, is palpable. Noah could have saved the entire world perhaps just by putting up a little fuss. He doesn't say a thing.

In fact, there are other ancient Near Eastern flood narratives. As the old biblical pun goes: There's a flood of flood narratives. And there are other flood heroes, Zuisudra, Atrahasis, even in the Greek mythology, Deucalion and Pyrrha. But in all these other cases, the ancient Near Eastern flood heroes put up a fuss. They say, we don't think this flood idea is a good thing. Perhaps you might want to reconsider. Not Noah—he builds a boat, gets in, that's the end of it.

One could often, one might often want to compare, could compare, Noah to the hero of the Babylonian flood epic. This is the story called the Epic of Gilgamesh, a very famous epic in antiquity, which has numerous parallels to the Bible. In the Gilgamesh epic, the hero was named Utnapishtim.

Utnapishtim is told by a god on the sly, "the other gods are going to wipe out the world, you build a boat, I'll save you." This is the benefit of a polytheistic society. The gods can work against each other.

So Utnapishtim, who's no dummy, decides to build a boat. In fact, his neighbors come along and they say to him, "Utna, why are you building this boat?" Utnapishtim says, "You know, there's this other god who is mad at me, so I'm building this boat to escape him." His neighbors, who are not too quick on the uptake—I mean why would you build a boat in the middle of the desert?—decide to help him, and they actually help. Utnapishtim brings on board not just animals but also craftspeople, musicians and metal workers. He's interested in saving society. He's pretty active about this. Not Noah. He just goes along with it.

But the stories are very well connected, as if the biblical writer knew the Gilgamesh epic and played upon it. Even in details, they are connected. Noah gets from God the dimensions on how to build the Ark. Utnapishtim gets from his god friend the dimensions on how to build the ark. And, in fact, neither boat has a rudder. The boats simply go where they will in the water and land where they will. And, of course, they both land on mountaintops.

There are people engaged in biblical archaeology, in the sense that they want to prove the Bible true, who are continually sending expeditions to Mt. Ararat in Turkey, which is where Noah happened to land.

If one were looking at the Babylonian epic, Utnapishtim actually lands not in Turkey, but on a placed called Mt. Nisir, which is in Kurdistan. Perhaps these archaeologists may, in fact, be looking in the wrong place.

When they get out of the ark, they both offer sacrifices. In the Gilgamesh epic, we read, "The gods smelled savor, smelled the sweet savor. The gods crowded like flies around the sacrificer." It had been a while.

In Genesis, 8:21, we have, "When YHWH smelled the pleasing odor, he said in his heart, 'I will never again curse the ground.'" The same sense of smell, the same sense of delight and sacrifice. But a very different result.

The comparison is spectacular here, too, because of what happens concerning immortality. Utnapishtim is rewarded for his faithfulness by the god who saved him, and he is the only human being who was granted, in the Babylonian epic, the gift of immortality. Gilgamesh, the hero, wanting to revive his friend, a guy named Enkidu, from death, seeks out how to become immortal, and he finds his way to Utnapishtim, and he says, "Utna, how do I do this? How do I become immortal?" And Utnapishtim says, "It's impossible. You can never achieve immortality." Just as in the Bible, you can't get back to the Garden of Eden.

But after much cajoling by Gilgamesh, Utnapishtim finally says, "Look, there's a flower. You can find it at the bottom of the sea. If you eat it, it will give you immortality." Gilgamesh, who is a major hero like Hercules, dives down to the bottom of the sea, pulls up the flower of immortality. But when he gets up on the bank, he's really exhausted. He's also not too bright. So he sets the flower down on the side of the shore, and he immediately falls asleep. As you might expect, along comes a snake who eats the flower, and the snake becomes immortal, and Gilgamesh will not be able to revive his friend, Enkidu. Visions again of Genesis, Chapter 3, with that snake always causing problems. One must worry about this.

At the end of Noah's flood epic, God decides to make a new covenant, a covenant with Noah, and "with Noah and all his descendants after you," as the text puts it. The Noachide Covenant even extends to the birds, the cattle, "every beast of the earth with you, as many as came out of the Ark." This is a royal grant covenant. It's like a promise to Noah and to all of Noah's descendants. We'll see that same type of covenant made with Abraham later and then, finally, with David.

And the sign of the covenant is the "bow." Most people think of rainbows, right, pot of gold at the end. But the "bow" here is not the rainbow or only the rainbow, it's the war bow. What God does is take a "bow" like a bow and arrow, a sign of war, and put it up in the heavens as a sign of peace. And he says he swears by this bow that never will he again destroy the world by flood. Which is why in the Book of Revelation in the New Testament, when the world is finally destroyed, it is destroyed by fire. One thing we might actually find some day.

Good things do happen. In an echo of that priestly writer's opening chapter, Genesis 1, Genesis 9 following repeats the command to Noah, "Be fruitful and multiply and fill the earth." Noah and his family will replace Adam and Eve, but they are not quite mirror images of Adam and Eve. There are some differences. For example, Noah and his family receive new dietary regulations. Adam and Eve got the business about don't eat from the tree. This is what Noah gets: "Every moving thing that lives shall be food for you. And as I gave you the green plants," this is the language of Genesis, 1:29, "now I give you everything." In other words, God makes a dietary concession to Noah and his family.

Prior to Noah everyone had been vegetarian; now they can eat anything. This almost complete freedom in diet, by the way, will be modified with Moses, who provides the Children of Israel particular dietary regulations, which enable them to distinguish themselves from their neighbors in terms of what you eat and how you eat it.

In terms of consistency with earlier biblical materials, as well, we have echoes of both Genesis 1:26, 27, the creation of human beings, and the story of Cain and Abel. God forbids humanity from eating flesh with its life, that is its blood, that's the precious blood from Abel that we saw. And goes on to say, "Whoever sheds the blood of a human being by a human being shall *his* blood be shed, for God made human beings in his own image." And that's the idea again. That if you kill one person, it is like killing God or like killing one-quarter of the world's population. This is the text that takes murder very, very seriously.

We might even see the hand of this priestly writer in an earlier verse. Most people assume, my students were convinced, that the animals went on the Ark two-by-two. As that old camp song went: "Two-by-two they went on, elephants and kangaroosies, roosies." Right? Not entirely. Yes, there are some verses that say they go on two-by-two. But there are other verses, for example, in Genesis, Chapter 7, they go on seven-by-seven.

Why? Well it doesn't work for campfire songs, because seven-by-seven doesn't scan, but this is the priestly writer coming in making the distinction between animals which are clean, animals people can eat that are permitted, and animals which are not. Moreover, it's very helpful, because if Noah is to offer sacrifice as soon as he gets off the Ark, you want to make sure he's not killing one of those animals that might not be able to reproduce again.

Now, just as forbidden fruit brings knowledge as well as shame, so Noah's next action, the establishment of viniculture, raising grapes, comforts even as it leads to disaster. Noah is introduced to the reader with the prophecy: "Out of the ground which YHWH had cursed, this one shall bring us relief from our work and from the toil of our hands." And that Noah is the first person whose birth is recorded after Adam's death makes this prediction, in fact, quite poignant. And the connection with Adam is reinforced by Genesis 9:20, which notes, "Noah was the first tiller of the soil." Actually, the Lord God sent Adam from Eden to till the ground from which he was taken. Noah is, in effect, a new Adam.

But with Noah, although he tills the soil, it turns out that too much of the good thing is just not good for him. He drinks the wine he raises, and as the text said, he becomes drunk and "lay uncovered in his tent." This is a frightful reversal of what happened in the Garden of Eden. We're back to a naked person, but now there is total shame. There's nothing good whatsoever.

And what happens next is, in fact, indeterminate. Perhaps an earlier story has actually been suppressed by the biblical writer. We are told only that Noah's son, Ham, saw his father uncovered and told his brothers. The brothers, with a cloak over their shoulders, walked backwards and covered their father so no one would see his nakedness.

But we're told also when Noah awoke from his wine and knew what his youngest son had done to him, he said, "Cursed be Canaan." Why Canaan, the ancestor of the Canaanites? Perhaps Ham or maybe Canaan in an earlier story had actually done something rather than simply see Noah. Ancient Near Eastern parallels, as well as Greek parallels, suggest this may have been a castration story. The Bible, of course, is not going to say that.

What does happen with Ham, in a terrible story, is that in post-biblical material Ham is considered cursed with dark skin, and it's that legend of the curse of Ham that led, for example, American slave owners to justify and legitimize their enslaving of people of African descent. That's misuse of the Bible, and it happens far too often.

In a positive light, Noah brings about viniculture, and that's something we can celebrate. In a negative light, the world will continue to go downhill, as we'll see in the next lecture with the story of the Tower of Babel and then finally God's call of Abraham.

Abraham, Sarah, and Hagar
(Genesis 11:26–21:34)
Lecture 4

> The primeval history is a story of humankind's increasing alienation
> from God, from each other, and from the land. ... This is the story of
> the Tower of Babel, in which humankind unites altogether on the plain
> of Shinar—that is by the way Babylon—in order to build a giant tower
> to get up to God.

The tower of Babel (Gen. 11) is humanity's final, united fall. Re-creation with Noah proves a failure, and God will have to start again. Babel may polemicize against Solomon's overextended economy and international labor force. It may parody the Babylonian *ziqqurats*, thought to be bridges between heaven and earth. Such bridges are not built through independent human initiative; they require divine partnership, as the next several lectures on the "patriarchal sagas" (Genesis 12–50) reveal.

The stories of the Patriarchs (Abraham, Isaac, and Jacob) appear to be set in the late Bronze Age, c. 1750 B.C.E., although the accounts were written centuries later, as evidenced by obvious anachronisms (e.g., references to Philistines [who did not arrive in Palestine until c. 1200, the early Iron Age] and domesticated camels). Some early modern scholars of the patriarchal sagas (the accounts of Abraham, Isaac, and Jacob) sought not only to locate their historical settings but also to prove their historicity; emblematic of this approach is the work of the so-called "American School," associated with W. F. Albright and G. Ernest Wright. Funded principally by church-run schools and seminaries, these scholars practiced "biblical archaeology" in the "holy land." Today, "Near Eastern" and "Mediterranean archaeology" has primarily turned from "proving the Bible" to understanding its cultural contexts. According to Wright, the acting of God in history is central to the proclamation of Israel's faith. If the Bible were shown to be historically invalid, people might be engaging in "false faith." The American School is well known for seeking biblical parallels in documents from the ancient cities of Mari and Nuzi. Neither source, ultimately, offered confirmation of the patriarchal sagas.

While the American School was positivistic and optimistic, the early "German School" might be classified as minimalistic, more interested in literature than archaeology, in determining why the stories were told than proving their historicity. The dominant figures are Albrecht Alt and Martin Noth. Alt associated the patriarchs with clan deities: the shield of Abraham, the Fear of Isaac, and so on. Noth posited that although the patriarchs were likely historical figures, the stories were conveyed, over time, in legendary or saga-based form. The school noted etiologies (stories of origin): the explanations of such practices as circumcision and dietary regulations; natural phenomena, such as the Dead Sea and free-standing salt pillars; and such ethnic interests as the fractious relationship between Israel and Moab (Hebrew *m'av*, "from [my] father," the child conceived incestuously by Lot's daughter after she made her father drunk [Gen. 19:30–38])—a story that echoes Noah's fate and anticipates an ethnic reference that reappears strikingly in the Book of Ruth.

Arguments for a relatively early origin to several tales include the recording of patriarchal practices that were offensive to the religious sensibilities of later times. Gen. 20:12, Abraham's insistence that Sarah is both his sister and his wife, is counter to Lev. 18:9 and Deut. 27:22. Jacob, Abraham's grandson, marries two sisters, contravening Lev. 18:18. The majority of biblical scholars today date the literary composition of the patriarchal sagas to the Judean royal court, c. 900, with the writing of the "J" source. Additions continued to be made until the text reached its (more-or-less) final shape sometime in the late 5th or early 4th centuries, with a possible final editing as late as Hellenistic times.

Because the patriarchal stories concern morality, responsibility, and faith, more than just historical approaches are necessary to their understanding. Theological, ethical, and literary questions also enter the discussion. How should Hagar's first flight to the wilderness be assessed? Is God abusive or protective for sending her back? Why does the text present a major theophany (appearance of the Deity) to a woman, a foreigner, and a slave?

What does this suggest about Hebrew/Egyptian relationships?

Genesis 12, Abram's introduction, threatens to repeat the disasters of the primeval history, yet Abram not only survives but thrives. His story provokes, but does not answer, questions of human and heavenly responsibility, as close reading demonstrates. Promised "a great nation," Abram's circumstances cast doubt on the promise; he himself is very old (seventy-five at his departure, Gen. 12:4); his (only) wife, Sarai, is infertile (Gen. 11:30); and his nephew, Lot, whom he takes to Canaan (anticipating that Lot will be his

The expulsion of Ishmael and his mother, Hagar.

heir?), separates from him (Gen. 13) and moves to Sodom. Canaan's famine prompts a sojourn in Egypt (a scene repeated by subsequent generations of Hebrews).

The particulars of each scene demonstrate a capacity for characterization. About to enter Egypt, Abram tells Sarai (his first words to her), "I know well that you are a beautiful woman, and when the Egyptians see you, they will say 'this is his wife'; then they will kill me … Say you are my sister, so that it may go well with me because of you …" On what is his knowledge based? In hoping that "it may go well with me," where is Abram's concern for Sarah? Abram's theology one of trust, self-interest, or test?

The Egyptian officials praise Sarai to Pharaoh, who takes her into his harem. For "her sake," he gives Abram "sheep, oxen, male donkeys, male and female slaves, female donkeys, and camels." Does Abram intend to tell the truth? If so, when? What of Sarai? Might she appreciate palace comforts after the camps of Canaan? Why is the Egyptian ruler not named; how does he compare with other Pharaohs (the Joseph saga; the Exodus)?

God afflicts Pharaoh's house with plagues. Appalled at Abram's lie—how he discovers it is not specified—Pharaoh gives him his wife and banishes him with "all that he had"; Gen. 13:1–2 reveals Abram to have become very wealthy. Gen. 12:17 reads, *al-d'var Sarai*, "concerning the matter of Sarai" (NRSV: "because of Sarah") or, literally, "upon the word of Sarai." Did Sarai's word, to the Pharaoh or to God, ensure her release? The plagues prefigure Exodus, where also Hebrews are enslaved. The stories of Egypt and Israel are thus intertwined. The "ancestress in danger" scene is repeated with both Sarah (Gen. 20:1–18) and Rebecca (Gen. 26:6–11). The "promise motif" (cf. Gen. 13:14–17), will be fulfilled outside the Pentateuch, although it continues to be threatened—by natural disasters, military campaigns, human weakness, and as we shall see in the next lecture, even divine action. ■

Suggested Reading

William G. Dever, *Recent Archaeological Discoveries and Biblical Research.*

Niels Peter Lemche, *Early Israel: Anthropological and Historical Studies on the Israelite Society before the Monarchy.*

Phyllis Trible, *Texts of Terror: Literary-Feminist Readings of Biblical Narratives.*

Questions to Consider

1. What evidence would convince a skeptic of the historicity of the patriarchs? Even if their existence were proven, how would one determine the historicity of the stories told about them?

2. It is often claimed that the patriarchal tales represent universal stories rather than temporally contingent ones. In what sense then are we like

Abraham, Sarah, and Hagar? If we identify with the characters, do we risk romanticizing the past?

3. Why would Israel present Abraham, its forefather, in a manner many readers find morally ambiguous?

Abraham, Sarah, and Hagar
(Genesis 11:26–21:34)
Lecture 4—Transcript

The primeval history, as we've seen, is a story of humankind's increasing alienation from God, from each other, and from the land. When last we met, we talked about the story of Noah, as if God was going to start creating the world again, and it looked pretty good for a while. Noah and his family and the animals survived the universal flood. Noah plants a vineyard, he produces wine, which pretty much everybody can appreciate. But the next thing you know, Noah gets drunk, he winds up cursing his son, and the world is going downhill again. Humankind seems somehow compelled to try to become like the gods. Try to strive to be more than what we are.

The last episode in the primeval history in Genesis 11 gives us that. This is the story of the Tower of Babel, in which humankind unites altogether on the plain of Shinar—that is by the way Babylon—in order to build a giant tower to get up to God. We see familiar stories like this in Greek mythology, piling mountain upon mountain to storm Olympus. But this is simply the Bible's version, and God up in heaven is not going to stand for it. Rather than allow humankind to become like the gods and storm heaven, God decides to confound humanities' language, that's why we speak in a multitude of languages, and, thereby, disperse people all over the world in different locations and different languages. They can no longer work together.

If the original commandment is to fill the earth, this is a very ironic way to have it actually be fulfilled. And there are other reasons for the Tower of Babel than simply this etiology, this story of origins, for why people are scattered everywhere and for why we have different languages. There are in the ancient Near East—we have their ruins today—terraced towers that the Babylonians built. They're called *ziqqurats*. These are temples that are supposed to be bridges between the Earth and the heavens. The idea was when you went to the temple you would gradually ascend as if you were coming up to where the gods lived.

By telling the story of the Tower of Babel, the biblical writer is saying, oh, those terraced temples that the Babylonians built, those aren't signs of bridges between the Earth and heaven, uh-uh, those are buildings of humankind, humankind's failed ability to reach Heaven. They're signs of God's power, not human's power. They're not bridges to heaven at all, rather they're simply leftovers from the flood.

It looks like at the end of the story of the Tower of Babel that God is going to have to start again, and that's in fact exactly what happens. When the primeval history ends with the Genesis 11, humankind has simply gone downhill. We are all left scattered, unable to communicate with each other, now having to figure out how to live in a world that's just basically a mess. And God has to figure out how He's going to commune with us. How do you find somebody who's actually going to listen?

And the story that we actually get, the story of Abraham and his wife, Sarah, may not be quite the story one would have expected, because Abraham and Sarah are not perfect characters. They are like you, and they are like me. They are flawed, sometimes they're tricky, sometimes they're quite clueless. But they are often faithful. They are often smart. And I think it's appropriate God seems to like them.

Abraham is called by God out of the blue as it were. A voice comes to him and says, "Abram," which is his name to begin with, he becomes Abraham later, "Abram, take your wife, Sarah, and go to this new land which I will promise you." And Abram gets up and goes.

God promises him he will be the father of a great nation, which sounds pretty good until we start looking at the details. Sarah, his only wife—and this is a polygamist society, he could have had others—Sarah, his only wife, is infertile. The land, the Promised Land, turns out, as soon as he gets there, to be in famine. He goes down to Egypt, Abram does, where immediately his wife lands in the harem of the Egyptian king, the Pharaoh. Abram's nephew, Lot, who goes with him to the Promised Land, is taken captive by an alliance of kings and eventually finds his way to Sodom, which is not a city with a great future. Sarah plans to have her slave give Abram a son, but that doesn't work out well. And then Abram gets commanded by God to kill his beloved son, Isaac. This is not a story that bodes well.

What's going on here in general? Could it be that Abraham's fidelity is being tested, that God is testing Abraham to see how much he can endure, whether he can still believe despite all evidence to the contrary? Or, perhaps in engaging the way he does with God, is Abraham testing God to see how God will remain faithful even despite Abraham's failings?

Before we can talk about characterization here, I'd like briefly to discuss the question of Abraham's historicity, because now we are no longer in myth, we are in saga. Abraham is much more like a real person than Noah or Enoch or Cain or Abel or Adam and Eve. And it was the case, particularly at the turn of the 20th century on up until about World War II, that biblical scholars were fascinated with the question of Abraham's historicity.

This raises the question of the historicity of the patriarchs, and that's simply the way we refer to Abraham, Isaac, and Jacob. Their wives, by the way, are the matriarchs. The history of the patriarchs in the patriarchal era—The stories seem to be set in the mid-Bronze Age, 1800, 1750, or so. But the accounts themselves are written much later, and we can tell that the accounts are later, because every once in a while there is a staggering anachronism, which most readers of the Bible wouldn't pick up because to most people antiquity is antiquity.

But we find in the patriarchal sagas, for example, references to the Philistines. They are about 500 years later. They won't show up until about the year 1200. We find references to domesticated camels, which is not something most of us care about. And it wasn't anything the people in the Bronze Age cared about, because camels wouldn't be domesticated until the Iron Age.

There are obvious anachronisms here. The biblical writers didn't care. They are simply telling a good story. And in telling that story, they are reflecting their own time period, rather than the actual time that the patriarchs are set.

Archaeologists also attempted to prove the Bible true. And we've already seen that, with looking for Noah's ark or looking for the walls of Jericho.

When it came to the patriarchs, biblical archaeology, as it was then called—now we speak of Mediterranean archaeology or Near Eastern archaeology—biblical archaeology thought they could actually locate the patriarchs. There was a school of archaeology typically called the American School, because it was run primarily by American academics funded by American churches and American Christian seminaries. The names most commonly associated with the American School are William Fox, Will Albright, and G. Ernest Wright. And those of you who have church libraries, I bet you will find books by them there.

This American School thought that not only could one prove the Bible true by archaeology, but it was necessary to prove the Bible true. In other words, the truth of the Bible guaranteed the truth of theology. As Ernest Wright put it: "The acting of God in history is central to the proclamation of Israel's faith." If the Bible were shown to be historically invalid, people might be engaging in false faith.

Well, for a while it looked like this American School, these biblical archaeologists, were digging up promising material. They found ancient archives at cities called Nuzi and Mari. And at first, it seemed like those archives were revealing to them material that matched up with the patriarchs. At first, they suggested these archives proved that a man could marry his sister. Well, it seems that Abraham was passing off his wife as his sister, perhaps that's the background. Or that it was common for women to provide their husbands concubines, in order to produce children who would become the women's legitimate heir.

There were many such examples of these partial connections with the Bible. But in the past several decades as scholars have begun to translate these texts more cautiously and do the rigorous historical work which is needed, it turns out that the American School's optimism was somewhat misplaced. The patriarchs cannot be proven by archaeology. For those who care about this from a religious perspective, the good news is you can't disprove it either.

In addition to the American School, there was another school in the middle part of the 20th century called normally the German School, which also was interested in the history of the patriarchs. For example, a German scholar named Albrecht Alt suggested that the patriarchs Abraham, Isaac, and Jacob may have originally been clan leaders, leaders of groups, and the clan leader would have his own special god, like a totem. And we do find in the Bible that God has different epithets, depending upon which patriarch is being discussed. We have, for example the Shield of Abraham or the Fear of Isaac or the Mighty One of Jacob.

Alt's idea was that there were originally separate clans, each with its own god. And as the clans merged together, eventually they combined their history, making the clan leaders relatives, one the son of another. And making gods all the same God, just with different names. So that Elohim and YHWH and the Mighty One and the Fear and the Shield were all names for the same God. That's possible, but again we simply cannot prove it. These may simply be stories. The patriarchs may not have been individual clan founders. They may have actually been related, or they may simply be a story that somebody made up in order to convey certain cultural considerations to their own people at their own time.

The stories about these clan gods might be looked at as etiology stories of origins. But, in fact, we do have in the Bible real etiologies, real stories of origin, and these sometimes we can determine are written well after the fact. Let me give you one example. Israel has two traditional enemies called Moab and Ammon. They are people who give the Israelites grief when they are wandering in the wilderness after they escape from Egypt. They always go to war with Israel, and Israel simply doesn't like them.

In Genesis 19, we have an etiology of how Moab and Ammon came to be, and the story goes like this: Sodom and Gomorrah are destroyed. They're wicked; God decides to wipe them off the face of the Earth. Living in Sodom happens to be Abraham's nephew, Lot. Lot, aided by a couple of angels, escapes Sodom. Lot's wife turns back and turns into a pillar of salt, because they had been commanded, don't look back. That, of course, explains why there are salt pillars in the Near East.

But Lot and his daughters eventually escape, and Lot, who is scared of everybody, eventually takes his daughters up to a cave. And the daughters conclude, "There is no one left alive to continue our father's name." So what do you do? Well, if you're Lot's daughters, you get your father drunk and then on successive evenings have sex with him, and you conceive by him. And that's just what happens. So the two daughters get their father drunk, perhaps rape him, at least have sex with him. They conceive children. One is called *m'av*, meaning "from my father," that's Moab; and the other is called *Benammi*, "son of my people," that's Ammon.

Those are etiologies, stories of origins, for Israel's traditional enemies. Israel is saying, in effect, we recognize these people as part of a family, but we also want to call them incestuous bastards, as it were. A nice story of origin.

But it does seem to be the case that some of the stories in Genesis are not made up well after the fact, because indeed sometimes people in Genesis do things which later Israel would have considered totally improper, against the law. The biblical law code, for example, forbids a man from marrying two sisters at the same time. But that's precisely what Abraham's grandson, Jacob, will do. He marries two sisters, Rachel and Leah. The biblical law code forbids a man from being married to his sister, but Abraham claims Sarah to be his sister, and the narrator says at least she's his half-sister.

There are several such cases, which suggest perhaps some of these stories really are quite old. That they really did, that they really were at least told, if not necessarily happened prior to the time that the text were written. They may actually be old. The majority of biblical scholars today date the literary composition of the patriarchal sagas to the Judean royal court sometime between 900 and 750. The same as we saw with, say, Adam and Eve or the flood stories.

In these particular stories, God is most often like the God of Genesis 2 and 3, not transcendent, but immanent. This is a God who wrestles with human beings, who talks to us all the time, who fights with us. This is a God who's sort of like another human, not quite so transcendent.

Aside from etiologies and history, what I find particularly helpful with these stories is how they function on a literary basis. I mean how they grab the reader. These are well-packed stories. They are exceptionally well written. It's simply great literature. They are marvelous.

We might, for example, look even just briefly at the story of Abraham's concubine. Sarah has a slave whose name is Hagar. Hagar in English. The name Hagar, by the way, means "the stranger." She's an Egyptian slave. And Sarah, who is infertile and who knows that Abraham has been promised children, decides at one point to take that promise into her own hands, and, in effect, puts Hagar into Abraham's bed. No one gives Hagar the choice. And Hagar miraculously conceives. But when she conceives, as the text said, "Her mistress became light in her eyes, a thing of no worth." But also you think Hagar is becoming increasingly pregnant, and Sarah consequently is looking less heavy, lighter.

Sarah can't take it. She simply can't deal with this younger woman who has just what she wants, that pregnancy. She begins to abuse Hagar, and Hagar, pregnant Hagar, flees from her into the wilderness.

And at that moment, an angel, perhaps God himself, actually appears to her. Now, here is the magnificence of the Bible. This divine manifestation, this theophany, an appearance of God, does not happen to Abraham, and it doesn't happen to Sarah, not to people of the promise. It happens to a slave, and an Egyptian, and a woman, and a pregnant one at that. That's the genius of the Bible. God shows up to people whom you wouldn't expect to receive that revelation.

The angel says to Hagar, "Hagar, where are you coming from and where are you going?" And Hagar responds, "I am running from the hand of my mistress, Sarah." But she never says where she is going, because she doesn't know. That's the genius of the characterization here. Just to listen to the dialogue.

The angel actually sends her back home, which some biblical interpreters have looked at as very cruel, to send a slave back to a place of abuse. And others have said, wait a minute, she's got a responsibility for a fetus here, you don't want her wandering around in the wilderness. At least let the child be born and have Abraham acknowledge him.

Later, Hagar will be thrown out. As we saw, Abraham listened to the voice of his wife. And eventually Hagar and her son, Ishmael, are booted out. But at that point, Ishmael also receives a divine promise, and he, like his younger brother, Isaac, will become the father of 12 tribes. It's extraordinary how this text matches up tit-for-tat, playing theme against themes, and through dialoguing characterization brings these people back to life.

But as you've seen, just when the angel commands to send Hagar back, there is some narrative ambiguity here. It's not exactly clear why characters do what they do or why God does what God does. To provide a more detailed look at this narrative ambiguity, I want to look more closely at the first full chapter we have about Abraham. This is the end of Chapter 11 and the beginning of Chapter 12.

We will find here themes sounded already in the primeval history. But instead of vague characters like Noah, more well-rounded characters, we can get a better handle on them. Abraham's introduction at the end of Genesis 11 threatens to repeat the disasters of the primeval history as we've noticed. Adam and Eve are given a garden, but they failed to maintain the residency requirements, so they are evicted. Noah is given a fresh start only to become drunk and naked. The post-diluvian, which is simply a fancy way of saying "after the flood," generation threatens to build a tower to Heaven to become like the gods—you might think of the snake's talk with Eve, "You will become like the gods, knowing good and evil"—only to be dispersed across the world.

And then there is Abram. Promised "a great nation," his circumstances cast doubt. He's 75 at the time God calls him. Now granted, we have people in their eighties and nineties, who were still producing children, but it doesn't happen very often. Sarah, as we know, is infertile. Abraham brings his nephew, Lot, along, perhaps thinking Lot might inherit. But Lot eventually winds up in Sodom, so that's not going to work. And when Abraham finally gets to the Promised Land, there is a famine. So Abraham does what any smart ancient Near Eastern person would do in times of famine: You go to Egypt, because Egypt is the bread basket of the ancient Near East. As long as the Nile floods, and the Nile is going to flood, Egypt will have grain. They are not so dependent upon rain.

Abraham and Sarah go down to Egypt. And, at this point, we finally find Abraham actually talking to his wife. He did not say to her, when God calls, "Hey, hon, you know God just spoke to me from Heaven, pack up." This is the first time he actually speaks to her. His first words: "I know well that you are a beautiful woman, and when the Egyptians see you, they will say, 'This is his wife.' Then they will kill me. Therefore, say you are my sister, so that it may go well with me because of you."

What do we do with this? Abraham is, in effect, asking Sarah to lie on his behalf. Is that ever morally appropriate? Are there times you have to? In saying to Sarah, do this so "it may go well with me," where is Abraham's concern for her? Or what choice does she, what would happen if she had said, "No, I don't think I'm going to lie for you?" They go down to Egypt, she says, "Oh, I'm gorgeous, that's true, here is my husband, they are going to kill him." That's the end of the story. God would have to start again.

And where is Abraham's theology here? Is it one of trust? Did he think, "Oh, God has called me. He's not going to let some sort of disaster happen. I'll fix it the best way I can, and I'll let God get me out of this mess"? Or is he testing God? What is God going to do? If Abraham was willing to leave his home, perhaps God ought to be willing to leave Heaven, to put in a little bit more effort for Abraham.

Well, what Abraham expected to happen, happens. Sarah is apparently gorgeous. Here is where some of those movies come in. In the movie version, this is Ava Gardner. I mean Sarah is just exquisite. And the Egyptian officials see her, they think gorgeous, and they praise her to Pharaoh and right on cue Pharaoh—the name, by the way, means "the house," it's a metonymy, like "the White House said;" Pharaoh is "the house" in Egypt, it's the ruling person, we'll just call it a king—the Pharaoh, right on cue says, "Oh, let me take Sarah into the harem," and for her sake, the Bible says, he gives Abraham "sheep, oxen, male donkeys, male and female slaves, female donkeys, and camels." I wonder, by the way, if this is where Hagar came from, one of those female slaves. We're never told.

But how is the situation to be resolved? Abraham is doing quite well right now, but he is supposed to get back to the Promised Land, and he is supposed to become the father of nations. And it's tough to do all that if you're in Egypt, and your wife is in the king's harem. Did Abraham ever intend to tell the truth, and if so, when?

And what of Sarah? Did she perhaps think, "Well, if I'm not having kids with Abraham, perhaps Pharaoh might do something a little bit better." Abraham has not yet had any children. And the source of Sarah's infertility may not be evident to her. Was she, in fact, tired of this man, this Abram who was dragging her from the comforts of Chaldea and then the comforts of Haran and taking her out to the wilderness of Canaan, which is not really prime real estate in the Bronze Age. Might she appreciate the palace comforts, the perfumes, the baths, the soft beds, as opposed to some nomadic camp?

And then there is the Pharaoh. Why is he not named? In fact, throughout Genesis and Exodus, we keep having references to Pharaoh, but never named. This is like saying the President and not telling us which one. Are Pharaohs supposed to be compared? This particular Pharaoh on whom Abraham plays a trick; a later Pharaoh we'll see with Abraham's great grandson, Joseph, who promotes Joseph to the prime minister of the land; or the later Pharaoh still whom Moses encountered; a Pharaoh who knew not Joseph, who enslaves the, the later Pharaoh who enslaves the Israelites. Are we to compare them simply because they don't have names?

Well, in this particular story, God does enter into history to protect the patriarchal promises. God afflicts Pharaoh's house with plagues. We'll see that come back again when Pharaoh's house is inflicted with plagues. That's the story of the Exodus. These plagues are not named, and there were not 10 of them.

And Pharaoh concludes—how he finds this out is not clear—that Abram has lied to him about Sarah. Pharaoh realizes that her presence in the harem threatens to make him, not to mention her—which he doesn't—an adulterer. And committing adultery anywhere is a bad thing. It doesn't matter whether you're a Hebrew or an Egyptian or a Babylonian. Summoning Abraham, the Egyptian king gives him his wife and banishes him with "all that he had." And by the time we're up to Genesis 13, verses 1 and 2, we find that Abraham has become exceptionally wealthy. He has made out like a proverbial bandit. Did God want all this to work this particular way?

And what about Sarah again? What might she have done during this problematic situation? And my question here is prompted by an ambiguous phrase in the Hebrew. In Genesis, Chapter 12, verse 17, we're told that Pharaoh spoke to Abraham *al-d'var Sarai*, usually translated "because of Sarah" or "about Sarah." Pharaoh spoke to Abraham about Sarah or concerning the matter of Sarah. Literally, *al-d'var Sarai* means "upon the word of Sarah." Does this mean that Sarah actually spoke a word to Pharaoh saying, "Hey, Pharaoh, I'm actually married? You might not want to take me in your harem." Or did Sarah actually say to God, "God, please get me out of this? This is not what I had intended." Was Sarah pro-active here, or was she simply silent through the whole thing?

I worry about her, as well, because it seems to me she's really the key to the promise. We find that this patriarchal line is ensured during the first generation, not through the father, because as we've already seen, Abraham has fathered another son, Ishmael, by Hagar. It's not the father who counts here; it's the mother. It's the line that goes through Sarah that will be important, not the line that goes through Hagar. So with the short tale of Abraham and Sarah's sojourn in Egypt, only a few verses, we've encountered rich characterization, complex and ambiguous action, a sense of both divine power and human reaction. And we've also got a partial template of stories to come. The comforts of the court remain in tension with the wanderings of the nomads. Here Pharaoh's court is a place perhaps of safety but also of danger to Abraham. Abraham is doing better when he's back on the road to Canaan.

The plagues as we've seen prefigure the Exodus. At first, Sarah is, in effect, enslaved by Pharaoh. She's taken into his harem; she has no choice. Then we find that Abraham is given Egyptian slaves, men and women. One of those slaves becomes Abraham's second wife, Hagar, and the mother of his son, Ishmael. Ishmael then becomes the father of his own tribe, the Ishmaelites. And we'll see later that the Ishmaelites are the ones who sell Joseph into slavery in Egypt.

And then Joseph, Abraham's great grandson, becomes a slave in Egypt. He eventually gains his freedom and his entire family follows him down there. But in the next generation, at the beginning of Exodus, as the text says, "There arose a Pharaoh who knew not Joseph," and he enslaved all of Joseph's population. The Israelites again become slaves in Egypt. What goes around comes around. The fate of Israel and Egypt will be and, ironically, even today is still intertwined. These stories have modern implications.

We also find the success of this new people of God, Abraham's people, will be built up through, well, in part, accepted political means like warfare and negotiation, but also in the early years, especially through trickery. This trickster motif, in which somebody succeeds not by military power, not by strength, but by brains, by cleverness, will reappear with Rebecca, Sarah and Abraham's daughter-in-law; her son, Jacob; Jacob's daughter-in-law, Tamar; the Egyptian midwives who save the Hebrew babies from death; judges such as Ehud. And if these names are not familiar, they will be.

The stories of the characters in the early part of the Bible are stories of people who were the underdogs, who do not have armies, who do not have power, and they get by because they are smart. And sometimes they have to lie to do it, and sometimes they have to cheat to do it. And back then, this was not a moral problem. These are tricksters who would have been celebrated by the people who told their stories. Much as today we can look at a picaresque novel and celebrate anti-heroes or in, for example, Native American mythology, coyote, the trickster figure. We do kind of like him a little bit more than people who simply play by the rules.

We also find trickster figures who are problematic. Abraham plays this trick on Pharaoh, and he gets away with it. That will also happen fairly frequently and particularly with some of the women.

It turns out that Joseph is the love-interest of his master's wife. Potiphar, who buys Joseph, has a wife. We'll call her Mrs. Potiphar. She doesn't have a name. Mrs. Potiphar is in love with Joseph, and she keeps saying, "Lie with me, Lie with me." And Joseph says, "Uh-uh, uh-uh, I'm not going to touch my master's wife." One day, he gets a little bit too close. She grabs his garment, and he flees away. And she says to the people in the household,

"Look, he tried to attack me. I have his garment here." And Joseph winds up getting thrown into prison. And you know what? She gets away with it.

Later on, we'll find the story of Samson and Delilah, Delilah who betrays Samson to the Philistines and gets a lot of money, and she gets away with it. What are these women signaling, as well? We might want to keep our eye on them. We also have, in the patriarchal tales, the motif of what's called the "ancestress in danger." Somebody's wife being placed in a harem—you think that's a one-time thing, but it's not. Later on, Abraham will take Sarah and place her in the harem of Abimelech, King of Gerar. And Abimelech then finds out that Sarah's his wife. And Abimelech is furious and says to Abraham, "How could you do this?" And Abraham says, "Well, you know, I said she was my sister. She's really my half-sister. I really didn't lie." Well, of course, he lied. She's also his wife.

What makes this even more problematic, Abraham's son, Isaac, passes off his wife, Rebecca, to the very same King Abimelech of Gerar, about whom one has to worry. Why are these ancestors doing this? And I suggest the idea here is the women really are important, and God is watching out for these people. The ancestors do what they can in order to ensure their future, but they need a lot of help, and that's God's job. Finally, the motif of the promise continues. God had promised Abraham a land, numerous descendants, and that Abraham would indeed be a blessing to other nations. Well, despite famine, despite problems in the family, despite problems with his wife, and as we'll see in the next lecture, even despite God's command that Abraham kill Sarah's son, Isaac, somehow that promise will come to be. With God's blessing and despite sometimes the patriarch's ineptitude, it's all going to work out okay in the end.

Isaac
(Genesis 21–22)
Lecture 5

God decides to test Abraham, so he tells Abraham to take his son, Isaac, and kill him, offer him up as a burnt offering. ... It's only 19 verses. This is one of the best short stories ever written. It is so packed.

The arguments for Mosaic authorship of the Pentateuch (Greek for "five scrolls") are scripturally based, but they face numerous problems. Scripture and early commentary do suggest Mosaic authorship. The term "the Books of Moses" appears in Ezra 6:18; Exod. 24:4; Josh. 8:31; and in the Old Testament Apocrypha, Ecclus. 24:23. Attributions of Mosaic authorship are suggested by the 1st-century C.E. Jewish historian Josephus (*Ant.* 4), the Jewish philosopher Philo of Alexandria's *Life of Moses*, and in Christian sources Mark 12:26 and Acts 15:21.

Arguments against full Mosaic authorship appear already in antiquity. Fourth Ezra (2nd Esdras) records (14) that Ezra rewrote the Torah after it was destroyed. Saint Jerome, in the late 4th century, makes a similar observation. The Christian philosopher Clement of Alexandria (3rd century) denied that Moses would tell such a lie as that of Noah's drunkenness (Gen. 9). With the Enlightenment, more rigorous criticisms of Mosaic authorship appeared. Why would Moses refer to himself in the third person? Is the Deity's name Elohim, YHWH, El-Elyon, El-Shaddai? ("God" translates "elohim"; "Lord" signals the Hebrew letters "Y-H-W-H," also called the *Tetragrammaton* [Greek for "four letters"]). There are (apparent) contradictions leading to such questions as, What came first: animals (Genesis 1) or humankind (Genesis 2)? Did Noah take animals two by two or seven by seven? Was the Torah given on Mt. Sinai (Exod. 19) or Mt. Horeb (Deut. 1)? Is Moses's father-in-law Jethro, Ruel, or Hobab? Repetition in the Bible have also contributed to criticism (The Ten Commandments, or "Decalogue" (Greek: "ten words"), appear in Exodus 20 and 34 and Deuteronomy 5, with thirty minor variations. The "ancestress in danger" appears three times. The three accounts of how Isaac received his name—Gen. 17, 18, and 21—differ as to who laughed and why.)

The divine names could reflect different aspects of the divine personality: YHWH for ethics, Elohim for transcendent manifestation. "Contradictions" may be harmonized or may result from a single author's mistake. Repetition may also represent authorial artistry, as we'll see in the next lecture.

In 1651, Thomas Hobbes had already claimed that much of the Pentateuch was post-Mosaic; shortly thereafter,

Click Art.

The trial of Abraham's faith.

Baruch Spinoza made similar claims. The major spokesperson for this model, now called the Documentary or Graf-Welhausen Hypothesis, was Julius Welhausen, who in 1878, working with the theories of Graf, published his *Prolegomenon to the History of Ancient Israel.*

Exegesis (from the Greek for "to draw out"), or scholarly analysis, includes source criticism and the various other methods that these lectures have already adduced. The method applied determines both what questions are brought to the text and the means by which answers are derived. Our test case is Genesis 22. How do we interpret the story? Anthropology suggests the *Akedah* may be an etiology explaining why the Hebrews do not practice human sacrifice. The practice was known: Jephthah sacrifices his daughter (Jdg. 11); Ahaz and Manasseh, their sons (2 Kgs. 16 and 21, cf. Mesha King of Moab, 2 Kgs. 3:27). Ezek. 20:26 even speaks of a divine command ordering child sacrifice. Exod. 22.29–30 suggests that all first-born children and animals belong to God (cf. Exod. 24:10–20 on redeeming first-born males). To offer a child was to offer one's most precious possession

(Carthage). However, Abraham is rewarded precisely *because* he is willing to offer his child.

For the Church, the *Akedah* prefigures the cross; the sacrifice of sons by fathers. Isaac carries his wood; Jesus carries his cross (Epistle of Barnabas). Jewish (Rabbinic) exegesis, sometimes considered a forerunner of deconstruction, concentrates on what is said and what is omitted. Explanation of the very detailed v. 2 in a remarkably condensed chapter. Interest in the silence between son and father. As Ishmael and Isaac face death; one is passive, the other, questioning. This introduces the motif of countering primogeniture. Hagar and Abraham both heed angelic messages: one in anguish, the other, silent. Might the *Akedah* also have been Abraham's test of God? Why does Abraham plead for Sodom but not for Isaac? Did Abraham recognize that his son's loyalty was to his mother? Gen. 23:1 notes, "Sarah died at Kiriath-Arba, that is, Hebron." But Abraham had "returned to Beer-sheva." Isaac brings Rebecca "into the tent of Sarah his mother"—"of Sarah his mother" is absent in some Greek manuscripts. "He took Rebecca, and she became his wife, and he loved her. So Isaac was comforted after his mother's death" (24:67).

We might wonder what effect the event had on Isaac. Compared to his father and his sons Jacob and Esau, he appears passive, weak, and repetitive, but perhaps he is more savvy than them all. The biblical stories were originally told orally, and what is conveyed—in person, through dialogue—may give quite another impression. We see this as we turn to the Jacob saga. ∎

Suggested Reading

Joseph Blenkinsopp, *The Pentateuch: An Introduction to the First Five Books of the Bible*, Anchor Bible Reference Library.

Carol Lowery Delaney, *Abraham on Trial: The Social Legacy of Biblical Myth*.

Jon D. Levenson, *Death and Resurrection of the Beloved Son: The Transformation of Child Sacrifice in Judaism and Christianity*.

Shalom Spiegel, *The Last Trial*. Translated by Judah Golden.

1. What moral judgment should be made concerning Abraham? Concerning God?

2. Sacrifice was as common in antiquity as television is today. Why did it become less common, and is it something that has been replaced or should be revived?

3. Why might Judaism have chosen this passage as the New Year (Rosh ha-Shanah) reading?

Isaac
(Genesis 21–22)
Lecture 5—Transcript

In the last lecture, we looked briefly at the story of Abraham and Sarah to discuss, among other things, the difficulties of situating them historically. But that does not preclude doing some sort of historical investigation on the patriarchal period, the period of the middle Bronze Age when Abraham, Isaac, Jacob, their wives, and their children lived. One of the ways we can approach the question of history is through a discipline known as "source criticism." So what we'll do in this lecture is we'll look briefly at source-critical questions: Who wrote the Pentateuch? Why is the Pentateuch sometimes assigned to Moses? And why do most scholars doubt that Moses had a hand in its composition?

And then, following a brief discussion of the various sources scholars have proposed, we'll look at one particular story, Genesis 22, the story of Abraham's near sacrifice of his son, Isaac, to try to determine what sources are there; but also to look at various other methodological approaches, because source criticism is only one of many as we've seen.

In fact, speaking of sources, you've already been exposed to some of them. You will remember, I hope, when we did Genesis, Chapter 1, that grand creation story where God said, "Let there be light." This wonderful transcendent God. I mentioned back then that that was usually assigned to the "P" or priestly writer who wrote sometime while the Jews were in exile in Babylon, and he was writing to provide an alternative to the Babylonian cosmogony, the *Enumah Elish*. So "P" is one of our four major sources for the composition of the Pentateuch.

And I hope you will also remember when we looked at Genesis 2 and 3, the Adam and Eve story, that the name of God changed. God, *Elohim*, in Genesis 1, God, YHWH, in English, Genesis 2 and 3, usually translated "Lord." And this Lord God has a much different manner of appearing. This Lord God is more immanent, gets his hands dirty in creating Adam, walks in the cool of the garden. Two different names for God. Two different sources.

The second source is usually called the "J" source. We should have called it the "Y" source, because we talk about YHWH. It's our luck that German scholarship got this first, and as Germans would pronounce "J" as "Y" as, for example, in the name Johan, so we talk about the "J" source. And they would actually talk about "JHVH" as opposed to "YHWH." But it's the same God. Those are two of our sources.

And when put together with two more sources, one called "E," which also uses the name, *Elohim*, probably written in the northern kingdom of Israel, also called *Ephraim*. We biblical scholars try to figure out various mnemonic devices, "E", *Elohim*, *Ephraim*, perhaps around the year 800 to 750 or so. And the final source "D," for the Book of Deuteronomy, which is very easy to remember, late seventh century. "J," "E," "D," and "P" provide us the four sources for Pentateuchal composition. And as we find those sources, when we go through various aspects of the Pentateuch—Genesis, Exodus, Leviticus, Numbers, and Deuteronomy—I'll flag those sources, so we can get a sense of not only where the sources are, but why the various writers wrote the way that they wrote.

Now, the four sources put together are referred to as the "documentary hypothesis," just a fancy name for this four-source theory. But the documentary hypothesis only really got going around the 18th century. Prior to that, pretty much everybody assumed that Moses wrote the Pentateuch. So before we can even talk about the sources that scholars now think exist, we have to go back, figure out why people thought Moses wrote the Pentateuch, and then determine why scholars think this is probably not the case. Don't think of this as so much an anti-Moses lecture, it's kind of pro-Moses, he did enough, but I don't think he wrote the Pentateuch.

We'll start with this: in terms of Mosaic—simply the adjectival form for Moses—in terms of Mosaic authorship, we actually have some hints in the Bible itself. For example, the term "Book of Moses" appears in the Prophet Ezra, Chapter 6. And the Book of Exodus itself in Chapter 24 claims, "Moses wrote all the words of the Lord." We also have some ancient documents not in the Hebrew Old Testament but, in fact, in the Old Testament Apocrypha, those Greek texts written by Jews in between the Old Testament composition and the beginning of the New. There is a book in the Old Testament

Apocrypha entitled "Ecclesiasticus," not be confused with Ecclesiastes. It's also called the "Wisdom of Jesus ben Sirach." Anyway, it dates to about 180 B.C.E, Before the Common Era. And what ben Sirach says in this text, is he talks about "the book of the covenant of the most high God, the law of which Moses commanded us." And if you took that word "law" out of the Greek and put it into the Hebrew, that would be the Torah that Moses commanded us. And as we've seen, Torah can be another name for the Pentateuch. So perhaps this particular author, writing in Hellenistic times, thought Moses authored the Pentateuch.

Mosaic authorship is also sponsored by first century writers, both Jewish and Christian. We have a first century historian named Josephus and a first century philosopher named Philo, called Philo of Alexandria, both Jews. Both claimed that Moses wrote the Pentateuch. And we have references to "the Books of Moses" also in the New Testament, in the Gospel of Mark and in the Book of Acts. So this idea of Mosaic authorship really took off pretty quickly.

There is a certain logic to it, actually. Moses is the main character of Exodus, Leviticus, Numbers, and Deuteronomy. At least he knew more or less what was going on. And further, the Pentateuch ends with his death, as if when Moses stops, here our collection stops.

Now some people have already wondered, in fact, they wondered about this in antiquity: How could Moses have recorded his own death? Which is not a bad question.

This is Deuteronomy, Chapter 34, verses 5 and 6: "So Moses, the servant of the Lord, died there in the land of Moab, according to the Word of the Lord, and He [that refers to God] buried him in the valley of the land of Moab, opposite Beth-peor. But no one knows where the place of his burial is to this day." So how could Moses have written this?

Some ancient sources said God was simply dictating, and Moses wrote this with tears in his eyes. I mean, I think that's lovely, I don't think it holds much water. Another ancient source, which is a bit less supernatural, says, oh, well, Joshua, Moses's successor, filled in the last little bit. But I don't think Moses wrote this at all.

There are explanations for the various reasons why people thought Moses wrote this text, but other explanations that, I think, are better for why he didn't. For example, it's true we have the expression, "the Books of Moses." But on the other hand, we have texts like "the Book of Ruth" and "the Book of Esther." And no one has ever claimed that Ruth wrote Ruth or Esther wrote Esther. The term "Book of Moses" could simply indicate that Moses is the main character. It doesn't necessarily have to mean authorship.

Nor does Moses actually anywhere claim to have written the Pentateuch. It would be nice if he said, "Hi, I'm Moses. (This is Exodus.) I'm now writing your Bible for you." It doesn't happen that way.

Even in antiquity, we have people who actually doubted Mosaic authorship. I find this fascinating. There is a first century document, first century Common Era, C.E., called Fourth Ezra. And in some collections of the Old Testament Apocrypha, it goes under the name Second Esdras. So those of you who have Bibles with the Apocrypha, you may actually be able to find this first century document about 90–95 Common Era, ostensibly written by Ezra, who was a scribe following the time of the Babylonian exile. So this is a back-dated text.

And this is what Ezra, quote-unquote, this first century author, says about Babylon's destruction of Jerusalem in the sixth century. Ezra prays to God: "Your law has been burned, and so no one knows the things which had been done or will be done by you. If I have then found favor in your eyes, send the Holy Spirit into me..." it sounds kind of Christian, doesn't it? "Send the Holy Spirit into me, and I will write anything that has happened in the world from the beginning." So in the first century, there is actually a fairly strong trade-in that suggests Ezra is responsible for the Pentateuch, the original having been lost. And Saint Jerome, obviously a Christian saint, in the late fourth century Common Era, also asserted that part of the Pentateuch was written by Ezra.

On the other hand, there were some Christians who, in fact, questioned Mosaic authorship, even in antiquity. One of my favorite among the Church Fathers is a fellow named Clement of Alexandria, wrote massive commentaries on both the Old Testament and the New. And at one point, Clement of Alexandria says he has his doubts about Mosaic authorship of parts of Genesis. Specifically, he says, "In Genesis, Moses says Noah got drunk. Moses would never have told such a lie."

Absolutely fascinating. With the Enlightenment, we all know the Enlightenment, more rigorous criticisms appear than that Noah got drunk and Moses would not have lied. The following data prompted the suggestion of different sources, which were ultimately combined by a particular editor. For example, why would Moses refer to himself in the third person? Right? The text read, "Moses went up on a mountain." "Moses gave the law." If Moses had written it, he probably would have said, "I". And "I" is a perfectly normal word for ancient Israelites to use. We see it in the prophetic text all the time. Isaiah uses "I;" Jeremiah uses "I." Why not Moses?

Moreover, they asked, why are there different names for the deity? God, *Elohim*; YHWH, the Lord. And why does the deity have different personality traits, transcendent on the one hand, immanent on the other? They also questioned why the Bible had such repetitions in it.

When we get into the law code, as we will in a lecture or two, we find that the Ten Commandments—they are actually called "ten words" in Hebrew, and the Greek is "Decalogue," which simply means ten words—they are actually given three separate times in Exodus 20, Exodus 34, as well as Deuteronomy 5. And it turns out that there are over 30 minor variations among the three accounts. One would think if Moses actually wrote the Pentateuch, he would have known what the Ten Commandments said, and he would have gotten it right each time. Why the changes?

Some of the critics of the Enlightenment also said, this Pentateuch could not have possibly have been written by single authors, because there are too many repetitions. No one author is going to tell the same story three times, but yet we have the same story of a patriarch passing off his wife as his sister. And we've already gone through one of those stories when we looked at Abraham and Sarah in Pharaoh's harem.

But there are other stories that are repeated, and sometimes in terms of contradiction. Abraham and Sarah have a son whose name is Isaac. His name has something to do with the Hebrew term, *yitzakh*, which means "to laugh." But his name is given in three different ways in Genesis 17, 18 and 21. All three agree that it has something to do with laughter, but they disagree on who laughed and why. You'd think a single author would have gotten it right.

And then there are those apparent contradictions, some of which we've seen. What came first? The animals, Genesis 1, or humankind, Genesis 2? How many animals did Noah take into the Ark? Did they go in two-by-two or did they go in seven-by-seven? When we get up to the law codes, we'll find that Exodus claims that the Torah was given on Mt. Sinai. That's normally a term familiar to people. But when we get to the Book of Deuteronomy, Deuteronomy tells us the Torah was given on Mt. Horab, same mountain, different sources.

When God speaks to Moses in the wilderness, he speaks in a place called the "tent of meeting," and that's where the Ark is, where the law is held. But is the "tent of meeting" outside the camp, so people won't have to come in contact with it, because it's one of these holy things? Is it outside the camp, so Exodus 33? Or is it in the middle of the camp, and all the tribes camp around it? That's Numbers 2. These various discrepancies have suggested that Moses probably did not write the Pentateuch, or at least that the Pentateuch did not have a single author.

Now, there are obvious ways of countering each one of these things. Yes, of course, God has different names. But on the other hand, people have referred to me as Professor Levine or as A.J. or as Mommy. That doesn't make me a different person, right? So, of course, God in his merciful manner may be YHWH and in his more transcendent judgmental manner may be *Elohim*. It could be the same author.

There is also no reason why Moses would not have repeated the Ten Commandments. They certainly bear repeating. And the story about the laughter isn't bad either. So maybe, in this case, Abraham laughed and, in that case, Sarah laughed. It's a good story, and we can have variance to that story. It's certainly culturally appropriate. Nevertheless, the weight of the evidence seems to convince scholars at the Enlightenment, Moses probably didn't write this material. And, thus, the documentary hypothesis was born.

In the 17th century, Thomas Hobbes, who may be familiar to you from tapes on philosophy, already claimed that much of the Pentateuch postdated Moses. And he did so not only on the basis of the material I've just cited, but also because of some of those anachronisms we've talked about before, like domesticated camels in the Bronze Age. Baruch Spinoza, a famous Jewish philosopher from the same time period, argued the same thing.

By the middle of the 19th century, scholars had, in fact, isolated those four sources, "J", "E", "D," and "P," and close to the end of the 19th century, they had even determined when those sources were dated.

As we continue looking at the biblical material, I'll let you know what these sources are and why they might be helpful. In fact, when we turn to our test case, Genesis 22, verses 1 through 19, we can immediately see that this is the "E" source, *Elohim*, because the first verse uses the name "God." Now if we think about *Elohim*, the "E" writer, writing some time in the eighth century, this is a time when the northern kingdom of Israel finds the kingdom of Assyria on the horizon. They know that their own kingdom is in jeopardy. For the "E" writer to tell the story of Abraham being told to sacrifice his son, perhaps they were thinking, "Ah, Isaac represents us, and we are in danger. Maybe God will allow us, at the last minute, some reprieve." The story would have meant different things to different cultures. But, of course, the story means a whole lot more than that.

So let's then look at Genesis 22. The story is usually called the *Akedah*. The word comes from the Hebrew term "for binding," because Abraham bound Isaac with ropes. And since that's the normal way in scholarly discourse the story is referred to, I'm going to say *Akedah*. It's also easier to say than Genesis 22, 1 through 19.

Here is the basic story line. God decides to test Abraham, so he tells Abraham to take his son, Isaac, and kill him, offer him up as a burnt offering. The next morning, Abraham actually gets up early, saddles a couple of donkeys, takes a few of his servants, his young men, his son, Isaac, and they trek off to a place—Abraham is not quite sure where it is, but they go anyway—and three days later, they arrive.

On the way, there is not much conversation, but Isaac, at one point, says to his father, "Dad, well, we've got the wood for the burnt offering, and we've got the fire for the burnt offering, but where is the offering itself, where is the animal?" Abraham responds, "God will provide Himself the lamb for the burnt offering, my son." In fact, you can read this in two ways. "God will provide the lamb, my son, so you don't have to worry about it." Or, "God will provide the lamb for the burnt offering: my son."

There is a question here, by the way, about how old Isaac is. All right? Most people assume Isaac is just a little kid. He may well be in his twenties or even in his thirties. This takes place well after Ishmael has been expelled from Abraham's camp. If you think of Isaac as an adult, the story takes on a different nuance, because then he becomes a willing sacrifice, rather than a kid who is literally scared to death.

On the mountain, Abraham builds an altar, sets out the wood, binds Isaac with ropes, puts Isaac on the pyre, lifts up the knife, he's ready to kill his son, and suddenly, good thing, an angel calls down from heaven and says, "Don't touch that kid, don't do anything to him." Abraham, at this point, lifts up his eyes, looks over and sees a ram caught in a thicket and thinks, "Aha," takes Isaac off the pyre, puts the ram on, slaughters the ram instead. So he has an alternative sacrifice. And then at the end, he names the mountain, "the Lord will provide" or "the Lord will see," in the sense of "see to it." An angel calls out again, repeating the promises made to Abraham about numerous descendants and to be a blessing to nations. And then Abraham returns to his servants, and they head back. That's the basic story. It's only 19 verses. This is one of the best short stories ever written, I think. It is so packed.

In terms of interpretations, depending upon what questions you bring, you will get different answers. Most students I've had, when I've asked them about this story, most students have heard it in one form or another, say, "Oh, yeah, we know the story. That's the ancient Israelite way of explaining why Israelites/Hebrews do not engage in sacrifice of human beings. Right?" And we know child sacrifice was practiced in antiquity. In Judges, Chapter 11, the judge sacrifices his daughter. We have accounts in the Book of Second Kings, of Ahaz and Manasseh, two actual kings, who sacrificed their sons during national emergencies, that's Second Kings 16 and Chapter 21. And in Second Kings, Chapter 3, King Mesha of Moab, who's losing the war against the Israelites, sacrifices his son, and the Israelites are so horrified they actually fall back, as if somehow that sacrifice, at least for a moment, were efficacious.

In fact, we have sacrifices throughout the ancient world. Those of you familiar with Greek mythology may recall the story of Agamemnon sacrificing his daughter Iphigenia prior to leaving on his sea journey to Troy for the Trojan War.

Even more to the point, there is an odd, odd verse in the prophet Ezekiel, who was, by the way, an odd, odd prophet, we'll get to him soon. Ezekiel even speaks of God ordering child sacrifice. This is Ezekiel 20, verse 26. "I made them surrender their eldest sons, so that I might fill them with revulsion." Was it the case, at the time of Ezekiel, that child sacrifice was actually practiced?

There is also an anthropological interpretation of a couple of verses in Exodus 22. This 22:29B. "The first born of your sons you shall give to me. You shall do likewise with your oxen and with your sheep." Now, we know that the oxen and sheep are sacrificed. Could it have been the case, prior to the incorporation of the law code into the Torah, that some form of child sacrifice was practiced? Thankfully, later on, Exodus says you will give me your oxen and your sheep, and your first-born sons you will redeem. Good thing.

We also have examples of child sacrifice in Carthage. This is extraordinary. Archaeologists have found a necropolis. *Necropolis* is the Greek term for "city of the dead," which has thousands of graves, jars of bones of little children. And what we've been able to tell from the inscriptions is that the parents sacrificed their children, probably their first-born, to the god Saturn, who, if you know your Greek mythology, was known for eating his own children. The idea was: Your first-born child would be with the god, and that child would somehow be in heaven protecting you and all your subsequent children.

Now, I mentioned in the first lecture that the ancient world is not our world, and they do things that are quite different than we do. To me this is heinous. I mean, how could you sacrifice a child? But in antiquity, the view was: If you loved the gods enough, you would give the gods the most precious thing that you owned. And what could be more precious than your firstborn child? And that's probably what was going through the minds of these Carthageneans.

So, is the *Akedah*, Genesis 22, the Hebrews' explanation for why they don't engage in sacrifice? Eventually, it was used that way, but I don't think that's why that story was written originally. In fact, Abraham winds up getting rewarded by God precisely because he was willing to sacrifice his son. Right? You know, if I were Abraham, I would have said to God, "No, I'm not going to sacrifice my kid. That's not a good idea." Abraham doesn't do that. Moreover, offering the ram is not God's idea. It's not God who comes up with this concept of substitution. That's Abraham's idea.

So it seems to me, at least in its earliest period, the *Akedah* had other functions. In terms of functions which have been attributed to it, and I want to jump ahead just a little bit, both the church and the synagogue have put their own interpretations on it. So just as some historians have said, well, this is not really a story about child sacrifice, it's a story of why we don't sacrifice children, the church came up with its own reading. It noted that Abraham put the wood on Isaac for Isaac to carry, and then it said, "Ah, when you go to the gospels, Jesus, at least in the Gospel of John, carries his own cross."

Already by the first century Common Era, there is a document called the Epistle of Barnabus. It didn't make it into the New Testament canon we have today, but it's in some early canonical collections. And Epistle of Barnabus actually makes that connection between Jesus and Isaac explicit. And you can see where they would have gotten it. Abraham, the loving father, sacrifices his son; God, the loving father, sacrifices his son.

The rabbis also talked about this story, and they were quite upset by it. Now rabbinic commentary, rabbinic study of the Bible—we'll use the term *exegesis* from the Greek, to read out, just a fancy way of saying "scholarship on" or "interpretation"—rabbinic exegesis of this text looks at every particular word that's used, and it becomes very attentive to gaps, as well as to repetitions. And when it looks at gaps and repetitions, it is, in fact, the forerunner of contemporary views of deconstruction. How does the story break down? What are we not being told? How can it be re-centered?

And, in fact, when rabbinic exegesis looks at this story, they say, "Oh, wait a minute. That first line has much too much detail in it." For a short story of only 19 verses, this first verse is simply too long. They note the first line, "Take your son, your only son, your son whom you love, even Isaac." And they say, there has got to be something else going on here. So they actually invent a dialogue between God and Abraham, which the Bible only gives us the first part.

God says, "Take your son." Abraham, not wanting to kill his kid in this particular rendition, says, "Uh, can't do it, I have two sons, Ishmael and Isaac, therefore, all bets are off." God says, "Uh, got to recoup on this one, take your only son." Abraham says, "No, I have only one son by Hagar and only one son by Sarah. Sorry, can't do it." God says, "Well, the son whom you love." Now, this is a question. We know that Abraham loved Ishmael his oldest son. We saw that right before Sarah convinces Abraham to banish Hagar and Ishmael into the wilderness. That's the story where we're told Abraham grieved over his son, Ishmael, but God told him to listen to the voice of his wife.

And you may recollect, that's exactly the wording that God says to Adam back in the Garden of Eden, "because you have listened to the voice of your wife." Abraham really does love Ishmael. It's not clear he loves Isaac that much. I like to think of God prodding him a little bit here: "Abraham, you really do love Isaac." And perhaps Abraham said, "Yes, I really do." At which point, so says rabbinic exegesis, God was ready to say "even Isaac," and Abraham was ready to yield here.

It's not a bad story. The rabbis also note that although the party travels for three days, no conversation is recounted. So they bring in Satan to try to tempt Abraham not to sacrifice Isaac, to try to tempt Isaac to run away. The irony here is that Satan won't be invented for a good 500 years subsequent to this period. And the rabbis were also particularly attuned to little irritants in scripture and that being attuned will actually bring us back to anthropology.

They noticed in 22:19 a major problem. This is what the text says, "So Abraham returned to his young men, and they arose, and they went together to Beersheba. And Abraham dwelled in Beersheba." And where was Isaac? Two go up the mountain; only one comes down. Well the rabbis say, well, Isaac simply went up to Heaven to go to Hebrew School to study Torah with some of those patriarchs before the flood. I don't think so.

It may well have been that the story of the *Akedah* was originally not a Hebrew story at all, but some local pagan story like the epic of Gilgamesh, which we've already seen the biblical writers happy to adopt and adapt. Perhaps in that original story, the child really was killed by the father, and the editors simply slipped up on this one. But that lack of Isaac is a problem.

What finally happened here? It's hard to say one way or the other. There is even some rabbinic exegesis that suggests, in fact, Isaac was killed. Why? Because in the Middle Ages, people were being martyred, and Isaac becomes an ideal prototypical martyr.

This is a quote from the 12th century Rabbi Ephraim Jacob of Bonn, who writes a poem, and about Isaac says, "Down upon him fell the resurrecting dew, and he revived." In other words, Abraham really did kill him the first time. "And then God raised him up again, and his father seized him then to slaughter him once more. Scripture bear witness. Well grounded is the fact. The Lord called Abraham a second time from Heaven," which, in fact, in Genesis 22 he did. There's a wonderful book by a scholar named Shalom Speigel called *The Last Trial*, where you may want to look at some of this additional medieval interpretation. Absolutely fascinating.

Well, like rabbinic exegesis, contemporary literary approaches also look at words and juxtaposition, and how they are used. We might actually look at Genesis 22 as a narrative foil to Genesis 21. In Genesis 21, Abraham's son, Ishmael, the child of the slave, Hagar, faces death in the wilderness, and he is saved at the last minute, when his mother lifts up her eyes and sees a well with water. Isaac, too, threatened with death in the wilderness, is redeemed when his father looks up and spots a ram. Both mother and father heed angelic messages, but where Hagar is desperate, Abraham is relatively sanguine about the whole thing. Hagar's anguish highlights Abraham's compliance. She protests; he doesn't. Abraham again, perhaps, is more concerned about Ishmael than Isaac. And I wonder if, in fact, Abraham was thinking, "Ah, Sarah made me get rid of Ishmael, let me take her son, the son she waited 90 years for, and see what happens if I kill him."

Indeed, the next account we have of Sarah, right after Chapter 22, is Sarah's death notice, as if she never saw Isaac again. And she dies in a different place than the place Abraham went back to when he left the mountain, as if Abraham and Sarah never talked again after this. Or, perhaps simply, Abraham is testing God like God is testing Abraham. Could be the case. Is God going to pull him through at the last moment here? Or is God waiting for Abraham to say, "Wait a minute, God, this isn't just"? And Abraham refuses. I wonder if, finally, Abraham and God have come to terms here, because after the *Akedah*, we never see the two of them talking together either. After this test, there maybe nothing left for the two of them actually to say.

And what of Isaac finally? Well, we have some psychoanalytic readings. I grant that psycho-biography is difficult. It's like saying, what was Hamlet's relationship with his mother? But, on the other hand, sometimes it can be actually quite profound. Although Sarah's death is described in Chapter 23, not until Chapter 24 does Isaac come to terms with his loss: "Then Isaac brought Rebecca into the tent of Sarah, his mother. He took Rebecca, and she became his wife, and he loved her, and so Isaac was comforted for his mother's death." By the way, that phrase, "into the tent of Sarah, his mother," is only in the Hebrew, it's not in the Greek. Perhaps the Greek was made a little nervous by Isaac's connection with his mother.

And as far as Isaac himself, is it because of the *Akedah* that he spends the rest of his life more or less passive at home in bed? And as we'll see in the next lecture when we look at the Jacob saga, bedridden, beguiled by his family, ruled by his wife, and tricked by his son. Fascinating stories continue.

The Jacob Saga
(Genesis 25–36)
Lecture 6

Form criticism is not designed to set out what is historical. Form criticism, like folktales, is designed to tell a good story using certain literary conventions that people will recognize, such as genealogies and annunciations. Close reading tells us that how that form is finally played out in terms of dialogue, plot description, juxtaposition, characterization, and motivation.

The form critic, influenced by folktale analysis, focuses on the units (*pericopae*, sing. *pericope*, from the Greek for "to cut around") that comprise the larger narrative and attempts to locate the social setting of that unit in its oral stage. The form critic seeks the "setting in life" (*Sitz-im-Leben*) of the tale before its incorporation into the biblical narrative. Form criticism notes the parameters of each *pericope*; the premise is that the stories originally circulated independently, perhaps even unconnected to the patriarchs. Although the form remains consistent, studies of oral cultures reveal that storytellers typically adapt their accounts to times, places, and audiences. The form does not, and cannot, guarantee a basis in historical fact.

Let's test this with Genesis 25; form critical observations on the stories of Jacob and Esau. The account begins with an etiology: "Two nations are in your womb, and two peoples, born of you, shall be divided; the one will outdo the other, and the older will serve the younger" (Gen. 25:23–24). Jacob (Israel) will prevail over Esau (Edom). The etiological couplet authenticates the oracle. Its relationship to earlier "annunciation" etiologies (Gen. 16:11–12) prompts comparison: Rebecca, like Hagar, is heeded by God and, again, the oracle is not entirely encouraging. Esau's description as "red and hairy" ("red": *admoni*; 25:25) connects him to Edom ("red"), one of Israel's enemies. *Seir*, "hairy," is a pun on Seir, Edomite territory (Gen. 32:3).

Literary analysis observes the effects of description (the Bible rarely provides physical description), names, and authorial remarks. "The first came forth red, his whole body like a hairy coat. So they named him Esau" (Gen. 25:25). He appears animal-like, brutish (the Gilgamesh epic describes the animalistic, uncivilized Enkidu as "wild and hairy"). He is introduced through physical features rather than action; there is little subtlety.

"Afterwards his brother came forth, and his hand had taken hold of Esau's heel, so his name was called Jacob" (25:26). The focus on action makes Jacob appear more subtle, less easy to read. He is "grasping" by nature. His name, "one who supplants," portends that he raises himself up by pulling others down. Is this name appropriate for Israel's (eponymous) ancestor? Does its change to "Israel … who 'struggles with God' and prevails" signal changed character?

When the boys grew up, Esau was a skilled hunter, a man of the field, while Jacob was an *ish tam*—usually translated "quiet man"—dwelling in tents (25:27). Is the hunter valued or seen as uncivilized? Does "man of the field" distinguish Esau from the patriarchs or equate him with the earlier first born, Ishmael? In what sense is Jacob *tam*? The term elsewhere connotes innocence and/or moral integrity; cf. Abimelech of Gerar, who explains (Gen. 20:5–6) he is *tam* because he did not know that Sarah was Abraham's wife.

Literary criticism also attends to motive, which the Bible usually suppresses: "Isaac loved Esau because he ate his game, but Rebecca loved Jacob" (25:28). Is Isaac self-centered, thinking with his stomach—as Esau did earlier? Does the father live vicariously through his son? Does Esau remind Isaac of his beloved older brother, Ishmael? Is Rebecca's love—minus an explicit motive—self-serving? Motivated by the oracle? Does she love Jacob because she can control him? Because he is more like her? Does she love Jacob because Isaac loves Ishmael?

Literary criticism also explores the effects of dialogue: "Once when Jacob was boiling pottage, Esau came in from the field and he was famished. Esau said to Jacob, 'Let me eat some of that red pottage, for I am famished'" (25:29–30). Esau does what the narrator says, in the same terms; there is no complexity. "Let me eat some of that red pottage, for I am famished" (RSV) misses the impact of the Hebrew: "Let me chow down on that red, red stuff." Jacob responds: "First today sell your birthright [entitlement to a double portion of the estate] to me." His deliberateness contrasts Esau's breathlessness. Narrative voice reinforces Esau's lack. The Hebrew reads, literally: "And he ate, and drank, and rose, and went and despised, did Esau, the birthright" (25:34a).

Literary criticism asks (moving to ideological criticism): What are its views of those holding power? Leaders need to provide food. Esau, a hunter, was famished; Jacob had food and knew how to bargain with it. The motif reappears with Jacob's grandson, Joseph, and with Moses.

Israel's national saga depicts the community as succeeding through brains (and trickery) rather than (military) might. But success, especially through trickery, comes at a price. God enters history, although Israel can never determine when. To obey divine commands may entail personal suffering. The oracle of Israel's success over Edom waits centuries until it is fulfilled (2 Sam. 8:12–14; 2 Chr. 25:11–14); this gives the nation hope in times of distress.

Literary-critical readers finally attend to aesthetics. Although perhaps originally independent, the Jacob stories satisfy artistically through repetition of motifs and plot lines. Action and counteraction. As Jacob tricks Esau with Rebecca's help, so Jacob is tricked by Rebecca's brother Laban. Working seven years for Rachel, Jacob wakes to discover he has consummated a marriage with Leah, she of "tender eyes." Leah resembles the blind Isaac. Was Isaac similarly duped? Laban's rationale—"It is not done so in our country to give the younger before the first born" (29:26)—repays Jacob for usurping Esau's birthright and blessing.

As Jacob tricked Isaac with false garments—the skins his mother prepared—so Jacob is tricked by Joseph's coat, dipped in goat's blood. Potiphar's wife uses Joseph's coat as false evidence of his attacking her (Gen. 39). Joseph's Egyptian clothes disguise his identity from his brothers. Judah, the inheritor of the promise, is tricked when his daughter-in-law,

Tamar (Gen. 38), removes her widow's clothes and wraps herself in a veil; Judah takes her to be a prostitute and has intercourse with her.

No mere historical accounts, the patriarchal sagas raise complex issues of morality, theology, and community identity, even as they provide aesthetic delight. The following lecture, on literary conventions, is our final foray into literary criticism. ■

Suggested Reading

Robert Alter, *The Art of Biblical Narrative.*

Questions to Consider

1. To what extent are the patriarchal sagas profitably compared with folktales?

2. Can, or should, various *pericopae* in Genesis be seen as funny? What delight might the original audience have found in them? In oral presentation?

3. Do the accounts of Esau (as well as Ishmael) indicate an ambivalent relationship between Israel and its neighbors? Does Israel regard these other nations as "in the family"?

The Jacob Saga
(Genesis 25–36)
Lecture 6—Transcript

Our focus has been, to this point, on various forms of how scholars engaged in *exegesis*, biblical interpretation. We have looked at some older methods, such as source criticism, the documentary hypothesis, as well as some of the newer methods in terms of literary criticism or even psycho-biography. The criticism, such as literary criticism/psycho-biography, and, as we'll see in the next two talks, some close reading, some attention to literary convention, are part of new type of biblical studies that begin actually in the 1960s and the 1970s.

It turned out before then most people who worked in biblical studies taught in divinity schools and seminaries, and the only people they ever talked to were theologians. But in the 1960s and in '70s in the United States, suddenly American universities and colleges founded departments of religious studies. And once biblical scholars found themselves in secular institutions and secular departments, they found themselves talking to historians and literary critics and sociologists, and whole new worlds of biblical studies opened up. So not only can one be a theologian here, one also can be, indeed should be, skilled in all the humane and social sciences in order to interpret the biblical materials.

So in this lecture, where our test case will be Genesis, Chapter 25, the story of Isaac's children, Jacob and Esau, and how they duke it out for who is going to succeed in terms of ruling the clan, we'll use some more of those close-reading concerns that literary criticism brings us. But we'll also include a little bit of an earlier method that was very popular at the turn of the 20th century, called "form criticism."

We'll start with form criticism. The context of form criticism is this: We today understand how literature functions; we understand how art functions. If somebody went into a library and ripped off all the covers and title pages of every single book, we would, 99 percent of the time, be able to tell what to do with that book, because of the form that the book takes. If we get a book, and it says, "take two eggs and beat them," we will know that we've got a cookbook. If it says, "On a dark and stormy night," we will think we've either got a mystery or a parody. We will know the form.

For another example, if I were to say to you, "The lions chewed up the bears last night." You would not think, I suspect, that there was some disaster at the local zoo. You would know that I'm using sports metaphors here. Or if I were to say something like "Saint Theresa beat Saint Matthew." Again, there is no war in Heaven. We understand the form. We understand the sports metaphors.

So the question for the biblical studies experts and for anyone looking at the Bible is: What are some of the forms that the Bible uses, and how can we understand them? Indeed, some biblical scholars have suggested that once we understand the form, we can understand the setting in life where it was used. In other words, we know what to do with a cookbook. We understand the form. We understand its setting. The term for "setting in life" most often used in the scholarly discourse is *Sitz im Leben*, because, of course, these are Germans, and they invented the term, and it simply means, "setting in life." And we will look for the *Sitz*, this setting.

Sometimes this actually works. It's very good with prophetic oracles. But we are not there yet. In terms of finding forms, you're already familiar with some of them—etiologies, stories of origin. You saw that, for example, in the story of Lot and his incestuous daughters, the etiologies, the origin stories, for Moab and Ammon. We know how those stories function. We recognize the form, etiology, and we recognize the *Sitz*, the "setting in life." The Israelites told those stories in order to explain why they're in enmity with certain tribes who sound like them and look like them and speak their same language.

To accompany form criticism, which can be fairly mechanical, we have the newer literary technique of close reading. This is much like rabbinic exegesis that we saw when we looked at the *Akedah*. To look at how words convey meaning, but also like a literary critic would, close reading looks at dialogue. It looks at what narrators say. It looks at how characters are described. It looks at what is said, and what's not said. For example, the narrator tells us that Isaac loved Rebecca. We saw that in the last lecture. He loved her, and he brought her into his mother's tent. But we're never told whether Rebecca loved Isaac or not. But we are told that Rebecca loved her son, Jacob, so we know she can love. But whom does she love?

And we look at dialogue, because dialogue can have multiple meanings. We look for literary motifs; not only etiologies and prophecies, but catchy phrases and reminders of previous stories.

So our test case then is Genesis, Chapter 25. This is the story of Esau, Jacob's older brother, and Jacob, and how Jacob manages to procure Esau's birthright. And I'm going to go through this verse by verse, because that's what form criticism would do.

The form critics say the first thing you do is, you identify your narrative unit. Their view, and they are influenced by folklore studies here, is that independent narrative units in the oral tradition simply were passed along. People would say, "Anybody got a good Jacob story?" And you would get a short Jacob story. And eventually the idea was that these were all combined together. So they look for where this story begins, and where the story ends. The technical term for this is the Greek term *pericope*. It means an independent narrative unit. What I tell my students is think of periscope without the "s," because that's how *pericope* is spelled. It's periscope without the "s". You're getting simply a snapshot, a narrative unit.

And we look at where the *pericope* begins, and we find it begins here in Genesis, Chapter 25, verse 19, with the reference: "This is an account of the descendants of Abraham's son, Isaac." Isaac is the beginning of the story. We also find out that the *pericope* ends in verse 26: "Isaac was 60 years old when they [that is, his twins] were born." Already, I've got some close reading to do here, because Isaac doesn't show up in the rest of the story and that makes me a little bit nervous. He's part of the frame, as if he is looking on from the outside, but he's not really part of the action. He's not part of the picture.

The opening verses also include a reference to Rebecca and, indeed, a genealogical notice. And genealogical notices, "who begot whom, who is related to whom," are a standard form in biblical exegesis. We find them all over the place, but we rarely find them attached to women. So here we have another concern for an anomalous form. By having a genealogy given for Rebecca—Rebecca "the daughter of Bethuel the Aramean of Paddan-aram, and the sister of Laban the Aramean"—we already know she is an exceptionally important character, because the genealogy for the woman is anomalous.

And then we finally get what looks like, on the surface, a simple petition and an equally simple etiology. Rebecca, like all the other matriarchs, had some fertility problems. She finally after decades gets pregnant. But it turns out the pregnancy is very difficult; she's having such pains. She is so uncomfortable. She's finally calls out to God and says, "If everything is okay, why do I feel like this? I can't go on living anymore." She's in such pain her language actually bespeaks her desperation. And then she gets an answer from Heaven. And it's not the sort of answer one might have expected. Right? Instead of being told, "Oh, you have a little bit of a problem here, but it's okay, take a couple of Demerol, and everything will be fine," this is not what she gets. She gets an answer in poetic couplet, yet another form. And when you have poetic couplet, the idea is, perhaps this is like a prophetic oracle. God is now speaking in poetry. His language is different than hers. Think of Charlton Heston booming down.

This is the answer Rebecca receives: "Two nations are in your womb, and two peoples born of you shall be divided." This is swell. The woman is carrying twins, and prenatally they are already fighting it out. No wonder she is uncomfortable.

Rebecca is also told: "The one will outdo the other, and the older will serve the younger." That's Genesis 25, 23, and 24. Yes, it's an etiology. It tells us that the two twins will eventually father two peoples and one, the children descended from the younger twin, will be superior to the children descended from the older twin. But there is a lot more going on here than that.

Again, we can pay attention to the poetry and see where it comes up again. We find it in major statements in the Pentateuch. Poetry is common in the Prophets, much less so in the Pentateuch. We'll see it again with Miriam crossing the Red Sea—actually it's the Reed Sea, but we'll get there—as well as with Moses. This is an important etiology. It's something we need to pay attention to.

But we can also pay attention to the form. This is an annunciation, a standard form. An annunciation is a form where God or an angel tells a woman, either that she is going to be pregnant, or a pregnant woman something about the children she is about to have. We've already seen one of these with Hagar, right, that first theophany to the woman, where Hagar is told: "You are with child, and you will bear a son, and you will call his name, Ishmael." And the annunciation goes on: "And he will be a wild ass of a man, and his hand will be against his brothers, and he will live at odds with all of his kin."

When we get annunciations, it's not all sugar and spice. Sometimes when God tells you something about your children, it might not be quite what you were hoping for. And I think it's the same thing with Rebecca. I don't think it's good news to be told that your children will be at war, and their descendants will be at war. So here we might want to compare Rebecca and Hagar, at least here they are in solidarity.

More of interest to me, and here we move a little bit more into psychology, what do we make of that prediction itself? Is this a gracious God telling Rebecca that her pains are not imaginary; she's not making it up? No, I don't think so. But is this setting Rebecca up? Can you imagine being told and knowing this was true that you will have two twins, you will have twins, and that one will succeed and one will not? And then how do you raise these children knowing what their fates are going to be, knowing one will prevail over the other? Does Rebecca even ever tell Isaac about this? We're not told. Does she tell the children?

Well, let's look at the children, and we can see a little bit more in terms of close reading. When the kids are finally born, we actually get a description of Esau. And the Bible rarely gives us descriptions of people. Every once in a while, we get a notice "so and so was beautiful, Rebecca is beautiful, Rachel is beautiful, David is beautiful." But even in cases like that we don't actually know what they look like. In fact, for some of these women, they might have been sort of short and fat, because that was the standard of beauty in the ancient Near East. That way you didn't have to worry about famine; you had enough packing.

But with Esau, we actually a description, which is very, very odd. Whatever the standards of beauty were in the ancient Near East, I don't think Esau conformed to them. This is what we get in Genesis 25:25. "The first came forth red, his whole body like a hairy coat, so they named him Esau." Well, the word "Esau" is connected with the word Adom, which means red, but Edom or Adom is also one of the countries, one of the nations, at war with Israel. The word *Adom* means "red." Here is Esau with a red hairy coat. Already Esau is set up to be one of Israel's enemies.

Moreover, and here is a pun you're not going to get in English, but it's there in the Hebrew, the word for hairy is *seir*, and the word for the Edomite major city is *Seir*. People in antiquity would have heard that. Esau is indelibly connected with the Edomites, Israel's enemy. And he, in fact, with his hairiness, seems a little brutish.

If we recall the story of the epic of Gilgamesh, where Gilgamesh wanted to find that flower of immortality for his friend Enkidu, Enkidu was a wild man, and he's identified as very hairy. That's one of the sigla in the ancient Near East for somebody who's not quite civilized. There is no subtlety to this introduction. Esau is what he is. Even before his twin is born, we might figure this is not the one to inherit the promise. And, in fact, we don't even need the description to be told that because we're already alerted: Elder sons usually don't inherit. And as elder, Esau is associated with Ishmael, the older son, the child of the fields. This two-brother motif keeps replaying—Cain and Abel, Ishmael and Isaac. And we'll continue to see that.

Well, while the text describes Ishmael, excuse me, while the text describes Esau physically, it describes Jacob by action, what he does. "Afterwards his brother came forth and his hand had taken hold of Esau's heel, so his name was called Jacob," which means supplanter. This focus on action makes Jacob look a little bit more subtle. When you look at him, you can't tell what you're going to get. You have to watch what he does. But I also worry about this grasping, this supplanting. Is this part of his nature, as if to take hold of life and to grab it? Or is he one who will pull himself up by pulling others down, which is what he does with Esau? And ultimately, we find out actually, he's one who will pull himself up and pull others up along with him. But that's something he's actually going to have to learn.

Quickly, the narrator passes over their childhood, unlike the story of Isaac, where we get at least a story of his weaning. And the next thing we find is that the boys have grown up, and we're into a new *pericope*, a new narrative unit. Here, close reading comes in again, and again the Hebrew conveys nuances that the English totally glosses over. We're told when the boys grew up, Esau was a skilled hunter, a man of the field, while Jacob was, the Hebrew is *ish tam*, usually translated "quiet man," dwelling in tents.

Well, we can first ask the question about the hunters. Are hunters to be considered valuable, or are we really more interested less in people who hunt, than in people who raise animals? Hunting is—it's kind of old fashioned. It's what Nimrod did way back before the flood. But it's a little violent, and Israel is not too keen on this. Esau's got the wrong job description. But then when we look at Jacob, this *ish tam*, I have to worry. Sometimes when I think of a quiet man, I think of that movie called *The Quiet Man* with John Wayne. Unfortunately, nobody watches John Wayne movies anymore. John Wayne, a quiet man, but when he has to go to battle, watch out. That may have some sense of what the word *tam* means.

But when I find that word used elsewhere in the Bible, it really doesn't mean "quiet." It has the connotations of moral integrity or innocence. For example, King Abimelech of Gerar finds out that Sarah is Abraham's wife, not his sister, and says to Abraham, "I am *tam* of heart." I am innocent of heart. I didn't know she was your wife. That's the way it's normally read, so I don't know quite what it means to say Jacob is an *ish tam*, an innocent man. Is the point when he eventually procures the birthright and blessing, that he did it innocently? It was all on the legal up and up. Perhaps. Or perhaps the term is simply ironic. Already I've got problems with Jacob, and he's barely born. Right? He hasn't done very much.

Another problem we have with the biblical text, which is to me what makes it so much fun and also so very frustrating, is that the Bible, when it talks about characterizations, usually suppresses motive. Modern novels, we have lots of interior monologue. The narrator tells us everything that main characters are thinking. But we don't often know what characters in the Bible are thinking. Very little interior monologue. Very little actual description of motive. So then I have to worry about what are Jacob's motives in getting Esau's blessing and birthright? What motivated Rebecca to help?

So let's look at some motives here, when they're shown and when they are not shown, to see how they show up and what they do. We get actually a motive in the next verse. "Isaac loved Esau because he ate his game, but Rebecca loved Jacob." I have a motive for Isaac's love. He liked the food. I'm not quite sure this is a good motive for loving one of your children rather than another. It seems to me it's a tad self-centered. But then I wonder, perhaps it's Isaac living vicariously through this elder son. Perhaps it's Esau who goes and does what Isaac can't do; Isaac who stays all the time, Esau who goes out and hunts, the kind of manly guy. Or is it more than that? Does Isaac actually love Esau not just because of the game, but because he knows Rebecca loves Jacob?

And why, when we're told Rebecca loves Jacob, don't we get a motive? The text could have said Rebecca loved Jacob, because he was good at cooking. The text could have said Rebecca loved Jacob, because he was like her, clever, a trickster. But it doesn't tell us. Is it Rebecca loves Jacob without reason? A pure love, a non-self-centered love? Or does Rebecca love Jacob because she knows that Isaac loves Esau? On the other hand, in a more mercenary sense, does Rebecca love Jacob, because she knows Jacob is the one who is going to win? Has she been manipulated by that divine oracle? Or, does she love Jacob because she can control him? We don't have the motive, and that adds to the richness of characterization of this text.

As the story continues, we find an increasing emphasis on Esau's beastly nature. And we also find through close reading, here looking at dialogue, that we can tell a lot about characterization. And again we have a problem, because the English translations miss the nuances of the Hebrew. The verses in question here are Genesis 25:29-30. The standard English translation goes like this: "Once, when Jacob was boiling pottage, Esau came in from the field, and he was famished. And Esau said to Jacob, 'Let me eat some of that red pottage for I am famished.'" With Esau, you know exactly what you're going to get. The narrator says he's famished. He comes in, and he says, "I'm famished." Complexity is not his strong suit.

Moreover, it actually sounds quite nice to say, "Let me eat some of that red pottage," that's relatively civilized. You could hear that on Masterpiece Theatre. But that's not actually what Esau says in the Hebrew. The Hebrew, for those of you who are interested in this sort of thing, says, "*halitanina min ha-adom ha-adom hazeh ki ayef anochi*." Which really means, "Let me chow down, please, on some of that red, red stuff, because I'm starved." *Ha-adom ha-adom hazeh*, that red, red stuff. This is not a man of great articulation. Granted he does say, "please," the Hebrew particle *na*. I have a little bit of sympathy for him, but not a whole lot.

Jacob, on the other hand, uses the form of the court, technical terms for birthright, technical terms for promising. And he says to his brother: "First today sell your birthright to me," which basically means give me your double portion because you, Esau, as older son, have the right of primogeniture. You will get more of the inheritance than I, the younger son. His use of legal terminology concerning the birthright contrasts with Esau's, "Give me some of that red, red stuff." These are two brothers with very, very different personalities.

Esau, meanwhile, is still on automatic. He says, "I'm about to die. Of what use is a birthright to me?" I kind of wonder, is he really that hungry? Frankly, the man is a hunter, couldn't he have found something out in the field and cooked it himself? I do worry about this. He's thinking with his stomach.

Jacob isn't done yet. He says, "Swear to me today," another imperative verb. And Esau actually swears, and he gives his birthright away, just for a mess of pottage, hardly worth it.

At the end of the story, most English translations read, "And he swore to him and sold his birthright, and he ate, and he drank, and he went on his way." The Hebrew actually says, in very direct form, "He ate and drank and rose and went and despised, did Esau, his birthright." Ba-boom, ba-boom. Esau again on automatic. And simply the way the Hebrew spells out this very compact *pericope*, we have a good sense of the characterizations of the two, simply by the way they talk. For Esau, rapid fire, hasty, not thinking. For Jacob, conniving, shrewd, subtlety.

And in support of this assessment, close reading—with them, look at the next story. We've already seen that juxtapositions are important, the sense of juxtaposing the *Akedah* with the expulsion of Ishmael. Here is another one. Chapter 26 immediately begins, "Now there was a famine in the land beside the former famine that was in the days of Abraham." And what have we just seen? We've seen Esau, the hunter, who doesn't have enough food and who was hungry. And we've seen Jacob who knows how to bargain with his pottage. When there is a famine in the land, it's Jacob we want to be our ruler, not Esau, because he knows how to distribute goods, as, in fact, will his son, Joseph, when Joseph becomes the prime minister of Egypt and distributes grain during seven lean years. Watch out for what these people do.

Prudent bargaining is also an appropriate trait for leaders, but it's one Jacob has to learn a little bit better. He is able to bargain with Esau, but that's like shooting fish in a barrel. Later on, to convince his father to give him the blessing as well, he needs his mother's help. And Rebecca will actually put hair from a goat on his arms, so that when he goes to Isaac to get the blessing, Isaac will say, "Well, the scent is the scent of Esau," because he can smell the animal, "but the voice is the voice of Jacob." Here Jacob needs his mother's help.

Later, Jacob will actually bargain for his wife. We'll see this in the next chapter. He'll try to bargain with Rebecca's brother, Laban, for Laban's daughter, Rachel. But Rebecca's brother is much like Rebecca. They are both two tricksters, and Laban actually winds up outwitting Jacob. What goes around comes around in this text. As we find out with Laban, he will substitute an older daughter for a younger daughter. As he puts it in Genesis 29: "It is not done so in our country to give the younger before the first born." Jacob usurps the rights of the first born from Esau. Laban switches his daughters. Jacob winds up with the unwanted first born, rather than with Rachel, the beautiful younger one. What goes around comes around in the Bible.

And these various plot motifs will continue, each echoing earlier events. We'll find, for example, that Jacob's favoring of his son, Joseph, like Rebecca's favoring of Jacob, will lead to inner family tension and turmoil. When parents play favorites in the text, when they play favorites today, bad things happen in the family.

And just as Jacob will trick Isaac with false garments, wearing those skins that his mother prepared for him, so Jacob himself will be tricked by garments. Jacob has 12 sons. He loves his son, Joseph, Rachel's son, more than all the others. And the other sons simply can't stand this, and they can't stand Joseph, who is an obnoxious kid. At one point, they eventually wind up selling Joseph into slavery. And they take his coat, and they dip it in the blood of a goat, and they show that coat to their father, and their father, Jacob, concludes "a wild animal must have eaten my son." As Isaac is fooled with animal hair, so Jacob is fooled with animal blood. Again, what goes around comes around.

As Jacob deceived his father by means of clothing, the lambskin, so Joseph will later deceive his brothers. Joseph becomes prime minister in Egypt, and when the brothers come down looking for grain, they see an Egyptian official standing there dressed in royal robes, and they don't recognize Joseph. Clothes, in this case, do make the man. They are tricked again.

And even Jacob's son, Judah, the inheritor of the promise, from whom King David descends, will himself be tricked. Judah has a daughter-in-law, whose name is Tamar. And in Genesis 38, Tamar, waiting to be married to Judah's youngest son and knowing Judah is not about to allow that, takes off her widow's clothes—she had been married to Judah's older sons, and they had both died—takes off her widow's clothes, wraps herself in a veil, goes down by the street corner, and here comes Judah tooling along. He mistakes her for a prostitute. Clothes make the woman. Eventually winds up having sex with her. She conceives. He finally acknowledges that they are his children after quite an adventure. And these children wind up becoming the heirs to the promise. Two more twins, one of them Perez, becomes the ancestor of David. Judah, who fooled his father with Joseph's coat, is fooled by Tamar wearing clothing he hadn't expected and being in a place he hadn't expected. The stories simply continue one after the other.

So where are we then in terms of our method? I don't think we have history here, because form criticism is not designed to set out what is historical. Form criticism, like folktales, as we'll see in the next lecture, is designed to tell a good story using certain literary conventions that people will recognize, such as genealogies and annunciations. And close reading tells us that how that form is finally played out in terms of dialogue, plot description, juxtaposition, characterization, and motivation. Through all of this material, we have a much better sense of who these characters are. Were they real people? I'm not so sure. And if they were, the one thing that I do know is that these various forms, these various literary conventions, mask their historicity. If there were a real Jacob, there were a real Esau or a real Rebecca, we would never be able to find them, because of the way their stories have been preserved. Fascinating material.

And we'll see in the next lecture, how those forms continue, when we look at something called "type scenes" or "literary conventions."

Folklore Analysis and Type Scenes
(Genesis 25–36, cont.)
Lecture 7

As we look at the Bible, it turns out that those motifs common to ... all folktales, actually show up in the Bible. The folktale analysis may be looked at as a type of form criticism.

Earlier approaches to the Bible, such as source and form criticism, find application in the study of conventional plot lines, or "type scenes." Rather than regard such repetition as indicating a retelling of a single episode by different sources, type-scene analysis shows how changes in the convention disclose narrative art, as well as convey information about community heroes and values. Because type-scene analysis owes much to the study of folklore (e.g., permutations of the Cinderella story or of modern "urban legends"), we begin with folkloric conventions. Our test case is the continuation of the Jacob saga. We then turn to type-scene analysis by examining various encounters of men and women at wells. This lecture also includes a brief foray into the Gospel of John, where another version of the type scene appears.

Folktale analysts, such as the Russian formalist Vladimir Propp, observe that traditional stories are composed of a number of set motifs. In tracing a few of Propp's motifs, our test case is the story of Jacob, beginning where the previous lecture ended, Gen. 27:41. (1) The hero is absent from home: Jacob is sent away both to escape his brother and to find a wife (Gen. 28:2,5). Abraham and Moses face similar displacements, as do Ruth, Esther, Jonah, and Daniel; their stories also are profitably interpreted as folktales. (2) Heroes are often aided by helpers. As Jacob is helped by God, so are Abraham and Moses. (3) An opponent seeks to thwart the hero. Jacob faces not only his father-in-law, Laban, and his brother Esau but also a mysterious wrestler at the Jabbok River. The number of opponents demonstrates his extreme peril, bravery, and ultimate good fortune. Moses confronts Pharaoh and his own people; David faces opposition from Saul and others. (4) The hero receives a mark or brand, usually indicating maturation or survival. "When the man saw that he did not prevail against Jacob, he touched the hollow of his thigh, and Jacob's thigh was put out of joint as he wrestled with him" (Gen. 32:25). Thereafter, he walks with a limp. Other examples include the mark of Cain (Gen. 4:15), Abraham's circumcision (Gen. 17:9–14, 23–27), and Moses's shining face (Exod. 34:29–35). And finally, (5) The hero is transfigured. As the frog becomes a prince, so Jacob is told (Gen. 32:28): "Your name shall no more be called Jacob, but Israel, for you have striven with God and with people, and have prevailed."

Jacob wrestling with the angel.

Recognizing the formulaic, audiences delight in the manipulation of details (hence, the popularity of situation comedies, game shows, teen slasher films). Although the Bible likely contains singular examples of what its original audiences would have recognized to be conventions, some cases remain evident, including birth annunciations, the "ancestress in danger," infertile women becoming pregnant, and perhaps the entire Book of Judges. Our test case, the meeting of a woman at a well, begins with a comparison of Gen. 29 (Jacob meets Rachel) and Gen. 24 (Abraham's servant meets Rebecca) and includes Moses (Exod. 2) and Saul (1 Sam. 9).

The pattern opens: The hero leaves home to find a wife. Gen. 24 offers the first break in the convention: Rather than Isaac, Abraham's servant fills the hero role. The story reinforces Isaac's passivity and confirms his association with substitutes: the ram at the *Akedah*, Rebecca's filling the gap caused by Sarah's death, the switching of the blessing. Unlike Abraham's servant, who travels with camels and gifts, Jacob leaves without money, fleeing his brother. He makes his own way in the world. Similarly, fleeing Egypt, Moses arrives at a well in Midian (Exod. 2:15b–21). Moses stumbles into fate rather than proactively engaging it; he is not planning on finding a wife, any more than finding a burning bush or freeing his people. Saul goes to a well not to find a wife but his father's donkeys (1 Sam. 9:11–12). Jesus goes to Jacob's well, meets a Samaritan woman, and discusses marriage with her (John 4).

The next step: The man meets the woman. Arriving at the well, Abraham's servant prays for matchmaking success; only this variant, in which the man is not explicitly a Hebrew, is marked by religiosity. Jacob, ever the negotiator, begins by speaking to the townsmen. This scene foreshadows Gen. 34, the rape of his daughter Dinah, in which Jacob is again more attentive to political alliances between men than to emotional alliances with women. Moses arrives at the well before the women. There, he meets not men, but the seven—indistinguishable—daughters of a Midianite priest. Moses's life will continue to revolve more around priestly than domestic matters. Saul meets a group of women. Rather than aiding the women, as Jacob and Moses do, Saul is helped by the women on the very banal question of those lost donkeys. Thus, from the beginning, Saul is dependent on others. His relationship with women is a minor theme; where it sounds, such as with his daughter Michal, who betrays him with David, it is generally negative. Jesus too meets a woman, but his initial interest in obtaining drinking water flows into a discussion of "living water."

Third, the hero obtains water. Rebecca draws water for Abraham's servant and for his camels. Her energy contrasts with Isaac's passivity. Gen. 24:16–20 makes her the subject of eleven active verbs. The recounting of this meeting is, like the water, drawn out: a complex introduction fitting Rebecca's complex character. The narrator adds that she is "beautiful and a virgin"; we know nothing of Isaac's appearance, let alone sexual status. In contrast to Rebecca, Rachel does little. Jacob draws the water and only after removing the stone over the well. The stone is Jacob's signature: he is, as Robert Alter puts it, "a man who sleeps on stones, speaks in stones, wrestles with stones, contending with the hard, unyielding nature of things, whereas in pointed contrast his favored son will make his way in the world as a dealer in the truths intimated through the filmy insubstantiality of dreams." Like Jacob, Moses faces blocks; in this case, hostile shepherds. For Moses, nothing comes easy and enemies arise from all quarters. Moreover, Moses does more than help the women; he "saves" (*hoshea*) them. Saul obtains neither water nor bride. To the contrary, he gets information about a local "seer"—the prophet Samuel. His dependence on Samuel remains throughout his tragic story. Saul leaves the well in search of donkeys; like his kingship, his type scene is aborted. It may be telling that Saul's successor, David, never participates in this type scene; he is "unconventional." Jesus never gets water from the woman; instead, he provides her "living water."

Fourth, the marriage is contracted. Laban notices the bracelets, anklets, and nose-ring Rebecca received. The family learns that Isaac is Abraham's only heir—he's the best catch in the Middle East. We might speculate on what motivates the family agreeing to the marriage, just as we might speculate about Rebecca's motives in favoring Jacob. It is Rebecca, not her father or her brother, who makes the final decision. Rachel's beauty is not mentioned until the discussion of marriage, where it is commodified in connection to the bride price. To possess Rachel, Jacob has to bargain, as he had earlier done with Esau. Complicating the situation is Rachel's older sister, Leah, of "weak" (or "tender") eyes. Is Leah like Isaac: more victim than actor? Will she too be passed over, less loved? Moses is encouraged to marry by the Midianite priest Jethro; Moses frequently needs to be prompted. Jethro will later give Moses guidance on community governance (Exod. 18:14–27). No marriage takes place between Jesus and the Samaritan. The woman, married numerous times, is currently living with, although not married to, a man.

Folktales and type scenes are told less (if at all) for the sake of historicity. They are typically presented as events attested by unconfirmed witnesses. They assume different facets as they move from teller to teller, culture to culture. They reveal more about cultural and character-based issues than about "what really happened." They can also influence the presentation of history, because "what really happened" can be conformed to the plot. Folktales and type scenes are not necessarily either easily recognized or easily classified. Identification becomes increasingly difficult when the accounts are more complex and the points of contact are less clear. An excellent example is "the Jew in the court of the foreign king."

Given what we've covered so far, the story of Moses to which we now turn should already be somewhat familiar. A child, like Isaac, is born under special circumstances; a people, like Sarah in Pharaoh's harem, is enslaved in Egypt; plagues brought upon Pharaoh and his house encourage him to free his captives; the hand of God shows fidelity to Moses in the covenant made with the patriarchs; the story includes the presence of strong—and tricky—women; it contains unexpected humor; and as in Genesis, it contains great pathos. ■

Suggested Reading

Robert Alter, *The Art of Biblical Narrative.*

Alan Dundes, *Holy Writ as Oral Lit: The Bible as Folklore.*

Susan Niditch, *Folklore and the Hebrew Bible.*

Questions to Consider

1. How do the annunciation scenes (Abraham, Hagar, Rebecca, Samson's mother [Elizabeth, Mary]) reveal different aspects of characterization?

2. Why are so many type scenes connected with women?

Folklore Analysis and Type Scenes
(Genesis 25–36, Cont.)
Lecture 7—Transcript

Enhancing the benefits of close reading and form criticism, our two topics of the last lecture, biblical scholars have been increasingly looking to folktale analysis and to folklorists for new methods by which to look at the biblical material and provide some analysis of it. In particular, a folklorist named Vladimir Propp has been very helpful. His book, *Morphology of the Russian Folktale*, which is exceptionally dry, turned out to be exceptionally rich for biblical scholars, because what Propp did is explain how different folktales shared motifs.

And as we look at the Bible, it turns out that those motifs common to Russian folktales, indeed common to all folktales, actually show up in the Bible, as well. The folktale analysis may be looked at as a type of form criticism, but I'd rather have a different analogy. If we think of form criticism as like a house, a split-level or a ranch or an apartment, the form is the house itself.

What the folklorists show us is that the house can be furnished with Danish modern, some sort of contemporary Louis XIV, old English. What we can do with the Bible is look at how the forms stay the same, but how the furnishings change. That's what happens in folktales. That's what happens in the biblical text.

The other thing that folktale analysis has been very helpful with is to point out again the question of conventionality, literary conventions. It is conventional, for example, in folktales for heroes to leave home, go on a quest, find some sort of treasure, and come back and take over. Everybody knows the plot line. We also find in the Bible certain literary conventions. The same story repeated over and over. The idea of the endangered ancestress is one.

What happens, then, when we look at some of these scenes and we notice the same story, the same form, but different characterizations? So, after a brief foray through some folktale analysis using some of Vladimir Propp's categories, we'll then use the analysis of literary conventions, called "type scenes," to take a look at one particular convention, how heroes meet their wives at wells, to find out a little bit more about each of these heroes. To look at this material in this way, brackets the historical question, but enhances extraordinarily the narrator's art, the artistry of the text.

So here we are looking at Vladimir Propp's folktale categories. There are 31 of them. Trust me, I'm not going to go through all of them. But I think a few are worth looking at. Here are Propp's categories. According to Propp, every folktale requires the absence of the hero from his or her home or proper place. In other words, the story has got to get started somewhere, and usually the folktale hero leaves home. Already we can think perhaps Isaac is not the idea folktale hero, but, in fact, Jacob is.

Folk heroes are often sent on a quest to go find something, and that's what we find with Jacob. We can pick up here in the Jacob saga right after the point we just left off. Jacob has tricked his brother out of birthright and blessing. Esau is furious. And Esau, this big hairy glunk, is going to go after his brother. Rebecca, therefore, has to get her son out of town quickly. She says to her husband, "Isaac, Isaac dear, Esau's wives, these local Canaanite women, are driving me nuts. Let's send Jacob back to Padam-aran to my hometown," so that he could find a woman from the old homestead. Isaac... Jacob is, therefore, sent off, ostensibly on a quest for a bride, but really to get out of the neighborhood before Esau can attack him. There is the quest.

And we find other heroes being sent off on similar quests. Abraham being sent off to find a new Promised Land on the voice of this unknown God. We'll find Moses putting himself on a quest, leaving for the land of Midian, escaping a murder charge. Heroes go on quests, but for different reasons and with different goals.

Propp next notices that heroes are often accompanied by helpers. In fairy tales and folktales, often birds—I think about the Disney version of Cinderella with the mice and the birds—but that's a standard folktale category. We find with Jacob, for example, that he could be seen as helping himself. He doesn't have any aid on his way. That tells us something about Jacob right there. He is somebody who helps himself. But other analysts have said, "Wait a minute. Jacob is helped by God. God follows Jacob all the way through."

And in fact, when Jacob is on his way to Padam-aran, he stops off at place called Luz, he will later call it Beth-El, House of God. And he has a dream there of a heavenly ladder, and angels ascending and descending, and he realizes that's a house of God. And then he knows God will take care of him. So in this case, Jacob is the folktale hero, God is the helper, and that winds up being standard in the Bible. Abraham is the folktale hero; God is the helper. Moses, the hero; God as the helper. And this continues on and on.

A third motif is that the hero encounters an opponent, because otherwise you really don't have a story. There is going to be something blocking the hero's way. In Abraham's case, it's the famine, something not human, something out of his control. In Jacob's case, he's got tons of things blocking him. He's got Esau on the one hand, and then on the other, when he actually arrives in Padam-aran, he's got Laban, his tricky father-in-law. He's got troubles coming and going.

In fact, there is a third block, overdone in the case of Jacob. When he's coming back home after marrying Leah, the older sister, and then marrying the younger sister, Rachel, and working 14 years for the both of them, on his way back home to meet Esau, he stops off on the banks of the Jabbok River. And before he is able to cross, during the evening, some mysterious opponent, a god, a man, an angel, wrestles with him, blocking his way until he's actually able to cross. The number of opponents Jacob faces tells us about the extreme peril that he's in, but also his bravery and tenacity.

Similarly, Moses confronts a Pharaoh, who will not let the slaves go. David faces opposition from King Saul. A folktale hero was no hero unless there is some sort of worthy opponent.

Fourth, here is to me where it gets interesting, Propp notices that folktale heroes are usually branded or marked in some way. They can change, as Cinderella does from a girl in rags to a beautiful woman in a grand ballgown in a grand coach. There is some sort of physical change. We find this, for example, with Abraham who was circumcised. That's his physical change as part of his being a hero.

Jacob, it's even more striking. When he battles this figure at the River Jabbok, what we're told in Genesis 32, verse 25, is "When the man saw that he did not prevail against Jacob, he touched the hollow of Jacob's thigh, and Jacob's thigh was put out of joint as he wrestled with him," which means from then on Jacob walks with a limp. He carries the result of the battle with him. It's not something he can forget about.

And other examples of this type of mark are, of course, the mark of Cain that we've already seen in Genesis 4. And I think also a mark that Moses had. We're told in Exodus 34 that after Moses spoke with God, his face was shining with rays of light, so shining, in fact, that he had to wear a veil when he came in front of the people. Moses, too, was marked by God or transfigured. And indeed, this transfiguration can be yet another folktale motif. The heroes are not only branded. They are also changed in some way. Jacob gets a new name, Israel, "one who strives with God." And the name is given to him by that opponent at the Jabbok River. Once you have a name change, you're something different.

We see the same thing with Abraham and Sarah, because they start out as Abram and Sarai. But once they become in covenant with God, their names change, they are transfigured, they are something new. We even see this when we get to the Book of Daniel, where Daniel and his three friends—you may have heard about these friends who get tossed into a fiery furnace, and if you haven't, we'll see them in Lecture 24—the friends actually have new Babylonian names, because when you go into another court, you become transfigured. And finally, even with Joseph who, when he goes into Pharaoh's court, is renamed *Zaphenath Paneah*. I think Joseph was simply easier.

Transfiguration of heroes, branding of heroes, opponents blocking heroes, all of these are folktale motifs. We would expect to see them in stories of heroes, and we find them in the stories of Genesis. And, in fact, the study of these folktale motifs can be applied to Noah's Ark, and the Prophet Jonah, and the Book of Esther. They are all over the place.

Literary conventions are also prevalent in the text. The problem here is they are less easy for us to spot than they would have been for people back then.

Yes, it's pretty easy to find folkloric motifs, but to find literary conventions one needs to know a little bit more about the culture that produced them.

Today, we know what our own literary conventions or artistic conventions are. We recognize a situation comedy. We can flip on the TV, and within two minutes, we know what we've got. We recognize a teen slasher film, somebody with a hockey mask, for example. Thirty seconds into the movie we can write the plot, because they are conventional. The reason we like these stories is because we're familiar with the form. We're at home with them. And the reason they work, and they don't all work, is because they play on the convention. It's not exactly the same story each time, but good storytellers will take what is conventional and transform it a little bit. Maybe make the hero somebody you wouldn't have expected, or make the killer somebody you wouldn't have expected.

The best example, I think, of this is the parody. Parodies only work because we recognize the convention. Take two old classics. There is a movie I absolutely adore called *Blazing Saddles*. It's a Mel Brooks movie, and it's a parody of westerns. The movie makes absolutely no sense if you've never seen movies like *High Noon* and *Shane*. But once you know the convention, the rest of it follows suit.

In the 1970s and '80s, there were disaster films galore. Ocean liners overturned, towering infernos, airplanes about to crash, and then parodies were made of them. And the reason the parodies worked is because we knew the disaster film convention.

Now, the problem with the Bible is we don't know all of the conventions that people had back then. And it may well be that a lot of stories we find in the Pentateuch or even later are actually plays on conventions that would have had people roaring in the aisles in the early Iron Age. We simply can't see them. But every once in a while, we can find them. The same story, the same form, the same split level, but furnished very, very differently.

This is, by the way, the counter to the documentary hypothesis. The documentary hypothesis, in part, is based on the idea that no storyteller would tell the same story over and over again. Folktale analysis and type scene, convention analysis, tells us, wait a minute, the same author can write the same story over and over again as long as the characters are changed. We become very familiar with the form and, thereby, appreciate the characters even more.

And that's what I'd like to show you by looking at one particular convention. This is the scene of a man meeting his wife at a well. We know it's a convention when we see it a second time. Right? And in Genesis 29, Jacob meets his future wife, Rachel, at a well. And then we think, "Ah, back in Genesis 24, Abraham has a servant whom he sends off to find a bride for Isaac, because, of course, Isaac doesn't go anywhere, and that servant happens to meet Rebecca at a well. I've got a convention."

And once I find that I discover other well scenes. It turns out Moses meets his wife at a well. King Saul meets some women at a well, but they don't get married. And for those of you who know the New Testament, Jesus meets a woman at a well in John, Chapter 4, and they actually wind up talking about marriage. And I think the author of the Gospel of John would have had his audience rolling on the floor, because they would have known the convention, and they would have taken delight in it.

Here is the pattern. We start out when the hero leaves home to find a wife. Genesis 24, the very first example, gives us the first break in the convention, because it's Abraham servant rather than Isaac who goes. And that already tells us something about Isaac. He's not going anywhere. More than reinforcing Isaac's immobility or passivity, this break in the convention immediately gives us the sense of Isaac and his connection to substitutes— the ram that substitutes for him at the *Akedah*; how Jacob substitutes by pretending to be his brother when getting the blessing. Isaac plays with substitutes, is substituted for. Here even, somebody by proxy goes out and finds his bride.

This scene also allows us secondary plot development, because when the servant—we'll call him Eliazar—actually finds Rebecca, she then becomes the only one of these brides who does not meet her husband at the courtship time. By the time Rebecca meets Isaac, the marriage has already been contracted between Rebecca and her family and Abraham's servant. So then we have to look at what happens when Rebecca finally meets Isaac. And here we have another one of those little scriptural irritants, a word that cannot be easily translated in the text.

Here is the story. Rebecca is on a camel riding back to Canaan to meet Isaac, and she finally catches a glimpse of Isaac walking in the fields and doing something. And the Hebrew word has no early cognates. It's not used anywhere else in the Bible. There are some later Arabic cognates, but those aren't terribly helpful, because they are too late. What intrigues me here is whatever he was doing, most translations read "meditating," but they really don't know. What we find out is that when Rebecca sees Isaac *something*, she falls off her camel. Now most English translations read, "she alit, she slid off, she dismounted." But the text is very clear, Genesis 24:64, "she fell off her camel." And then I really wonder what was Isaac doing, and what was Rebecca's reaction when she first saw Isaac—shock, horror, and, one would hope, delight.

Let's move to the next type scene. This is the story of Jacob. Unlike Abraham's servant, who shows up at the well with camels and gifts and other sigla of importance, Jacob only shows up with his walking stick, because he's still on the lam from his brother, and he had to leave town quickly. And this tells us something about Jacob. He's got to make his own way in the world. He's not going to have proxy. And in fact, he will be on the road away from home a very long time before he actually succeeds.

And we can look at some of those other stories. After killing the task master who was beating a Hebrew slave in Egypt, Moses thinks he's gotten away with it, but the next day he finds out the news of the murder has become known. And he runs away to Midian, and he lands at a well. And in fact, he's just sitting there. And suddenly come along seven daughters of a Midianite priest. This is typical for Moses. He just stumbles into his fate. He's on no mission. He's running away. Things catch up with him. Moses does not volunteer to do things. He's got to be kind of pushed into it, typical for Moses.

The convention appears again in First Samuel, Chapter 9. This is our first introduction to the first king of Israel, King Saul. The scene begins promisingly enough. Saul leaves home and goes to a well. Unfortunately, he is not there to find a wife. He's actually looking for some donkeys his father had lost. Saul, in effect, misses the boat. He's supposed to go, according to the convention, to a well to find a wife. He goes, but for the wrong reasons. Already I suspect his kingship is going to be in danger.

And according to the Gospel of John, since I mentioned it, Jesus actually leaves home from the Galilee and journeys to Samaria and goes to a well, and the well is called "Jacob's Well," which sends us back to Genesis.

The next step in the pattern is that the hero actually meets a woman. And in this part of the convention, I think the woman is drawing water, which is what she is supposed to do, may actually symbolize the bonds that are to be created between the woman and the man at the well.

Well, here we go. Arriving at the well, Abraham's servant prays for matchmaking success. Only in this version does somebody pray, but only in this version is the person who prays not a Hebrew. So here we have the Gentile who prays. And increasing the irony, this is the servant who would have inherited Abraham's estate had Isaac not been born. And here in a great amount of generosity, he prays for a successful match, so that Isaac will have a wife, and then Isaac will have children, thereby disinheriting himself even more. This is a good sort of servant to have.

Jacob, perhaps, a bit less pietistic, but no less practical, begins by speaking to the townspeople, because this is the sort guy Jacob is, he will negotiate. He will talk 'til he's blue in the face in order to get his way. We've already seen that with Esau, bargaining carefully. He's interested in possible political alliances. And we'll see this throughout his biography that the Bible gave us. In fact, for all of Jacob's protestations of his love for Rachel, he spends more time talking to men than he ever does talking to her.

In Exodus, Chapter 2, Moses is in flight from Egypt. He arrives at the well before the women. He is first on the scene. He is the leader despite what he might want to do. And there he meets not men to begin with, but actually seven daughters of a Midianite priest, who's variously called Jethro or Reuel or Hobab. The women he meets, these seven daughters, are relatively undifferentiated. It doesn't really matter with Moses and women. He's not terribly interested in women. He's going to talk to guys like his father-in-law, and he's going to talk to God. Even in this courtship scene, we get a sense of how Moses and his wife will relate, and Moses, later, and his father-in-law will relate, because it's the father-in-law for Moses who was the more important relation.

Saul encounters a group of women coming to draw water. It looks promising. Knowing the convention, we expect him to be invited home, meet a set of parents, and contract a marriage. At the very least, we should expect him to aid the women. Jacob actually helps to draw water for Rachel. Moses helps to draw water for the daughters of the Midianite priest. But not Saul, no. He says to the women, "Do you know where I can find a seer to help me locate my father's lost donkeys?" And the women say, "Oh, yes, there is a seer down the street." We're also told, by the way, that another word for "seer" is "prophet." And the seer they are talking about is the Prophet Samuel, who was the major prophet in this book, First Samuel. And Saul never makes the match. He goes off in search of his donkeys and finds quite a difference, a different fate, as well.

Jesus, too, meets a woman, but his initial interest in drinking water, which Jesus is actually the only one who actually lands at a well in order to get water, flows into a discussion about his identity and theology.

Well, third, the hero has to obtain water somehow. This is the convention. But in the first one, it's not Abraham's servant who draws the water, it's Rebecca. And she doesn't simply draw water for the servant, she draws water for his camels in a flurry of activity. In Genesis, Chapter 24, verses 16–20, she is the subject of no fewer than 11 active verbs. She is just a flurry of action. She captures the scene. You can't resist looking at her. And this emphasis suggests her exceptionally active, very complex character. And, again, a contrast with Isaac, activity again not being one of his strong points. We already know Rebecca will dominate every scene in which she appears.

The narrator in Rebecca's scene also adds, very quickly, "She is beautiful and a virgin." That is, she's got all the right qualifications for being the second matriarch. We, by the way, know nothing about Isaac's appearance, let alone his sexual status. Now, in complete contrast to Rebecca, Rachel does very little. Jacob draws the water, and then only after removing the stone from the well. On the one hand, the stone blocking the well may symbolize blocks on Rachel's fertility. And it certainly represents other blocks that Jacob will face. Jacob only obtains Rachel for a wife after working for his father-in-law, Laban. And as we've seen, the first time he attempted to get married, Laban substituted the older daughter for the younger. Jacob has to work another seven years for Rachel, 14 years in all.

I think the stone can even be regarded as Jacob's signature motif. And here I'm dependent upon biblical scholar Robert Alter, who is, in fact, the one who brought biblical scholars to the idea of type scenes and helped us with this. Robert Alter describes Jacob as a man who sleeps on stones and wrestles with stones, somebody who contends with the hard, unyielding nature of things. And he contrasts that to Jacob's son, Joseph, who makes his way in the world as a dealer in truths based on filmy things, like dreams. How different these people are. By the way, in terms of sigla, motifs, just as Jacob is associated with stones, we'll find that Moses is associated with water, and, later, Samson is associated with fire. They are motifs that carry the folklore along.

Finally back to the type scene, in contrast to the extended engagement between Abraham's servant and Rebecca, Jacob and Rachel hardly talk, and that lack of communication will continue through their marriage.

Well, like Jacob, Moses faces blocks. In this case, he has to drive away hostile shepherds so the women can obtain water. For Moses, nothing comes easy, and enemies arise from all quarters. But here is something else in terms of this scene, again something missing in the Hebrew. Moses does more than help the women, the Hebrew says, he saves them. The root is *hoshea*. Moses is a savior. Already he's saving women. Saving is a bit strong for drawing water from a well. So the word carries more import than we might have think, than we might have thought.

And this connection of Moses with saving will continue on and on. Indeed the connection of Moses with drawing water is part of his own birth story. When Moses is floated down the Nile, the Pharaoh's daughter sees him and says, "I shall call him Moses, because I drew him out of the water." And that's why, according to the Hebrew text, he's called Mosha. Actually, Mosha is not someone drawn out, it's the active form, "one who draws." Moses remains the active figure.

By the way, the word really doesn't mean "to be drawn out of water," the name Moses is really an Egyptian name, like Thutmose and Ramses; that "mss" form simply means "to be gotten of a god." Like Ramses is Ra's son, and Thutmose is the son of Tut. Moses actually has a good Egyptian name, but we'll see that in the next lecture.

Well, moving on to Saul, Saul obtains neither water nor bride. To the contrary, he gets information about the local seer. He leaves the well and, in effect, aborts the type scene, and that's appropriate, because we'll find when he goes to battle with King David, that his own kingship is aborted. And speaking of the ending Saul's kingship and the transfer of authority to David, note, although David is married several times, he never meets a woman at a well. David is, in effect, unconventional. He doesn't follow the type.

Jesus, of course, never gets water from the woman, instead he provides her living water, but that's another story for another lecture series.

The fourth step in the scene is the contracting of the marriage. Well, Laban, Rebecca's father, notices his daughter wearing bracelets and anklets and nose rings, which was high fashion back then—all the jewels and gold that the servant had given to Rebecca, and Rebecca herself could hardly fail to notice this as well. The family, thus, learns that Isaac is Abraham's only heir. Abraham is a very wealthy clan leader, plus he's got a god protecting him. Isaac is, in effect, the best catch in the Middle East. So, of course, they are perfectly happy that Rebecca is willing to marry Isaac. But we can also speculate on what motivates them—piety, family loyalty, greed. And it turns out to be Rebecca, not her father and not her brother, who makes the final decision. Rebecca will always call the shots.

Rachel's beauty winds up getting mentioned not when Rebecca's does, when we first meet her, but a little bit later on, when the discussion of marriage begins. That's when we find out she is just a knock-out. But since it occurs in the discussion of marriage, we find out that for Jacob and Rachel, Rachel's beauty is a commodity. It's something to be traded here, and it comes at a price. To possess Rachel, Jacob has to bargain with Laban, as he had done earlier with Esau.

And making things more complex, as you know, Rachel has an older sister, who, like Esau, has a problematic physical description. Esau is hairy; Leah, the older sister, has either weak or tender eyes. The Hebrew could be translated either way. So I wonder here, will she too be passed over like Esau was, less loved? Or perhaps like Esau, might Leah gain in the end? Esau eventually winds up becoming the father of the Edomites, a great nation. Leah, actually, will become the ancestress of David. The promise goes through her, not Rachel.

Moses's type scene concludes not with Moses and the women, but with Moses and his father-in-law. In fact, it's the Midianite priest who basically encourages Moses to get married. Moses doesn't ask; the Midianite priest simply gives. And Saul's marriages are passed over in almost complete silence. They are simply not important. He doesn't fulfill the type scene, and his children will not become heirs to the kingdom. And of course, there is no marriage between Jesus and the Samaritan woman, but they do, in fact, talk about marriage.

Now, by now you've got the tools to see how type scenes function—the ancestress and danger. Go back and look at the plays on the scene. Or annunciation scenes, to whom is the announcement of a child made? What are the words that are used, what is the fate of that child to be? We might find other plot motifs and other scenes, and we can see through these scenes the incredible complexity of the characterization. How these scenes obtain different facets as they move from teller to teller and scene to scene and book to book. This is great stuff.

And from what we've seen so far, we're ready in our next lecture to move into the Book of Exodus, because we've now got all the tools we need, almost, in order to figure out how to interpret this material. We already know what we might want to look for. We might look for a child born under special circumstances, that's Moses. We might want to look for people enslaved, because we've already seen Egyptians enslaved to Hebrews and Hebrews enslaved to Egyptians. That will come around again. A Pharaoh who has no name and questions as to whether he is benevolent or malevolent. The hand of God showing fidelity to the people when they are in the depths of despair and in utmost trouble. Questions of historicity, questions of archaeology, questions of trickery. Women who help out in the most unexpected of ways. Great humor and incredible pathos. All of which and more we'll find when we get into the Book of Exodus.

Moses and Exodus
(Exodus 1–15)
Lecture 8

There is nothing in the Egyptian records nor in any other records. If I
were an Egyptian record keeper, the escape of a group of slaves from my
troops is not something I would care to record. Moreover, this group of
slaves might have actually been quite small, but the Bible has increased
the numbers and increased the importance. Whether historical or not,
we simply can't prove it.

Slavery in Egypt: Although Hebrew slavery in Egypt is unnoted in
external sources, slavery itself in the ancient Near East is well attested,
and Genesis anticipates the Egyptian circumstances. Sometimes,
ancient bondage was less what we think of as slavery than a kind of extended
forced labor, or *corvee*. An inscription from Thutmosis II (c. 1490–1436
B.C.E.) depicting Asiatics engaged in brick work has the taskmaster say,
"The rod is in my hand; do not be idle." The Egyptian poem "Satire on the
Trades" describes the brick-worker: "He is dirtier than vines or pigs from
treading under his mud. His clothes are stiff with clay … He is miserable …
His sides ache … His arms are destroyed. He washes himself only once a
season. He is simply wretched through and through."

Egyptian slavery fulfills patriarchal predictions and, thereby,
indicates that nothing has gone awry with God's promises to the
patriarchs. The Lord said to Abram, "Know for certain that your
descendants will be sojourners in a land which is not theirs, and will
be slaves there, and they will be oppressed for four-hundred years"
(Gen. 15:13–14). The Egyptian slave Hagar is, with her son Ishmael,
exiled—with anticipation of death—into the wilderness. The Ishmaelites
sell Joseph into slavery, and the Egyptians enslave Sarah's descendants
and threaten their sons. The Pharaoh "who knew not Joseph" is, like the
pharaohs encountered by Abraham and Jacob's sons, unidentified. (The title,
meaning "Great house," is a metonymy, cf. "The White House announced

… .") The absence of the name may result from *damnatio memoriae*, the erasing of a name from history (cf. The monotheistically inclined Amenhotep [Ikhnaton]). The omission enhances theological implications. Ancient Egyptians viewed Pharaoh as divine; a contest between God and Pharaoh opposes rival claimants for divinity. It enhances folkloric connections.

Text criticism also complicates the story. This approach attempts to determine the earliest literary version; it is applied often in cases where the Hebrew (MT) and Greek (LXX) accounts differ. The Hebrew of Exod. 1:22 reads: "Then Pharaoh commanded his people, 'Every son that is born you shall cast into the Nile.'" The Septuagint, Targums, and Samaritan Pentateuch add "[born] *to the Hebrews*." The conventional wisdom in text criticism is that the more difficult reading (*lectio difficilior*) is likely to be original. The additional detail included in the Septuagint appears to be a later clarification; it is easy to determine why it was added, but less so why it may have been deliberately removed. The more indeterminate Hebrew heightens Pharaoh's ineptitude.

Ironically, several women—Moses's mother and sister; the Pharaoh's daughter, along with the midwives Shiphra and Puah—through deception, subvert royal power. The midwives confirm Pharaoh's view of the Hebrews as "other" than normal. By adopting the child, Pharaoh's daughter flouts her father's order. Moses's sister arranges for him to be nursed (for wages) by his own mother. Moses's initial display of his commission is a simple magic trick: Aaron's staff becomes a snake (Exod. 7:8–13); the court magicians perform the same trick, only to have their staffs swallowed by Aaron's. The magicians also turn water into blood (Exod. 7:22), hardly what Egypt needed.

But what about Moses? His early life, also unattested in Egyptian sources, evokes cross-cultural folktales and Israelite cosmogonic motifs. His infancy parallels that of Sargon of Akkad: protected by women from execution by an evil king, placed in a reed basket, and rescued. The term for Moses's basket is the same for Noah's ark (*tevah*). And Moses escapes drowning, as does Noah.

Moses's initial action opens the folktale motif of the hero's leave-taking. Moses's self-imposed exile is prompted initially not by Egyptians but by Hebrew slaves aware of the taskmaster's murder. Moses flees from Pharaoh, who "sought to kill" him (Exod. 2:15). The motif is repeated when Moses returns to Egypt (Exod. 4:24–26), but the Lord is the agent of death. Again, Moses is rescued by a woman, his wife, Zipporah, by apotropaic magic. Foreshadowed are both Moses's breaking the power of slave-masters and his struggles with the slave generation.

The finding of Moses.

Click Art.

Although the ten plagues have received "scientific" explications (earthquakes; Atlantis [!]), the biblical text is interested not in rationales but in divine power. Inclined after each plague to free the slaves, Pharaoh has a "change of heart." In Exod. 4:14, ten times Pharaoh hardens his heart; ten times God prompts this change. Biblical Hebrew associates emotions with physiology: Jeremiah (4:19) cries: "My bowels, my bowels, I writhe in pain!" (RSV: "My anguish! My anguish!"). "In the night my heart instructs me" (RSV, Ps. 16:7); the Hebrew is "My kidneys afflict me." The hardening of the heart is the ossification of one's vital principle. It indicates, as Nahum Sarna eloquently observes, "a state of moral atrophy."

Theologians wrestle with the question of morality. Some explain the apparent contradiction between Pharaoh's action and divine responsibility as expressing the intractable problem of fate and free will. Others note that Pharaoh had established himself as callous and inconsistent. God then prompts him to manifest his true self. The Bible has its own explanation.

Exod. 10:1–2 (cf. Exod. 9:15–16): "Then the Lord God said to Moses, 'Go in to Pharaoh, for I have hardened his heart and the hearts of his servants, that I may show these signs of mine among them.'" "And that you may tell in the hearing of your children, and your children's children how I have toyed with the Egyptians and what signs I have done among them, that you may know that I am the Lord." God responds not only out of compassion, then, but also because of remembering the covenant he made with the Hebrew people.

Exodus culminates with the splitting of the sea and the escape of Israelites and others. "Reed Sea" (LXX, "Red Sea") may explain the miracle: The Hebrews escaped through marshes, but Egyptian chariots got stuck in the mud. The word for "reed" is the same as the material of Moses's basket. His escape from watery death had prefigured the Exodus.

Theologically and ethically, Israelite existence is interpreted through the Exodus. Deut. 5:15 (cf. Exod. 20:11): "Remember that you were a slave in the land of Egypt, and the Lord your God brought you out from there with a mighty hand and an outstretched arm; therefore remember the Lord your God commanded you to keep the Sabbath day." Exod. 22:21 (cf. Deut. 23:7): "You shall not wrong a stranger or oppress him, for you were strangers in the land of Egypt." Deut. 24:17–18: "You shall not subvert the rights of the fatherless … remember that you were a slave in the land of Egypt and that the Lord your God redeemed you." ∎

Suggested Reading

Jonathan Kirsch, *Moses: A Life*.

Göran Larsson, *Bound for Freedom: The Book of Exodus in Jewish and Christian Traditions*.

1. What is the moral vision of this material, given Moses's killing of the taskmaster and hiding the body and God's hardening of Pharaoh's heart? Do the Egyptians "get what they deserve"? Does anyone "deserve" the death of a child?

2. To what extent is Aaron highlighted in the story, and how do those episodes reflect priestly (P) interests?

3. Is there any means to distinguish "fact" from "fiction" in this narrative?

Moses and Exodus
(Exodus 1–15)
Lecture 8—Transcript

The Joseph saga, to which we will return in Lecture 23, describes how this son of Jacob, sold into Egypt and slavery, eventually rises to become Pharaoh's second in command and winds up saving all of Egypt and, indeed, all of the Middle East from famine. Through Joseph's generosity and initiative—and it helps to have Pharaoh on his side—Joseph actually winds up bringing Jacob, his 12 sons, his one daughter, Dinah, and the rest of the family from Canaan down to Egypt. The Israelites settle in the land of Goshen, which some of my students had always thought was Lantic Ocean, but it's land of Goshen. And they multiply and they multiply. And, "There arose, at one point, a Pharaoh who knew not Joseph, but when he saw the Hebrews multiplying in Egypt, he became afraid." And he winds up enslaving them and, thus, begins the story of the Exodus, in the Book of Exodus, the second book of the Pentateuch.

What we'll do in this lecture is look at a couple of historical notes, such as what was slavery like in antiquity, and who was Moses and how is his story told. We also look at the ten plagues, which were used by God to encourage Pharaoh to let the slaves go free. And we'll look at the motif called the "hardening of Pharaoh's heart." Why is it that after each of these plagues, Pharaoh at first says, "This is not a good thing, I think I'll let them go," but then changes his mind? And why is it sometimes it seems that God changes Pharaoh's mind, that God hardens Pharaoh's heart?

And in terms of the deity directly, I'm going to reserve, in general, conversations about God for the next lecture, because I think God deserves a lecture just about God. But here we are in terms of Exodus and the slavery.

It turns out, as you can probably imagine by now, that we're having difficulty at this early period in Israel's history finding external biblical evidence to confirm what the Bible says. So we have no external evidence for a group of Israelites being enslaved in Egypt. There is nothing in the Egyptian records nor in any other records. This would not be terribly surprising. I think if I were an Egyptian record keeper, the escape of a group of slaves from my troops is not something I would care to record. Moreover, this group of slaves might have actually been quite small, but the Bible has increased the numbers and increased the importance. Whether historical or not, we simply can't prove it.

We do, however, know something about the type of slavery that took place in the ancient world. And slavery in antiquity is not the way we typically think of slavery today when we think of, for example, the enslavement of people in the United States prior to the Civil War. Exodus, Chapter 3, for example, gives us an idea that slavery was not the sort of thing that broke up families. Slaves were allowed to own their own property. They lived in their own neighborhoods. Here is an example. Exodus, Chapter 3, suggests that the Israelite women had social connections with local Egyptians. As the text says, "Each woman shall borrow from her neighbor and any woman lodging in her house." In other words, these Hebrews actually could take in boarders. "'They should borrow objects of gold and silver and clothing, and these,' says God, 'You shall put on your sons and daughters when you leave Egypt.'" This is not the way we typically think of slaves, borrowing clothes from the neighbors like a cup of sugar, taking in boarders.

And, whereas I doubt the Egyptians themselves would have seen it this way, it may be that that particular notion of borrowing could have been to the Hebrews a sense of being paid for their slavery. We have a hint of this in the Book of Deuteronomy. This Deuteronomy is 15:13–15: "'When you set your slave free,'" as you have to do according to Deuteronomy after seven years, "'do not let him go empty handed. Furnish him out of the flock, your threshing floor, and your wine vat with everything the Lord God has blessed you. Bear in mind that you were slaves in Egypt, and the Lord God redeemed you; therefore,' says God, 'I enjoin upon you this commandment today.'" So it seems appropriate, at least, that the Hebrew slaves got something from the Egyptians when they left.

We do know something about Egyptian programs of mass slavery. It's less slavery the way we would think of it than it is forced labor. The technical term is *corvée*, forced labor of portions of the population for an indefinite period of time. Actually King Solomon engages in *corvée* slavery when he builds the temple in Jerusalem, which is not something we would normally think that Solomon would do. But if you look at First Kings, Chapter 5 and Chapter 9, you will find it.

The Egyptian *corvée,* like most *corvées,* meant people worked in degrading conditions without any money for long periods of time. And what did they do? There were gangs who built pyramids, who built irrigation ditches, who did construction, brick making, canal digging. We find from Exodus that the Hebrew slaves were entrusted with building the two storage cities of Pitom and Ramses. So forced labor for construction.

Slavery itself is, in the Near East, well attested in both in art and architecture. For example, there is an inscription dated to the time of a Pharaoh called Thutmose II, about 1490 to 1436. This is old stuff. This scene depicts Asiatics, non-Egyptians, building and laying bricks. And the taskmaster is represented as saying in hieroglyphics, "The rod is in my hand; do not be idle." Slavery was nothing to mess around with.

There is also an Egyptian wisdom poem, and we'll get to wisdom later in these lectures. This one is called "Satire on the Trades." And the poet says of the brick worker—and remember the Hebrews are the business of building and laying bricks— "He is dirtier than vines or pigs from treading under the mud. His clothes are stiff with clay. His leather belt is going to ruin. Entering into the wind, he's miserable, his sides ache, his arms are destroyed with technical work. He washes himself only once a season. He is wretched through and through." Upshot, nobody wanted to be a slave. It's nothing to be romanticized whatsoever.

Whether the Hebrews were actually slaves in Egypt or not, and whether their conditions were not so bad—taking in lodgers, borrowing cups of sugar— or totally degrading, at the very least we can say, again from a literary perspective, that slavery in Egypt was something that the reader would have anticipated from reading Genesis. In other words, according to the biblical text, it's true the Hebrews were enslaved, but nothing had gone wrong. In fact, Abraham knew about it way back in Genesis. This is Genesis 15, early on: "The Lord said to Abraham, 'Know for certain that your descendants will be sojourners in a land which is not theirs, and they will be slaves there, and they will be oppressed for 400 years.'" This is the covenant Abraham signed on to.

And Joseph, too, expected problems. After he reunites with his brothers and his entire family moves to Egypt, he comments in Genesis 50, the last chapter in the book, "God will surely take notice of you and bring you up from this land to the land which he promised on oath to Abraham, Isaac, and Jacob. And when God has taken notice of you, bring my bones back with you." So he knows that his brothers, his family, his fellow Hebrews, are going to be in Egypt quite a long time.

And in terms of the plot, we've already seen Sarah being placed in Egyptian harem—that's a type of slavery; Sarah taking her own Egyptian slave, Hagar, and putting her into Abraham's bed, more slavery; Hagar's son, Ishmael, giving rise to a group of people called the Ishmaelites, who sell Joseph into slavery; and now the Hebrew people themselves enslaved in Egypt. The connections with Egypt and slavery are intractable. They are always going to be there.

But now we come to that Egyptian slavery itself and to the pharaoh "who knew not Joseph." It's not clear who this pharaoh is. He's traditionally identified as Ramses II. The timing works out. But I think the identity of the pharaoh really doesn't matter. What does matter is what he does and how he acts. If you're concerned about the lack of name, we might note that the pharaohs in Genesis are not named either.

Some have suggested, perhaps, that this lack of name may not simply be due to the idea that all pharaohs are alike, but rather because Egypt practiced something known in Latin here as *damnatio memoraie*. The idea was if you really didn't like somebody, like a government leader, you would erase any sign of that leader. The Egyptians did this with a Pharaoh named Ikhnaton, who worshiped one god. As soon as he died, they wiped out every bit of evidence they could find—obviously not all of it, because we know about Ikhnaton—that they could find of his cult. I think people in Stalinist-era Russia did the same things, where you can find photographs that have been doctored and people written out.

Could this Pharaoh's name have simply been written out of the text? I don't think so. I think the name is simply not there to suggest that any Pharaoh, any leader, could be like that. And I think the lack of name has another effect. The Pharaoh in Egypt is divine. The Pharaoh is a god. Having a lack of name suggests God the Pharaoh fights the God of the Hebrews, and we know who's going to win. And finally, although Pharaoh, the important one, doesn't get a name, the two midwives who minister to the Hebrews and refuse to kill the Hebrew babies even though Pharaoh ordered it, the two midwives, we have their names, Shiphra and Puah. How nice the two midwives get named, but the head of the country, his name is not preserved or perhaps erased.

In terms of this Pharaoh, he's not too bright. That sometimes happens with government leaders. This is what he decides. He determines, "The people of Israel are too many and too mighty for us. Come, let us deal shrewdly with them, lest they multiply. And if war befall us, they join our enemies and fight against us and escape from the land." But then the Pharaoh learns the more they were oppressed, the more they multiplied, and the more they spread abroad. In other words, the Pharaoh keeps giving them more work and the more work he gives them, the more babies they produce. Perhaps less work or a different type of work might have been more helpful.

Pharaoh decides he's got to do something, so he launches on a plan to decrease the Hebrew population. But to understand exactly what he does and why this is peculiar, we need yet another method in biblical studies, and this is called "text criticism."

Text criticism is the method that tries to determine the earliest or, perhaps, the correct reading. Now why is that a problem? Because in addition to the Hebrew text, we have the Greek translation of the Old Testament. It's called *Septuagint*. And we have Aramaic—Aramaic is a language like Hebrew— Aramaic paraphrases from the first and second centuries of the Common Era. And we have Latin versions and Syriac versions. And sometimes these texts, particularly the Hebrew and the Greek, do not always agree. It's not necessarily always the case that the Hebrew preserves the earlier reading, because, in fact, our Hebrew manuscripts are medieval, except for those found among the Dead Sea Scrolls.

So here is a case in Exodus 1:22 where the Greek says one thing and the Hebrew another. This shouldn't disturb you too much. You've already seen it when we talked about Isaac. How the Hebrew has, "Isaac brought Rebecca into the tent of Sarah, his mother." And the Greek simply has, "Isaac brought Rebecca into the tent." Right?

Here is another example. The Hebrew of Exodus 1:22 reads: "Then Pharaoh commanded his people, 'Every son that is born you shall cast into the Nile, but you shall let every daughter live.'" Now think about this for a minute. "Every son that is born you shall cast into the Nile." It might have been helpful if Pharaoh had specified every son that is born to *whom*. And, in fact, that is precisely what the Greek and the Aramaic and even the Samaritan Pentateuch do. They read, "Every son that is *born to the Hebrews* you shall cast into the Nile." Now I think that's what Pharaoh intended, but now I've got to worry, why does the Hebrew text lack "to the Hebrews?" Which is the original reading?

I think what the Hebrew text is doing is trying to show how stupid this Pharaoh is. Moreover, there is a kind of pathos here, because we find out later the tenth plague will be the death of the first-born children in Egypt. By issuing this original command and not being specific, Pharaoh has, in effect, foreshadowed the death warrant that will be assigned for those Egyptian children.

Why does the Greek and the Aramaic and the Samaritan add it in? Because it's logical. I can understand why text would add in "and to the Hebrews." It makes it clearer. I can't understand why the Hebrew text would have taken it out. So I think here the Hebrew was the original reading, and it shows us just how dumb this Pharaoh is. That is, in fact, how text criticism is usually done. Take the more difficult reading, because you can figure why somebody would correct it, but not why they would make it wrong.

Nor is Pharaoh's foolishness, I think, limited to this type of ineptitude we see in the Hebrew. The sly opening is confirmed by a couple of other little tidbits. For example, the midwives disobey him, which means Pharaoh's own workers won't listen to him. And even worse, when this little baby comes floating down the Nile River, Pharaoh's own daughter sees the baby says, "Ah, this must be a Hebrew child." I mean, who else would it be? It's not the brightest thing to say. But she's right. And instead of saying, "Ah, my father says all these babies shall be killed," what does she do? She adopts this baby, and she even winds up procuring this baby a nurse, because it turns out the baby's sister happens to be there. And who is the nurse? The baby's own mother, who, in fact, gets wages for nursing her own child. Pharaoh is thwarted at every turn, in fact, by women who don't even obey him.

There is a great lack of awareness here. Pharaoh's incompetence continues even when Moses and Aaron, his brother, do meet him. Moses has been commissioned by God at the burning bush and told, "Go back to Egypt and say to Pharaoh," you all know this, "Let my people go." Moses hesitates for a while. God says, "Fine, your brother, Aaron, who is apparently a better speaker, can go with you." But they have to go. And Moses arms...Moses is armed by God, as is Aaron, with particular magic tricks. So that when they go to Pharaoh's court, it's not just they're saying "Let my people go." They can actually demonstrate God's power.

Well, it turns out that the Egyptians have court magicians, and they can do the same sort of magic tricks that Moses and Aaron can do. They are not such a big deal. For example, Aaron's staff becomes a snake, and it slithers on the ground. So Pharaoh's magicians turn their staffs into snakes. Well, it turns out that Aaron's staff eats the other snakes. You know, his staff is bigger than theirs. But that's not really much of a great trick. Once the plagues start, it gets more interesting.

God creates ten plagues to be put on the Egyptians. The first plague is a plague of blood, such that all the waters in Egypt, including the Nile River, turn into blood. This is staggering, because it means the entire population is going to be without drinking water, fields can't be irrigated. This is a major disaster. What do Pharaoh's court magicians say? "Oh, we can do that, too." And they, in fact, make more blood, which is not quite what you want. The second plague is the plague of frogs, which crawl out of the Nile and get into everything. What do the court magicians say? "Oh, we can make frogs," and they make even more frogs. It turns out that not only is Pharaoh inept, his court magicians make things worse in Egypt by adding to the plagues. These are not people you actually want on your side.

And his foolishness and ineptitude may be confirmed by the motif of the hardening of his heart. But before we turn to this account, I think we need to talk a little bit more about Moses. Moses's early life is, of course, unattested in Egyptian sources. But the description we have in the Bible does evoke some of those cross-cultural parallels we've seen before. His infancy story, being floated down the Nile, being rescued by some women, and eventually growing to greatness, mirrors exactly the story of one Sargon of Akkad, who ruled in the middle of the third millennium B.C. It is a convention in fairy tales and folktales in the ancient Near East to float babies down rivers and have them found, and then they become great rulers. Indeed, both are protected by women from execution by a king; both are placed in reed baskets.

Moses's infancy account also resembles the primeval history. Here is another one of those problems that the English glosses over, but the Hebrew has. The word for the basket that Moses is placed in is *tevah* in Hebrew. And *tevah* is the word for the "ark" in which Noah floats. So, in effect,, Moses is in a new ark, and he, like Noah, is saved from drowning in the water. There is the connection.

Moses's mom places Moses in this ark in the reeds or the bullrushes. And the word for "reed" is *suf*. But it also turns out that later Moses will bring the children of Israel through a particular body of water. The Hebrew is *yam suf*, sea of reeds or sea of bullrushes. Some of you may have heard the expression "Red Sea," that's the Greek. The Hebrew Moses is, in fact, floated through bullrushes and eventually brings his people through bullrushes. The connections simply continue.

And as you know, because we've talked about this already, while Exodus 2 provides a Hebrew etymology for the name Moses, *Mosha* in Hebrew, that really is a good Egyptian name, like Ramses and Thutmose. Moses's initial action after his infancy opens the folktale motif of the hero's leave-taking, and we've seen this. His self-imposed exile is prompted initially, not by the Egyptians, but by Hebrews slaves saying, "Ah, you killed a taskmaster. Are you going to come down on us now, too?" Which shows that Moses will always have trouble, not just with the Egyptians, but also with his own people. Moses can't take loyalty for granted.

Moses flees from Pharaoh, who sought to kill him, and the motif is later repeated when Moses returns to Egypt, where we're told in Exodus 4, "The Lord sought to kill him." And in Exodus 4, Moses is rescued by his wife, Zipporah, just as, back in his infancy stories, he is rescued by a woman. Now strikingly, I think Moses's own leadership role is anticipated by these women. How so? Because the midwives and Moses's sister and Pharaoh's daughter achieve power the only way they can. Not through warfare, but by taking a stand and fighting against a type of injustice. And that's, in fact, what Moses is going to have to do. And he does it with God on his side, which is lovely.

And so we come to the ten plagues. These are difficult. The ten plagues have received "scientific" explanation. There were shows on TV like *Mysteries of the Bible* and *In Search of Ancient Mysteries*, which say, "Oh, the Nile turning to blood is really certain forms of plant life that's red, and the frogs were caused by the plant life, and the darkness is caused by wind storms." And some people even think it has to do with the blowing up of Atlantis, which is using one fictional story to explain something else that may be fictional.

The point is not whether the plagues can be explained naturally or whether they can't, because the ancient readers didn't care about it, they simply assumed these were plagues. The question here is: (a) How were the plagues recounted? and (b) Why did there have to be ten of them? Why does Pharaoh keep changing his mind?

We actually find out that in addition to the Book of Exodus, the plagues were mentioned in two other places, in Psalm 78 and in Psalm 105. But they are not quite the same plagues, and there aren't ten of them. I suspect in antiquity there were several versions of this story with different plagues and different orders, and the authors of Genesis and, excuse me, the authors of Exodus simply gave their particular version, leaving the Psalms, perhaps quite early Psalms, to give theirs.

Now, in part, the problem for the plagues is that Pharaoh has a change of heart. And we're told that that's going to happen right at the beginning. Exodus, Chapter 4. Has God informed Moses? "See that you do before

Pharaoh all the miracles which I have given to you to put in your power." But God goes on: "I will harden Pharaoh's heart, so that he will not let the people go." And this is a problem. Why would God, who is supposed to be a liberator, keep the people there and then engage in all these plagues, which certainly are no help to the Egyptians?

Between Exodus 4 and Exodus 14, ten times Pharaoh hardens his own heart; and ten times God prompts the hardening. They seem to be working together on this. This makes Pharaoh appear not only doltish and malevolent, as he did with the babies, but also without any sort of rational control. He offers to let the people go; he changes his mind. He offers to let them go; he changes his mind. He's vacillating. And the plagues are becoming increasingly worse. What's going on?

Briefly, in terms of hardening of the heart, for the ancient Hebrews, inner organs were seats of emotion. And we have today, too. You say, you know, "I with a heavy heart feel something." For example, the bowels are the seat of strong emotion. Jeremiah, in Chapter 4:19, cries out: "My bowels, my bowels, I writhe in pain." The Revised Standard Version puts it more delicately: "My anguish, my anguish." Right? And although the Revised Standard Version translates Psalm 16, verse 7: "In the night, my heart instructs me," the Hebrew was actually: "My kidneys afflict me"—I'm getting a little bit nervous here, because the kidneys are the seats of conscience.

And the heart is, for the Hebrews, the seat of inner life. The hardening of the heart is like the ossification of your vital principles, the numbing of your soul. Biblical scholar Nahum Sarna put it this way, "It is a condition of moral atrophy," and that's what Pharaoh has.

In terms of the contradiction between Pharaoh hardening his own heart and God doing it for him, there were several explanations. Some suggest that this is the intractable problem of fate and free will. As Rabbi Akiba, a second century Jewish martyr put it, second century Common Era, "All is determined and free will is given." God knows what you're going to do, but you're responsible for your actions anyway. Maybe this is one way of showing it. God planned it, but Pharaoh takes responsibility. On the other hand, perhaps God is simply pushing Pharaoh in the direction that he had started. This is what Pharaoh decided to do, and God is just going to make it worse for him, because he deserves the punishment. That's more of an existential reading, I suppose.

The source critics, our old friends from the documentary hypothesis, have their own explanation. Oh, "J" is the one who comes up with Pharaoh hardening his own heart, because "J" is interested in character. And "E" is the one who comes up God hardening Pharaoh's heart, because he wants that nice transcendent God in charge of everything. I don't find this convincing, but it does show up in some of the books.

Exodus gives us its own explanation, and here is where things get really morally problematic. According to Exodus 10, "Then the Lord God said to Moses, 'Go into Pharaoh for I have hardened his heart and the hearts of his servants that I may show these signs of mind among them, and that you may tell in the hearing of your children and your children's children, how I have toyed with the Egyptians'"—or made sport, but really "toyed" with the Egyptians—"'And what signs I have done among them, that you may know that I am the Lord.'" Why is God hardening Pharaoh's heart? Because it provides an excuse for yet another plague, and yet another plague, and, thereby, not only the Egyptians, and not only that present generation of Hebrews, but their children and their children's children will know about God's might.

This, for me, provides a theological problem. It's not easy here. I want God to be a liberating God, and that's the way we normally think about God. But, in fact, this is not necessarily just a liberating God. God is more complex. Indeed, even when we look at God's rationale for freeing the people, normally we think, "God"—and we hear this as well—"God heard the cries of the people, that they were enslaved, and he responded to their oppression." But remember, they have been there for 400 years, and they just didn't start crying out in year 398. The reason He finally responds is not simply because of compassion, but because, this is Exodus 6, "I heard the groanings of my people, and I remembered my covenant with them that I will bring you into the land which I swore to give to Abraham, to Isaac, and to Jacob." He responds out of compassion, yes, but he also responds because he's in a contract with these people, and this is part of his terms of the contract. Now, I suspect all of these readings are probably correct, a little bit. There is the covenantal model. And there is the fate and free will model. And there is the idea that God wants his power to be manifest.

My teenage daughter, when she heard this story a while back, and I read to her this business about making Pharaoh's power, making God's power manifest, said "Well, God's just on an ego trip." Sometimes children actually have pretty good insight. But I think it's more than that. Because remember, their world is not ours. These are stories that the Hebrew people would have celebrated: "Look at how strong this God is. Look at how strong our God is. See how He manifested His power in history. He can punish those who do wrong, just as He can reward those who do right." So that when the Hebrew people leave Egypt, go to Mt. Sinai in the wilderness and enter into a covenantal relationship with God, they will know this is a God Who can reward. And it's a God Who can punish. And it's a God Who, as we already saw back with Cain and Abel, is not one Who works on automatic. God who chooses to do what God wants to do at God's own time.

Exodus culminates with the splitting of the Reed Sea and the escape of the Israelites. And as I've mentioned, Red Sea is the Greek; the Hebrew is Reed Sea. Here we have some other images evoked from Genesis. By parting the waters, that's like a new creation. And by having the waters close again over the Egyptians and their chariots, that's like Noah's flood where the waters come back again. It is as if God re-creates the world, when he allows the Hebrew people to pass through.

And, therefore, Exodus becomes not only a new creation with this new people, but, in fact, it becomes the template of all future redemptions from oppression and from slavery. Theologically, as well as ethically, Israel's existence becomes interpreted through the Exodus. For example, this is Deuteronomy 5, and we find the same thing in Exodus 20: "Remember that you were a slave in the land of Egypt, and the Lord your God brought you out from there with a mighty hand and outstretched arm. Therefore, remember the Lord your God commanded you to keep the Sabbath day." That's that second explanation beyond the "P" code in Genesis 1, which says you keep the Sabbath day, because that's when God rested. Here, it's because you were slaves, and you know what it's like to work.

Here is Exodus 22, repeated in Deuteronomy 23: "You shall not wrong a stranger or oppress him, for you were strangers in the land of Egypt." Morality and ethics are grounded in the experience of slavery. Deuteronomy 24: "You shall not subvert the rights of the fatherless. Fatherless, you shall not take a widow's garment and pawn. Remember that you were a slave in Egypt, and the Lord your God redeemed you from there. Therefore, do I enjoin upon you even this commandment." Even the dietary regulations, to which we will turn in two lectures, are connected to the Exodus event. Leviticus 11: "You shall not defile yourselves with any swarming thing that crawls upon the earth, for I am the Lord your God who brought you out of the land of Egypt to be your God, and you shall be for me a holy people." And in Exodus 14:31, we read: "And Israel saw the great work which YHWH had done among the Egyptians, and the people feared YHWH and the people believed in YHWH and in his servant, Moses." And what they believed, we'll find out in the next lecture, when we return to this biblical God.

The God of Israel
(Exodus 1–15, cont.)
Lecture 9

This God responds to Moses: "Ehyeh asher ehyeh." "I am what I am" …
This is a God of being, a God of process, a God of future orientation. A
God who takes whatever form this God wants to take. … Subsequently,
whenever this God is referred to, … he is referred to, as "YHWH,"
which actually translates the Hebrew, "He will be" or "He is what
He is."

More than an account of the liberation of Hebrew slaves, the
opening chapters of Exodus also provide insight into the name of
the Deity and the sources used in the Pentateuch's composition.
When Moses is told to rescue his people, he asks (Exod. 3:13), "If I come
to the people of Israel and say to them, 'The god of your fathers has sent me
to you,' and they ask me, 'What is his name?' what shall I say to them?" In
other words, "Which god are you?" The question makes excellent sense in
the polytheistic Near East. The voice responds with a name both cryptic and
revelatory, "I will be what I will be." The Deity's name is given in Exod.
3:14, and only here, in the first person, *ehyeh asher ehyeh*, meaning both "I
will be what I will be" and "I am what I am." All other Hebrew references
appear in the third person form: "he will be" (YHWH). Into Greek, the active
"I will be" becomes the static "I am" (*ego eimi*).

Sometimes called the *Tetragrammaton* (Greek meaning "four letters"),
YHWH is composed of four consonants (early Hebrew manuscripts lack
vowels). The name eventually received vowels (called "points") taken from
the Hebrew for "my Lord," *Adonai*. This resulted in the term "YaHoWaH,"
which gives us, finally, "Jehovah." The *Tetragrammaton* was probably
pronounced by the Hebrew priests. Legend has it that the name, attributed
with increasing holiness, came to be recited once a year, on Yom Kippur (the
Day of Atonement), by the high priest in the Holy of Holies of the Jerusalem
Temple, at the moment that chanting from the Temple choir swelled.

Readings of the *Tanakh*, as well as prayers in Judaism, substitute the Hebrew "My Lord" (*Adonai*) for the *Tetragrammaton*. Some Jews will even provide circumlocutions for *Adonai* (e.g., *ha-Shem* ["the name"]) to preserve the holiness of the name. The Jewish mystical tradition asserts that the name is ineffable; were it to be correctly pronounced, says one legend, the Messiah would come. Other writers speak of myriad pronunciations.

In Hebrew culture, names are more than labels. To "call one's name" or to know one's name signals power. Given mastery over the woman, Adam "calls her name Eve" (Gen. 3:20). A name change signals a change in one's fate and the fate of one's descendants—Sarai to Sarah ("princess"), Jacob to Israel. Etymologies provide insight into character and fate. Isaac is "laughter"; Israel is "one who strives with God"; and Jacob is "supplanter."

Hebrew words are typically built on tri-consonantal roots (stems). Analogous would be the root SNG, whence: sing, sang, song. The root of YHWH is that the root is unclear. The most common derivation is from the root meaning "to be, become, make happen." This future emphasis matches Hebrew's verbal orientation. It fits embedded uses of the term, such as Exod. 6:6–8, "I am YHWH, and I will bring you out from under the burdens of the Egyptians, and I will deliver you from bondage, and I will redeem you with an outstretched arm and with great acts of judgment. And I will take you for my people, and I will be your god, and you shall know that I am YHWH ..." A second possibility is the root for "to fall." The connotations are both to make a sudden appearance, like a meteor, and to cause rain to fall. This derivation would strengthen the connection of YHWH to Near Eastern storm and nature gods, such as the Canaanite Baal. The name may have originated as "Yah," a battle cry. Perhaps the origin is deliberately vague or overdetermined: YHWH is never fully known.

Even were we to locate the name's origin, it may yield little about the origins of YHWHism. For this question, we return to source criticism. According to Exod. 3:16, usually assigned to E (Elohist, Ephraimite), YHWH ("Lord") appears first at the burning bush. Earlier, the deity was "Elohim" (God). Exod. 3:1 locates the bush on Mt. Horeb, another term (probably E) for Mt. Sinai. The Hebrew for the "bush" is (ironically?), *Sineh*, like "Sinai."

The Israelites resemble the bush: small but invincible; threatened but never consumed; humble, yet strong. Gen. 4:26–27 quotes Eve at the birth of Seth: "God [Elohim] has appointed for me another child instead of Abel … To Seth also was born a son, and he called his name Enosh. At that time, people began to call upon the name of the Lord [YHWH]." This verse, in possible contradiction to Exod. 3, is usually assigned to J. And finally the priestly (P) commentary is found in Exod. 6:2, which observes, "God [Elohim] said to Moses, 'I am YHWH. I appeared to Abraham, Isaac, and Jacob as El Shaddai ["god of the mountain"; perhaps, "of the breasts"; cf. Gen. 17:1] but my name YHWH I did not make known to them.'"

Perhaps in its earliest cultic history, Israel's chief deity was El (generic "god") not YHWH; later, the two were assimilated. "Israel" is based on "el," not "YHWH." Deut. 32:8–9 casts YHWH as one of El's sons: "When the most high (Elyon) gave to the nations their inheritance, when he separated humanity, he fixed the boundaries of peoples according to the number of divine beings. For YHWH's portion is his people, Jacob his allotted heritage." Characteristics of the Canaanite sky-god El are assimilated to YHWH. Ugaritic and Canaanite texts depict El as an elderly, bearded man enthroned in a divine council. So, too, YHWH is sometimes depicted (Ps. 102; Job 36; Isa. 40; Dan. 7:9, and so on) as an aged patriarch, enthroned in a divine assembly (1 Kgs. 22; Isa. 6: Ps. 29, 82, and so on).

Theories of the cult's origin are similarly complex. The "Kenite hypothesis" suggests that the Israelites learned of YHWH, the god of Mt. Sinai, from Moses's father-in-law, the Midianite priest. Exod. 18:12: "Jethro, Moses' father-in-law, took a burnt offering and sacrificed it to Elohim; and Aaron came with all the elders of Israel to eat bread with Moses' father-in-law." Thus, the Kenite Jethro hosts a cultic meal. Cross-cultural influence is likely during the period of settlement: Judges 1:16 notes, "The descendants of the Kenites, Moses' father-in-law, went up with the people of Judah … into the wilderness of Judah, which lies in the Negev near Arad, and they went and settled with the people." In Judges 4–5, the heroine Jael is married to a Kenite. First Chronicles 2:55, although a late source, associates the Kenites with the Rechabites, a group known for rigorous personal piety. Countering this view: theophoric (god-bearing) names associated with YHWH appear before Exodus 3; for example, Moses's mother Yocheved ("YHWH is glory"). But the name may be a later insertion; Exod. 2, her introduction, records no name.

Another explication returns to the theory of the patriarchs as independent clan heads: YHWH is the patron of Moses's clan, cf. Shield of Abraham (Gen. 15:1); Mighty One of Jacob (Gen. 49:24). Clan gods may have been attractive to semi-nomadic peoples whose identity is more determined by family than by land. This thesis could also explicate the first words the Deity speaks to Moses: "I am the god of your father" (Exod. 3:6). Exod. 15:2, the very old "Song of Moses": "Yah [Hebrew shortened form] is my strength and my song, he has become my salvation. This is my God and I will praise him, my father's God and I will exalt him."

The covenant community told their God's story less through etymologies or cosmologies than through recounting divine actions in history, and they described their relationship to this Deity through covenants, as the next lecture demonstrates. ∎

Suggested Reading

Samuel E. Ballentine, *The Torah's Vision of Worship.*

Walter Brueggemann, *Theology of the Old Testament: Testimony, Dispute, Advocacy.*

Mark Smith, *The Early History of God: Yahweh and Other Deities in Ancient Israel.*

Questions to Consider

1. What would "wrongful use of the name of the Lord your God" (Exod. 20:7) be?

2. YHWH is sometimes considered a wilderness deity, found on Mt. Sinai in the desert. What changes in YHWH's presentation occur as the Israelites build YHWH a temple in Jerusalem?

3. Why is YHWH not imaged? Why are images (idols) in general forbidden (Exod. 20:4)?

The God of Israel
(Exodus 1–15, cont.)
Lecture 9—Transcript

The Exodus is more than simply an account of the liberation of the Hebrew slaves from bondage under Pharaoh. The Exodus, particularly the beginning of this book, provides us incredible insight into the nature of God, and we get that insight in part through the manifestation at the burning bush and also through the discussion of the divine name. Is it Elohim? Is it YHWH? Is it El-Shaddai or El-Elyon? So for this lecture, we'll return to Moses at the burning bush, and we'll try to figure out, moving from that theophany, that manifestation of God, on through the rest of the Pentateuch, who is this deity? What does the name mean? Who, exactly, are these people worshiping?

So we start off at the burning bush. Here is Moses. He had split Egypt after having committed murder. He lands at a well, he meets some ladies, he marries one of them, and then he happily engages his new career: He is busy tending sheep on behalf of his father-in-law. And here is what happens when we actually get to the text. This is Exodus 3: "Moses led the flock along, and he came to Horab," and this will turn out to be another name for Sinai, same place. "He came to Horab, the mountain of God, and there an angel appeared to him as the fire was blazing out of a bush. Although the bush was on fire, it was not being burnt up." A miracle.

Moses turns to take a closer look. I think anybody would. But when he gets a little bit closer, a voice calls out, "Moses, take your shoes off, you're standing on holy ground. Do not approach any closer." And then voice says, "I am the God of your father, the God of Abraham, Isaac, and Jacob." And at this point, Moses is, no doubt, completely stunned. This is not what your average shepherd might have been thinking. But we, as readers, are stunned, too, because we know that the Hebrew people have been enslaved for about 400 years. We've been waiting to see what's going to happen. And we've been waiting for Moses to get his hero's call.

It turns out, like many of the judges and indeed prophets after him, Moses is not terribly anxious to accept this commission. When the voice from the bush says, "Go and redeem my people. Tell Pharaoh, 'Let my people go.'" Moses demurs. He doesn't want to do it. He's afraid he's not a good speaker. He's simply a shepherd. Okay, he was raised in the royal court. But he really doesn't want to do it. He needs some sort of assurance, not only that the Pharaoh will believe him, but also that the Israelites will believe him. They have no reason to trust him.

So Moses asks in Exodus 3:13: "If I come to the people of Israel, and I say to them, 'The God of your fathers has sent to me to you,' and they say, 'What is his name?' What am I supposed to tell them?'" In other words, which God are you? And in a world of polytheism, this is a very good question. And how do we identify you? If names convey a sense of the person, a sense of the Being, how we have a sense of this God? What is your name? The question makes a great deal of sense. The problem is the answer remains mysterious. Here is the response. The bush, this God, responds to Moses: "*Ehyeh asher ehyeh*." "I am what I am" or "I will be what I will be." The Hebrew can take either meaning. If God had simply said, "My name is Zeus, or my name is Asher, or my name is Baal," everybody would know what this God was talking about. But, "I am what I am. I will be what I will be." This is a God of being, a God of process, a God of future orientation. A God who takes whatever form this God wants to take. The deity's name is given here in Exodus only in the first person: "I am." Subsequently, whenever this God is referred to, it is referred to, or he is referred to, as "YHWH," which actually translates the Hebrew, "He will be" or "He is what He is."

But then we have worry about, what does this name mean and where does it come from? We'll stop briefly just to look at the name "YHWH" itself. As you've heard in earlier lectures, the term is sometimes referred to as the *Tetragrammaton* and that's simply Greek for "four letters," which in English come out to be Y-H-W-H, YHWH. The pronunciation YHWH is simply a convenience, because ancient Hebrew, biblical Hebrew, as well as, in fact, modern Hebrew, lacks vowels. We simply have consonants. Vowels have been put in in some texts much, much later. Those are called points.

In terms of YHWH, that's the best guess we have for pronunciation. We also have some sense, from the first couple of centuries of the Common Era, that that's how the name was pronounced. Our old friend, Clement of the

Alexandria, the one who was concerned about Noah being drunk, actually gives us a transliteration in Greek of the name YHWH. So with Greek letters, it looks sort of like YHWH. That could be the case. We also have, from the sixth and fifth centuries Before the Common Era, papyrus remains from a Jewish military colony, no less, from Elephantine, which is located in Egypt. They are under Persian patronage, and they are simply there to keep the Egyptians from revolting. This community built its own temple, had its own legal system, its own architecture, its own judges. We have their letters that go back and forth from Jerusalem.

But in this temple, as their letters describe, they worship a God whose name seems to be "YHW ("Yahu")," Y-H-W without that final "H" on the end. And it does seem to be pronounced "Yahu." These are Jews. They are problematic Jews in antiquity, because in addition to this God YHW, they also have a goddess, Anat-Yahu, or Mrs. YHWH, as it were. But here is another possibility of the pronunciation, YHW. The name YHWH itself, simply the pronunciation, is being increasingly used in Christian worship, so you might hear in churches, YHWH. Jews in temples and synagogues would never use that term.

Whenever the *Tetragrammaton* in a temple or a synagogue comes up in the prayer book or comes up in biblical reading, Jews will, instead of reading YHWH, read the word, *Adonai*, which simply means "my Lord." And sometimes more orthodox Jews will not even say, outside of a liturgical context, *Adonai*. They'll use another circumlocution like *Adoshem* or simply *ha-Shem*, which means "the name." This means not only is the *Tetragrammaton* a sacred symbol when written down, but even the pronunciation is so sacred in the Jewish context that one needs a circumlocution and then a circumlocution for the circumlocution.

In terms of another way of pronouncing YHWH—this fascinates me— we've seen the word *Adonai*, that means "my Lord." What some people in Germany wound up doing is taking the Y-H-W-H, and, of course, they would pronounce it with a J, J-H-W-H, and they would put in the vowels from *Adonai*. And if you take the letters from the *Tetragrammaton* and the vowels from the Hebrew for "my Lord," and you pronounce it with a German accent, you get *Jehovah*. And that's where the term *Jehovah* comes from. It's simply a construct with a little bit of a German accent.

In terms of the *Tetragrammaton* itself, it was probably pronounced by the priests in the temple. We have legendary accounts that suggest eventually, in the second temple period after the Babylonian exile, the *Tetragrammaton* became so holy it was only pronounced by the High Priest once a year on the holiest day of the Jewish calendar, Yom Kippur, the Day of Atonement. He only pronounced the name in the Holy of Holies, the innermost sanctum of the temple. And when he pronounced it, the choir swelled, so that, in fact, the only person who could hear this pronunciation was God, which is really the only person who really needs to hear it.

Jewish mystical tradition asserts the name is ineffable, unpronounceable. And, indeed, if somebody did come up with a pronunciation, the world would end and the Messiah would come. Others suggest that there are a myriad of pronunciations, that nobody can quite latch on to all of them. The name remains a mystery.

I want to share with you one very problematic ancient rendition of the *Tetragrammaton*. Hebrew reads from right to left. English, as you know, reads from left to right. Greek, like English, reads from left to right. We have, from the first and second centuries of the Common Era in Egypt, texts called *Magical Papyri*. They are actually incantations, spells, love charms, health potions, and what not. We, on occasion, have in the *Magical Papyri* invocations to a great God called *Pipi*, who was actually signaled by a chicken head with legs. This astounded scholars for years. They couldn't figure out where this comes from. What actually happened was if you take, written out in Hebrew, the letters for YHWH, and you read them backwards, and you think you're reading in Greek, the letter "H" in Hebrew looks sort of like the Greek letter *pi*, and the two other letters, that are actually a *yud* and a *vuv* in Hebrew, actually looked like the *iota* in Greek. So if you read it backwards, it looks like "*pipi*." And as you can imagine, "*pipi*" is simply onomatopoeic for chicken in Egyptian.

The point of this is not how silly these people who wrote these *Magical Papyri* are. It's the fact that even pagans recognize this name has power.

Even if they couldn't pronounce it, even if they couldn't read it in the right direction, the very letters themselves suggest that this is God one is evoking. This is fascinating to me.

That the divine name would have particular power is, in fact, consistent with the way the ancient Israelites thought about names. To call one's name, to know one's name, suggests that one might have power over that person. Right at the beginning of human history, in Genesis, Chapter 3, we learn that "Adam called the name of his wife, Eve, mother of all living." And the fact that he can name her suggests, thereby, his domination over her. That's one way we see that initial curse being played out.

Jacob, as you know, seeks the name of his opponent who wrestles with him at the Jabbok River. It's not clear who that opponent is, whether it's Jacob's own inner turmoil or an angel or God. Whoever the opponent is he refuses to give Jacob his name, but instead he renames Jacob "Israel, one who strives with God." And the change of name here indicates something about Jacob's future identity.

By the way, other scholars have suggested that the name "Israel," which can mean "one who strives with God," also can convey the impression, convey the connotation, of someone who was happy or someone who was successful. So here again, we have a particular Hebrew term with more than one possible meaning. The Bible leaves it with struggle, but I wonder if people who considered themselves Israelites in antiquity would have thought of themselves as happy and fortunate, because that's partially what the name can mean. We've already noted the importance of names, the changes of Abram and Sarai's name to Abraham and Sarah, Isaac and laughter, Esau and red for Edom, et cetera.

There are also meaningful names as we go all the way through. My favorite name is actually the name of Jacob's eldest son. His name is Reuben, which may be familiar to you. Reuben is the child of Leah, the unloved wife. And when she finally has the son, she thinks Jacob will be really pleased, she's given him what he wants. *Reu* means "look here," and *ben* means "a son." Which means that every time Jacob will look at his son Reuben and call his name, he will think, "Look, a son." Leah is simply pointing out to him,

"Look at what I did." And this sort of, what, pregnant name will show up also when we get to the prophets. Isaiah's children and Josiah's children have meaningful names.

Now, biblical scholars began to think, if we could figure out the etymology of a term, if we could get to the root of that name, that YHWH name, perhaps we could get a sense of YHWH's origins and YHWH's identity. Hebrew words, for the most part, are built on tri-consonantal stems. I mentioned before that to do religion you need a little bit everything. Here is linguistics. Most words are based on tri-consonantal stems, which is simply three letters. If we think about the English, S-N-G, we have sang, and sung, and song. And we can hear the connections among them, as well as the sounds. So the idea would be, if we could figure out what the three letters were in the *Tetragrammaton*, four letters, we might be able to get a hang on YHWH.

Part of the problem is we also have false etymologies. S-N-G could also give us snug and snag. So when we look to those four letters and try to figure out which are the three letters upon which the name is based, we come up with a multitude of responses. Typically, we normally look at the most common derivation from the Hebrew verb, "to be" or "to become." Hebrew actually only has two tenses, completed action and incompleted action, the perfect tense or the imperfect tense, which is why YHWH can be translated, "He will be what He will be," or "He is what He is." But not, "He was what He was."

If this word is from "to be," if YHWH originally has this "to be" connotation, then we have the sense that YHWH is always present, YHWH is always active, YHWH, the one who will be, as having a future orientation. Someone who creates. Someone who moves history. Someone who makes history happen.

This also fits the Greek translation of the Hebrew Bible, where YHWH is translated, *ego eimi*, "I am." And that is, by the way, Jesus, the way Jesus refers to himself in the Gospel of John. There is also the embedded use of the term "YHWH," which has the connotation of "to be." This is Exodus 6: "I am YHWH, and I will bring you out from under the burdens of the Egyptians, and I will deliver you from bondage, and I will redeem you with an outstretched arm and with great acts of judgment, and I will take you for my people, and I will be your God, and you shall know that I am YHWH, your God, who has brought you out from underneath the burdens of the Egyptians." So when we get the sense of the name, YHWH, we get a sense of action, divine manifestation in history, and YHWH, who does what He wants to do, when He wants to do it, will be what He will be in time.

A second possibility, etymologically for the name, is that it might come from the Hebrew root meaning, "to fall," as in the sense of rain falling down. That's also quite possible, because YHWH, on occasion, gets assimilated to the Canaanite god whose name is Baal, which is basically a word that means "Lord." Baal is a nature god, he's a thunder god, he is the one who causes rain to fall. So there may be a partial connection there, as well.

A third suggestion is that the name comes from the root meaning, "to blow." And not only to give a blow to somebody, to punch somebody, the warrior type, but also to blow, like to blow up a storm, or to blow wind—again, connections with the nature god, but also a sense of the warrior. And we know, as we've seen with the plagues, YHWH can certainly put up a good fight. Others have suggested roots like "to desire," or "one who loves" or "speaks." I'm not convinced by that.

But there is one other possible etymological origin, which actually intrigues me. I don't know if it's true, but I want it to be. And that is that it's originally a battle-cry. People go into battle, and they go, "Yah!" And why do I think that might be the case? Because there is actually some hint of it at Moses's "Song of the Sea," where we are told "YH," the shortened form, "is my God." So it may have some connection there, as well.

It seems to me, even if we can't figure out historically or etymologically for sure what this term means—I do think it comes from the Hebrew for "to be"—the fact that other possible interpretations accrue to it, seems to me entirely appropriate. Because this is a God who's not going to be constrained by one particular meaning. And if there are certain connections with Baal, the Canaanite god, so much the better. Because when Israel is put into competition with Canaan, and YHWH goes one-on-one with Baal, it helps if YHWH has Baal's attributes.

In terms of how else Israel might have identified the name, we note when Moses talks to this bush, or the bush talks to Moses, that suddenly we get the sense that YHWH had not been used before. Now we have to move back to source criticism. Now, if you had been frustrated with all this information about "J", "E", "D," or "P", this may be probably the last time you'll have to deal with it, maybe once or twice more. But it is important. Here is Moses at the burning bush. This is typically assigned to the "E" source. How do we know that? Because it starts out by using *Elohim*, the word for God, and also because the location is Horab. That's up in the northern kingdom. That's an "E" term. "J", the other writer, will use Sinai.

By the way, the word for bush is *sineh*, and then Sinai sounds awfully like this. This may be a pun, that when you get to the burning bush it is as if you get an early glance at what Mt. Sinai is. And I think, as long as we're talking about this bush, that it's a pretty good symbol, not only for God, but also for Israel. Something that you can throw fire at, and it's not going to get consumed; something that's small, but yet invincible; something that's relatively humble, and yet strong. And in the same way that Moses feels compelled to turn and look at this bush, the idea is, in the ancient Near East, from the Israelites' perspective, one is compelled to turn and look at Israel. You have to pay attention to this nation, because YHWH's on its side. Okay.

According to the "E" source, YHWH tells the people his name is YHWH at the burning bush. According to the "J" source, the people have been calling upon the name of YHWH as early as Genesis, Chapter 4. This is Genesis 4:25 and 26: "Adam knew his wife again, and she bore a son and called his name Seth, for she said God, *Elohim*, has appointed for me another child. To Seth also a son was born. He called his name Enosh. At that time, people began to call *besame* YHWH, upon the name of YHWH."

The "P" writer harmonizes this all, because "P" is the editor who puts it all together. This is what the "P" writer says in Exodus 6: "God, *Elohim*, said to Moses, 'I am YHWH. I appear to Abraham, Isaac, and Jacob as El Shaddai,'" usually translated, "God of the mountain," sometimes "God almighty," and, indeed, sometimes "God of the breasts," which may be, in fact, two mountains next to each other, but I think it also has that connotation of nursing care. That's Genesis 17, where El Shaddai shows up. But "P" goes on, "But my name, YHWH, I did not make known to them."

Perhaps in its earliest cultic history, Israel referred to its God not as YHWH, but as *El*, because *El* is simply the Hebrew generic term for god, God with a small "g". But it's also the name of the head of the Canaanite pantheon, it's Baal's father. And that would fit nicely into the Israelites' settlement in Canaan. Why not take the name of their god and assimilate it to the name of the Hebrew god? And it may well have been that's what the Hebrews did, because *El* shows up with a variety of epithets. El Shaddai we've just seen; El Elyon; El Roi, the god of seeing, not the son on the Jetsons. Right? So that these various El's all become assimilated to the one God.

Deuteronomy 32 actually casts YHWH as one of El's sons. This is how the text read: "When the most high," this is El Elyon, "gave to the nations their inheritance, he separated humanity and fixed the boundaries of the people. To YHWH, his portion is his people; Jacob, his allotted heritage." Which sounds like El is divvying up humankind among the gods, and YHWH, fortunately enough, winds up with Israel.

There are also characteristics of the Canaanite god, El, which somehow connect with YHWH. El in Canaanite and Ugaritic text is typically pictured on a big throne surrounded by a court, and he is often seen as an elderly man, white hair and a beard. And YHWH, typically, is also pictured in a heavenly court. We already saw that in Genesis 1, with the "let us make humankind." He's normally seen sitting on a great throne, and sometimes he's seen as an old man.

This is Isaiah, Chapter 40. "Do you not know? Have you not heard? Were you not told long ago?" That's good prophetic rhetoric, say the same thing three times. "Have you not perceived"—say it four times—"since the world began that God sits enthroned on the vaulted roof of the world?" But that's exactly how El is depicted. And in terms of the god being elderly, Daniel, Chapter 7, verse 9, "As I was looking, thrones were set in place and the ancient of days took his seat, his robe was white as snow and his hair like lamb's wool, pure white." There are the connections with El, perhaps.

In terms of the origins of Yahwism, we return to our friends, the Kenites, whom we met in connection with Cain. Biblical scholars speak about the "Kenite Hypothesis," the idea that Moses learned about YHWH from the Kenites. Whom in particular?—His father-in-law, Jethro, the Midianite priest, because Midianites and Kenites overlap. This could be. According to Exodus 18: "Jethro [Moses's father-in-law] took a burnt offering, sacrificed to God, *Elohim*, and all the elders and the people came and joined him for dinner." Is this an initiation rite, a cultic sacrifice? Could be.

We know that the Kenites remained within the covenant community, but distinct. So they are there, and they could conceivably promulgate their religion. And First Chronicles, which is a very late post-exilic source, nevertheless, in Chapter 2, associates the Kenites with a group of people called the Rechabites. And the Rechabites, mentioned in Jeremiah 35, are an ultra-orthodox sect, heavily pious. So the Kenites do have this heavy connection with God-worship, with the Sinai Peninsula, which is where they are located to begin with, and with ultra-orthodoxy. So it's certainly possible that the Kenites could have given YHWH to Moses.

I'm not convinced of this, however, there are certainly good explanations against it. For example, Jethro was never called a priest of YHWH; he's a priest of Midian. It may be that the cultic sacrifice Jethro offers is not a sacrifice to YHWH, it's simply your basic cultic sacrifice. And since the people happen to be on Jethro's turf, he gets to offer it. And, indeed, the people might have thought, by the time they wrote their text, YHWH and whoever the Kenite god was were the same anyway. Could the Hebrews have picked up YHWH from the Kenites? It's possible, but it's certainly not definitive.

Another explanation for the origins of YHWH is that somehow YHWH was associated with those clan gods. And we've already seen this thesis in discussing the patriarchs, Abraham, Isaac, and Jacob, as if originally they were separate clan leaders, each with his own God: the shield of Abraham, the mighty one of Jacob. And as the clans merged together, the gods merged together. Might it be possible, therefore, that YHWH is Moses's clan god, and as Moses led the people, he gave them his God or at least his conception of divinity? It could be. Clan gods would have been attractive to semi-nomadic people, because, unlike gods, say, Marduk, the Babylonian god, clan gods are not restricted to particular locations. You can take them with you as you wander. And YHWH, as you know, is not stuck in a particular location. YHWH is portable. YHWH is a god of time, as we saw in Genesis 1, not a god of space so much.

Why a clan god for Moses? Here's Exodus 3, verse 6: "I am the God of your father." And that would fit with other identifications of God as father. The fear of Isaac. Laban swears by the God of Nahor, his grandfather. So that fits. According to Exodus, Chapter 15, verse 2, this very old "Song of Moses," I've already cited: "Yah is my strength and my song. He has become my salvation. This is my God and I will praise him, my father's God and I will exalt him." So it may be that Moses has taken on this God or developed the God concept he had already inherited, and then shared it with the people.

In Exodus, Chapter 18, we are told that Moses's second son by his wife Zipporah, Eliezer, has a name meaning, "The God of my father was my help and delivered me from the sword of Pharaoh." Now the name Eliezer doesn't mean all that. It simply means, "my God is help." But I'm intrigued by the fact that the editors feel compelled to add, "the God of my father," making that connection with Moses, as well.

So finally a bit of conjecture on this one. According to the Book of Exodus, under Moses's leadership, a mixed multitude comes out. The people who leave Egypt are not simply Israelites, they are probably other slaves, other people disenfranchised from the Egyptian government. This is Exodus 12:38. All these people appear to have accepted YHWH as Moses's clan god. So if there was a Moses, and that is a big if, since outside the Bible he's not attested in any other source, his connection with Yahwism would be a major factor, if not the major factor, in determining at least the origins of Israelite theology.

But Israelite theology remains incredibly difficult to determine. Because, even if we knew the origins of Yahwism, if we could get it back to the Kenites, and even if we understood the etymology, if we knew that it came from "to blow" or "to fall" or "to be," that may not have been what the authors of the Bible thought the word meant.

I mean think about how etymologies function today. Right? We have lots of names that have very good solid etymological bases, like Moses and the connection with "be begotten by an Egyptian." But, of course, the Bible erases that entirely. The Bible gives us an etymology for Moses "to be drawn out of water." But I think if you ask the average person on the street today, where does the name "Moses" come from? Besides telling you "the Bible," they would not be able to give you the etymological background. And it may well be for the Bible itself, they had the name YHWH, they might not have known the background, they simply knew it meant something like, "He will be what He will be." And that's how they wound up discussing their God, ultimately.

The biblical God is not found so much by linguistics. And it's not found so much by these kinds of thick descriptions. The biblical God is found in the god's manifestation in history. That's how the Israelites conveyed their sense of God. What has God done for us? What will God do for us? So in order to get a handle on this God, what we will need to do, as we will do in the next lecture, is to look at how God manifests in history: what aspects of that history the people decide to celebrate, what aspects of that history make them a little nervous.

And we find that this God of the Exodus manifests in particular historical ways, through miracles and theophanies, such as the plagues and the burning bush, but also through covenants. We've seen that already with Noah and the covenant of the rainbow. We've seen it with Abraham and the promise for mighty nations. We will see it with David, and we will certainly see it in the next lecture, when we deal with the covenant on Sinai to Moses. The god manifests through laws. God gives the human people laws, and we then proceed to follow them out. That's how we become united to God.

And, finally, through theological developments. But, in fact, we really won't get precise theological developments until we get to the prophets. It's not yet an issue for the people. Upshot, the covenant community told their God-story less through etymologies and, indeed, less through cosmologies than by recounting divine action in history, and then describing, in particular, their relation to this God through covenants. And it's to covenants we'll turn in the next lecture.

Covenant and Law, Part I
(Exodus 19–40, Leviticus, Deuteronomy)
Lecture 10

One of the major ways that the Israelites related to their God is through covenants.

The Hebrew term for "covenant," Berit, may be familiar through such organizations as B'Nai B'rith, literally "children of the covenant." A covenant is a contract, a legal agreement between parties. The prophet Jeremiah speaks of "the new covenant" written on people's hearts (Jer. 31:31–34). The Greek expression for this contract, he kaine diatheke, is also the expression "New Testament." The Hebrew expression for "covenant making" is c'rat berit, literally, "to cut a covenant," as in the English idiom "to cut a deal." The "sign of the covenant" is circumcision, a ceremony even today in Judaism known as the Berit (Bris, in Eastern European pronunciation), Milah, "covenant of circumcision," or simply Berit.

The *Tanakh* provides two forms of covenants. The "vassal or suzerainty treaty" formulation underlies the covenant at Sinai (the Mosaic covenant, or the covenant mediated through Moses). The "royal grant" model is associated with the covenants to Noah, Abraham, and David (cf. Psalms 50, 81, 89, 32). Both forms are explicated by what may be called an "I-Thou" relationship or contracts between unequals: lord and vassal, humanity and God. The terms of the contract are binding on both parties. The two models are attested in ancient Mesopotamia from over 4,500 years ago. The Hittites, an Asiatic group, used Akkadian (Semitic) covenantal models, which may suggest that the form originated in the Mesopotamian basin. The earliest extant example is the Stele of the Vultures; this text, written before 2500 B.C.E., charmingly depicts vultures devouring corpses of the covenant party's enemy.

The covenantal form has six primary parts, each attested in biblical material. The first part, the *preamble* opens with the titles of the superior party. This appears at the opening of the Decalogue (literally, "ten words"): "I am the

Lord your God" (Exod. 20:2a). The second part, the *historical prologue* assures the party of the second part (Israel) that the party of the first part (God)

can fulfill the contractual terms (typically, protection from invasion, economic alliance). In royal grants, the prologue delineates the reasons both for the vassal's obligations to the king and for the king's desire to reward the vassal. The historical prologue appears next in the Decalogue: "Who brought you out of the land of Egypt, out of the house of bondage" (Exod. 20:2b). God's motivation for freeing the people was the covenant obligation to Abraham, not, *pace* many theologians, the injustice of slavery itself.

Moses coming down from Mount Sinai.

Click Art

The third part, *regulations/ stipulations* make up the third and typically the longest section. These delineate the responsibilities of the co-signatories. Treaties typically insist that the second party (the vassal) show loyalty only to the lord and avoid additional alliances. Exod. 20:3–6 mandates, "You shall have no other gods before me; you shall not make for yourself a graven image, or any likeness of anything that is in heaven above, or that is in the earth beneath, or that is in the water under the earth; you shall not bow down to them or serve them." In this third section, the Mosaic code presents a relatively uncommon element. Ancient Near Eastern covenants typically present *casuistic* ("cause-and-effect") law; that is, they list crime and punishment. The Babylonian Code of Hammurabi (from the time to which Abraham is dated), for example, offers (ll. 142–43): "If a woman so hated her husband that she has declared, 'you

163

may not have me,' her record shall be investigated at her city council; if she was careful and not at fault, even though her husband has been going out and disparaging her greatly, that woman, without incurring any blame at all, may take her dowry and go off to her father's house. If she was not careful, but a gadabout, thus neglecting her house and humiliating her husband, they shall throw that woman into the water." The Decalogue's formula is *apodictic*: command apart from result. "You shall not murder; you shall not commit adultery; you shall not steal; you shall not bear false witness against your neighbor; you shall not covet your neighbor's wife, or his manservant, or his maidservant, or his ox, or his ass, or anything else that is your neighbor's" (Exod. 20:13–17). The Mosaic code also has a proportionally higher number of positive injunctions than its ancient Near Eastern counterparts. More than a list of "thou shalt nots," it contains a fair number of "thou shalts": "Remember the Sabbath day and keep it holy. Six days you shall labor and do all your work; but the seventh day is a sabbath to the Lord your God; in it you shall not do any work: you, or your son, or your daughter, your manservant, your maidservant, or your cattle, or the sojourner who is within your gate ... Honor your father and your mother ..." (Exod. 20:8–12). And finally in the stipulations section, vassal/suzerainty treaties concentrate on the vassal's obligations (here, injunctions placed on Israel) in surety for future service and loyalty. The royal grant, associated with Noah, Abraham, and David, stresses the Lord's obligations in responding to loyalty shown by the vassal. Typically, this formulation involves the granting of land. In the Bible, it includes guarantees of safety from universal destruction (Noah); promises of land, descendants, and blessing (Abraham); and promises of an eternal throne (David).

The next set of covenantal forms is not included in the Decalogue proper. Part four requires the safe *deposit* of the contract and regular *public readings*. Deut. 10:5 specifically mentions depositing the tablets of the law in the Ark of the Covenant. Deut. 31:9–13 offers provisions for recitation: "At the end of every seven years, at the set time of the year of release, at the Feast of Booths [Tabernacles], when all Israel comes to appear before the Lord your God at the place which he will choose, you shall read this law before all Israel in their hearing. Assemble the people—men, women, and little ones, and the sojourner within your towns—that they may hear and learn to fear the Lord your God, and be careful to do all the words of this law." Other examples include Joshua 24 is a covenant renewal ceremony and Ezra giving a public reading "before the assembly, both men and women and all who could hear with understanding ... and the ears of all the people were attentive to the Book of the Law" (Neh. 8:2–3).

The fifth primary part of covenants—like all legal contracts—list *witnesses*. Usually the witnesses are the gods of the co-signatories. Given Israel's lack of other gods, the Bible improvises: Josh. 24:22 has the people function as both signatories and witnesses. Josh. 24:27 uses natural phenomena: "And Joshua ... took a great stone, and set it up under the oak in the sanctuary of the Lord. And Joshua said to all the people: 'Behold! This stone shall be a witness against us, for it has heard all the words of the Lord which he spoke to us.'"

And finally the last section introduces *blessings* on those who abide by the covenantal terms and *curses* on those who forsake them. These materials fulfill what is implied in apodictic formulations. Deut. 28:1 promises, "If you obey the voice of the Lord your God, being careful to do all the commandments ... blessed will you be in the city and blessed will you be in the field." Deut. 28:15ff. warns, "If you do not obey the voice of the Lord your God or be careful to do all his commandments ... cursed shall you be in the city, and cursed shall you be in the field ... in all that you undertake to do, until you are destroyed and perish quickly ... The Lord will smite you with the boils of Egypt, and with the ulcers, and the scurvy, and the itch of which you cannot be healed ..." As in Leviticus (19:18), "You shall love your neighbor as yourself," the responsibilities of the suzerain are to the weakest in the community.

The specific laws concerning morality, diet, marriage, and so on, as we see in the next lecture, ensure the covenant community's status as a holy—or separate—people, as vassals to the Lord their God. ■

Rolf Rendtorff, *The Covenant Formula: An Exegetical and Theological Investigation*, Margaret Kohl, trans.

1. Is it correct to claim that Judaism prioritizes the Mosaic (suzerainty/vassal) model and Christianity, the royal grant? As used in the biblical narrative, are these forms in tension, complementary, or both?

2. What are the possible implications for worship if the believing community is related to its Deity by contract?

3. How would the biblical suzerainty contract, or apodictic laws, be enforced?

Covenant and Law, Part I
(Exodus 19–40, Leviticus, Deuteronomy)
Lecture 10—Transcript

One of the major ways that the Israelites related to their God is through covenants: royal grant covenants, a particular type of covenant, with people like Abraham and Noah and, especially, King David, and a second type of covenant called the suzerainty-vassal model, which we will unpack in this lecture. That's the covenant that describes the relationship Moses brokered between God and the Israelites.

In fact, the covenantal forms are known throughout the ancient Near East. They are not surprising. They are not inventions that the Israelites came up with. The more we know about the form and how the Israelites adapted that form, the better sense we can get of how they perceived themselves as a covenant community—what their own self-identification was—as well as how they perceived their relationship with God.

In terms of covenant itself, we need to begin with basic language. The word for "covenant" in Hebrew is *berit*, but some of you may be familiar with it actually as it comes in its English form. Some of you may have heard of the organization, B'Nai B'rith. But *b'rith* is simply another way of pronouncing *berit*, and *b'nai b'rith* simply means "children or sons of the covenant." The covenant itself is symbolized, and we know this from the Book of Genesis, by the sign of circumcision, that injunction that God put upon Abraham and all of Abraham's descendants. In contemporary Jewish practice, you may have heard of the expression, a *bris*, which is Eastern European pronunciation for the "Brit covenant." Circumcision is, in fact, called in Hebrew, *berit milah*, "covenant of the circumcision." So here is one of those odd examples where we have an ancient Hebrew term which comes into English, but nobody quite knows where those terms come from.

The idea of the covenant actually has major impact on early Christian self-definition, as well. So before we return to the ancient Israelites, a brief stop over into Christianity. The prophet Jeremiah talks about arranging a new covenant, not inscribed on the flesh, but inscribed in one's heart. This is

Jeremiah 31. The Greek expression for new covenant, *he kaine diatheke* in Greek, is also translated, "New Testament." So that's where these various terms come from. The New Testament is, in fact, for the Christians, a "new covenant."

We go back to the Hebrew. The Hebrew expression for making a covenant is *c'rat berit*, which means to cut, literally to cut a covenant. That doesn't really have something to do with circumcision. It's more the sense that we would have in English of "to cut a deal." And that actually works, because covenants are, in fact, contracts. And to understand the relationship between God and the Israelites that Moses mediates, this suzerainty-vassal model, is basically to understand contract law. It is as if God and the Israelites have a contract. And each party—God, the party of the first part, and Israel, party of the second party—have particular responsibilities within that contract. So we need to see how this works out.

The well-known German Old Testament specialist, Walter Eichrodt, suggested that covenants were the dominant way that ancient Israel perceived of itself. Actually, the term "covenant" doesn't start showing up in great measure until the seventh century or so. And covenantal language winds up getting re-inscribed back into earlier material. It is, however, a major way that the people did look at themselves.

Let's look now at the Mosaic—from Moses—type of covenant. This is called a suzerainty-vassal treaty. A suzerain is simply an "overlord." The "vassal" is somebody dependent upon that overlord, sort of like a junior lord or a petty prince. That's the Mosaic model. The Davidic model, the Abrahamic model, is called a "royal grant," also between an overlord and somebody who's underneath him. But the covenants actually wind up having different forms.

We might think of the covenantal form in the Bible, I guess here with a nod to theologian Martin Buber, as an "I-Thou" relationship. God establishes the terms, but the people have to respond. So here we go. For the specific form of the covenant, we actually turn to Mesopotamian sources. We have covenants as old as 4,500 years ago, standard contracts from the ancient

Near East. These, as you can imagine, are written materials people are likely to put in archives, which is why we happen to have a good many of them.

The ancient group most often associated with this type of covenant are the Hittites. And they actually used Semitic models. So for Israelites to use covenantal forms fits right within their cultural context. The earliest example we have of a covenant in inscriptions dates to 2500 B.C.E., right, two millennia and a half before Jesus. It's called "The Stele of the Vultures." A *stele* is simply a tall pillar on which is writing and sometimes illustrations. The Stele explains a particular covenant between two peoples.

And, as we'll see, part of the covenant, the end part, are part injunctions, which say what happens if you break the terms of the covenant. And it's usually that the suzerain will come and punish you. The Stele of Vultures charmingly depicts, on the top of it, vultures devouring the corpses of those who violate the terms of the covenant. Which means when you enter a covenant, you do not mess around. Okay.

Here is the form of the covenant, and watch how this plays out, because it should give you a different sense of how the Decalogue, the Ten Commandments, function. The laws there are not arbitrary in form. Covenants throughout the ancient Near East always start out with a preamble, and the preamble opens with the titles of the superior party. This is the party of the first part. Contemporary contract law does the same thing. Right? "I, Mr. Smith, the owner of such and such a store," and then we go on. The preamble for God is to make absolutely sure who this Deity is whose making the covenant, hence the Decalogue, the Ten Commandments, begin in Exodus 20: "I am the Lord, your God...." Now we know who we are dealing with. That's the party of the first part.

Part two of all covenantal formulations is an historical prologue, which not only continues the identification of the God directly, but also provides evidence that the party of the first part, the suzerain, is capable of carrying out the terms of the covenant. Right? If the suzerain is to be in the role of protector to the vassal, the vassal needs to know that the suzerain has the ability to protect, to support, when necessary. That's usually done by a listing of the suzerain's past actions.

Go back to the Decalogue. We've begun, "I am the Lord, your God…;" next line, "who brought you out of the land of Egypt, out of the house of bondage." That's the second part of the covenant. That's the historic preamble. And this also returns us to the lecture we had on Exodus, which suggests that God brought the people out, not only because he heard the cry of the oppressed, and not only because he had compassion on them, and not only because he saw the injustice of their situation, but because he's bound by contract to Abraham, Isaac, and Jacob. That's part of the benefits of that contract law.

Now, throughout the Decalogue, we will find additional aspects. The third part of the covenantal formulation are the regulations and stipulations of the covenant. And this is, as you can imagine, is the longer part. Right? If you make a covenant to purchase a piece of land, you spend most of that time in the contract explaining what the borders of the land are, what the markers are, what the resources are. Here are the stipulations of the covenant. Basically, what the vassal has to do, and usually the stipulations begin with some sort of pledge of loyalty. The vassal is only a vassal to one suzerain, not to a bunch of them.

Back to the Decalogue: "You shall have no other gods before me." So again, we have that covenantal model. And God goes on, just to make really sure that there won't be any other gods worshipped except for the YHWH, except for YHWH God, "You shall not make for yourself a graven image, or any likeness of anything that is in heaven above, or in the earth beneath, or in the water that is under the earth." This is the kind of three-tiered model of the universe. "You shall not bow down to them, and you shall not serve them." This is covenant. God simply could have said, "Don't have any other gods," that's the end of it. But that wouldn't be the model. When you're making the contract, you need to be as explicit as possible.

Now, in most covenants from the ancient Near East, along with these stipulations, after loyalty is pledged, then we have a bunch of laws: the vassal is supposed to do this; the vassal is not supposed to do this, how much taxes get paid, how many men the vassal has to give to the suzerain for war concerns. In most ancient Near Eastern treaties, the laws that are listed under these stipulations are "causal laws," conditional laws. Which say, "If you do this, then this will happen. If you don't do this, then this will happen." So we have cause and effect.

One example of these ancient covenantal formulations we have in the well-known Code of Hammurabi, which dates—it's a Babylonian text, and it dates from the time to which Abraham is normally dated, the middle Bronze Age, sometime around 1700-1750 B.C.E. Here is one example of case law, conditional law, from the Code of Hammurabi. "If a woman so hated her husband that she has declared to him, 'You may not have me'"— this is the ancient way of getting divorced in Babylon—"her record shall be investigated in the city council. If she was careful and not at fault, even though her husband has been going about in the city and disparaging her greatly"—negative reputation doesn't count—"that woman, without incurring any blame or penalty at all, may take her dowry"—the money she brought into the marriage—"and go off to her father's house." So here is the if–then situation. If, however, she were not careful but a gadabout, "neglecting her house and humiliating her husband, they shall throw that woman into the water." Now, I'm not sure if they throw her in and just leave her to drown, or if this is just some sort of public humiliation. The point is this is case law. "If you do this, then this will happen. If you do that, then that will happen."

The Bible does have certain examples of case law, and we'll get to them. But the biblical formulation, which is pretty much, not 100 percent, but pretty much distinct from what we have in the ancient Near East, is *apodictic* or absolute law. Where it's not an if–then circumstance, it's simply, "thou shall" or "you will" or "thou shall not," without a listing of penalty. You do it because God says you do it.

And we go back to the Decalogue. "You shall not murder." "You shall not commit adultery." "You shall not steal." "You shall not bear false witness." And the last one, which is highly detailed, "You shall not covet your neighbor's wife." Clearly, these are laws addressed only to men, right. "You shall not covet your neighbor's wife or his manservant or his maidservant, or his ass or his donkey, or anything else that your neighbor owns." Just to get it all in there.

And the Mosaic Code, by the way, in terms of its laws, both *apodictic* as well as causal and conditional, actually has a fair number of positive injunctions. It's not just a series of "thou shall nots." We've already seen that when we looked at Genesis, where the First Commandment is the very positive, "Be fruitful and multiply and fill the earth." So here we have instead of just don't do this and don't do that, we have positive injunctions.

Here is one back in the Decalogue: "Remember the Sabbath Day and keep it holy. Six days you shall labor and do your work, but on the seventh day, it is a Sabbath to the Lord, your God. In it, you shall do no work." And here is that legal formulation detailing again. You, your son, your daughter, your manservant, your maidservant, your cattle—animal rights, here, you can't go out and plow, right—or even the sojourner who was within your gate. That's Exodus 20.

And the reason we have for this in Exodus 20 harkens back to the "P" code in Genesis, Chapter 1: "For in six days, the Lord made Heaven and Earth and the sea and everything that is in them, and on the seventh, he rested." When you go to Deuteronomy, which replays the Decalogue, replays the Ten Commandments, you get the same commandment, "Honor the Sabbath and keep it holy," in Deuteronomy 5, but there, Sabbath rest is based on the Exodus from Egypt, "You were slaves in Egypt." Same law, different rationale, and both positive.

For another positive law in the Decalogue, this one is my favorite, "Honor your father and mother." Very positive here. And later on, we'll find law codes, I won't read them out to you, you can look them up yourself, where we find out if children hit their parents or totally dishonor them, then you can put the children to death. It's not clear people actually did that, but I like having it on the books.

In stipulation sections, we can see differences, as well, between suzerainty-vassal models, which is the Mosaic Code, and the royal grant model, which is the Davidic model, the Abrahamic model. The suzerainty model, the Mosaic Code, concentrates primarily on the vassal's obligations, what the party of the second part has to do. And that's where all the thou shalt's and thou shall not's come from.

But the royal grant associated with Noah and Abraham and David rather puts most of the burden, the concern of the covenant, on the suzerain, on the Lord. Royal grants are promissory contracts, usually given in response for past services. So if you are vassal and you have been, oh, the best vassal there ever was and you've done everything your Lord could possibly want, your Lord in beneficence, or in hopes that you might do even more, might give you a royal grant, giving you extra land, breaks from taxation, additional peasants to work the land for you. They tend to be promises for things that have already occurred and guarantees of hope for future alliance.

Here is Genesis 9, verses 8–14, this is Noah's covenant: "God said to Noah and his sons, 'I am now establishing my covenant, *berit*,'" same word, "'with you and with your descendants after you.'" Because royal grants tend to be continuous. Once the father gets it, everybody else gets it unless somebody does something truly awful. "'And then my bow I set in the heavens to be a sign of the covenant.'" Or Genesis 15, this is the Abrahamic covenant: "That day the Lord made a covenant with Abraham and said, 'I give to your descendants,'" that future continuation, "'this land from the river of Egypt to the great river, the river Euphrates.'" Those are, by the way, the borders of David's kingdom. So we see the royal grant given to Abraham and the fulfillment of that when David becomes king. And we'll see that in a lecture or two.

This is typical for royal grants. They often give you formulas for the gift of land and protection from enemies. That's exactly what we have for David in the Bible.

The next set of covenant forms is not found in the Decalogue proper, but we're still going down that suzerainty-vassal model. We've had the prologue, we've the preamble, we've had the stipulations. Next, there comes a requirement for safekeeping. Right? If you've got a contract you're going to put it in your safety deposit box. We simply need the ancient Near Eastern version of that. And also, along with safekeeping, you need a guarantee that these covenants are going to be read to the people at regular intervals. Because just because one generation signed on, that does not necessarily guarantee in a suzerainty-vassal treaty that the next generation is going to sign on. So it is for the Bible as if every generation has to re-up to God's covenant.

Deuteronomy, Chapter 10, verse 5, specifically mentions the ancient Near Eastern safety deposit box. This is the Ark of the Covenant, which is built in order to house the laws that Moses received from God on Mt. Sinai. This Ark of the Covenant, to which we shall return in a lecture or two, when we get up to First Samuel, is the same ark that some of you may be familiar with from those movies, *Raiders of the Lost Ark*. That's the ark that they're talking about.

Deuteronomy 31 offers provisions for the recitation of these laws at regular intervals. Here is what the text says: "Moses commanded the priests, the sons of Levi, and the elders,"in other words, the people who are running the cult, "at the end of every seven years, at a set time of the year of release," when you let your fields lie fallow, "at the Feast of Booths or Tabernacles," this is the Fall Harvest Festival, "when all Israel comes to appear before the Lord, your God, at the place he will choose," which, of course, winds up being Jerusalem, but technically we don't know that yet, right, "you shall read, *et hatorah hazeh*, you shall read this law, this Torah, to all Israel in their hearing. Assemble the people, men, women, little ones," because the children are here the guarantee, and you find continual references to children throughout the law code, "and even the sojourner within your towns," because you don't want them making mistakes, "that they may hear and learn to fear the Lord, your God, and be careful to do all the words of this law," all the words of this Torah. "And that their children, who have not known it, may hear, and they, too, may learn to fear the Lord, your God, as long as you live in the land"— and then Moses adds, "which you are going over the Jordan to possess."

These laws were probably, I would say certainly, but I can't prove it, written well after the time that the people actually entered into the land of Canaan. But here they are backdated and put on Moses's lips as a promissory note to say, when you get over into Canaan, here is what you do. But fascinating, nevertheless, is the fact that this idea of repeated readings is a part of the covenantal formulation from the ancient Near East. If the Bible didn't have it, the ancient Near Eastern population would have seen something to be missing.

Joshua 24 gives us another example of this. Joshua 24 is, in fact, a covenant renewal ceremony. You have to keep doing it. When the children of Israel are in the wilderness, they are there for 40 years. By the time they get into the land, that first generation, with the exception of only Joshua and Caleb, has died out. We have to do the covenant all over again. How does Joshua do it? Exactly the way anybody would do it, if they knew anything about ancient Near Eastern law codes. Joshua begins by reciting the great deeds of the "God of your fathers," by talking about Abraham, Isaac, and Jacob, by talking about Moses and Aaron, by talking about the period in the wilderness, the plagues, the release from slavery, the protection from scorpions, all the materials that God has provided the people, all the good works God has done, that's the preamble.

And then he says to the people, "Will you serve God, even though you know that this means you have to be obedient to what God wants?" So the people get a say in this, like contract law. And the people replied, "We shall serve the Lord, our God, and his voice we shall obey." And then we're told, Joshua wrote all these words in the Book of the Torah, the Law of God. So Joshua, Chapter 24, is, in fact, in a nutshell an entire suzerainty-vassal model.

For public readings, one more example—and I do this one because when we were talking about Mosaic authorship of the Pentateuch, and I mentioned we have a text called Fourth Ezra, where it's claimed that Ezra perhaps wrote the Pentateuch—here is the original text from which fourth Ezra got the idea. This is Nehemiah, Chapter 8. Ezra has returned from Babylon in the Second Temple Period. The temple has been burned down, several generations before. Ezra re-does the law and needs to read it to the people. Ezra gives a public reading: "From early morning 'til noon," takes a long time to read the Torah, "before the assembly, both men and women and all who could hear with understanding, he read the Book of the Law of Moses, and the ears of all the people were attentive to that book." So there is the connection.

Now, following the provisions for storing the covenant and for reading it at set times, like any good contract, the next thing you need, as you know, this is "witness." Right? You can't just make a covenant. You have to go to a notary or you have to get witnesses. Now in ancient Near Eastern covenantal formulations, the witnesses are usually the gods of the people who are party to the covenants. Right? So if you're a vassal, you would have your gods, and if you're an overlord, you would have your gods. And you would simply, as they say in English, "swear to God," or back then, in a polytheistic system, "swear to the gods." Right?

Now the problem we have with the Israelites is there is only one God. So then you've got to worry about by whom they are going to swear. They improvise, which is what you would have expected. In Joshua 2, the people function as both signatories to the covenant, the party of the second part, and witnesses. And they say, "We will be witnesses." That's sort of double dipping, but in the ancient Near East that was okay. Joshua, who may have realized this, also adds in a second set of witnesses. These are natural phenomena. "And Joshua took a great stone and set it up under an oak in the sanctuary of the Lord." This is at Shechem, which by the way will become the capital of the northern kingdom generations down. "And Joshua said to all the people, 'Behold, look. This stone shall be a witness against us for it has heard all the words of the Lord which he spoke to us.'" Not that the stone is going to talk, but it's not a bad idea, because it suggests that whenever the people saw that stone, they would be reminded of their particular contract. I guess it's like setting up a landmark that people have when they buy certain pieces of property.

The last section of any suzerainty-vassal model ancient Near Eastern covenant are the blessings upon those who abide by the covenant and the curses upon those who don't. I find these fairly juicy. This material, by the way, fills in what's missing in the *apodictic* formulations. So although the Decalogue says don't do this, don't do this, by the time you get down to the blessings and curses, you can pretty much figure what the payoff is.

The blessings are not bad, and they are pretty much what most people would expect if you're living in the ancient Near East. This is Deuteronomy 28:1: "If you obey the voice of the Lord, your God, being careful to do all the commandments, the Lord, your God, will set you high above the nations of the earth, blessed will you be in the city, blessed will you be in the field.

Your crops will grow, your women will be fertile, you will not be attacked by external enemies." It will just be perfect. This, by the way, for Deuteronomy raises a problem, because it does suggest that people who are doing well are doing well because they behaved properly. And people who are doing poorly are doing poorly because they have sinned. Right? That's the model that underlies this. And we'll see, when we get to the Book of Job, that not everybody bought into that system. There are alternatives.

More fun are the curses. This is Deuteronomy 28:15 and following, and I'm just picking and choosing. You can, at your leisure, go look up the rest of these curses. And by the way, these are nowhere near as bad as some of the curse formulations we have from the ancient Near East. This is Deuteronomy: "If you do not obey the voice of the Lord, your God, or be careful to do all his commandments, cursed shall you be in the city, cursed shall you be in the fields." So you can see this mirror image. "The Lord will send upon you curses, confusion, and frustration in everything that you undertake to do until you are destroyed and perish quickly."

And if that's not enough, "Your dead body shall be food for the birds of the air, and there will be no one to drive them away. The Lord God will smite you with the boils of Egypt," which I guess are the worst type of boils you could get back then, "and with ulcers and with scurvy and with an itch from which you cannot be healed." Right? These are palpable. You can feel them in your body. And I suspect that if people heard this read aloud to them every seven years, this would be, at least partially, the material that would have stuck. This actually fits quite nicely.

It may be that because the suzerainty model is based with God as the party of the first part, that there is a different sense of what some of the stipulations will be. How the people, the party of the second part, will identify themselves. Yes, this is contract law. Yes, this is a standard formulation. But at least one of the signatories is not your average signatory. So some of these laws that we have are quite different than what we find in the ancient Near East. And it may be because God is the one, according to Deuteronomy and Exodus, Leviticus, and Numbers, Who is explaining what these laws are.

Among the laws, Leviticus 19:18: "You shall love your neighbor as yourself." Which could also be rendered, "You shall love your neighbor who is a human being like you are." In this suzerainty model, all the parties of the second part are equal. And that's different from normal models, where the suzerain makes a covenant with the vassal, but then the vassal has lots of underlings who have little to no say in this. Here, everybody is equal. Exodus 22: "You shall not afflict any widow or fatherless child, and if you do afflict them and they cry out to me, I will surely hear their cry." So in this case, the responsibilities to the suzerain are specifically to the most weak and most vulnerable members of society. Not standard in most contracts, but I think it's helpful here.

Now, to be sure, the Book of Exodus does not cover all the proverbial bases. In particular, in this model, it makes no provision for a monarchy. That will come in with the Book of Deuteronomy. Because when you're dealing with a suzerainty-vassal model in which the suzerain, the party of the first part, is God, it's not always easy to enforce the stipulations. Right? That's the problem with Deuteronomy, in general, where if you behave properly, you get rewarded, but what actually happens if you don't? Because God does not always step into history and punish those people who fail to heed the commandments, in Hebrew, the *mitzvot*. It helps if you have some sort of formal government, a monarchy who actually can serve to enforce or, at least safeguard, those laws. We'll eventually find that, and Deuteronomy will finally hint at it. There are other laws that we have in terms of sanctions, and every once in a while God does step in.

Now I've been holding off on this, because everybody knows about it, and I think it's blown out of proportion. But there is one particular example where the people, after making covenant, immediately break it. You all know this story. Moses comes down with the two tablets of the law. You've seen it in art. You've seen it in the movies. Right? Except the first tablets don't last, because as soon as Moses comes down the mountain, he sees that the people, under his brother Aaron's direction, have built a golden calf, and they are dancing around it and worshipping it, as if the calf is their new God. This, by the way, would make sense in the ancient Near East. Calves, usually two of them together, are often used as thrones for God. So it may well have been, early on, that there was this story where these built these two calves.

They idea was that the God of heaven would come down and sit upon them, as if these were God's cushions. But the way it plays out in Exodus, these people have built an idol. This is terrible, obviously, because the people aren't supposed to do this. This is Exodus 31–32. We're told that the faithful Levites do execute those guilty of idolatry. So that's one way that "thou shalt have no other gods before me" gets played out.

But then God gives a sort of *coup de grace* here, and here is how it reads: "The Lord spoke to Moses, 'Set out you and your people'"—you and your people you, Moses, have brought up from the land of Egypt—"'Go from here to the land which I promised to Abraham, Isaac, and Jacob,'" that's that covenant. "'My angel will go ahead of you.'" (God actually stops and says, "I'm not going to go with you myself, because I might get angry and bad things will happen, but I'll send my angel.") "'But a day will come when I shall punish them for their sins.'"

So the punishment does come in eventually. And as we'll see two lecture hence, the punishment is at least, in part, the enforcement of the idea that none of the people who committed this type of idolatry will ever set foot in the land of Canaan. The only two people from the wilderness generation to make it in are Joshua and Caleb. But before we can get there, we have to look at a few more of these stipulations. So in the next lecture, we'll talk about the relationship between covenant in the ancient Near East and the law that we have today. And then we'll look at some specific laws, like dietary regulations and laws regarding human sexuality.

Covenant and Law, Part II
(Exodus 20–35, Leviticus)
Lecture 11

I hope through this to be able to show the distinction between covenant and law, and why translating Torah instruction as law is probably not as accurate as we might want.

Although the extent to which this comparison works is debated, the following distinctions in purpose, sanctions, geographical limits, temporal focus, and solemnity presented originally by George Mendenhall (*The Tenth Generation*) remain provocative. *Purpose.* Covenants create new relationships in accordance with previously established stipulations (e.g., a marriage contract, a mortgage). Individuals may choose to participate. In contrast, laws regulate existing relationships. One does not, for example, have a choice about whether to participate in the U.S. legal code. One enters the covenant via assent and often by external signs (e.g., public pledge); in a legal system, one is "in" as soon as one enters the territory it governs. For Scripture, the sign is (male) circumcision: a symbol of fertility and maturity, as in the expression "circumcised fruit trees" (trees mature enough for harvesting). Women are exempted from this sign; Scripture likely sees woman's identity as a component of family identity.

In covenantal systems, rewards and punishments are meted out by the suzerain or the suzerain's agents; in Scripture, this usually means divine blessings and curses. Under law, punishment is defined and administered by the state. The covenant model, especially as Deuteronomy presents it, has inevitable problems with *theodicy* (literally, "justice of God"; the issue of why the good suffer and the wicked prosper), because it implies that the good life indicates righteous living; suffering suggests a proximate cause, such as evil behavior. The Book of Job challenges this view. Legal models typically lack reward or blessing. One is punished for disobeying the law but not—manifestly—rewarded for obedience.

Geographically, covenants are unlimited; consequently, one can live within covenantal and legal systems simultaneously. Laws are territorially bound. Where the general principle is that the "law of the state is the law" (e.g., Hebrews must obey the laws of Egypt when in Egypt), covenantal stipulations prevail in cases of conflict (as the Book of Daniel 1–6 demonstrates).

Covenants are also primarily *future-oriented* and may be regarded as solemn promises (again, cf. the marriage analogy, "in sickness and in heath"). Conversely, laws have a past orientation. We do not typically reflect on the fact of our existence in a legal system but rather note this existence when the law is broken and we are caught. The future orientation of laws exists only insofar as courts have standards for punishments, yet even here the future orientation has a past component; that is, the standards are also designed to function as deterrents.

The *solemnity* of the covenant, but not law, is marked by ritual (again, cf. marriage). For three days at Sinai, the people remained in a state of ritual purity: they washed their clothes, did not engage in sexual intercourse, and observed: "Whoever touches the mountain shall be put to death. No hand shall touch him, but he shall be stoned or shot ..." (Exod. 19:10ff.). The covenant is established in a theophany: "Mt. Sinai was wrapped in smoke, because the Lord descended upon it in a fire ... and the whole mountain quaked greatly" (Exod. 19:18). The ritual of rereading and reaffirming the covenant also differs from the legal system, where the laws remain "on the books" and are recited not for public assent, but in cases where they are challenged (e.g., the Senate) or broken (e.g., the court).

In a legal system, one either obeys the laws or suffers consequences mandated by the state. In the covenantal system, one chooses to obey. Some Christian theologies hold that biblical laws are an (ineffective) means for earning salvation. However, Jewish texts from that early period until today do not follow such a view; indeed, the covenantal model precludes it. Covenantal stipulations (*mitzvot*) do not earn one standing or election: standing or election are presupposed. One obeys commandments because one is a member of the covenant community.

Among the most well known of the so-called "ritual" laws (see Lev. 11) are those of diet (Hebrew: *Kashrut*, cf. the expression "keeping kosher"). For example, the following are forbidden: Animals that do not chew the cud and have a split hoof (e.g., pigs, rabbits, camels); animals that live in water but lack fins and scales (e.g., shellfish, crustaceans); animals that eat carrion (e.g., vultures); and anything containing blood (see Lev. 17:10–14; 19:26). Other ritual laws include: Injunctions against planting a field with two types of crops (Lev. 19:19), injunctions against wearing a garment made of two different materials (Lev. 19:19), injunctions against cross-breeding animals (Lev. 19:19), and prohibitions against tattoos and scarification (Lev. 19:28).

But where do such laws come from? Dietary and comparable regulations are normal aspects of culture and religion. Religious systems do not divorce bodies (what enters, what leaves) from the holy. All cultures maintain dietary parameters regarding what is permitted, required, or expected (e.g., the Eucharist, matzah, turkey on Thanksgiving) and what is forbidden or avoided: (e.g., blood, certain meat [in the United States, dogs, cats, rats, horses], human flesh).

Such regulations can be explained. The laws have a salutary component for one's health. Pork causes trichinosis if undercooked; shellfish frequently are diseased or cause allergic reactions. However, other ancient Near Eastern peoples were also aware of cooking procedures, and this rationale does not encompass the majority of the laws. Other rationale for the regulations could include the following. Economic reasons: Pigs are expensive to raise and contribute little in return. This rationale hardly fits laws forbidding rabbit. Syncretism: Israelites are enjoined against Canaanite (i.e., pagan) cult practices, such as the sacrifice of pigs. Again, this rationale is insufficient; Canaanites also sacrificed and ate sheep, goats, and bulls. Allegory: As the Jewish philosopher Philo of Alexandria proposed in the 1st century C.E., we avoid pig, lest we hog resources; we are like sheep, not vultures. The model is not comprehensive; camels are forbidden, but why not be camel-like and conserve resources? Or some regard injunctions as arbitrary forms of self-discipline. Most anthropologists argue that taboos are consistent across categories. A coherent explanation would consider what the dietary injunctions have in common with other laws, such as those listed above.

With some modification, the model proposed by anthropologist Mary Douglas offers a start: "Holiness requires that individuals ... conform to the class to which they belong." The classifications may be partially arbitrary, but they are relatively consistent. Animals appropriate to the water have fins and scales; animals that live in the water but lack these characteristics—shellfish, crustaceans—are forbidden. Permitted mammals are ruminants with a split hoof. Pigs lack one; camels, the other. Blood is a sign of life; animals to be eaten are dead. The combination creates a category confusion. Concern for separation and taxonomy explains planting and clothing regulations. Separation is connected to wholeness, and wholeness is connected to holiness.

The interest in avoiding category confusion extends to sexuality, including homosexuality: "You shall not lie with a male as with a female; it is an abomination. You shall not lie with any beast and defile yourself with it; neither shall any woman give herself to a beast to lie with it; it is a perversion" (Lev. 18:22–23; cf. Lev. 20:13). Are the laws intended to prevent participation in Canaanite cults? There is no clear evidence homosexuality marked Canaanite worship. To cast sexual aspersions on one's enemy is a common form of *maladicta*.

Homosexuality is forbidden because it entails misuse of semen. One locus of the argument, the story of Onan in Gen. 38, falters: Onan practiced *coitus interruptus* for birth control. A second locus are laws stating that anyone with a seminal emission is ritually impure until appropriate actions (e.g., a bath) are taken and time passes (cf. Lev. 15). Yet one is also impure—which is not a "sin"—after heterosexual intercourse. The third locus, Sodom and Gomorrah (Gen. 19), concerns violence (the Sodomites seek to "know" [here, "to rape"] the strangers). The threat concerns the assertion of power by "feminizing" the strangers (as is stereotypically associated today, for example, with prisons and prep schools). The main concern seems to be violence rather than homosexual acts. Other forms of "wasting seed"—masturbation, oral or anal (heterosexual) intercourse, intercourse with pregnant or menopausal women—are not forbidden. Category confusion again provides a helpful explication: A man who lies with "a male as with a female" puts the male in the woman's role. Lesbianism is omitted (but see Rom. 1) likely because for the Israelite, sexual intercourse was defined as involving penile penetration.

A few of the many other notable texts in the legal corpus include: The only "trial by ordeal" is the "test of bitter waters" (Num. 5:11–31), designed to appease a man overcome by a "spirit of jealousy" in suspecting his wife of adultery. Moral laws encompass the majority of the *Mitzvot*: care for the poor and the stranger, justice in the courts, honesty in the marketplace, peace in the family, and so on. Israelite tradition did not distinguish between "ritual" and "moral" laws. Both were mandated by the Deity as parts of the covenant. Both enabled the people to be "holy." Finally, we come to the laws concerning holy war. For these we turn to the Book of Deuteronomy (Deut. 20–21) and to the Deuteronomic History, which begins with the Book of Joshua, a book of war. ∎

Suggested Reading

Mary Douglas, *Purity and Danger: An Analysis of Concepts of Pollution and Taboo.*

Howard Eilberg-Schwartz, *The Savage in Judaism: An Anthropology of Israelite Religion and Judaism.*

Victor H. Matthews, Bernard Levinson, and Tikva Frymer-Kensky, *Gender and Law in the Hebrew Bible and the Ancient Near East.*

Saul Olyan, *Rites and Rank: Hierarchy in Biblical Representations of Cult.*

John F. A. Sawyer (ed.), *Reading Leviticus: A Conversation with Mary Douglas.*

1. What particular benefits do the covenantal and legal systems offer?

2. Does explication of a commandment influence, one way or another, the decision to keep it?

Covenant and Law, Part II
(Exodus 20–35, Leviticus)
Lecture 11—Transcript

In the previous lecture, we discussed the covenant, both as a literary form well known throughout the ancient Near East and as a particular way that the ancient Israelites attempted to describe the relationship between themselves and their God.

In this lecture, we'll continue our discussion of covenants, first by looking at the difference between life within a covenantal community, such as that which ancient Israel had, and life in a contemporary legal system, such as what we have in the United States, because they really are quite different systems. And I hope through this to be able to show the distinction between covenant and law, and why, in fact, translating Torah instruction as law is probably not as accurate as we might want. So when we look at this material, we'll look at in terms of purpose and sanctions and signs, because there are differences all the way through. Here, I'm basing my work on early scholarship by George Mendenhall.

In terms of purpose, nice place to begin, covenants set up something new, like a contract. There wasn't something there, you make a contract, then you have something. So covenants, in terms of purpose, create new relationships, often by using older forms, like the suzerainty-vassal model. But something new is being created, and you sign on to something new. You have a choice as to whether you want to enter a covenant or not.

Here, perhaps, the best analogy for covenants is the idea of marriage, which is, in fact, a contract between you and your spouse. Legal systems, you have no choice. You're born into the system. I can't go up to the lawmakers and say, "I don't particularly like this law; I want to be able to have a say on whether I want to abide by this or not." One doesn't. The law is simply there. We, as citizens, can protest, but for the most part, we don't, every five or six years, renew the entire law code or even recite it.

Because the covenant requires some sort of assent, because we sign on to it differently, it's often marked by external signs, such as a public pledge. We can already see that the covenants are marked by external signs, most notably the *berit milah*, the covenant of circumcision. Law codes don't have such signs. We're simply in them. No one has to come up to you, if you're in the United States, and ask you if you're part of a particular law code. But they might want to know if you're part of a covenant community, because it's not necessarily the case that you would be. And it helps if you have an external sign, not that this one is one you want to display in public.

Women within the covenant community do not bear this external sign, and that's because, in antiquity, when these covenants were developed, we are dealing with a patriarchal society, not patriarch in the sense of Abraham, Isaac, and Jacob, but patriarch in the sense of "determined by male interests."

In terms of sanctions, rewards and punishments within a covenantal model are meted out by the suzerain—in the biblical case, the suzerain would be God—and sometimes the suzerain's agents. But when we see those sanctions as spelled out in the biblical covenantal forms, those are the blessings and the curses. Right? If you abide by the covenants, you are blessed; if you break the covenant, you are cursed. The covenantal model, as we've seen, has problems with theodicy, the "justice of God." Why sometimes do the wicked prosper? Why aren't they punished?

But that's not a problem that we have within the legal system. In the legal system, in fact, if you behave wickedly, you are, in fact, punished. And you are punished not by a divine model, but by laws of the state. So the sanctions within the covenantal model for Moses are meted out by God; the sanctions within a legal system, such as that which we have, meted out by the state. And, moreover, when the state metes out punishments, that's all it does. The covenant, you get rewarded. If you behave properly, there are blessings. The state tends not to bless us if we follow the laws. The state only kicks in when we do something that we weren't supposed to do, when we transgress the laws.

In terms of geography or where the regulations are applicable, if you are a member of a covenant community, that covenant goes with you wherever you go. It fits along with the idea of God being manifest in history and over time, rather than located in only one particular space. So if you are a member of the Israelite covenant community, and you happen to move to Egypt or are forcibly moved to Babylon, you are still a member of that covenant community. And where the laws of the state in which you are living differ from the terms of the covenant, ideally, the covenant will prevail. And we'll see that many lectures hence, when we get to the Book of Daniel, where Daniel is brought into Babylon, and the Babylonians make laws which force him to transgress the covenant. And Daniel says, "Absolutely not, I refuse." He abides by the laws of the covenant. That's, in fact, how he lands in the lion's den.

Laws, obviously, are territorially bound. We don't move laws from the place to place. For example, one can drive heaven knows how fast on the autobahn in Germany, 80, 90, 100 miles per hour, but you cannot do that in most streets of the United States, or those sanctions kick in. In other words, the police come to get you. Covenants have not only a geographical concern—in other words, they are portable, they last wherever you go—but they also have a temporal focus. Specifically, covenants tend to be future-oriented. We might think of them as external promises. If you sign onto a covenant, as if you enter into a marriage, or engage in a legal contract, the covenant has a concern for the future. That's when it kicks in.

Laws, on the other hand, are past-oriented. They are already on the books. We don't have to think about them. And, in fact, until we wind up breaking them, or we get caught breaking them, we usually don't. They don't, in that sense, operate as a social reality. When we go through life in the United States, we follow U.S. laws. We tend not to think about them, we simply do them. But the idea of the covenant is, it's future-oriented, you're always engaged in it, you always think about it.

There is also a difference in terms of solemnity. If you make a covenant, particularly if you make a covenant with God, there has to be some sort of, oh, symbolic process. Again, think about a marriage. Yes, you can get married by just going to a justice of the peace and having a couple of words said on you. But marriage, in a traditional sense, is a solemn concern, with flowers and caterers, and a white dress, and a groom, and rings, and, at the very least, you register for china. It's a ceremony. That's a covenant.

The covenant we have in the biblical code is certainly a ceremony. It's certainly something you would pay attention to. This is the covenant from the Bible: "For three days at Sinai, the people remained in the state of ritual purity. They washed their clothes, they did not engage in sexual intercourse. And they observed the injunction put upon them by Moses: 'Take heed that you don't go up the mountain or even touch the border of it. Whoever touches the mountain, shall be put to death.'" That's pretty solemn. "'No hand shall touch the person who touches the mountain, but you shall stone him.'" You don't even get a second-order touch. It's that important.

The covenant is then established in theophany, by manifestation of God. "Mt. Sinai is wrapped in smoke," the Bible tells us, "because the Lord descended upon it like fire. And the smoke of it went up like the smoke of a great oven, and the whole mountain quaked greatly." That's solemn, that's important. By the way, it's probably ahistorical. This seems to be the description of either of a volcano or, perhaps, a volcano and an earthquake together. But there are no active volcanoes in the Sinai peninsula.

The people knew what a covenant was when you make it with God. We don't have that with the legal system. Every once in a while, you can see a president or a governor using a special pen and enacting something into law. But for the most part, laws are simply created day after day in various localities, local, state, federal, and we tend to pay very little attention to it. It doesn't have that sort of solemnity.

If we think about the rationale for obedience, we also have a difference. One is obedient to the covenant, because that's what one wants to do. You sign on to the stipulations, because you want to do so. In this sense again, covenants are like marriage. When you marry someone, ideally, you and the person to whom you're married try to help each other out, work for the best. And sometimes if your husband or your wife asks you to do something, you might actually do it because you want to, and not because there is a law on the books saying you have to. That's covenant. Law, you have no choice, it's simply there, it's not voluntary. The rationale for obedience is it's part of the system, you have no choice.

Some Christian theologians, following hints in St. Paul from the New Testament, have suggested that the laws of the Torah are there in order for the people to earn their way into Heaven. In other words, if you follow enough of those laws, God will reward you. There would be a scale at the end of your life, and if your obedience was heavier than your disobedience, then you got into Heaven. And if your disobedience was heavier, you'd land in Hell. But that's actually not the way covenants function at all, either the biblical version or, indeed, Judaism ever since. One does not follow the law in order to earn one's place into God's kingdom. The covenant already tells you, your place in election is presupposed, it's already there once the covenant is made. And then you follow the stipulations, because that's what you have agreed to. Again, the covenant is like a marriage.

Covenantal stipulations, just for a word of definition, are called *mitzvot*. *Mitzvot* translates the Hebrew term, "commandments." But the term *mitzvot*, *mitzvah* in the singular, has a different connotation. You may have heard the expression *bar mitzvah* or *bat mitzvah*. *Bar mitzvah* is actually is an Aramaic term, meaning "son of the commandment." And *bat mitzvah* is "daughter of the commandment." Eastern Europeans would say, *bas mitzvah*. This means, as well, that not only are the *mitzvot* commandments, but they have the connotation of good deeds. There is an expression, "to do a *mitzvah*," which does not mean to follow a law, it means to do something that God would want you to do.

So the commandments already have, in terms of connotation, a sense of something good, of something pleasing, in the same way you would want to do something for your husband or for your wife. I tend not to think of the U.S. legal system in that type of marital terms.

Let's move to those regulations themselves, fascinating stuff. Among the most well known of the so-called ritual laws, as opposed to those moral laws, like don't oppress a widow or be nice to your neighbor, are the dietary regulations. Most people are familiar, in general, with some of these, the idea that within the covenant community, one is not supposed to eat pork, one is not supposed to eat shellfish. One is not supposed to consume any food with blood in it. You can't carry on like a vulture, for example. The question is, why are they there? Right?

So we'll look at some of these laws, not only the dietary regulations, but also some other laws. Why? Because in order to understand the biblical law code, I think it helps not to separate all the laws out and say, this law is here for this particular reason and that law is here for another reason, but rather to see if they hold something in common. Is there some sort of rationale behind at least many, if not most, of these ritual laws, or are they simply arbitrary?

So, in addition to looking at laws regarding diet, we might consider laws that say, you can't crossbreed animals, or you can't plant a field with two different types of crops, or, indeed, you can't wear clothing made of two different materials like linen and wool. Men can't wear women's clothes; women can't wear men's clothes. Where did these come from? And how would we come to understand them?

Before we begin specific explanations, just a word or two on some of these dietary concerns. Many of my students, when I start pointing out to them this business about not eating pork—and I live in Tennessee, where barbecue is really, it's the state dish, right?—they don't understand it, and they say, "This is primitive, it's silly." It makes no sense to them. But, in fact, all cultures maintain dietary regulations, and all religions maintain dietary regulations. The only reason the biblical ones look silly is because they are not biblical people.

And I think some of the dietary regulations that we have today might have looked peculiar to people back then. For example, Christians have particular dietary regulations in terms of positive injunctions. Most Christians will go into church and, at some point, participate in a Eucharistic celebration or a communion meal. And even on the more general cultural level, we think about eating Easter eggs at Eastertime, and if you don't, there is something not quite right with you. Jews will eat *matzah*, unleavened bread, at Passover time, to commemorate the exodus from Egypt. In the United States, we also have a kind of civil religion. What's Thanksgiving without turkey? Right? It's just not right. Or even going to a baseball game and not having a hot dog.

These are part of our civil religions. And, indeed, all cultures have, if not laws on the books, then a view that certain foods, although full of protein, nutritious, are simply forbidden to eat. Most people don't eat human flesh. We could. We simply don't want to.

In certain cultures, things like sheep's heads and goats' eyes are delicacies. Not in my house, because my children would simply revolt. We don't do that. We don't eat those foods, because they are not part of our culture. We would feel peculiar with monkey brains and goats' eyes. For other cultures, perhaps some of our concerns with, you know, pizza might look a little bit problematic, let alone what we get in some fast food restaurants.

So we ought not to look at the biblical dietary regulations as peculiar in and of themselves. What we need to do is figure out, why these particular regulations and not others? There have been several explanations regarding the dietary laws, and I think they all, to some extent, may have some validity, but I'm not convinced that they all work. The most common explanation my students give me when I say, "Well, why does the Bible have these laws?", is that they are for hygiene purposes. Right? Because the one thing that most of my students remember is the pig is forbidden. And they say, "A pig, if you don't cook it long enough, causes trichinosis. You can die." And then, invariably, somebody will raise her hand or his hand and say, "Well, I'm allergic to scallops," or "I'm allergic to shrimp." So, perhaps, the people in the ancient world knew about allergies and, thereby, they forbade pig, because of health concerns, and shellfish, again because of health concerns. I'm not convinced.

Other people in the ancient Near East ate pig. They knew how to cook it. They knew if you didn't cook it long enough or properly, they would all die. They also knew about allergies. They also knew some people couldn't eat shellfish, and they also knew that sometimes shellfish got bacteria in them. It's not as if the Israelites were the only smart people in the ancient Near East, or the only people who had doctors. Other cultures knew this, as well, so I think there must be some other explanation.

More recently, I've heard that some of these dietary regulations have to do with economics. The idea is one ought not to raise pigs, because they eat a lot, but they don't really produce much back for you. Right? Sheep, you can get wool, for example; cows, you can get milk. But you can't get much out of a pig, except for decent barbecue. They are expensive, so, therefore, don't raise them. But this business about economics, although it might work for pigs, really doesn't work for most of the other animals. If you want to raise an animal that's edible and cheap, raise bunny rabbits. They multiply quickly, they are easy to eat, they are easy to cook, but they are also forbidden, according to the biblical law code, because the biblical law code forbids any animal that does not chew a cud and have a split hoof. And bunnies don't fall under that category. So that doesn't work.

Another popular explanation is that pigs and rabbits, for example, were used by Canaanites as part of their religious practices. This is the view that says, "Well, the Canaanites are offering sacrifices to Baal, and they are sacrificing pigs, so, therefore, don't eat pig, because it might remind you of sacrifices to Baal." I don't buy that one either. It's true the Canaanites did sacrifice pigs, but they also sacrificed sheep, and goats, and bulls, and so did the ancient Israelites. If the idea is to avoid Baal culture, syncretism, the merging of religions, just give up on the sacrifices entirely. Perhaps a connection. I don't think so.

And still others have proposed allegory. Isn't it fascinating how people keep wanting to find these explanations? Even in the first century, Philo of Alexandria, who we mentioned before, said, you know, those laws are there for behavioral reasons. One ought not to act like a pig who hogs resources. Now actually that pun does not work in the Greek, which is the language Philo wrote, but it's apt. Right? You don't want to act pig-like. You don't want to act like a vulture, stealing, eating carrion, picking on others' remains, so you don't eat vulture. This is the modern, the modern saying, "You are what you eat." It could be.

But there are certain animals that are forbidden that, at least in terms of metaphoric potential, make sense to me. Why not eat camel? Be like a camel and conserve resources. So the allegory may have some connection, but it doesn't really get me too far. And moreover, none of these examples provides me a means of moving from the dietary regulations to the other law codes. And what I'd like to be able to find is a rationale that gets me from what you can eat to what you can wear, to what you can plant, to what you can do with your animals.

There is an anthropologist named Mary Douglas, who, a couple of decades ago, set out what I think is probably the most helpful explanation. She looked at questions of categories and said that holiness—and holiness is something the biblical law codes are very much concerned with—holiness requires that individuals, plants, animals, materials, conform to their particular categories, as if everything has a place. And if your categories get confused, if taxonomy, categorization, is messed up, then you lose your holiness, as if holiness is connected to wholeness. You don't want category confusion. The idea is the Israelites are Israelites and the Canaanites are Canaanites, and you don't mix them.

The classifications regarding food may seem arbitrary to us, but, indeed, they do fit a particular notion of category. For the ancient Israelites, the category of permissible animals is an animal that both chews the cud and has a split hoof. And if an animal lacks either of these or both of these, the animal falls out of the appropriate category.

Moving to shellfish. For the biblical law code, an animal that swims in the water and has fins and scales, fish, that's permitted. But if it lives in the water and it doesn't have fins and scales, it's out of place. And that would be things like clams and lobsters. They are defining their terms as to what's appropriate and what's not. In terms of planting two different crops in the same field, of course you wouldn't do that. That's category confusion. And, of course, you wouldn't wear garments made out of linen and wool, because you don't want to mix. And, of course, a man wouldn't wear women's clothes and a woman wouldn't wear man's clothes, because it's category confusion again.

The biblical code is interested in categories. Everything needs to be in its place. And, indeed, the idea of categories follows all the way through, as well as to some other laws, which have caused problems not only for ancient Israel, but, in particular, for people today interested in legislating sexual morality. I think this idea of category confusion actually explains what's going on when the Bible forbids homosexual action. And I think it would be irresponsible of me to give a lecture series on the Bible and not raise these particular questions, because they are so prevalent in contemporary discussions about what we should and should not do.

The Bible clearly forbids male homosexual activity. It says, paraphrasing the Hebrew here, "You, the male person, shall not lie with another male person as if he were a woman." Technically, the text reads, "Thou shall not lie with a man the lyings of a woman." A male shall not treat another male sexually, as if the other male were a female.

Why is that on the books? Here are some of the explanations you'll find in the literature. Extremely common is the assertion that ancient Canaanites engaged in homosexual activity for ritual practices. This is sacred prostitution. They may well have, but we don't have any good evidence of that from Canaanite sources. The Bible hints at it. But to cast aspersions on one's enemies' sexual activities is very, very common. You don't like somebody, suggest the person you don't like is inappropriately having sex. Standard *maledicta*, it's a standard curse.

A second argument is that homosexuality is forbidden, because it involves a misuse of semen. The idea is here that whenever you, the male person, have sex, it should be for procreative purposes only and, therefore, only with a woman. It's true that the Bible does encourage procreation. A man is not to sleep with a woman while she's menstruating, which means he will sleep with her when she is in her most fertile period. But the Bible, on the other hand, does not condemn misuse of semen elsewhere.

We have the example of Onan in Genesis, Chapter 38, and sometimes this example of Onan, who as the text says "spills his seed upon the ground," is cited as an injunction against masturbation. But that's not, in fact, what Onan was doing. He was actually practicing birth control, *coitus interruptus*. And that was only in Onan's case, not in anyone else, not for anyone else. In fact, the Bible never forbids masturbation. It never forbids oral sex, if it's a man and a woman, and that's not going to let you conceive anything. Or any other sort of sexual position between a man and a woman. Nor does it forbid sexual intercourse with a woman who is pregnant—she's not going to get pregnant again—or sexual intercourse with a menopausal woman. Although granted in the ancient Near East, she might actually conceive if she is 90. But, for most people, this is not going to happen.

Others have suggested that the laws against homosexuality are there because of Sodom and Gomorrah, Genesis, Chapter 19. Let's visit that for just a moment. Abraham's nephew, Lot, is in Sodom. At one point, two divine messengers, angels, come to visit him. And the men of Sodom, from the greatest to the least, crowd around Lot's store, and they bang on the door, and they say, "Send out the strangers, so that we may know them." "Know" can simply mean "get to know someone." But "know" in the Bible, K-N-O-W, can have the technical sense of have sex with—"and Adam knew his wife Eve and she conceived." And I think what these people are actually asking, these Sodomites, is "Send these people, so that we might rape them." And since they are men, and the visitors are men, this becomes a homosexual concern.

But actually what's going on with the Sodom and Gomorrah story is not so much a condemnation of homosexuality. It's a condemnation of rape and violence. And how do I know that? Because the same story of strangers in a town and townspeople saying, "Send out the strangers that we may know them," shows up in Judges, Chapter 19. And at that point, the people involved cast out a woman—we'll see this in a few lectures when we get to Judges—and she is raped to death. The concern here is violence, the power that the townspeople want to have over the strangers, and not homosexuality per se.

It's true the Bible does not like homosexual activity. The question, however, remains, why? And I simply come back to the idea that it's a question of category confusion. The ancient Near Eastern view of sex was a man penetrating a woman. For a man to penetrate a man—again think of the wording, "don't lie with a man the lyings of a woman"—puts one male in the woman's role. And that's category confusion. By the way, in the Old Testament there is no reference to lesbianism, because the Old Testament view of human sexuality meant a man doing some sort of penetration. The New Testament picks up on that particular gap.

There are a few, many, a few of the many, many other notable laws, so we can end with a few, if not non-controversial, perhaps at least not quite so controversial. Let's move from homosexuality to abortion. The text never actually talks about abortion. But there is one passage that has been used by both pro-life and pro-choice advocates. This is Exodus 21: "When men strive together and hurt a pregnant woman so that she miscarries but she herself is not hurt, the one who hurt her shall be fined. However, if any harm follows," as the biblical text says, which means "if the mother dies as well," then, the text goes on to say, "you shall give life for life, eye for eye, hand for hand, foot for foot, burn for burn, wound for wound, and bruise for bruise." This is the so-called *lex talionis*, the "eye for an eye."

So what does this mean? It means, at least according to the Hebrew text, miscarriage does not result in an eye for eye and a life for a life. The biblical code here does not consider the fetus to be a fully formed human being. It becomes monetary compensation if the fetus is injured or dies, compounding the problem. In some manuscripts of the Greek translation of this very passage, the Greek says, even if the fetus dies, it's an eye for an eye and a tooth for a tooth. Which means the biblical law code can be used either by pro-choice people or by pro-life people. It simply depends upon which manuscript and which textual tradition, the Greek or Hebrew, you want to depend on.

The Bible is not easy when it comes to locating contemporary morality. With homosexuality, we worry about the rationale. With abortion, the text is not actually talking about the woman's choice here. This is when she is injured. But we can always debate whether the Bible considers the unborn to be a human being or something, perhaps, less.

A couple more quick points. These are easier. According to Exodus, Chapter 34, when Moses came down from Mt. Sinai with the two tablets of testimony in his hand, he did not know that his skin shone like rays of light. We've seen this before when we talked about the folktale, about the hero being transformed, transfigured. And why is his skin shining? Because he had been talking to God. And the people become so afraid of his transfiguration that he has to wear a veil when he speaks to them, and then when he speaks to God, he takes his veil off.

Now, here is where it gets interesting. The Hebrew uses the term *keren*, it means a ray, coming out of Moses. But when the Greek text translated the Hebrew, it read, "horns," and so we have the image of Moses with horns coming out of his head. The Hebrew can bear this connotation, but the Greek formalized it, and so we came into Latin. In fact, *keren* sounds much like *cornu*, horns in Latin, whence cornucopia. And that's where we get Michelangelo's Moses with the horns coming out of his head. And more tragic, in fact, a legend, which I've still heard in Tennessee and I heard in North Carolina, that Jewish people have horns. And that's one of those Christian calumnies that's still around.

Moral laws, ethical laws, encompass the majority of the *mitzvot*, the commandment. Care for the poor and the stranger; justice for everybody, regardless of class, from the rich to the poor, honesty in the marketplace, peace in the family. And also holy war, because these laws concern not only morality and the home, but morality when one engages in war. And this brings us to the first major holy war played out in the Book of Joshua. This is the story of what happens when the people leave the wilderness, and they come into the land, and they discover its inhabitants. They'll have to fight those inhabitants to take the land promised to them. That's the next lecture.

The "Conquest"
(Deuteronomy 20–21, 27–31; Book of Joshua)
Lecture 12

If you read the Book of Joshua quickly ... it looks like the Book is presenting a blitzkrieg. Joshua and the Israelites get into the land, conquer Jericho, conquer the city of Ai, make it all the way through, and finally at the end, they make a covenant renewal ceremony at Shechem.. This was the greatest battle program ever enjoined. And, in fact, if we had been reading the Bible through, this is what we would have expected.

This lecture moves to the second part of the *Tanakh*, the *Nevi'im* (Prophets), with its first volume, the Book of Joshua. The Book of Deuteronomy provides the thematic framework for Joshua–2 Kings. The pattern is one known from suzerainty/vassal models: Those who follow God will prosper; those who stray will be cursed (Deut. 28:1–68). We shall discuss the laws of Deuteronomy in greater detail in Lecture 19, because the volume appears to have been implemented under King Josiah in the late 7th century. This lecture notes the details of Moses's death.

Moses is forbidden to enter Canaan (Deut. 31:2; 32:51–52). The Lord told Moses to "command a rock to bring forth water, but Moses struck the rock twice with his staff" (Num. 20:2–13; see also Exod. 17:1–7). "The Lord said to Moses and Aaron, 'Because you did not trust in me, to show my holiness before the eyes of the Israelites, therefore you shall not bring this assembly into the land that I have given them'" (Num. 20:12). Moses's final moments prepare Israel for the next stage of existence (Deut. 31). He blesses the tribes as a father would his children (Deut. 33:1–29; cf. Gen. 49). He is buried in Moab, but "no one knows his burial place to this day" (Deut. 34:6). He was 120 years old: his sight was perfect; his body, whole.

God had promised the patriarchs, Moses, and the covenant community the land "flowing with milk and honey" (Deut. 27:3), but they have to fight for it. A priest reminds the soldiers of the divine presence in battle. Officers discharge anyone who has built a new home, planted a vineyard but not enjoyed its fruit, and become engaged but not yet wed, and the faint-hearted. The ordinances enjoin against uncontrolled destruction (Deut. 20–21). The first initiative is to offer terms of peace at the price of forced labor. If surrender is denied, all adult males are to be killed, not women and children. Trees are not to be cut down. A captive woman is allowed a month's mourning period (to avoid rape). She may then become a soldier's wife; he is not permitted to sell her or to treat her as a slave. The exception to sparing lives: For a town "that the Lord your God is giving you as an inheritance, you must not let anything that breathes remain alive" (Deut. 20:16).

The Book of Joshua appears initially to be a straightforward recounting of the Israelites' "holy war" in the "promised land." The narrative impression of the "conquest" of Canaan receives archaeological support. The Hyksos, an Asiatic group, moved into Egypt in the 1720s. This could be seen to match the time when Joseph served as advisor to Pharaoh. With the rise of Egypt's Eighteenth Dynasty, c. 1570, the Hyksos were expelled. According to Exod. 12:40, "the time that the people of Israel dwelled in Egypt was 430 years"; 1720 - 1310 = 410. The Exodus Pharaoh is traditionally viewed as Ramses II, c. 1290; 1720 (Hyksos' arrival) - 1290 (Ramses II) = 430 (the number of years Exodus places the Hebrews in Egypt). This would date the conquest to the late 13th century. Archaeology attests a number of Canaanite cities destroyed in the late 1200s, including Beth-El, Debir, Lachish, Megiddo, and Hazor.

Josh. 1–11 contains several etiologies. The conquest of Ai (Josh. 7–8) is problematic: the name means "heap." Perhaps later Israelites developed the story to explain Benjaminite possession of the ruined site. The Jericho *tel* (an artificial mound of city debris) indicates consistent inhabitation from the Calcolithic (4,000–3,000 B.C.E.) through the Middle Bronze (1800–1500) Ages, but not in the Late Bronze Age (1500–1200), although the *tel* experienced severe erosion), which is the time of the conquest. Perhaps the prostitute Rahab's story is an etiology explaining Canaanite presence in the community, even as the story of Jericho explains the ruins. Josh. 10:16–27 offers an etiology of the unusually large stones blocking the entrance to the plain of Makkedah: the story of the entrapment of the five kings. Judges 1 provides a list of negative possessions—Beth She'an, Dor, Megiddo, Gezer, Acco, Sidon, and so on—indicating that occupation was at best incomplete.

A famous alternative, known as the "immigration model," has also been proposed. The immigration model is a relatively peaceful migration into the sparsely populated hill country. The tribes may represent population waves. Six "Leah tribes" (Reuben, Simeon, Levi, Judah, Isacchar, Zebulon) and four "concubine tribes" (Dan, Naphtali, Gad, Asher) settle west of the Jordan. The Rachel tribes (Ephraim, Manasseh, Benjamin) arrive with Yahwism (cf. exhortations to "put away the gods which your ancestors served beyond the river and in Egypt and serve the Lord" [Josh. 24:14]). Simeon and Levi settle in the central hills but scatter under pressure from nearby Shechem (cf. Gen. 34, 49). Judah annexes Simeon, and Levi loses its land grant. Both tribes are absent from the Song of Deborah (Jdg. 5). Fragments of Reuben are absorbed into Judah and Gad; Reuben's relations with Bilhah, Jacob's concubine, provide the etiology for tribal disintegration.

The Amarna Letters hint of a peaceful process of resettlement in Canaan by outsiders (including the Apiru). Issachar's area, including Shunem and Mt. Tabor, is cited in the Amarna Letters about Megiddo's king, who forced people from Shunem to act as slave-porters. Gen. 49:15 says of Issachar: "He saw that the resting place was good and that the land was pleasant, so he bowed his shoulder to bear and became a slave at forced labor." Perhaps Issachar acquired its territory by serving for it; the tribe's name can be translated "worker for wages."

The immigration model also explains mysterious references to the Tribe of Dan. Josh. 19:40–48 connects Dan with Philistine settlements on the Mediterranean. Jdg. 5:17, the Song of Deborah, asks why Dan "lingered by the ships." Gen. 49:16: "Dan shall judge his people as one of the tribes of Israel"; an odd statement, unless Dan is originally alien. Is this a connection to a group of sea peoples called the Denyen, Danaoi, and/or Danuna?

Other tribes may also carry non-Hebrew pedigrees. Asher from Assur (the Assyrian god) or Asherah (the Canaanite goddess). Gad is a Canaanite god.

Zebulun, which means "of the princes," is an epithet of the Canaanite Baal. The covenant-making ceremony at Shechem (Josh. 24) raises historical problems. Joshua mentions the Exodus and the wilderness and invokes Abraham, Isaac, Jacob, Esau, Moses, and Aaron but omits reference to the Sinaitic covenant. Perhaps the Exodus experience represents the collective memory of one group and the Sinaitic theophany, the experience of another. Shechem may have been occupied by Hebrews before the "conquest" (cf. Gen. 34), and the Amarna Letters locate Apiru in Shechem.

Prompted in part by studies in social revolution, some scholars—sparked by the work of George Mendenhall—posit a revolt by an indigenous population. To avoid oligarchies, the revolutionaries made the struggle for power an illicit assumption of divine prerogatives. Yahwism provided the catalyst for this new organization and ideology. Because the removal of kings was done by indigenous groups, no major military action was involved and, thus, no major story recorded.

The so-called "conquest" is likely a composite story of internal and external groups motivated by various political, religious, economic, and ideological concerns. They eventually established common cause and, later, common history. The Book of Joshua, joining history and folktale, represents a point toward the end of that process, when the traditions were becoming harmonized. One might view Joshua as part of a Hexateuch, a six-scroll collection, which completes the patriarchal promise. The Book of Judges, to which we turn next, offers testimony to the role of independent tribal units, even as it anticipates the creation of the monarchy. ∎

Suggested Reading

Susan Niditch, *War in the Hebrew Bible: A Study in the Ethics of Violence.*

Questions to Consider

1. Is holy war simply "wholly war," or is it ever justified? If the latter, and based on what you have read in the Bible to this point, does the Book of Joshua describe such an occasion?

2. Is Rahab a hero, a traitor, or a self-serving survivor ?

3. According to Deut. 31:10, "Never since has there arisen a prophet in Israel like Moses, whom the Lord knew face to face." Is it appropriate that he be denied entry into the promised land? That he have no memorial or tomb (compared, for example, to the patriarchs and matriarchs at Hebron; Rachel's tomb)?

The "Conquest"
(Deuteronomy 20–21, 27–31; Book of Joshua)
Lecture 12—Transcript

With this lecture, we move out of the Pentateuch, out of the Torah, and into the second division of the biblical canon, in Hebrew, the *Nevi'im*, the Prophets. The first part of this corpus is known as the Deuteronomic history. And here we mean by Deuteronomic history, Joshua, Judges, First and Second Samuel, and First and Second Kings. They are called the Deuteronomic history, because they follow that same general rubric of the Book of Deuteronomy. Kings who behave properly are described as being rewarded. Kings who behave improperly, which is most of them, are described as being punished by God. So the history here has an editorial gloss, an ethos, that springs from the concerns of the Book of Deuteronomy. The history itself was probably not edited until well beyond the time of the Babylonian exile, after the fifth, maybe fourth, or even as late as the third, century B.C.E.

So let's go back to the beginnings of the Deuteronomic history, the Book of Joshua. And, indeed, let's backtrack just a little bit more to the death of Moses. Because in order for Joshua to take over, the reins of leadership must be passed on.

As you already know from discussing the Mosaic code at the end of the Book of Deuteronomy, we have a record of the death of Moses. But it does raise the question, why does Moses, after all the trouble he went through to get the people out of Egypt and to lead them through the wilderness for 40 years, why when he's finally on the borders, is he not allowed to cross over? Which has always seemed very unfair to me. The Bible actually provides us an answer. I'm not really happy with the answer, but here is how it goes. According to Deuteronomy 31, and repeated in 32, Moses is forbidden to enter Canaan because he disobeyed a divine order. "The Lord had told Moses," here I'm citing Numbers 20, "command a rock to bring forth water." In other words, "speak to the rock." But we're told Moses struck the rock instead with his staff. He was told to speak to it; he hit it. And the Lord says to Moses, "Because you did not trust in me to show my holiness before the Israelites, you shall not bring this assembly into the land that I have given them." In other words, if Moses had spoken to the rock, it would have been a miracle. If he had hit the rock, heaven knows, maybe he hit a fissure. God is upset. Moses was disobedient. The miracle was not as glorious.

Some readers may well conclude that God's reason is petty. Others may find it, perhaps, fitting. There was no good reason to keep Moses out of the land, no good moral reason or ethical reason. But it may also be the case that Moses is like, oh, say, Winston Churchill. During a particular period of a nation's history, you need a particular type of leader. And when the nation's historical setting changes, when you go from war to peace, or when you go from a community wandering into the desert and into a community that has to conquer a new land by military might, new leaders are called for. Winston Churchill, or Moses, has done his job. And, perhaps, it's also appropriate that he remain outside the land, in solidarity with the people he led for those 40 years, because, as you know, only two who came out of Egypt will ultimately go into the land. I look at Moses on the outside as if he is a guardian watching over. It's not a bad image.

So at the end of Deuteronomy, Moses blesses the Israelites as a father would bless his children, and then we're told, the great leader dies. He is buried in Moab. And, "No-one knows his burial place until this day." Nor did they need to, in fact, because Moses's memorial is the Torah and those people who keep it.

And this brings us to Joshua, the transfer of leadership and the question of how the people enter the land. God had promised to the patriarchs, to Abraham, Isaac, and Jacob, that they would have land. Here is the fulfillment of that patriarchal promise. The covenant community will get a land "flowing with milk and honey," but they have to fight for it.

Oh, by the way, on "milk and honey," since we just completed in the last lecture talking about dietary regulations, why milk and honey? When you think about it, these are two of the very, very few foodstuffs that one can obtain without anything plant or animal dying. It's quite interesting. Renewable resources.

How do you take the land? Holy war. And holy war is not like regular war. There are specific laws, injunctions that the Bible lays down to tell people how to engage in a battle being fought on God's behalf. For example, you always bring the troops into battle. This is the modern English, "Praise the Lord and pass the ammunition." A priest will be there. Indeed, often the Israelites would bring the Holy Ark into battle with them. Officers are required to discharge certain people. For example, if a man has just built a new home, but he hasn't had much occasion to live in it. If he has just planted a vineyard, but has not enjoyed the fruits, literally, of his labor. If he has become engaged, but has not yet gotten married. And, of course, the faint-hearted are discharged. So we have the 4-F version from the Bible.

Ordinances are then made against uncontrolled destruction. For example, the first initiative is that the rulers should be offered terms of a truce. The initiator of the holy war here, Joshua, is to go to the rulers and say, "We will come take over your land and put you in forced labor. Do you agree?" And if they agree, then that's fine. We wind up with slaves. But if they don't, one can engage in war, but at least there is a possibility of a treaty here. If surrender is denied, all adult males are to be killed. Trees are not to be cut down. This is like the modern smart bomb; it kills people but it doesn't kill natural resources.

If a woman is taken captive, she is to be allowed one month to mourn her dead family members, and this prohibits rape. Right? She may then become the soldier's wife. But if he decides he does not like her, he is not permitted to sell her off as a slave or, indeed, to treat her like a slave. If he takes a woman captive and she becomes his wife, she is legally his wife; she is not some sort of second-order product.

Soldiers are required to be ritually pure, in the same they had to be literally pure when they stood before Mt. Sinai. Which means they cannot engage in sexual intercourse. And I mention this now because it will become very important to when we get to the story of David and Bathsheba.

We are told any town that the Lord, your God, is giving you as an inheritance, any town in Canaan, you must not let anything that breathes in it remain alive. Total destruction. The irony is when we actually look at what Joshua does, the first major campaign is the campaign against Jericho, and, indeed, surviving Jericho is Rahab the prostitute and her family. So although there is an injunction, "destroy everybody," it turns out these injunctions are not necessarily heeded, even by characters in the narrative. But these are the general laws, and so the Israelites prepare to enter Canaan under Joshua.

Now, if you read the Book of Joshua quickly, you don't look at the footnotes, and you don't really pay a whole lot of attention, it looks like the Book is presenting a blitzkrieg. Joshua and the Israelites get into the land, conquer Jericho, conquer the city of Ai, make it all the way through, and finally at the end, they make a covenant renewal ceremony at Shechem. Everything worked perfectly well there. There were no glitches. This was the greatest battle program ever enjoined. And, in fact, if we had been reading the Bible through, this is what we would have expected. We know the patriarchs had promises that they were going to get the land. Joshua fulfills those promises. Indeed, some biblical scholars have argued that what we have in the biblical text is not a Pentateuch, a five-book beginning, but rather a hexateuch, a six-book beginning, with Joshua showing the fulfillment of the promises made to Abraham, Isaac, and Jacob.

Not only does this blitzkrieg model seem to fit with what we would expect to have had happen based on the promises, but one can very cautiously, very, very cautiously, perhaps match up Joshua's conquests with external historical evidence. It's extremely tentative, but here is how it works. I'm going to go step-by-step, because I have to use math here, and math is not my strong point.

Step one. There is a group of Asiatics, they are called Hyksos—the name actually means rulers of foreign lands, interesting name for a group. They are from Syria, Palestine, and they move into Egypt around 1720–1710. That's more or less the timeframe for Joseph to have been the grand vizier. Perhaps background for Joseph, perhaps not. With the rise of Egypt's 18th dynasty in 1570, the Hyksos are expelled from Egypt. That's step two. And the native Egyptians take over. That may be the rationale for why Exodus talks about "a Pharaoh arose who knew not Joseph," because perhaps this new group of pharaohs are not from the Hyksos ethnic group, and they don't retain the same historical memories. That's step two.

Step three. According to Exodus 12:40, "The time that the people of Israel dwelled in Egypt was 430 years." Step four, the Pharaoh of the Exodus—if you're confused by now you can check the booklet—the Pharaoh of the Exodus is traditionally viewed as Ramses II, whose rule began approximately in 1290 B.C.E. So if you take the time of the arrival of the Hyksos in 1720, and you subtract from it the time of Ramses II's ascension to the throne in 1290, you wind up with 430, and that's the number of years Exodus places the Hebrews in Egypt. It actually matches up. Perhaps then, the Hyksos are the background for the story of Joseph, and Ramses II really is the pharaoh of the Exodus, and the Hebrew people really were enslaved in Egypt. It's possible.

And if this is true, then that date would put the conquest of Canaan sometime in the late 13th century, the 1200s, and that actually matches up with archaeology, as well. Archaeological investigation in the area of Israel suggests that a good number of cities were destroyed at this particular time. For example, at Beth-El, the House of God, where Jacob had his dream of that heavenly ladder, we have archaeological evidence of a violent destruction at the end of the 13th century.

Evidence also indicates that cities like Debir and Lachish were destroyed, and then only later re-inhabited. Lachish has yielded bowls, clay bowls, with inscriptions mentioning the fourth year of the reign of Merneptah, a pharaoh in Egypt. This is circa 1220, after the so-called time of the conquest. But it does suggest new things are happening. Perhaps people from Egypt came over. Could be.

In the north, cities like Megiddo and Hazor are also destroyed at the end of the 13th century, and the list goes on. So could it be, in fact, that archaeological evidence proves the story of Joshua? Well, this is biblical studies, of course, everybody is going to have doubts here or there. And, indeed, biblical scholars have their doubts about this, as well.

Israelite attack, ruling by Joshua, and coming into the community may explain these debris layers, these destruction layers. But a destruction layer is a destruction layer, and unless you have, you know, a sign saying, "Joshua was here, conquered at such and such a date," it's very difficult to tell what caused the destruction. Inter-city warfare, very common in Canaan. The Philistines are now on the scene, coming over the Mediterranean, perhaps they are involved. A fire could destroy a city-state very easily; natural problems can happen. Internal revolt, which does happen on occasion. A destruction layer only proves that something has been destroyed. It does not tell us who did the destroying.

So we go back to the Book of Joshua, and we look for confirmation. Was there really a blitzkrieg? But now we read carefully. And it turns out that Joshua, particularly Joshua 1–11, the blitzkrieg section, does not actually tell us that Joshua and company conquered everything. The stories are a little bit problematic.

For example, Joshua, Chapters 7 and 8, describe the conquest of a city called Ai, A-I. It's a great story. The problem is the name "Ai" already means "heap of ruin," which is not the sort of name most people would give to their city. And archaeological investigation suggests that in the 13th century, Ai was already a heap of ruin. It would have been debris, destruction layer, when Joshua and company arrived in the first place. What the Book of Joshua may well give us is an etiology, a story of origin, explaining why this city is destroyed. In their imagination, well, of course, Joshua did it. But did he actually do it? Archaeological investigation suggests no.

And then we have that very famous story of Jericho. When archaeologists engage in their investigation, what they look at is something called a tell. It's an artificial mound created by successive layers of cities that are built and then fall into ruin, and then you build another city on top of that, and another city on top of that. And the archaeologists looks at this tell, this artificial mound, as if it's a layer cake, and you can slice through, and you can find community destruction layer, different community destruction layer. And people have done this with the tell at Jericho.

And what has archaeological investigation yielded? We've got inhabitants at Jericho in the Calcolithic period, 4,000 B.C.E. This place is already inhabited. Ad it's inhabited through the Middle Bronze Age. The problem is when we get up to the beginning of the iron age, which is when Joshua is starting, that's the one time when there seems to be no evidence of inhabitation at all.

Now granted, the tell has suffered severe erosion. Perhaps the evidence that was there has been washed away or blown away. But it remains problematic.

Even the story of Jericho remains problematic, because this where we meet Rahab the prostitute. Joshua and company outside the land send in spies to scout out Canaan, to scout out the city. And the first thing these spies do is they land in Rahab's house, and Rahab is running a brothel. She is a prostitute. Now one can raise lots of questions as to why those spies went to a brothel first thing when they got into Canaan, and the easier explanations are that's where you could get information about city defenses, or that's where you could hide out, nobody would much pay attention. And there are other reasons that we won't go into.

But what happens is when they get into Rahab's house, Rahab has to hide them, and then word comes to the King of Jericho, Rahab is hiding spies. What happens? Rahab agrees to protect the spies as long as the Israelites, when they attack Jericho, preserve her and her family. And she actually will hang a red cord out of her window, so that the Israelites, during the conquest, will know where she is. And then Rahab says to the King of Jericho, "Well, we understand who these Israelites are. We know that God is on their side. We know that God will force everyone to yield to them." Rahab, the Gentile, the prostitute, the Canaanite, recites Israel's salvation history, recites the mighty deeds of God. Which is one of those nice ironies, because taking booty from these cities actually wind up being some of the Hebrews, and they wind up paying for it.

This may be an etiology, by the way, to explain why there are Canaanites yet in the land even though Joshua and Moses before him were commanded "Wipe out the Canaanites before you." The Canaanites are still there. Rahab is somebody who, it seems, deserves to be there.

There are several other etiologies in the text. There is a lovely one in Joshua 10 that describes why there are unusually large stones blocking the entrance to a cave. And it turns out, according to Joshua, that's where five kings of the land hid. I also like this story because for Joshua to conquer this land, he prays to God, and God causes the sun to stand still. That's where we get the idea that we have a geocentric, rather than heliocentric, universe. But it suggests to me knowing something about modern physics and modern astronomy. That this is not an historical record, but rather a bit of folklore, folktale, replayed back into the time of the conquest.

And finally, arguing against the full historicity of all this material is the beginning of the Book of Judges, to which we will turn in the next lecture. Judge, Chapter 1, provides us a list of negative possessions—cities the Israelites did not conquer: Beth She'an, Dor, Gezer, Acco, Sidon, major cities. The modern analogy would be, someone, I won't suggest whom, conquered the United States, but among the cities still left standing, New York, Washington DC, Philadelphia, Chicago, Detroit, Los Angeles, Atlanta. It's not that much of a conquering effort, if the major cities are still left standing.

So because there remain archaeological problems here, both in terms of textual evidence in the Book of Joshua and in terms of evidence on the ground, what people can dig up, other models for how the Israelites got into Canaan have been proposed. The most famous of these alternatives is known as the "immigration model." And this is the idea that the various tribes, the twelve tribes of Israel, came over the desert and gradually entered the land, settling first in the sparsely populated hill countries, and then only gradually moving down into the plains, so that the original entry of the Israelites into the land was more of a peaceful than a warlike one, and it's only when they began to outgrow the land, where they originally settled, that some battles began.

You can actually find some hints of this if you read the biblical tradition again carefully. For example, why are there twelve tribes divvied up among Jacob's wives. Six Leah tribes, the Rachel Tribes, and tribes associated with Rachel and Leah's maids, Bilhah and Zilpah, who wind up being Jacob's concubines. Perhaps it worked this way. Perhaps the six Leah tribes and the four concubine tribes came in first, and then the Rachel tribes arrived later with Yahwism.

And then the communities begin to split up. We already know from Joshua, and then Judges, that certain tribes lose their land very quickly. The tribe of Reuben, for example, loses its land. But what do we have in Genesis? We have Jacob cursing Reuben for sleeping with Bilhah. And what's his curse? He's going to leave his land, lose his land. Joshua plays it out. Simeon and Levi lose their land very, very quickly. Genesis 34 has Jacob curse Simeon and Levi for "making him odious in the land, because they attacked the city of Shechem and killed all the men." So what we may have with Genesis are foreshadowing etiologies for what actually happened to the individual tribes when they got into the land.

My favorite example of this is when you go to the specific tribes and look at their names and look at their backgrounds, you can actually find suggestions that they were maybe even residents of Canaan to begin with, and if not, came over separately. Here are a couple of examples. According to Genesis 49, speaking of Issachar, one of the tribes, "He saw that his resting place was good and that the land was pleasant, so he bowed his shoulder to bear and became a slave at forced labor"—corvées. Now, it's possible that Issachar gained its tribal land by serving for it, by becoming enslaved and then eventually throwing off the yoke of the enslaver. The tribe's name Issachar can actually mean a "worker for wages." But we do have possible background for this.

According to the Amarna Letters, texts preserved in Egypt, we have a reference to the area where Issachar settled around Mt. Tabor, and we're told that the king there, the king of Megiddo, the major city, forced people from Mt. Tabor and Shunem to act as slave porters. So perhaps Issachar's entry is backed up by the Amarna Letters.

Here is an even better one. These are the strange journeys of the tribe of Dan. Joshua, Chapter 19, connects Dan with Philistine settlements on the Mediterranean. Quite possible. But look at some of the other statements regarding Dan. The Song of Deborah, one of the oldest pieces of biblical literature we have, in Judges, Chapter 5, says of the tribe of Dan, "Why did you linger by the ships?" Which is a very odd question to ask a group of people who ostensibly just came over the desert. Suddenly these are shipbuilders. They are maritime people. Odd. Genesis 49:16, Jacob's blessings to his sons reads, "Dan shall judge his people as one of the tribes of Israel." Which is an odd statement, unless Dan was not one of the tribes of Israel to begin with. Perhaps they are not originally connected with this covenant community. Perhaps they are indigenous to Canaan. Perhaps they are part of that Mediterranean group, like the Philistines, who came over. Judges, Chapter 18, asserts that the Danites, the members of the tribe of Dan, were "seeking for an inheritance to settle, because until then no inheritance among the tribes of Israel had fallen to them," as if they came late, and they lost out on the initial land grant.

And finally, and perhaps most tellingly, we have external evidence of a group of sea peoples, that is population groups that entered Canaan from the Mediterranean, who were called variously the Denyen, the Danaoi, and the Danuna. And my suspicion is that the tribe of Dan is not related to Jacob, related to Israel from Genesis. What we have with Dan is a group of people that made common cause with the Israelites very, very early on. And, ultimately, were accepted into that tribal group.

Other tribes may also fall into this category, because the names of some of the other tribes suggest Canaanite origins. The tribe of Asher could be from Assur, the Assyrian god, or even Asherah, the Canaanite mother goddess. Gad, a tribe, is also the name of a Canaanite god. And Zebulon, yet another tribe, which means "of the princes," is an epithet for the Canaanite god, Baal. Odd names for Israelite tribes to be having, but entirely appropriate names for part of the indigenous population of Canaan who made common cause with the Israelites.

So here we have, perhaps, some evidence of a gradual penetration, but also some evidence of yet a third model: Perhaps some people indigenous to Canaan rose up against their overlords, rejected city-state government, and then, under the aegis of Yahwism, formed common cause with some of the tribes who came in from the wilderness. What we have in the Bible is a cleaned-up version of probably what was an exceptionally complex ancient history.

In terms of this complexity, let's go back to Joshua 24, that covenant ceremony at Shechem, which we've already talked about. Here, we get some hints of different tribes with different historical memories. In Joshua's recitation of the history to the people, this is part of that covenant model, the historical prologue, Joshua mentions the Exodus. He mentions the wilderness experience. He mentions Abraham, Isaac, and Jacob, Esau, Moses and Aaron.

He leaves out the reference to Mt. Sinai, the Sinaitic covenant, which is a very odd thing for him to be leaving out at a covenant renewal ceremony. One would have thought that would have been the high point of the wilderness journey. Why leave it out? Some biblical scholars suggest that the Exodus from Egypt represents the memory of one group of people who eventually comprised Israel, and the Sinaitic experience represents the experience of another group. And yet other groups, other tribes, had different experiences, perhaps those indigenous to Canaan. And, ultimately, they all come together, and they develop a common, a group memory.

And that should not be surprising, as well, because we in America do the same thing. My ancestors did not come over on the Mayflower. I am from Massachusetts, but my family does not go back quite that far. But every year, when I was a child, and now my children, celebrate Thanksgiving. And on Thanksgiving Day, we pretend, and I think we actually believe that we, too, are pilgrims, we, too, landed on Plymouth rock, and we, too, celebrate religious freedom, and we, too, eat turkey. Right? In other words, Americans have developed a communal memory. We all came over on the Mayflower. We were all somehow involved in the process of gaining freedom from England. People in Tennessee are still fighting the Civil War, or "The War of Northern Aggression," as my neighbors refer to it. Even if they are not indigenous to Tennessee, even if they are not from the South, they take on the collective memory of the region of the country. And that may well have been what the ancient Israelites did.

So where are we then? It's possible that there was some sort of conquest. I certainly wouldn't rule that out. And it's certainly possible that Joshua's responsible for some of it. But I also think the model based on immigration, gradual penetration by different people at different times, also makes a good deal of sense. And there is a part of me that's attracted to that third model. You might consider it an ancient version of the revolt of the proletariat, where some people rejected the city-state governans, rejected their marginalization, rejected the cults, the religion of the city-state, and left, thought there must be a better place somewhere else, and made common cause with some of these other people marginal to the city-states.

How is this all eventually put together? The so-called conquest is, therefore, probably a composite story. Some fictional, based on etiology; some historical, but the history coded by folktale and legend. And we've already seen how literary convention causes people to change the way they tell history. The Book of Joshua, therefore, conjoins history and folktale and explanations for ruins, and, perhaps, all these different tribes from different places, and brings them altogether. By the end of Joshua, the people have made common cause. They are united into one covenanted community.

When we turn next to the Book of Judges, we find out that this is really all fiction. The tribes have not united. They are at war not only with Canaanite city-states, they are at war with each other. They have not conquered the entire land. To the contrary, Canaanite city-states are oppressing them left and right, disasters are occurring. The Book of Judges shows us, perhaps, what might be a little more of the case, the Israelites trying to get on their feet, and the Israelites, here as well, entering the Iron Age and finding the wonders of new technology, with iron chariots and new forms of warfare and new enemies and new problems to face. That's the Book of Judges and that's the next lecture.

The Book of Judges, Part I
(Judges 1–8)
Lecture 13

Gone is the time of miracles, the sun standing still, or the trumpets
blaring and the walls of Jericho falling. In fact, gone is the time when
you can tell the difference between the good guys and the bad guys.
When we move to the Book of Judges, it is as if we are coming closer to
our own world.

The Book of Judges is, as Mieke Bal describes, "a book about death."
Repeating the type scene of apostasy, punishment, repentance, and
rescue, the book ultimately spirals into idolatry, rape, and near-
genocide. Yet the barbarity is broken by moments of delight. Judges plays
on traditional definitions of the hero: tricksters like Ehud, mothers like
Deborah, cowards like Gideon, tragic figures like Jephthah, even blockheads
like Samson. Offering high comedy and profound tragedy, Judges continues
to raise historical, theological, and moral challenges.

Judges is set c. 1200–1000, at the beginning of the Iron Age. The narrative
suggests a long editorial process culminating shortly before or during
Babylonian captivity in the 6th century. Individual tribal legends are
combined in the Deuteronomic editorial framework: the view that fidelity
is rewarded and apostasy punished. The type scene guides all but the last
several chapters. The basic pattern appears with the first judge, Othniel, in
3:7–11: "The people of Israel did what was evil" (3:7). YHWH gives them
to Cushan-Rishathaim of Mesopotamia for eight years (3:8). The people cry
out to the Lord, and "the Lord raised up a deliverer for the people of Israel"
(3:9). Othniel receives the divine spirit, wages war, and prevails (3:10).
Othniel judges Israel forty years, then dies (3:11), "and the people of Israel
again did what was evil" (3:12). Even this introductory pattern is broken
by textual anecdotes. Othniel is less stalwart than his betrothed, Caleb's
daughter Acsah. Acsah and Caleb function as ironic foils to Jephthah and his
daughter (Jdg. 11).

The first variation, the account of Ehud, is so sexual and scatological that it was just as likely a favorite of ancient Israel even as it is rarely cited from pulpits and bimas today. Ehud the trickster prevails by means of brains, not brawn. Like cross-cultural tricksters (Pan, Loki, Hermes), he is left-handed. This trait allows him to conceal his weapon: he "girded [the sword] on his right thigh under his clothes" (Jdg. 3:16). A sexual undertone begins.

King Eglon, the enemy, also possesses an unusual characteristic: he is "very fat" (3:17). Because kings are military leaders, Eglon is already shown to be unworthy. That *eglon* means "fatted calf" hints that he will be sacrificed to that hidden sword.

The judge's victory is filled with sexual and scatological imagery common to folktales. Ehud states (3:19), "I have a message for you, O king," and the king, stupidly, orders everyone except Ehud away. "Ehud came to him, as [Eglon] was sitting alone in his cool roof chamber" (3:20). "Ehud reached with his left hand" (the hand used for handling genitals; 3:21). He "took his sword from his right thigh, and thrust it into Eglon's belly ... the hilt went in after the blade, and the fat closed over the blade." The image is of perverse intercourse. Reading 3:22 euphemistically: "And the dirt came out"; more directly, the king defecates—there is an emission, but the wrong kind. Eglon's servants, believing that the king is relieving himself, avoid entering and, thus, permit Ehud to escape. "They waited until they were utterly at a loss; but when he still did not open the doors of the roof chamber, they took the key and opened them, and there lay their lord, dead on the floor" (3:25). Shamgar is the next judge, though little is said of him. He provides a break between the account of Ehud and the Song of Deborah.

The story of Deborah (Jdg. 4–5), told first in prose, then in poetry, plays on the themes of mothers, violence, and seduction. Deborah's introduction challenges military, gendered, and maternal conventions. Underneath her palm tree, the judge presides before the military problems arise. Most translations render 4:1 "wife of Lappidoth," but no such character appears. The phrase could be translated "woman of flames," which complements the name of her general, Barak ("lightning"). Her relationship to Barak complicates gender roles. Barak refuses initially to battle: "If you go with me, I will go; but if you will not go with me, I will not go" (4:8). This passage may be read, however, as Barak's testing of Deborah. Deborah agrees, but at the price of his honor: "The road on which you are going will not lead to your glory, for the Lord will sell [the enemy] Sisera into the hand of a woman" (4:9).

The "woman" who claims the honor Barak loses is Jael, the second "mother." Jael is married to the absent but frequently mentioned "Heber the Kenite [who] had separated from the Kenites, the descendants of

Deborah, the only female judge.

Hobab the father-in-law of Moses." (In the next lecture, we shall see how far Moses's household has fallen.) Sisera, the enemy general, fleeing Barak, goes "to the tent of Jael, the wife of Heber the Kenite, for there was peace between Jabin the King of Hazor and the house of Heber the Kenite." But what of Jael: Is she Israelite, Kenite, Canaanite? To whom are her loyalties? Are we to be reminded of Cain: a murderer, yet protected?

Jael inverts Near Eastern concerns for hospitality and conventions of motherhood. Her invitation is more seduction than protection: "Jael came out to meet Sisera, and said to him, 'Turn aside, my lord, turn aside to me; have no fear'" (4:18). Maternally: "She covered him with a rug. And he said to her, 'Pray, give me a little water to drink, for I am thirsty.' So she opened a skin of milk and gave him a drink and covered him" (4:19). Then "the wife of Heber, took a tent peg, and went softly to him, and drove the peg into his temple, until it went down into the ground, as he was lying fast asleep from weariness. So he died." The imagery evokes Eglon's death: sword and tent peg, trickster assassins, bedroom demise.

The Song of Deborah offers one of the oldest examples of Hebrew poetry. The song restages Sisera's death: he is standing as he dies, and his unmanning becomes even more manifest:

> She struck Sisera a blow
>
> She crushed his head
>
> She shattered and pierced his temple.
>
> He sank, he fell.
>
> He lay still at her feet.
>
> At her feet he sank, he fell;
>
> Where he sank, there he fell, done to death.

The song also mentions a third mother. Unlike Deborah and Jael, Sisera's mother is inside a home, not under a tree or in a tent; she has all the luxuries of the city-state, yet she lacks peace:

> Out of the window she peered.
>
> The mother of Sisera gazed through the lattice.
>
> Why is his chariot so long in coming?
>
> Why tarry the hoofbeats of his chariots?

Before Deborah's song allows too much sympathy, Sisera's mother develops her own explanation.

Are they not finding and dividing the spoil?

A womb or two or every man?

Spoil of dyed stuff for Sisera … ?

She will receive neither.

Gideon's story (Judges 6–8) reveals increasing problems with charismatic leaders who are less confident and less capable. The convention expands description of the judge's appointment: In the modern idiom, "good men are becoming harder to find." Gideon complains about the weakness of his tribe (Manasseh), family, and personal ability. He also complains about divine inaction. As Gideon is beating wheat in the winepress to hide it from the Midianites, an angel announces, "The Lord is with you, you mighty man of valor" (6:11). Given Gideon's position, the sarcasm is palpable. Gideon responds: "Pray sir, if the Lord is with us, why then has all this befallen us? And where are all his wonderful deeds, which our ancestors recounted to us, saying, 'Did not the Lord bring us up out of Egypt?'" Gideon risks trivializing divine ability by continually testing God. He taxes God's patience—and the reader's: "Let not your anger burn against me; let me speak but this once. Pray, let me make trial only this once with the fleece; pray let it be dry only this once on the fleece, and on all the ground let there be dew" (6:39).

This unpromising beginning matches his unpromising end. Gideon's other name is "Jerubaal," "Let Baal contend," a Canaanite "Israel." His final action, one of apostasy, confirms his fall: "Gideon made an ephod of [the gold captured from the Midianites] and put it in his city in Ophrah; all Israel whored after it there, and it became a snare to Gideon and his family" (8:27).

One of his sons, Abimelech ("my father is king"), will prove to be a false judge. With his tenure, the benefits of the charismatic leader become increasingly insecure. As we shall see in the next lecture, the role of the judge must eventually cede to that of the king. ∎

Suggested Reading

Susan Ackerman, *Warrior, Dancer, Seductress, Queen: Women in Judges and Biblical Israel*, Anchor Bible Reference Library.

Mieke Bal, *Death and Dissymmetry: The Politics of Coherence in the Book of Judges*.

Gail Yee (ed.), *Judges and Method: New Approaches in Biblical Studies*.

Questions to Consider

1. Is Judges "funny"?

2. What are the functions of such motifs as scatology, perverse sexual humor, and reversed gender roles (military women, mothers who kill, generals who seek protection from women) in a community's national epic?

3. What is the "theology" of Judges?

The Book of Judges, Part I
(Judges 1–8)
Lecture 13—Transcript

As we move from the Book of Joshua and into the Book of Judges, we change worlds. Gone is the time when the tribes are working in unity to gain the Promised Land. Gone is the time of miracles, the sun standing still, or the trumpets blaring and the walls of Jericho falling. In fact, gone is the time when you can tell the difference between the good guys and the bad guys. When we move to the Book of Judges, it is as if we are coming closer to our own world. There are fewer miracles, more divisions among the tribes, and individual charismatic leaders fighting individual battles with individual enemies. The tribes are no longer united. This is a new world.

It begins on an extremely promising note, but, by the time we get to the end of the Book of Judges, we find this covenant community spiraling out of control into chaos and into anarchy. So what ultimately happens in the Book of Judges is that we have an apology for the monarchy, an excuse to explain why the covenant community commissioned to be a nation independent and under God suddenly finds itself with King Saul and then King David pretty much like all the other nations of the world.

The Book of Judges is difficult to read. Scholar Mieke Bal refers to it as "a book about death," and that is, in fact, what it is, but, especially at the beginning of the text, the chaos and the anarchy and the tragedy are broken by moments of great humor, indeed, moments of farce. So we'll take two lectures to look at the Book of Judges. This first lecture will look at the initial judges, where we have a little bit more humor than we have tragedy.

We'll look at the judge Othniel to begin with, and Othniel actually establishes the pattern for the Book of Judges. We've already talked about type scenes, literary conventions such as the ancestress in danger or the annunciation to a woman that she will have a child. The Book of Judges can be looked at as an enormous type scene that fits a particular pattern where the people begin a form of apostasy. They begin worshipping foreign gods or idols. God punishes them by turning them over to a foreign nation, and they are enslaved or repressed. The people repent. God hears them and raises up a judge to rescue them. The judge rescues the people, defeats the foreign enemy, judges for a set number of years, and dies. Then the pattern begins again as the people sink into apostasy.

But this is not simply a repetition, over and over the same pattern. There are variations on the theme, which we'll notice, and we'll also see that each time the pattern is repeated it becomes more and more tragic, as if the people are ultimately spiraling out of control, so that at the end of the Book of Judges, in fact, there are no more judges—there is only chaos.

We start with the judge Othniel, we'll move to Ehud, and then to Deborah and then to Gideon. Things are pretty good at this point. Before we start with Othniel, just a brief mention of the setting of the Book of Judges. Judges is like Joshua set at the beginning of the Iron Age, but it's simply telling us what Joshua didn't. Joshua gives us a very positive notice, a full conquering. Judges says, not quite, not quite. We didn't quite conquer everything. The Book of Judges is, like Joshua, however, presented within a Deuteronomistic framework, which means that the editor, the Deuteronomic editor, is very concerned that people who behave properly, who worship God in the appropriate way, will be rewarded and people who sin will be punished. We will see some of that comeuppance that occurs to some of these judges who do not particularly behave well.

Here we go with the basic pattern. We're going to start with Othniel. This is Judges, Chapter 3. Othniel is the first judge. The pattern begins with apostasy: "The people of Israel did what was evil. Forgetting the Lord their God, they started to worship Baalim and Asherah," the Canaanite divinities. God gets upset. YHWH leaves the people to the consequences of their action and delivers them over into the hand of the enemy, the King of Cushan-Rishathaim—it's a Mesopotamian government—and the people are then oppressed. Israel repents, and God finally hears them and raises up a judge.

The judge here is Othniel, nephew of Caleb, and we will remember Caleb from his excursions into the Promised Land with Joshua. Caleb's line continues. But already we have a slight variation on the theme to begin with. It turns out that Othniel had actually been introduced to us a couple of chapters before—we already know he's on the scene. So here we have the book already letting us know we're going to have literary conventions but we're not going to be static about it.

Othniel comes on the scene because, the rulers of the community explain, we are under oppression. Caleb announces, I will give my daughter—her name is Acsah—to the ruler, to the judge, who was able to defeat the enemy. Othniel says, I'll take her. I will volunteer. And, in fact, Othniel winds up defeating the enemy. But here is another play. Othniel's wife Acsah winds up taking the lead. After their marriage she is the one who goes to her father and demands wells for water. She's the one who demands better land. So we see right at the beginning a judge who is capable of military conquest but not quite capable of getting what he specifically needs in order to thrive. That becomes his wife's job.

We'll also see even implanted in this very first story the problem of vows. Here is a story of a father who vows his daughter to a military leader pending conquest. In our next lecture we'll encounter the judge Jephthah, who vows to sacrifice to God the first person, the first being, who comes out of his house should he win the victory in battle. When fathers promise their daughters or make vows—this is a good example with Jephthah—we see the negative side. Themes are already implanted. Othniel judges for a set number of years; he dies. The people of Israel sink back into apostasy. The pattern will continue.

The next judge we find is the judge Ehud. I need to warn you that the story of the judge Ehud is both sexual and scatological. Most people who read the Bible do not assume that the Bible has such material in it. This is supposed to be, according to contemporary views, a holy book, a divine book. If we think back to Clement of Alexandria saying, "Moses would never have said that Noah got drunk," you can see the difficulty people might have. But the Book of Judges is like Israelites on the frontier. For people trying to establish a nation—the minority group within the major Mesopotamian area of numerous stronger kingdoms—people in such situations need to tell stories that will bolster them, that will serve to humiliate the enemy, that will serve to entertain. We might think of these as stories told by soldiers out in the encampment. They are not going to pull punches, and they are going to use whatever humor, earthy as it may be, in order to get their views across.

So now that you've been warned about the judge Ehud, let's watch his story. Here is the first variation on the scene. We are told that Ehud is left-handed, which, back then as well as today, does not encompass the majority of the population, and we've got to figure we're being told that for a particular reason. Ehud is not only left-handed, he makes himself an 18-inch-long sword that he straps onto the inside of his right thigh. You can picture where the sword is and how Ehud is functioning. When Ehud goes to the enemy king—his name is Eglon, which means, by the way, "fatted calf," not a great name for a king, and we're also told Eglon is very fat—when Ehud goes to Eglon, we might expect something tricky to occur, and that is precisely what happens. Ehud has his sword strapped onto his thigh. He is patted down by Eglon's soldiers. They do not find the sword. Ehud gets into the king's court, and he says to Eglon, "I have a message for you, O king, in secret."

Now, if I were an ancient Near Eastern king, I would have my entire army standing there (knowing anything about the Israelites) just for protection. Eglon the fatted calf has a brain like a cow. He immediately sends out all his soldiers, he retires to his upper roof chamber of his summer palace, and Ehud is invited in. The two men are alone, in private. Ehud comes to him as Eglon is sitting in his cool roof chamber, the text says. But, rather than receive the message that Ehud has promised him, Eglon receives death. Ehud reaches with his left hand—and the left hand, by the way, in the ancient world as well as, in fact, in the contemporary Middle East, is the hand that's normally used by men to handle genitalia—he reaches with his left hand underneath his clothes, he pulls out his sword, and he sticks the sword right into the fatted calf's stomach. We're told that the sword stayed in. It's an image of perverse intercourse.

To people in contemporary society, it sounds disgusting. I think, to people at the beginning of the Iron Age, people who are struggling to maintain a national identity and want to see their heroes succeeding, they would have loved—they would have loved—this story. Worse, the perversity of this intercourse continues with scatology. We have the Hebrew idiom, talking about Eglon, "and the dirt came out," which is simply an idiomatic expression for "he defecated." So not only do we have the sword penetrating him in front, we have an emission. It's sexual. It's scatological. The people in antiquity would have loved it.

What happens in the plotline? Eglon's soldiers are waiting outside the room, and they are expecting the king to call him and they are waiting, and they are waiting, and they are waiting, and he hasn't opened the door. They think to themselves, "Well, maybe he's in the bathroom." The text actually says this. Finally, when they can wait no longer, they break in the doors, and they find their king lying there with Ehud's sword still stuck in him. Meanwhile, Ehud is able to escape. He rallies the Israelite troops. He gains his men, and they wind up killing 10,000 Moabites. That's Chapter 3, verse 29. That's the story of Ehud, the trickster judge who kills the king through secrecy, through beguiling him, and I think people would have laughed. That's our second judge.

The third judge comes in only a verse or two. His name is Shamgar, son of Anath. Already we have a problem here because Anath is one of the Canaanite goddesses. So we might worry a little bit about Shamgar's background. Shamgar offends the literary convention in a variety of different ways. There is no mention of public infidelity. There is no account of oppression by an enemy. There is no account of Shamgar's judging or how long he judged or even his death. We're simply told that Shamgar takes an oxgoad and kills 600 of the Philistines with it. That's it.

Offending the plot line even more, in various early manuscripts of the Hebrew text, the story of Shamgar does not show up here at the end of the story of Ehud. It shows up well later in the Book of Judges, after the story of Samson—as if the biblical editor, the Deuteronomic editor, thought, "Well, we'll put this story last because he, Shamgar, is so offensive to the pattern to the literary convention. It seemed like he might make the last judge." This also tells us how unstable that early text is. The judges can, in fact, be interchanged to some extent.

I think the story of Shamgar might also be there to give us, in effect, a commercial break in between the long story of Ehud and the story we come to next, which is the Song of Deborah and the account of Deborah in prose narrative. This is Judges, Chapters 4 and 5. The thematics of this story, the prose narrative of Deborah and the Song of Deborah, play on the thematic of mothers: good mothers, dangerous mothers, honorary mothers, and biological mothers. The play on the type scene begins immediately, for we see Deborah sitting underneath her palm tree (Judges 4:4). She's already there prior to any sort of need for military commission. But there does occur oppression. The people have gone into apostasy, and Deborah now, our only female judge—again a play on the convention—becomes the official who will commission the general to go into war.

We have problems with Deborah right from the beginning even before her commission, and we'll see this immediately in Chapter 4, verse 4, her introduction. She's called a prophetess. That's fine, although we don't really technically have prophets yet. She's also identified in Chapter 5, verse 7, as a mother in Israel, but it's not clear she actually has any children. Indeed, it's not clear she's actually married. Most English translations identify her as the "wife of Lappidoth." Mr. Lappidoth actually never shows up in this text. Husbands are a rare commodity in the Song of Deborah, as we'll see. Mr. Lappidoth is not there. Moreover, the expression "Lappidoth" can mean "of flames." So instead of looking at Deborah as "Deborah, wife of Lappidoth," we might just as well translate "Deborah, woman of flames;" which makes a good deal of sense, actually, because, when we come to her general, whose name is Barak, Barak in Hebrew means "lightning." So here is this war machine—flames and lightning going against the enemy. That may well be the case.

Deborah's relationship to Barak is also slightly problematic. Barak is the general. He is supposed to do all that military conquest, manly material. But when Deborah says to Barak, "Go into battle," Barak says, "I'm not going unless you come with me." Now, on the one hand, in a positive sense Barak might be thinking, "Well, put your money where your mouth is, lady. If you're going to send me into battle, you come, too." But I also have a sense that he's not quite ready to untie those apron strings. Deborah represents God, and she is going to go with him into the field. So Deborah says, "Yes, I will go with you. However, your honor will be lost here." As she puts it, "God will give the enemy into the hand of a woman." So because Barak is unwilling to go into battle without the woman by his side, the honor normally due to him as military leader will be taken away.

At first we might think that the woman to whom the honor will be given is Deborah. It turns out not to be the case. There is another woman in this story—her name is Jael. I really like Jael, but I find her very mysterious. Let's look at Jael for a minute. We are told that she is married. Her husband is identified as "Heber the Kenite," and this brings us back to those Kenites we've seen, already connected perhaps with Cain, connected with the Kenite hypothesis, the idea that the Kenites provided Israelites some knowledge of YHWH, the idea of the Kenites as resident aliens in the community but not fully absorbed. Heber the Kenite actually doesn't show up, and we're not technically told to what ethnic group Jael belongs. We don't know if she is Kenite or Israelite or Canaanite. She's already a mystery.

What we do know about the Kenites is they were in alliance with Israel, except that Heber the Kenite, Jael's husband, had made a treaty with the enemy. So here we have some disloyalty already shown, and then the question comes about: Whose side is Jael on? Will she fight for the Israelites? That's normally whom the Kenites would fight for. Will she fight for her husband's allies? Will she fight for herself? What are her motives? As we've already seen even back in Genesis, motives are frequently suppressed. I know what Jael does; I'm still not quite sure why.

In terms of what she does, here we go. Sisera, the enemy general, has been routed by Deborah and Barak and their troops. Sisera is using iron chariots—this is the beginning of the Iron Age—and his chariots have gotten stuck in the mud. His entire military effort is doomed. Sisera takes off on foot, and, as he is running away, he goes to the tent of Heber the Kenite because he knows Heber is loyal to his boss, the enemy. Coming out of the tent, coming out to meet him, is Jael. In the English, she says, "Turn aside, my Lord. Turn aside to me. Don't be afraid." But Hebrew has her purring like a cat coming out: "*Sura adoni, sura elai al tira.*"

She entices him in, and he comes into her tent. In fact, he says to her, "I'm thirsty. Could I have some water?" And she gives him milk. Then he lies down, and she covers him with a rug. She's a good mom. She gives milk. She covers him. She tucks him into bed. Sisera then says to her, to the woman, "Stand by the door of the tent, and, if anybody comes by and asks, 'Is there a man here?' say no." No problem for Jael. She has already unmanned him.

She's now standing guard; that should be the soldier's role. There is, in fact, no man in the tent because the manly activity is being accomplished by Jael.

Then we're told Jael, the "wife of Heber," took a tent peg and went softly to Sisera and drove the tent peg into his temple, and it went down into the ground, and he died. This is not the sort of mother most people would want. So here we go from Deborah, the mother in Israel, the battle leader who may not have any children of her own, to Jael, the false mother, who gives you milk, tucks you in, and then takes a tent peg and kills you. Here again we have, of course, another inversion to the pattern. Normally it is the judge who dispatches the enemy. Here it is a second woman unexpected—neither Barak nor Deborah but Jael—and no motive is given. We do not know why Jael does this. Deborah says in her song it's out of loyalty to Israel. But the prose narrative never actually tells you.

At the end of the prose narrative, Jael, seeming to me much like a spider inviting a fly into her parlor, goes out to meet Barak, who has finally chased Sisera down, and she says to Barak, "Come into my tent and let me show you what I have." Barak comes into the tent as he is pursuing Sisera, and there lies Sisera dead, Barak finds, with the tent peg in his temple. And thereby Barak the general also becomes unmanned. His honor is usurped by this woman, Jael. Fascinating.

But that's just the prose narrative—let's go to the poem in Chapter 5. The poem in Chapter 5 may, in fact, be one of the oldest pieces of literature we have in the entire *Tanakh*. It's exceptionally ancient. In fact, before we look at the story of Deborah and Barak and Jael and Sisera in the poem, let's just do a little bit of background information. How early is this? Although it seems like in Deborah's Song she is calling all the tribes to unity, there are certain tribes who are missing. Simeon and Levi are not mentioned. Perhaps they had already been absorbed into some of the other tribes. More striking yet, the tribe of Judah is not there. Perhaps this is a song created by people up in the north originally, where Judah is the kingdom of the south, but his absence is conspicuous and problematic.

Now to the Song of Deborah. The poem restages Sisera's death. The prose narrative is nasty, it's problematic, but it's logical because we're told Sisera is lying down out of weariness. He's exhausted, which means it's very easy to plug him with a tent peg if he's lying down. In the Song he's standing up. Now, I don't think Jael went up to Sisera with a tent peg and said, "Hold still while I kill you." This has to be looked at on a metaphorical basis, and we can actually see him dying slowly, losing his honor, losing his ability, losing his manliness. Listen to the poem. "She struck Sisera a blow. She crushed his head. She shattered and pierced his temple." This is good Israelite poetry, to say the same thing several times: "He sank, he fell. He lay still at her feet. At her feet he sank, he fell. And where he sank, there he fell, done to death."

You can picture this being recited to a group of people who are perhaps losing a war, who need a little bit of bolstering, who want to see that enemy general really tent-pegged, as it were. And this actually works. The Song of Deborah then goes on to mention Sisera's mother, who never actually shows up in the prose narrative. Here is the third mother, and, in fact, the only biological mother of the three. Sisera's mother is pictured standing in a window behind the lattice. This idea of this woman framed in a window is a standard ancient Near Eastern artistic convention. We actually have ivory depictions of this. It's very, very common. We'll see it again, actually, with Jezebel, who meets her ending by—she puts on makeup first—and then she stands in a window, and she calls out to the people who will eventually engage her death.

But here's Sisera's mother behind the lattice, as if she's trapped. She's not like Deborah out in the field or Jael in her tent. She is comfortable, and she is there with her ladies-in-waiting, and she begins to ask, "Why is my son's chariot so long in coming? Why tarry the hoofbeats of his chariots?" But then she provides herself her own answer. She answers her question: "Are they not finding and dividing the spoils—a womb or two for every man?" Most texts read "a damsel or two," "a maiden or two," but this is a much more earthy text. What happens in war? Soldiers capture women—we've seen this in descriptions of holy war—and bring them back either for sexual objects or for servitude. This is what Sisera's mother is expecting, and that's, in fact, where she's left. She will not get stuffs, spoils, she will not get a servant from the women of Israel, and her son will never return to her. She is left in that window waiting, and that's the poet's part, the Song of Deborah in ancient text, but over the centuries I think it still has that power to grab.

After Sisera dies the land stays at rest for 40 years, and then the pattern continues, and we move on to Judges, Chapters 6 through 8. This is the story of Gideon, and here, in terms of the convention, the opening is substantially expanded because Gideon, like Moses before and like Saul later, typically rejects his commission. God calls him, and he's not too sure he wants to go. Here we go. Hesitant to accept his command when the angel calls him, he says, "Wait—my tribe, the tribe of Manasseh, is weak; my family is small; I'm not that able." It's as if he's saying, "Who, me? You want me? This is crazy." We actually see him at first when an angel comes to him, and we're told that the angel comes to him when he is hiding in a winepress beating wheat, but out of the eyes of the Midianites so that they can't see him.

There he is, hiding and beating this wheat, and the angel comes to him and announces, "The Lord is with you, you mighty man of valor." Now, if you were a military leader out in the camp, it makes a good deal of sense to say that. But the fact that he's hiding suggests that this opening might be a little bit more humorous than we would expect. The angel commissions him, but Gideon is not quite willing to go. He responds to the angel, "Pray, sir, if the Lord is with us, why has all this befallen us? Where are all his wonderful deeds which our ancestors recounted to us, saying, 'Did not the Lord bring us up out of Egypt?'" Gideon raises a good question. "Where are all those good miracles—what's happening? I'm stuck here in a winepress beating wheat." Something better has to happen.

He more or less accepts his commission, but he continues to put God to the test. He puts a fleece on the ground and says, "Tomorrow let it be dry," and then he says, "but tomorrow let it be wet." He continues to test God with these little petty miracles just to make sure that God will actually come through. Finally Gideon engages in battle, but, consistent with his hesitancy, just as he tested God, he will test his own men. He starts out with 22,000 men. He whittles it down to 10,000 and then finally to 300. And, by the way, for those of you familiar with the Gideon Bible, it's in this particular section that the Gideons from the Gideon Bible took their name. I actually looked it up in the Gideon Bible. This is what the opening passage says: They take their inspiration from Gideon, "who led a small band of men dedicated to the service of God." Those are those 300.

Gideon actually routs the enemy with his 300. Everything looks terrific. It's going great. Then problems begin again. Gideon's other name is "Jerubaal," which means "let Baal contend." There is a pagan background here, a Canaanite connection, and Gideon's final action is one of apostasy. We're told that Gideon made an *ephod*, some sort of idol, out of the gold captured from the Ishmaelites—a group of his enemies—in fact, from their earrings that they were wearing, that Gideon's men had taken in booty. From this gold he fashions an *ephod*, and we're told that this became a snare to Gideon and his family. Gideon and his family go astray.

The people come to Gideon, and they say, "Become a ruler after us, you and your sons and your sons following." In other words, establish a dynasty. Gideon says, "No, God is your ruler. God will be the one who will protect you." And that may be just as well, given his apostasy. But it turns out that Gideon has many sons. He has one son with the problematic name Abimelech, which translates "my father is king." One worries about a man who on the one hand denies dynastic rule but on the other hand names his child "my father is king." We will come to Abimelech in the next lecture. He will prove to be a false judge, and, with his tenure, the benefits of the charismatic leadership become increasingly insecure.

So we'll end this talk with just a brief mention of what happens with Gideon, and then we'll prepare for this downhill battle as we move from Abimelech, the false judge, to Jephthah, the judge who kills his daughter, to Samson, the judge who doesn't even realize his own commission to the people out of control. Here is the end of this section as we have it. After Gideon's death the Israelites again "whored after the Baalim and Baal-Berith." Most texts say "went astray;" the Hebrew actually says "whored after." This is a standard Hebrew idiom for apostasy. We'll see it especially in the prophets. And who are the people going after? The Canaanite gods, but, worse, not only Baalim, Canaanite gods, but a god called Baal-Berith, which translates "Lord of the Covenant"—a false god but with echoes of the Israelite deity. The text goes on, "They were unmindful of the Lord their God who had delivered them from all their enemies around them." What will then happen? We'll have to wait until the next lecture to see.

The Book of Judges, Part II
(Judges 8–21)
Lecture 14

A judge is not simply someone who would sit in a courtroom and engage in decision making over land disputations or over whose ox gored whose. To the contrary, judges are charismatic leaders imbued by the spirit of God. ... In the second part of the Book of Judges, that the entire institution begins to break down as the judges don't immediately receive the spirit or don't receive it at all as they make rash vows, and, by the time we get up to Samson, they are not even aware of what their divine commission is.

Abimelech, the false judge, embodies the threat of dynasties. His usurpation of power highlights the inevitable dynastic problem: competition. Gideon rejected dynastic rule (8:22–23) in favor of rule by God. Abimelech, the child of Gideon's Shechemite concubine, convinces the Shechemites that he, rather than one of the seventy sons of Gideon's wives, would make their appropriate leader: nepotism triumphs over legitimacy and qualification. Abimelech kills all his seventy brothers save Jotham, the youngest (9:5). Throughout the Deuteronomic history, dynastic succession exists in tension with the traditions of charismatic leaders and the ambivalence concerning primogeniture. Although Gideon consistently receives divine aid, God sends an "evil spirit" between Abimelech and the Shechemite lords (9:23); rulers require divine as well as political support. Abimelech exacerbates his father's idolatry. Gideon (Jerubaal) made an *ephod*, likely an image of a local god (8:27). Abimelech, supported by his Shechemite mother's relatives, receives funding from the Shechemite temple of "*Ba'al Berit*" (ironically, "Lord of the Covenant" [9:4]). The scene evokes Gen. 34, the rape of Jacob's daughter by Shechem (the prince of the land and, symbolically, the entire city). Abimelech is killed when "some woman" (9:53) drops a millstone on his head. Horrified at this ignoble end, Abimelech orders his aide to kill him (9:50–57). The scene ends not with a reigning judge and peace, but a dead judge and a curse.

Jephthah (11:1–12:7), the tragic judge, shows the problems with appropriate selection. "Jephthah ... the son of a prostitute, was a mighty warrior ... When [Gilead's] wife's sons grew up, they drove Jephthah away, saying to him, 'You shall not inherit anything in our father's house, for you are the son of another woman'" (11:1–2). The opening recollects Ishmael and Isaac (Gen. 21:10). It anticipates David: Both rulers function initially as outlaws (Jdg. 11:3; 1 Sam. 25).

Jephthah is commissioned not by God, but by his town's leaders: "Are you not the very ones who rejected me and drove me out of my father's house?" Yet he agrees: "*If you bring me home again* ... I will be your head" (11:9). The reversal of the convention and the absence of divine involvement indicate the breakdown of the political system. The conditional response anticipates the rash vow Jephthah later makes. The desire for "home" increases Jephthah's tragedy.

Later (11:29), "the spirit of the Lord" comes upon Jephthah. He immediately vows: "If you will give the Ammonites into my hand, then whoever comes out of the doors of my house to meet me, when I return victorious from the Ammonites, shall be the Lord's, to be offered up by me as a burnt offering" (11:30–31). The lateness of the commission raises questions of divine culpability. The vow has no excuse. Jephthah appears incapable of accepting his own worth.

At the victory, Jephthah's daughter emerges—as is typical for women—in celebration: "She was his only child. He had no son or daughter except her" (11:34). The verse echoes the *Akedah*: "your son, your only son ..." Jephthah blames his daughter: "Alas, my daughter, you have brought me very low. You have become the cause of great trouble to me ..." (11:35). She supports him: "My father, you have opened your mouth to the Lord; do to me according to what has gone forth from your mouth ..." The sacrifice is delayed while the daughter mourns her virginity. This becomes "a custom in Israel," perhaps a puberty or premarital rite. Or, as J. Cheryl Exum suggests, is "she" "an example" of daughters sacrificed to fathers' interests (cf. Othniel and Acsah; later, Saul and Michal)?

Jephthah's victory comes at the expense of tribal unity when Ephraim revolts. The problem is now internal to Israel, not external. His household tragedy assumes national implications.

Samson, Israel's Hercules (13:1–16:31), will eclipse, like the sun that is his leitmotif. Samson's nativity spoofs conventional annunciations. His parents are childless, and there is no indication that they want children, unlike their Genesis counterparts. Mrs. Manoah meets an angel in the field who announces, "Behold, you are barren and have no child." This is news? The angel informs Mrs. Manoah that she will become pregnant, the child should be a Nazirite, and he will deliver his people from the Philistines. She accepts this oracle without question; the same cannot be said for Manoah (13:6). Manoah, after a ridiculous conversation with the angel, invites the angel to lunch (cf. Gen. 18:1–15); the angel suggests offering a sacrifice instead, which he does. When the angel ascends in the flames, Manoah fears he and his wife will die, because they have "seen God." His wife retorts, "If the Lord had meant to kill us, he would not have accepted the burnt offering …" (13:23).

Samson and Delilah.

Samson's career spoofs, then tragically reverses, that of other judges. Breaking his Nazirite vows, Samson consumes honey from a lion's carcass. He thus violates the commandment against eating (from) carrion. He insists

235

on marrying a Philistine, against his parents' objections. When Samson is betrayed by his wife, his "military" action is against his bride's family. Samson burns Philistine fields; the Philistines burn Samson's wife and her father.

Delilah, the woman "from Sorek" whom Samson loved, is a complex figure. Viewed as Philistine, Delilah has a Hebrew name (cognate to *Layla*, "night"); she is the inverse of Samson, the symbol of sun and fire. Viewed as immoral, she never lies to Samson, but she does betray him to the Philistines. Viewed as mercenary, her motives are unexpressed: Might she fear Philistine reprisal? Is her cajoling a warning?

The story can be read at its end as if it is a tragedy like the story of Oedipus. Why does Samson reveal his secret to Delilah? She arranges to have his hair, the source of his power, shaved off. Returned to a state of infancy—bald, sightless, and helpless—Samson eventually regains hair, strength, and a modicum of maturity. He dies pulling down the Philistine temple. Thus ends the period of the judges.

With the Danites, the type scene is fully broken; chaos follows. Micah's story hints of Samson's and anticipates that of the Levite's concubine. Micah is "in the hill country of Ephraim," the Levite's home (17:1; 19:1). He obtains from his mother the "cursed" eleven hundred pieces of silver (17:1), the same amount received for Samson's betrayal. He buys a Levite and procures Teraphim, but the Danites steal both. The Danites represent the descent of the community into apostasy (18:1–31). Jonathan, son of Gershom, son of Moses (some manuscripts read "Manasseh"), and his sons were priests to the Danites until the exile. Dan and Beth-el held the Northern Kingdom's major shrines: perhaps this story and the next developed c. 622, during Josiah's reform, which included disenfranchising Levites and centralizing sacrifice in Jerusalem. The story is prefaced by "In those days there was no king in Israel" (18:1).

The story of the Levite's concubine reprises Sodom's destruction (Gen. 19), without divine intervention. The narrative opens with a text-critical problem. The Septuagint (19:2) reads that the concubine "became angry with [the

Levite]." The Hebrew reads, "she played the whore" (anticipating prophetic metaphors). The Levite follows her "to speak tenderly to her" (19:3). The expression recollects Shechem, Dinah's rapist, and, again, anticipates prophetic metaphors.

The story replaces Sodom with a Benjaminite city. The Levite bypasses lodging in the non-Israelite city, Jebus; this is Jerusalem. When they enter Gibeah, another Ephraimite gives them lodging. The Benjaminites, "a perverse lot," demand of the stranger, "that we may know him." The old man, like Lot, offers his own virgin daughter and Levite's concubine. The Levite "seized his concubine and put her out to them. They wantonly raped her, and abused her all the night until the morning" (19:25). In the morning, the Levite, seeing her "lying at the door of the house, with her hands on the threshold," commands: "Get up; we are going" (19:27–28). "She made no reply." The concubine's body now summons, and symbolizes, broken Israel. The Levite, in a perverse sacrifice, hacks her body into twelve pieces, which he distributes to the tribes. The attendant message is: "Has such a thing ever happened since the day that the Israelites came up from the land of Egypt?" (19:30). The tribes gather; the war leads to more loss as Benjamin's existence is threatened. To preserve the tribe, hundreds of women are given to Benjamin; rapes escalate. The text ends with the refrain "there was no king in Israel; every man did what was right in his own eyes" (21:25), and so sets the stage for the monarchy. ■

Suggested Reading

Phyllis Trible, *Texts of Terror: Literary-Feminist Readings of Biblical Narratives*.

See also works listed for Lecture 13.

Questions to Consider

1. Does the sacrifice of Jephthah's daughter provoke a reconsideration of the *Akedah*?

2. Why does Delilah, along with other women who trick men (such as Potiphar's wife in Gen. 39, a story we have not directly addressed) escape narrative judgment?

3. How does the story of Moses from Exodus through Deuteronomy contribute both to supporting the institution of the charismatic leader and undermining this system in favor of a dynastic monarchy?

The Book of Judges, Part II
(Judges 8–21)
Lecture 14—Transcript

From the stories of Othniel and Ehud and Deborah and Gideon we can see that a judge is not simply someone who would sit in a courtroom and engage in decision making over land disputations or over whose ox gored whose. To the contrary, judges are charismatic leaders imbued by the spirit of God. The spirit actually enters into them. Then they function primarily as military leaders but also as public figures who can lead the land both into safety and then into peace. The problem is, in the second part of the Book of Judges, that the entire institution begins to break down as the judges don't immediately receive the spirit or don't receive it at all as they make rash vows, and, by the time we get up to Samson, as they are not even aware of what their divine commission is.

So in the second part of discussion on the Book of Judges we'll see how the community descends into chaos as the office of judge itself falls apart. We'll first meet Abimelech, whom we've already encountered in the last lecture, the false judge. We will move on to Jephthah, the tragic judge. Then we'll see Samson, judge as farce. Finally, at the end of the book where there are no judges, we'll see the apostasy of the tribe of Dan and then finally the rape of the Levite's concubine, a rape that signals finally the complete and total chaos into which the covenant community has sunk.

We begin here with Abimelech, Abimelech whose father is Gideon and Abimelech whose name is "my father is king"—that's what the Hebrew means. He is, however, a false judge, and we know he is set up right from the beginning to be a problem. Gideon has many, many wives and many sons. This will, of course, be a problem with Solomon and David and questions of dynastic succession. But here Abimelech is not the son of the legitimate wife; he is the son of a concubine. Concubinage was a perfectly normal category in ancient Israel. One took a wife to produce a legitimate heir, and, if one were a king, one would take a wife for alliance concerns. One takes a concubine for sexual pleasure, and, if the concubine happens to conceive a child, there is no guarantee that that child will inherit anything from the estate of the father.

So here is Gideon, the child of the concubine. He wants to inherit. He takes matters into his own hands. How is he going to get rid of all of his brothers? He winds up murdering them all. This is not a great way to start. What we're told in Judges 9, verse 4, is that he begins association with a group of reckless and worthless fellows, and he kills his brothers, the 70 sons of Jerubaal. That's Gideon. He butchers them all on the same stone block, with only his youngest brother Jotham escaping. Already this is abundantly evident: we have a false judge here.

Moreover, Abimelech, in order to ensure support, goes to his mother's family, and it turns out his mother is from Shechem, that location where Joshua engaged in covenant making but also the place back in Genesis, Chapter 34, where Jacob's daughter Dinah had been raped, and we'll encounter Shechem later on as well. It will become finally the capital of the northern kingdom of Israel, and, after the Israelite fall to Assyria, Shechem becomes renamed Samaria, one of the later enemies of Israel. So Shechem is a problem. And the god of Shechem is identified as Baal-Berith—we've encountered this before. The expression means "Lord of the covenant," but what we have here is a false judge and a false god. What we want is the Israelite God of the covenant, not this Shechemite god, false god. Abimelech gets money from his mother's family. He kills his brothers. God simply will not stand for this.

Finally, God, instead of sending a good spirit, a holy spirit, into Abimelech, sends an evil spirit into the people, and they revolt against Abimelech. The Shechemite Lord said, "We have had enough of this," and, as the text said, this was done in order that the violent murder of the 70 sons of Jerubaal might recoil on their brother, Abimelech, who committed the murder and might also recoil on the people of Shechem who encouraged him to do that. That's Judges 9:24.

A war occurs, and Abimelech is killed himself in the same sort of ignominious manner in which Sisera is dispatched. During the fight a woman from an upper apartment drops a millstone used for grinding bread on top of Abimelech's head and shatters his skull. Abimelech thinks with his dying breath and his dying thought, I can't have it be said that I was dispatched by a woman, so he calls one of his soldiers to run him through with a sword so it will not be said that Abimelech was killed by a woman. But Abimelech has died, and at this point YHWH is getting annoyed with these people, upset with these people. The convention continues—apostasy, apostasy. And YHWH says, "I am not going to raise up any more judges for you." We can hear his anger in Chapter 10. YHWH states, "Did I not deliver you from the Egyptians and the Amorites and the Ammonites and from the Philistines and from the Sidonians and from the Amalekites?" and he goes on and on and on—"There will be no other judge."

But the people again sink into apostasy, and then they repent, and they need a judge, and nothing is happening. So here, in a variation on the scene, the people raise up their own judge. They call a fellow named Jephthah, and he becomes our tragic judge in a story of enormous pathos. This is Judges, Chapter 11. Jephthah also has ignominious beginnings. Abimelech is a child of a concubine. Jephthah is the child of a prostitute. So obviously he's not going to inherit anything from his father. It turns out that his father has numerous other legitimate sons, and they want to drive Jephthah away. As the text said, "They drove him away, saying, 'You shall not inherit anything in our father's house for you are the son of another woman.'" We might be reminded here back in Genesis of Sarah saying to Abraham, "Drive out the slave girl and her son, Hagar and Ishmael, because the son of the slave woman will not inherit with my son, Isaac." We'll see this over and over again, Judges replaying scenes in Genesis. But whereas in Genesis God almost invariably comes to the rescue, in Judges he rarely does.

Jephthah is driven away, and he gathers about himself reckless and worthless fellows just like Abimelech, indeed, just like King David. But all three have different fates. Abimelech is the false judge: his reckless and worthless companions are of no help to him. Jephthah is the tragic judge: his reckless and worthless companions become part of his army. David is the ideal king: he takes over. There is no worthlessness, there is no tragedy, in his companions.

Jephthah has, in effect, an army of brigands with him, and the townspeople come to him, and they say, "Be our ruler, be our judge. Help us remove the oppressive forces which are pushing us down, oppressing us." Jephthah says to the townspeople, "Aren't you the very ones who rejected me and drove me out of my father's house?" But Jephthah, the tragic judge, is yearning for a home, yearning for some stability, and he responds finally, "Yes, I will lead you if you bring me back home." In fact, they agree to that.

So Jephthah becomes the leader, and he turns out to be the most faithful Yahwist of all, the most faithful in terms of the covenant community's religious basis. Instead of immediately going to war he goes to the enemy, and he actually begins by pursuing peace. He says, "What have we done against you? We don't want to go to war with you. We simply want to inherit and settle in the land that God has promised us." He recites Israel's salvation history, and only after that are we told he received the spirit of the Lord. God relents on his thought, "I will not raise up a judge," and actually gives the Holy Spirit to Jephthah.

But then we here have a problem because immediately after Jephthah receives this Holy Spirit he makes a vow. He vows to God, "If you will give the Ammonites into my hand, then whoever comes out of the doors of my house to meet me when I return victorious from the Ammonites shall be the Lord's to be offered up by me as a burnt offering." One wonders already about the culpability of God here sending the Holy Spirit and then finding this rash vow. I also wonder about many biblical scholars who have commented on this particular verse. One frequently finds in Bible notations or in textbooks the idea that Jephthah was really expecting a puppy dog to come out of the house. I think this is a cop-out on the part of scholars. The vow is rash. There is no excuse. We don't even know if he has a dog. The fact is, Jephthah simply cannot believe that good things will happen to him. He sets himself up for failure.

And indeed that is precisely what happens. Jephthah has a victory, and, coming out of the house, as we might expect, is his daughter, because whenever the men have a victory the women always come out in celebration with dancing and tambourines. We've seen it with Miriam; we will see it again with the women celebrating David's victories. But we're told about this particular celebration, his daughter comes out and, the text reads, "She was his only child. He had no son or daughter except her." Here are the parallels with Isaac—we recall from the *Akedah*—"your only son, the son whom you love." Jephthah realizes the result of his vow, what will have to happen, and Jephthah simply can't deal with it, and he does the only thing that he possibly can. He strikes out at his daughter. He says, "Alas, my daughter, you have brought me very low. You have become the cause of great trouble for me." Or, as one biblical paraphrase puts it, "You have broken my heart." It's not exactly what the text says, but I think that captures the meaning.

The daughter, ensuring his compliance with the vow and providing him solace at the same time, responds, "My father, you have opened your mouth to the Lord. Do to me according to what has gone forth from your mouth." It's as if she can't bring herself to use the word "sacrifice." Before her death, however, the daughter requests two months to mourn her virginity, as the text says, with her friends, and they go up to the mountain. This may be an etiology for a woman's festival, perhaps a puberty rite or prenuptial rite, and it became a custom in Israel, so we are told, that the daughters of Israel went year by year to lament the daughter of Jephthah, the Gileadite, four days during the year. This becomes a custom.

Jephthah does to her as he had promised. We do not see the daughter again. Biblical scholar J. Cheryl Exum suggests that "not only did Jephthah's daughter's mourning become a custom in Israel, but in fact Jephthah's daughter is for the Book of Judges a custom in Israel." We've already seen this with the story of Othniel, with parents like Caleb vowing their daughters for military victory. But, whereas for Caleb's daughter Acsah it worked out well, for Jephthah's unnamed daughter tragedy accrues, and indeed the tragedy will continue to accrue. The chaos continues. Jephthah has won the battle, but suddenly the difficulties come from inside Israel rather than from outside. The tribe of Ephraim revolts against Jephthah. They say to him, "Why did you cross over to fight the Ammonites and did not call us to go with you? We will burn your house over you with fire." Who knew? People wanted to go to war, they didn't get summoned, and now they revolt.

The Gileadites, Jephthah's group, arranged to fight the Ephraimites, and they wound up killing 42,000 of them. Indeed, they guarded a river, the Gileadites did, and whenever the Ephraimites attempted to cross they put a test to them. They said, "Say the word 'shibboleth.'" It has come into English as a code word or a password. It turns out the Ephraimites could not pronounce the word. They wound up saying "sibboleth." So the Gileadites could tell by their accent, again signaling a break in the community, who were their friends and who were their enemies. Forty-two thousand dead Ephraimites: the problem is now violence internal to the community rather than violence on the outside. We can see Israel spiraling down.

And so we come to the next judge, Samson. Samson is like Hercules, only stupid. He's also like the sun, which is his leitmotif. Indeed, ultimately we will see that Samson, like the sun, burns himself out. We begin, actually, the story of Samson with yet another type scene, yet another literary convention. This is the annunciation type scene, the model of an angel or priest or seer explaining or promising to a woman that she will have a child who will go on to do great things. Indeed, the beginning of the Samson story starts out pretty much the way several of those stories in Genesis started.

We find out that there is an Israelite couple, and they have no children. We have an infertile wife. Except in this type scene, which seems to be a parody, this Israelite couple does not much seem to care that they are infertile. The wife is not saying to the husband, "Give me children or I shall die." There is no indication that they want children at all. Samson's father's name is Manoah. His wife is not named. We will call her Mrs. Manoah for lack of a better term. Mrs. Manoah is out in the field one day, and an angel appears to her and announces, "Behold, you are barren and have no child." This is news? But then he says to her, "You will become pregnant and you will have a son. You will make him to be a Nazirite," a particular holy person within Israel known for not cutting their hair and also from refraining from any sort of wine or strong drink. Nazirite vows are usually taken for a set period of time. Samson is to be a Nazirite from the day of his birth. The mother says this is fine.

She goes back home, and she announces to Manoah, "I met an angel in the field. He told me I'm going to get pregnant. I'm going to have a son." Manoah is a little concerned about this and starts asking his wife lots of questions. Finally he says, "Listen, the next time you are out in the field and the angel appears to you, come get me so I can see what's happening." And lo and behold the next day she is out in the field, and an angel appears, and

Manoah comes out. Manoah says to the angel, "What have you been saying to my wife?" and the angel, who is getting somewhat frustrated here—you can see how this is a play on the original annunciation type scenes—said, "Look, your wife has already told you everything. I've already told her. Why do you need for me to repeat it?" But the angel does.

Manoah, then, after listening to all this, invites the angel to lunch. We've already seen this back in Genesis when the three men representing God come to Abraham and Abraham invites them to a meal and they predict that Abraham will have a son. But the angel says, "Well, lunch is not really quite what is needed. Perhaps"—hint, hint—"you might offer a sacrifice to God." Manoah picks up on the hint and offers a sacrifice to God, and the angel goes into the flames and ascends into heaven, at which point Manoah thinks, "We've just seen God. We'll die." Mrs. Manoah has to explain to him, "Look, dear, it's unlikely we're going to die because I'm supposed to have this baby. If we die right now I will not have this child and this child will not redeem his people. Therefore, don't worry about it." Samson, as we'll see, very much takes after his father.

Samson's career, like his nativity scene, basically spoofs that of the other judges, at least at the beginning. Samson's play on the convention is that he has long hair. That would have meant something to people in the ancient Near East, where we have lots of inscriptions and artistic depictions of rulers with long hair, usually seven long locks. They are what used to be called "banana curls" for those of you of a certain age. Gilgamesh is usually depicted with these seven long locks. This is where Samson's strength resides—it's the sign of his Nazirite vow.

But it's not entirely clear that Samson realizes he's a Nazirite. Nazerites are supposed to keep themselves in states of ritual purity, but one of the first adventures Samson has is to encounter a lion and kill it and later on notice that bees have taken up residence in the lion's carcass. Samson eats some of the honey that the bees have produced. One is not supposed to eat anything dealing with blood. One is not supposed to deal with an animal which is carrion. That is entirely unkosher, and Samson eats it. Either he doesn't know his vow, or he doesn't take it seriously. Then next he insists on marrying a Philistine woman, and his parents say, sounding like many parents even today, "Look, can't you find a girl from your own family, from your own tribe?" But Samson insists, "She pleases me. Get her for me," and the parents yield, and he marries this Philistine woman.

As part of the wedding ceremony, Samson tells a riddle, and the answer to the riddle is, in fact, this lion with the honey in its carcass. Part of the riddle is, whoever guesses it gets riches from the riddle's teller. So the wife's relatives come to the wife and they say, "Get the answer for it so we can obtain from Samson his wealth." And the wife goes up to Samson and she starts cajoling him, day after day after day, "Tell me the answer to your riddle." Finally Samson gives in, and it's a good thing, too, for the wife, because the Philistines had said to her, "If you don't get the answer we're going to burn you and your father and your household." Good thing for the wife.

So she gets the answer, and she tells the Philistines, and the Philistines, on the last night of the wedding feast, say to Samson, "We have the answer to your riddle." Samson responds in good idiomatic Hebrew, "If you had not plowed with my heifer you never would have come up with the answer to this riddle." He is furious. He's absolutely furious because he has been betrayed. He winds up setting fire to the Philistine fields, and the Philistines, of course, are simply furious as well, and they wind up burning alive Samson's Philistine wife and her father. For the wife there is no way she can win, and she represents the tragedies of women in this book to come.

And poor Samson, he's now without a wife. He encounters a prostitute in the next scene. That's not going to get him anywhere. Finally he comes to a woman whose name has become legendary—Delilah. We don't actually know very much about Delilah. She's usually identified as a Philistine, but her ethnic background is never given. She may well be an Israelite. She's entirely independent. She is not somebody's daughter. She is not somebody's wife. She's on her own. She seems to own her own house, and she hobnobs with the rich and famous in the Valley of Sorek, where she lives. The Philistine leaders know all about her. We are told that Samson loves her, but we are never told that she loves him. One can hear echoes of Isaac and Rebecca back here.

The Philistines come up to Delilah, and they say, "We will give you a huge sum of money if you give Samson over into our hands," and Delilah proceeds to do precisely that. But, again, what's her motive? Is it to betray Samson to the Philistines because she is loyal to the Philistines, or does she know what the Philistines are capable of? They've already killed one of Samson's wives. Perhaps they will now kill her, Samson's lover. I'm not sure why she acts, but she does it quite well. She needs to find out from Samson the secret of his hair, and she starts cajoling him and cajoling him and cajoling him, and we readers, recognizing Samson's general dimwittedness, realize that the poor schlemiel is going to tell her the secret to his strength in any case, and finally he does.

The irony here is that Delilah signals to Samson time after time what she's doing. The first several times Samson lies to her, and she responds, "Samson, the Philistines are upon you," and he breaks his bonds and fights them off. He knows exactly what she's doing. She never lies to him. She never withholds the truth. And he's experienced these Philistines coming at him. Why he finally tells her the truth remains an open question. Is he trying to find some woman whom he can finally trust? He couldn't trust the Philistine wife to begin with. He can't trust the prostitute. Is he looking for trust here?

The Philistines actually capture him because he gives Delilah the secret: "My strength lies in my hair." So Delilah shaves his head, and, as he's resting on her knees, like an infant, bald and helpless, the Philistines come, and they attack him, and they put out his eyes, and they take him in chains, and they bring him to the city of Gaza. Here is Samson, like an infant, totally helpless, sightless. But slowly and inexorably his hair starts growing back, and his strength starts coming back. Finally his fidelity comes, and he prays to God, "Oh, Lord God, remember me, I pray you, and strengthen me." And through God's response and his long hair, Samson finally is able to accomplish what he was meant to accomplish. Chained to pillars holding up a Philistine temple, he pulls the pillars down, and the Philistines die all around him, and Samson dies in the rubble. He brings to death more Philistines during his death than he ever did at his life.

The story can be read at its end as if it is a tragedy like the story of Oedipus. The hero, blinded, finally comes to some sort of self-awakening, but it is a tragedy, and Samson, like the sun, is finally and totally eclipsed.

From the story of Samson we move on to the account of the shrine of Micah, which begins with a refrain that will echo again in Judges: "In those days there was no king in Israel." Here the type scene is fully broken. We will have no more judges. What we have is a guy named Micah living in the hills of Ephraim, and the first thing he does, we are told, is he steals a substantial amount of money, silver, from his mother—1,100 pieces of silver—and that turns out to be precisely the amount of money that the Philistines paid Delilah. Is Micah's mother Delilah? We don't know because we never actually find out what happens to Delilah.

But Micah admits to his mother he has stolen the silver, and the mother says, "Dear, it's all right. We'll use some of the silver to make an idol." You can see how downhill this tribe is going. So they make an idol, a pagan image, a molten image, and Micah sets up the shrine in his home, and first he has one of his sons become the priest, but later he encounters a Levite, and he says to the Levite, "I will give you 10 pieces of silver a year and a suit of clothes and your living. The priesthood is up for sale." And the priest becomes the priest to Micah's house.

Meanwhile, the tribe of Dan, who, as we have seen before, is looking for an inheritance in the land, stops by Micah's house to check with the Levite to find out if he's got any information on this. It turns out, they think to themselves, perhaps having a Levite is not a bad idea. So they say to the Levite, we're going to take you away, and, when the Levite complains, the tribe of Dan responds, "Keep quiet. Put your hand to your mouth and come with us and be to us a father and a priest. Is it better for you to be a priest in the house of one man or to be a priest to a tribe of a family in Israel?" In other words, it's a bigger job, it's an advancement in his career. We're told the priest's heart was glad, and he took Micah's *ephod*, his idol, as well as his *teraphim*, his family tribal signatories, perhaps gods, as well as a graven image, and he went in the midst of the Danites.

The Danites, of course, represent the descent of the community into apostasy, for, in their new city which they named Dan, the Danites set up the graven image for themselves, and we're told Jonathan the son of Gershom the son of Moses and his sons were priests to the tribe of Dan until the day of the captivity of the land. Moses' grandson, Moses' children, are also sinking into apostasy. Not surprisingly, there are some manuscripts which, instead of reading "Moses" read "Manasseh," as if certain scribes could not bear the idea that Moses's descendants would sink so low. The pagan encroachment has gone from one family to an entire tribe, and it will get worse because the final episode of the Book of Judges, beginning again, "There was no king in Israel, and every man did what was right in his own eyes" starts out with a man, again from the hill country of Ephraim, and he has a concubine, and we already know concubines are dangerous.

The concubine becomes angry with this man. The man is a Levite, a priest. The Hebrew actually reads, "She played the whore against him." The Greek simply says, "She became angry." I think the Hebrew might have been added on later, somehow to justify what happens to this woman. But in fact nothing justifies her fate. The concubine runs away to her father's house, but we already know the father's house is no place of safety for women in Judges. The Levite comes after her to speak tenderly to her. It's the same expression Shechem uses to Dinah, the girl he has already raped. And the father finally says, "Take my daughter and go," and they begin to go back home.

They bypass the town that will eventually become Jerusalem because they want to stay in a city that is an Israelite city—they think they will be safe. They enter the town of Gibeah, which is a Benjaminite city—it should have been okay—where another Ephraimite provides them lodging. Here we have a replay of Lot and Sodom, with visitors coming in to find lodging, but here the scene is worse than Sodom because these are not pagans. These are Benjaminites; they are in the family. The Benjaminites come out to the house of the man who has taken in the Levite and his concubine, and they say, "Send out the stranger that we may know him." Lot in Genesis 19 offered his two virgin daughters to the Sodomites. But Lot and his daughters were protected by the angels who had come to lodge with him. There is no angelic protection here.

The Levite seizes his concubine and pushes her out the door, and they wantonly rape her all night long and abuse her until the dawn. In the morning the Levite opens the door, and the text says, "He sees her lying at the door of the house with her hands on the threshold." He commands her, commands her, "Get up, we're going." And the text again says, "She made no reply." It's not even clear she's dead yet, but she is certainly dying. The Levite puts her on his donkey and brings her home and, in the most perverse sacrifice of all, hacks her body into 12 pieces and sends the pieces off to the 12 tribes of Israel with the attendant message, "Has such a thing ever happened since the days that the Israelites came up from the land of Egypt?"

The tribes gather, and they go to war against Benjamin, and the Benjaminites are almost wiped out. But then the tribes realize, we are a 12-tribe league. We cannot have genocide of one particular tribe. How does one repopulate Benjamin? They go find other women, other virgins, and give them to the Benjaminites, so one rape leads to more rapes and leads to more rapes after that. And the book ends in Chapter 21, verse 25, "In those days there was no king in Israel. Every man did what was right in his own eyes." Clearly a monarchy will be the only solution.

Samuel and Saul
(1 Samuel)
Lecture 15

First Samuel does not begin with a monarchy. To the contrary, it begins
with the birth of Samuel and what looks like a very calm and pleasant
society, as if somehow we're back to the good old days.

The tribal confederacy under the leadership of judges had disintegrated,
but the increasing threat of Philistine power made a centralized
government desirable. Samuel, who represents the transition from
charismatic leader to prophet, combines the roles of priest, prophet, and
judge. His wife's personal emptiness symbolizes the problems of the nation.
Unable to have a child, Hannah recollects Sarah, Rebecca, and Rachel.
Mocked by her fertile co-wife, she resembles Sarah. So distressed about her
infertility, when her husband asks, "Am I not more to you than ten sons?" (1
Sam. 1:8), she can make no answer.

At Shiloh, her encounter with the priest Eli anticipates the fall of Eli's
house and implies the rejection of the priest as national leader at this stage
of Israel's history. Hannah prays passionately for a child; Eli, seeing her
lips move but hearing no words, assumes she is drunk and berates her. Eli
cannot control his sons, who take the best portions of the sacrifices (1 Sam.
2:12–17) and have intercourse with women at the sanctuary (2:22). When
Hannah relates the truth, Eli prophesies her pregnancy and, thereby, evokes
the annunciation type scene. She promises to dedicate her son to God; he
will, therefore, replace Eli's sons.

Hannah's hymn, "The Song of Hannah" (the model for Mary's Magnificat
[Luke 1:46–55]), introduces extensive political concerns. It predicts social
upheaval: the mighty brought down; the weak uplifted. It predicts Hannah's
own changing circumstance: the barren made fertile. It locates the monarchy
under divine support and direction.

Samuel's commission comes while he is under Eli's care. Weaning Samuel, Hannah brings him to Shiloh; each year, she returns, bringing him a knitted coat (2:19). The "word of the Lord" (3:1), "rare in those days," comes to Samuel when he is "lying down in the temple, where the ark of God was" (3:3). Eli's promise of a dynasty, offered in 2:30, is revoked, and Samuel becomes God's agent: "All Israel from Dan to Beersheva knew that Samuel was established as a prophet of the Lord ... for the Lord revealed himself to Samuel at Shiloh ..." (3:19–4:1). Samuel combines the strengths of Israel's earlier leaders: Like Moses, God speaks to him; like Aaron, he has priestly duties; like Joshua, he unites the people and sets up a witness-stone (called "Ebenezer," stone of help, 7:12), like Deborah, he "judged Israel all the days of his life" (7:15).

That Samuel and his role as judge, prophet, and priest will not prevail is foreshadowed by the capture of the ark, the first event to occur under his leadership (1 Sam. 4–7). The ark's peripatetic journey adds unexpected humor. When the ark is brought to the Philistine temple at Ashdod, Dagon the idol keeps bowing to it. Re-erected, the idol falls apart. Ashdod's residents ship the ark to Gath, the home of Goliath. Breaking out in "tumors" (RSV) or "hemorrhoids" (JB), the Gathites ship the ark to Ekron. The people of Ekron cry, "They have brought around to us the ark of the God of Israel, to slay us and our people" (5:10). Finally, the Philistines tie the ark to two cows, which head to Beth Shemesh. There, the Levites detach the ark and sacrifice the cows. The ark remains in Keriath-Je'arim for twenty years, until David establishes his capital in Jerusalem (2 Sam. 6).

Samuel's history frames the ark narrative: It begins when he takes office; it ends with a mention of his latter years. "When Samuel became old, he made his sons judges over Israel ... his sons did not walk in his ways, but turned aside after gain; they took bribes and perverted justice" (1 Sam. 8:1–3). The "unworthy son" motif (Moses, Gideon, Eli) continues the polemic against dynastic succession. Given that the judge, priest, and prophet cannot establish permanent leadership, government must derive from a new source.

We see arguments both for and against kingship in 1 Samuel 8–11. The people want a king "to govern us like all the nations" (8:5). Their request undermines YHWH's kingship and compromises the tradition's egalitarian impulse. Samuel notes: kings take sons to populate armies; daughters, for the palace staff. "He will take a tenth of your flocks ..." "And you shall be his slaves" (8:17). 1 Samuel 9 offers a pro-monarchical perspective. Samuel appears not as the national prophet but as a local "seer." The Deity appears to favor not a king, but a prince: "I will send you a man from Benjamin, and you shall anoint him to be a prince over my people Israel." The impetus is practical: "He shall save my people from ... the Philistines" (9:16–17).

Ambivalence about kingship is complemented by ambivalence about Saul. His introduction implies that his qualifications are looks and wealth. "There was a man of Benjamin whose name was Kish ... a man of wealth. And he had a son whose name was Saul, a handsome young man. There was not a man among the people of Israel more handsome than he; from his shoulders upward he was taller than any of his people" (9:1–2). Saul's first action is his failure to fulfill a type scene. He "meets young maidens coming out to draw water" (9:11), but his mind is set on finding Kish's lost donkeys. He finds, not donkeys, but royal anointing. Like Moses and Gideon, Saul is a reluctant leader; he is also reluctantly anointed. He is only "a Benjaminite, from the least of the tribes of Israel: "And is not my family the humblest of all the families of the tribes of Benjamin?" (9:21). Samuel first anoints Saul in secret, as if God only minimally accedes to the people's demand. When Samuel makes a public announcement, the process makes the choice of Saul anticlimactic: Lots are cast to see whom God will choose for the king. The lots fall on Saul, but "when they sought him he could not be found. So they inquired again of the Lord ... and the Lord said, 'Behold, he has hidden himself among the baggage'" (10:22). Samuel asserts: "Do you see him whom the Lord has chosen? There is none like him among all the people."

As Israel struggles to harmonize traditional egalitarianism with a centralized monarch, Saul also has difficulty negotiating his role. Samuel may have plotted his failure, "Samuel did not come to Gilgal, and the people were scattering. So Saul said, 'Bring the burnt offerings here to me, and the peace offerings'" (13:8–9). The king usurps the priestly role. As Saul completes the sacrifice, Samuel arrives to pronounce condemnation: "Your kingdom shall not continue" (13:14). Instead of sacrificing the spoils of the Amalekite raid, "Saul and the people spared Agag [the king], and the best of the sheep and the oxen and the fatlings, and the lambs, and all that was good, and would not utterly destroy them" (15:9). God "repents" of making Saul king. Condemned by Samuel, Saul repents, but too late: "Samuel hewed Agag to pieces before the Lord at Gilgal" (15:33). "Samuel did not see Saul again until the day of his death" (15:35).

Saul's untenable political position culminates in his final tragedy. Suffering when the "evil spirit from

The death of Agag.

God" (16:23) overtakes him, Saul is comforted only by his harp player. His torment is divinely caused. His harp player will usurp his throne. Saul's son and daughter will betray him. His death confirms the fragility of his rule. Facing Philistine onslaught, Saul finds himself needing Samuel's advice. Yet Samuel is dead, and "Saul had put the mediums and wizards out of the land" (28:3). Saul, contravening his own law, seeks a medium. Attesting to the ineffectuality of Saul's national policies, his soldiers quickly find one in Endor.

The medium tells Saul, "I see a god coming up out of the earth" (28:13). When he inquires about its appearance, she responds: "An old man is coming up, and he is wrapped in a cloak." The term matches that used for the coats Hannah had made, and Saul knew that the man was Samuel. Told by Samuel that he will lose the battle, the king refuses to eat; the medium—whose livelihood and life were threatened by Saul's policies—feeds him dinner. The next morning, Saul and his son Jonathan die in battle. Making lament for them is their rival, the next king, David, to whose story we turn in the next lecture. ■

Suggested Reading

David Jobling, *First Samuel*.

Questions to Consider

1. Why is Saul made a sympathetic character?

2. Considering the previous seven biblical books, what model of political leadership would appear most beneficial for Israel?

3. What is compromised in the egalitarian (if androcentric) nature of Israelite religion, under the covenant, by the monarchy?

Note: The Book of Ruth appears between Judges and 1 Samuel in Christian canons. Both because most scholars date the book's composition to a period later than these texts and because in the MT, it appears in the *Ketuvim* (Writings), discussion of Ruth is reserved for a later lecture.

Samuel and Saul
(1 Samuel)
Lecture 15—Transcript

The very loosely knit tribal confederacy under the charismatic leaders called judges has now completely disintegrated, but some need for a government still remains because the Philistine threat is still there. Consequently, when we move into First Samuel we will find the need for the monarchy recited over and over again. But First Samuel does not begin with a monarchy. To the contrary, it begins with the birth of Samuel and what looks like a very calm and pleasant society, as if somehow we're back to the good old days when people were not being raped or chopped into bits.

The beginning of the story of Samuel portends good things for Israel. We have an account of a married couple, and we haven't seen them in a while. But here is a married couple who actually seem to love each other— Hannah, a woman, and her husband Elkanah—and every year they go up to the local shrine at Shiloh to offer sacrifices. Nobody attacks them on the way. It looks quite good. But it turns out that Hannah is distressed because Hannah has no children. We've seen this before, and not only does Hannah replay the literary convention, the type scene of a barren woman to whom an annunciation will be given, but it may well be that Hannah in her loneliness, in her barrenness, represents the loss that the community still feels, that somehow she embodies a sense of hope, a sense of needing to be fulfilled. She represents the community here on a very positive level.

She also resembles all those infertile women from Genesis. Like Sarah and like Rachel, there is a fertile co-wife there; her name is Peninnah. Hannah simply cannot bear the fact that her husband has children with a co-wife. So every year when they go up to the shrine at Shiloh, Hannah prays for a child. Her husband simply can't understand why Hannah is so desperate, and he says to her at one point, "Am I not more to you than ten sons?" And she answers not, because, for a woman who can't have a child, in Hannah's case, the answer is "No, you're not."

Hannah goes up to the shrine and prays passionately for a child, and she actually offers a vow, but here a positive one, unlike Jephthah's. She prays, "Lord of hosts, if you will only take notice of my trouble and you will remember me, if you will not forget me but grant me offspring, then I shall give the child to the Lord for the whole of his life, and no razor shall ever touch his head." He, like Samson, will be a Nazirite. Samson the Nazirite is a fool. Samuel the Nazirite is a genius.

She prays her prayer, and Eli the priest at Shiloh looks at her and notices that her lips are moving and her eyes are closed and she is fervently praying, and he thinks she's drunk. He says to her, "Put away your wine, woman. This is not the way you should behave at the house of God." And she explains to him, "No, I've been praying for a child," and Eli recognizes the depth and concern that she shows, and here's another annunciation. He tells her, "Yes, you will have a child." Eli is ready to recognize true piety. The lives of Eli and Hannah and Hannah's child, Samuel, will be intertwined because, just as Eli originally is unable to realize the depth of Hannah's prayer, so, too, there are gaps in his own life.

It turns out he has two sons who were also priests, but he simply cannot control them. We learn as early as Chapter 2 that his sons are serving at the sacrifices, and they are taking the best cuts of meat for themselves, and, worse, they are actually having sex with some of the women who are coming up to the shrine. This simply cannot stay. And we learn that, although God had promised Eli that his children would always, the expression goes, "Go in and out before me forever, always serve as priests at YHWH's altar," God simply cannot stand this apostasy in which the priests are engaged, and he says, "That promise is now revoked." So God's loyalties will shift to Samuel.

In celebration of her motherhood, because Hannah does, in fact, become pregnant and does, in fact, have a child, she sings a magnificent hymn called the "Song of Hannah." This is a staple, the woman making celebration not only over victory but also over pregnancy. We've seen women's victory songs with Deborah. We've seen a short victory song with Miriam at the Song of the Sea. And for those within the Christian tradition, Hannah's song becomes the model for Mary's Magnificat at the beginning of Luke, when Mary celebrates the birth of Jesus. This song is, however, less a paean into childbirth, it's less thanking God for the fact that Hannah herself has had a child, than it is, well, a political manifesto. Hannah is expressing national yearnings. She predicts in her song social upheaval where the mighty are brought down and the weaker raised up. She also speaks about her own changing circumstances, but in broader terms. The barren are made fertile. And that will finally be what will happen to the kingdom of Israel.

Hannah bears her son, Samuel. She nurses him, and when she weans him she makes good on her vow. She takes him up to the shrine at Shiloh and puts him in trust to Eli the priest, and Samuel begins to serve at God's altar. That's where his call comes from. As he's there serving for God, and, by the way, his mother never actually leaves him. We're told in this very, very delicate note that every year Hannah would come up to the shrine at Shiloh with a little coat, a little cloak that she had made for him. The mother's love continues. Hannah has not forgotten Samuel and neither has God.

Finally, "the word of the Lord," we're told, "was rare in those days," but it comes to Samuel when he is lying down in the temple where the ark of God is. We're now in First Samuel, Chapter 3. Samuel hears a voice. He thinks it's Eli the priest calling, so he runs into Eli's room and says, "What can I do for you?" and Eli says, "Go back to sleep. I didn't call." By the third time Eli realizes, "Ah, it's God calling," and he tells Samuel to be prepared and to tell God that he, Samuel, is ready. God commissions Samuel to be his messenger, and, by the end of Chapter 3, we're told Samuel grew, and the Lord was with him. As the expression goes, "Let none of his words fall to the ground." In other words, everything that Samuel said was heeded by the people, and everything that Samuel said was given to him by God. "All Israel from Dan to Beersheba, from top to bottom, north to south, knew that Samuel was established as a prophet of the Lord," as the text continues, "for the Lord revealed himself to Samuel at Shiloh."

This portends great things for Israel. It looks really good. Samuel combines the strength of Israel's earlier leaders like Moses: God speaks to him and the people listen. Like Aaron, he's got priestly duties because he's serving at the shrine. Like Joshua, he is able to unite the people from Dan to Beersheba, and they listen to him. Samuel, indeed, sets up a witness stone in testimony to his truth, just like Joshua did at the covenant ceremony at Shechem.

And, like Deborah, we're told about Samuel, Chapter 7, he judged Israel all the days of his life. He looks like the perfect leader. He's got the ear of the people, and God loves him. But there is still no centralized government, and the Philistines are still out there, and somebody has got to help out. We actually find out that a need for a centralized government and a standing military is not only just a need but it's essential.

The story of Samuel, his birth, and then his death notice provides the frame for what's called the ark narrative. Samuel, as we know, had been at the shrine of Shiloh with the ark, but, when the Israelites go into battle, the ark goes with them. What happens in Chapter 4 is that the ark is captured by the Philistines, and, during that capture, the two sons of Eli, those wicked, apostatizing priests, are slain. When the ark is captured, a Benjaminite who happened to be fighting on Israel's side comes to Eli, who is 98 years old at the time and blind, and he tells Eli, "The ark of the Lord has been captured. Your sons are slain." Eli, who is sitting on a stool— and we're told he's very heavy—falls over and he dies. The news also comes to his daughter-in-law, the wife of Phinehas, one of his children. She's pregnant, and she gives birth prematurely, and in her last moment she names her child. She calls him Ichabod, which means "the glory has departed from Israel." So here again a child represents the community's fate.

At this point the Deuteronomic historian, whom actually we've already seen in the Book of Judges, can move from farce to pathos and farce very quickly. The historian actually moves from this highly emotional scene of a dead priest and a dead daughter-in-law and a premature baby to a farce, and we have the ark narrative, the story of the peripatetic ark being dragged from Philistine city to Philistine city. In fact, some biblical scholars have suggested this, too, is a literary convention. We have, from the ancient Near East, stories of gods represented by their statues being moved from town to town to town, either being in exile because of war or deserting their people because they don't like the way their people are behaving.

Here is the ark representing God. The Philistines bring the ark to the Philistine temple at Ashdod, and there is an idol there called Dagon. Unfortunately, Dagon the idol keeps bowing down to the ark, so the Philistines have to upright Dagon again, and then Dagon bows down again and falls to pieces.

The citizens of Ashdod say, "We better get rid of this ark," so they ship the ark off to Gath, which is where Goliath is from. We'll meet Goliath when we finally meet King David.

What exactly happens to the people in Gath is not quite clear. It depends upon how you want to translate the Hebrew. They either broke out into tumors, or they broke out into hemorrhoids. Either way, it's not a good scene. So the Gathites ship the ark to Ekron. The people in Ekron cry out, "They have brought around to us the ark of the God of Israel to slay us and our people." So the people of Ekron don't want it either, and they finally, after consulting with their own priest, come to the conclusion that they will leave it up to some god, either theirs or the one of Israel, to determine what to do with the ark. They tie the ark to two cows that have just calved, two milk cows.

The idea is, if you are a cow—unlikely to happen—and you have just had a calf, you need that calf to nurse because otherwise you, the cow, will simply explode with built-up milk. The idea is the cows would probably stay in Philistine territory to be near their calves. But what we're told is the two cows, looking neither left nor right, mooing as they go, head back toward Israelite territory and bring the ark back home. They head to Beth Shemesh, where the Levites pick up the ark and dispatch the cows as a sacrifice to God, and the ark remains in Israelite territory for 20 years until David establishes his capital in Jerusalem in Second Samuel 6 and brings the ark up there.

But God will not always rescue the people quite as easily with tumors and falling down idols. We need a king to help out, and that's what we get next. When Samuel became old, we're told at the end of the ark narrative, he made his sons judges over Israel, "but his sons did not walk in his ways. They turned aside after gain, they took bribes, and they perverted justice." Well, the story of Samuel is not done. He will continue up through the rest of this book. But we're already told early on that Samuel cannot establish his dynasty. Some other sort of ruler is needed. The judge isn't going to work—we've seen that from the Book of Judges. Charismatic leaders cannot hold. Samuel the prophet and priest cannot hold. A new type of leadership is needed. In First Samuel, Chapters 8 through 11, we have a compromised view of the monarchy. The upshot is, kingship is to be granted to these people, but the king must be subservient to God. God will still be the people's ruler; it will be God who chooses the king.

It used to be thought that these particular chapters were the combination of two different sources, one a pro-monarchical source and one an anti-monarchical source. That may be the case, but these days biblical scholars think that, in fact, both views are written by the same Deuteronomic historian, expressing the historian's own ambivalence about the kingship. It's necessary, but it's not quite what Israel was founded to be, and we can see that ambivalence even in Samuel's own discussion with the people. The people come up to Samuel, and they say, "Give us a king to govern us like all the nations." Samuel responds, "Look, God is your king. If you take a king like all the other nations you'll be undermining YHWH's rule."

Moreover, what happened to the egalitarian impulse of Yahwism that we saw underneath the covenant, where everybody is equal? A king establishes class distinctions, and a monarchy thereby entails Israel's loss of unique status. Under YHWH they are not like all the other nations; they are a nation holy and distinct apart. And, if the theological explanations were not sufficient, Samuel gives the people practical explanations for why they shouldn't want a king. Kings will take your sons, he says, to populate their armies, and they'll take your daughters for the palace staff. They'll take a tenth of your flock. They'll take the best of your cattle. They'll take your donkeys. And you shall be, Samuel says, the king's slaves. The conclusion at this point is, kingship is not good for the people, and it's an offense to God, but, despite what Samuel says, the people are resolved.

The irony is, by the way, that everything Samuel said actually came true. By the time we get up to King Solomon we find all of these predictions have come true. King Solomon has a corvée, forced labor. We already saw that with slavery in Egypt. He has a major capital center with a temple, with a palace, with the entire infrastructure that a capital center requires, both to work for the monarchy and to work for the centralized cult. He's got a royal priesthood. He's got a royal harem with international gods. He's got an overextended economy—too much importing, too little exporting. He's got a heavily taxed and increasingly frustrated peasant class, and there will be a revolt after he dies. In the Bible, like everything else, be careful what you ask for, right?

Nevertheless, although tepid, the Bible also offers a somewhat pro-monarchical condition. This is First Samuel 9. We see already the change in the perspective and the change in the description of Samuel. Here he's no longer the one who has the ear of the people from north to south. He's simply a country seer. He's a local fortune-teller, a finder of lost objects. And here the deity actually seems to favor some sort of monarchical rule. But God doesn't quite ask for a king yet. God says, "it's okay if you have a prince," and this brings us to the story of the prince who becomes King Saul. Here is the description: "I will send you a man from Benjamin, and you shall anoint him to be prince over my people Israel. He shall save my people from the hand of the Philistines, for I have seen the affliction of my people because their cry has come out to me." We've seen this before. A new leader will be raised up—but a different type of leader.

Saul's introduction is a tad on the problematic side. I get the feeling, when looking at it, that his primary job qualifications are good looks and wealth. Here is how we meet Saul: "There was a man of Benjamin whose name was Kish, a man of wealth, and he had a son whose name was Saul, a handsome young man. There was not a man among the people more handsome than he. From his shoulders upward he was taller than any of the people." He's rich, and he's drop-dead gorgeous. Other than that it's not clear what his qualifications are to lead the people. Nor are we sure he will make a good leader when we finally see him in action, and, indeed, we already have.

Think back to the type scene of men who meet women at wells. This is where we first see King Saul. He meets some young women coming up to draw water in Chapter 9, verse 11. But he's not looking for a bride. He is, as you will recall, looking for his father's lost donkeys. And the women sent him on his way, "Go to the local seer;"—and that turns out to be the prophet Samuel— "perhaps he will help you." The type scene, as you know, was aborted. Saul will not marry these women in the same way that he will not complete his kingship.

He goes to Samuel, and Samuel says to him, "You're going to be king." Saul, in typical fashion—you might think of Gideon or Moses in the background—is reluctant. He says, "I'm a Benjaminite. It's the least of the tribes of Israel," and he goes on, "Is not my family the humblest of all the families of the tribe of Benjamin?" Fat chance. We already know that his father is wealthy. Perhaps given both Saul's own doubts and Samuel's as well, Samuel anoints Saul in secret. It's not time for the public inauguration yet. When Samuel finally does make a public announcement regarding Saul's anointing, the events are not really auspicious. The tribes are collected, and lots are cast to determine whom God will choose to be king. The lots fall upon the tribe of Benjamin and then to a particular clan and then to Saul's household, and finally the lots fall upon Saul.

The people looked for Saul, "but when they sought him he could not be found, so they inquired of the Lord." I'm citing Chapter 10 here. And the Lord said, "Behold, he has hidden himself among the baggage." When Samuel then asserts, "Do you see him whom the Lord has chosen? There is none like him among all the people," I wonder about the tone that he would have used because kings do not usually hang out among the baggage. Some of the assembled crowd immediately shout out, "Long live the king!" It's in the Bible; we didn't invent it from the British monarchy. But some fellows called "worthless" by the narrator ask, "How can this man save us?" and it seems to me that the question is, in fact, not without merit.

So as Israel struggles to harmonize its original egalitarian tradition underneath the covenant with this centralized monarchy, we also find Saul trying to deal with this new change, not only in Israel's status but within his own. Saul is in a very difficult spot because Samuel himself is quite ambivalent about this kingship idea. It seems almost as if Samuel is setting Saul up for failure. Saul does go to war against the Philistines, and for the most part he is winning. But at one point in the midst of a military campaign he and Samuel had agreed to meet for Samuel to offer sacrifice, and Saul waits, and he waits, and he waits, and the people are beginning to leave, and he needs them to be gathered together. But Samuel has not shown up.

We're told Saul waited seven days, the time appointed by Samuel, but Samuel did not come to Gilgal, which is where they were, and the people were scattering from him, so Saul finally said, "Bring the burnt offerings here to me and the peace offerings" (First Samuel 13). Thereby the king usurps Samuel's role. The king is not supposed to be the one to offer sacrifice. That's the job of the priest. As Saul completes his sacrifice, Samuel arrives but only to pronounce condemnation. He says to Saul, "Your kingdom will not continue," which is not what you need to hear when you're a military leader, right?

The account of Saul's transgression is, in fact, given a different spin in Chapter 15, where his culpability, his guilt, and the situation of his rejection are even worse. There is a raid against the Amalekites, but this is holy war, and within holy war one is supposed to take every bit of that booty and dedicate it to God, and the men who are captured are supposed to be killed. We've seen this already. But Saul preserves some of the booty, and Saul and the people spare the king of the Amalekites—his name is Agag—as well as the best of the sheep and the oxen and the fatlings and the lands and all that is good and refuse utterly to destroy them. This is totally against the rules of holy war. Saul is here in violation of divine commands. We're told at this point God repents of making Saul king.

Samuel arrives and accuses Saul of transgressing the dictates of holy war and of failing to honor God, and Saul repents, but it's too late. We're told, "Samuel hewed Agag to pieces before the Lord at Gilgal"—Samuel's sacrifice to God. We're also told at that point that Samuel did not see Saul again until the day of his death. Saul's untenable position culminates in his final tragedy. God causes an evil spirit to come upon Saul. He can't get rest. He has no peace. We'll see in the next lecture that it's only through David's playing his harp that Saul gains any sense of serenity. His torment is divinely caused. His people are not entirely loyal. We discover that his harp player, the young David, will usurp his popularity and then usurp his throne. His daughter, Michal, who is in love with David, will betray him. His son Jonathan will also betray him because Jonathan's loyalty is to David. His remaining children and grandchildren will either be killed or stripped of their power. Saul will be left a solitary tragic figure, and his death confirms the tragedy as well as the fragility of his role.

Again, facing Philistine onslaught, Saul realizes he needs Samuel's support, Samuel's help, but not only has Samuel not spoken with him since the incident at Gilgal, Samuel is dead. Saul is stuck; he needs to speak to Samuel. What's he going to do? Worse, the one way you can speak to somebody who is dead is you get a medium to cause the ghost to come out of the ground. But we're also told that Saul, in one of his executive orders, had put all the mediums and wizards out of the land. So Saul, contravening his own law, seeks a medium. He goes to his servants, and he says, "Seek out for me a woman who is a medium, that I may go to her and inquire of her." Attesting to the total inability of Saul to rule and the inefficacy of his laws, the servants find a medium. Nobody was paying much attention to what Saul says.

They go to the land of Endor, and for those of you who know that old TVshow *Bewitched* and Endora, that's where the name comes from. The witch there, the medium of Endor, conjures up the spirit of Samuel, and the medium tells Saul, "I see a god coming up out of the earth," and when Saul inquires, "What is his appearance?" she responds, "He is an old man coming up, and he is wrapped in a cloak." It's the same word used for the cloak that Samuel's mother, Hannah, used to bring to him when he was at the temple in Shiloh. It's an odd word, so, in fact, we know this is Samuel. And Saul knows it is Samuel, and Samuel says to Saul, "You will lose the battle." Saul then refuses to eat, and ironically and graciously, the medium whose life had been put in danger by Saul's executive order kills a fatted calf and gives him dinner and says, basically, "You need your strength because you've got a battle on the morrow." The next morning Saul and his son Jonathan die in battle.

Here is the tragedy. The next day when the Philistines came to strip the slain they took armor and jewelry. They found Saul and his three sons lying dead on Mount Gilboa. They cut off his head, they stripped him of his armor, and they sent messengers through the length and breadth of their land to carry the good news to idols, to their gods, and to the people alike, because here they have prevailed over Israel. They have killed Israel's king. They deposit his armor in the temple of Ashtoreth as a sign that they have won, and they nail his body on the wall of Beth Shan. So even in death Saul is humiliated.

But when the inhabitants of Jabesh Gilead, a town Saul had protected, hear what the Philistines have done to Saul, all of the warriors among them set out, and they journey to recover the bodies of Saul and his sons from the wall of Beth Shan. They bring him back to Jabesh, they burn the bodies, and they take the bones and they bury them underneath the tamarisk tree in Jabesh Gilead, and for seven days they fast. That's the end of the story of King Saul, but it's not the end of the story of the monarchy—the pro-monarchical forces, the pro-monarchical voices, actually, right?

The Philistines are on the horizon. Somebody needs to help out. Somebody needs to retain the kingship. And thereby we come to King David. But, as we'll see, King David will replace some of these same conventions that we saw back with the judges and back even with Saul. An inauspicious beginning, association with worthless and reckless fellows—King David will even make an alliance with the Philistines. In the same way that the Israelites had to fight their way into Canaan, David is going to have to fight his way into the kingship. Will he succeed? Yes. And why? Because finally, for one more time, God has changed his mind, and he will establish his kingdom.

The final scene that we'll see that guarantees this kingdom is that royal grant covenant that we already know God will give. So David gets what Saul never had, the covenant with God, the royal grant like Noah had and like Abraham had, the promise of eternal kingship. In the next lecture we will meet King David hanging about with worthless fellows—beloved of God, a player of the harp, a slayer of Goliath, and a man who finally loses his role again by committing adultery, by having his sons go to war against him, and finally by dying a lonely, cold, old man alone in his bed.

King David
(1 Samuel 16–31, 2 Samuel, 1 Kings 1–2)
Lecture 16

David's accession anticipates a period of tribal unification, prosperity, and peace with neighboring kingdoms; the royal grant by which the Deity adopts David and guarantees that his descendants will hold the throne of Israel in perpetuity (1 Sam. 7) appears to confirm his promise. However, David's own failures lead to familial strife, civil war, and the bloody route to Solomon's throne.

The story of David is worthy of an entire course. His story encompasses myriad roles, including the erstwhile shepherd whose music soothes King Saul's spirit (1 Sam. 16); the armor-bearer whose shot kills the Philistine champion Goliath (1 Sam. 17); the enemy of Saul, but the intimate of Saul's son Jonathan and husband to Saul's daughter Michal (1 Sam. 18 *passim*); the leader of a gang of malcontents and the Philistine vassal (1 Sam. 22–27); the king granted an eternal covenant (2 Sam. 7); the adulterer who arranges the death of his lover's husband (2 Sam. 12); the father whose beloved son, Absalom, wars against him (2 Sam. 13–20); and the old man who cannot find warmth (1 Kings 1). David can be viewed as a culture hero, similar to King Arthur. David's history receives no uncontested support

Click Art.

King David playing the lyre.

from external evidence. An inscription possibly reading "house of David" has been found among fragments of Iron Age pottery. Some archaeologists claim that the inscription testifies to David's existence; others question both its date and its age. The attribution to him of Goliath's death may be an example of form criticism at work: The story remains the same, but the characters change. Second Sam. 21:19 attributes Goliath's death to David's soldier, Elhanan.

The opening verses signal political and personal deficiencies; David's domestic failures foreshadow and serve as a microcosm of the ensuing civil war. "In the spring of the year, the time when kings go out to battle, David sent Joab with his officers and all Israel with him, and they ravaged the Ammonites ... but David remained in Jerusalem." Clearly, he was not attending to his duties. "It happened, late one afternoon, when David rose from his couch and was walking about on the roof of the king's house, that he saw from the roof a woman bathing; the woman was very beautiful." Is this David, described as "skilled in music, a man of valor and a warrior, sensible in speech and handsome in appearance, and the lord is with him" (1 Sam. 16:18)?

Interpreters question Bathsheba's complicity in David's downfall. Does she see him as he sees her? Had she planned to be seen? Does she know the king's movements?

David's relationship with Bathsheba is premeditated: "David sent for messengers and inquired and said, 'Isn't this Bathsheba ... the wife of Uriah the Hittite?" The scene recollects David's other relationships, including: His marriage to the clever Abigail, after complicity in causing her first husband's death (1 Sam. 16:1–25). His marriage to Michal, who loves, then despises him, and "who had no child to the day of her death" (2 Sam. 23).

Whether David can "love" is an open question. Jonathan loves David, to such an extent that he, Saul's son and heir, betrays his own father and king. David makes public lament over the prince's dead body: "I am distressed for you, my brother Jonathan/greatly beloved were you to me. Your love to me was wonderful/passing the love of women" (2 Sam. 1:26). David even orders the song to be "taught to the people of Judah" (2 Sam.1:18). But David does not say he *loved* Jonathan. The more cynical reader would see the lament as opportunistic.

"So David sent messengers to get her, and she came to him and he lay with her. (Now she was purifying herself after her period)" (2 Sam. 11:4). Did David abuse his power? Had Bathsheba a choice when the "messengers" arrived? Is this rape? Is this the "romance" of popular legend? Had David read Deut. 22:22 on the punishment for adultery? And what of Bathsheba? Is this the fulfillment of her plans? Why does the text explicitly note that "she came to him"? Is she depicted as faithful in her ritual practices, or simply as not pregnant?

"The woman conceived, and she sent and told David, 'I am pregnant'" (11:5). David is the father, because Bathsheba was introduced as purifying herself at the completion of her menstrual cycle. What does Bathsheba want David to do with this information? First, the coveting of the neighbor's wife, then adultery, then murder? David recalls Uriah and encourages him to "go down to your house and wash your feet." This is an invitation to connubiality, because "feet"—Hebrew: *reglayim*—is a euphemism for genitalia. Uriah refuses: "The ark and Israel and Judah remain in booths ... shall I then go to my house, to eat and to drink and to lie with my wife? As you live, and as your soul lives, I shall not do such a thing." David even gets Uriah drunk, but still he demurs. Finally, David sends him back with a sealed letter to Joab: Place Uriah "in the forefront of the hardest fighting, and then draw back from him, so that he may be struck down and die" (2 Sam. 11:15).

Bathsheba—after a time of mourning—marries David and bears a son. But "the thing David had done displeased the Lord" (11:27). Initially, it is not clear what the "thing" is: Rape? Adultery? Uriah's murder? Marriage to Bathsheba? Sinning against God? How can one atone for voyeurism, adultery, murder, and cover-up? oes David recognize his protection under the royal grant? God speaks to David through Nathan: "You have struck down Uriah the Hittite with the sword, and have taken his wife to be your wife... now therefore the sword shall never depart from your house ... I will take your wives from before your eyes, and give them to your neighbor, and he shall lie with your wives in the sight of this very sun. For you did it secretly, but I will do this before all Israel" (2 Sam. 12: 10-12). Adultery is never private: It involves messengers, coworkers, confidants. It affects even one's children: Amnon rapes Tamar, and Absalom—leading a civil war against his father—will rape David's concubines on the palace rooftop.

David admits his sin, and Nathan tells him that his sin has been passed over ... at least in God's purview. Psalm 51 is titled "A Psalm of David, when the prophet Nathan came to him after he had gone in to Bathsheba." Despite David's repenting, Nathan predicts, "the child that is born to you shall die" (12:14). David and Bathsheba have a second child who, with the machinations of his mother and the prophet, obtains the throne. His name is Solomon. ∎

Suggested Reading

J. Cheryl Exum, *Fragmented Women: Feminist Subversions of Biblical Narratives.*

Stephen L. McKenzie, *King David: A Biography.*

Marti J. Steussy, *David: Biblical Portraits of Power.*

Questions to Consider

1. How might the story of David function as later propaganda for the monarchy?

2. Should rulers' personal lives enter the assessment of their governing capabilities?

3. Is David admirable despite his (major) failings? If so, how? If not, what does one make of the royal grant?

King David
(1 Samuel 16–31, 2 Samuel, 1 Kings 1–2)
Lecture 16—Transcript

With the introduction of David, soon to become king in Israel, the Deuteronomic historian provides us a hint of prosperity to come, tribal unification, and the royal grant covenant finally put into play. Israel, after all those disasters in the period of judges and the difficulties between Samuel and Saul, will finally have a time of fulfillment of those promises made to the patriarchs Abraham, Isaac, and Jacob. Indeed, David captures the imagination so much I suggest he's actually worthy of a course in and of himself.

How best then to look at King David, this magnificent hero, this charmer, this rogue, this scoundrel? Let's take a quick look at some of the various characterizations by which the Deuteronomic historian portrays David. Then what I'd like to do is look very, very closely at one particular scene, the very well-known story of David and Bathsheba, because in this one story one finds an epitome of everything that makes David so compelling: his charm, his fidelity, his conniving, his trickery, and ultimately his piety to God and God's love for him but also God's refusal to let him get away with murder and with apostasy.

So here we go with the story of King David. In effect, who is he? He begins as an erstwhile shepherd, the youngest son of a man named Jesse, who is called to the royal court to soothe King Saul's spirit when Saul's spirit is troubling him. In this sense he's also the psalmist whose hymns to God reach the heights of poetic artistry. When one looks through the psalms one finds numerous of these psalms ascribed to King David. Could he have actually written them? If there were a King David, it's possible.

He's also the King's armor bearer. He is a warrior. But in this wonderful story, the stuff of legend, I fear, we're told that he eschews Saul's armor—it's simply too big for him—and he will go up against the Philistine champion, Goliath of Gath, with only a slingshot, and with that slingshot he brings down the giant and thereby the Philistine forces.

He's also the enemy of King Saul, the reigning monarch. David is fighting for his own throne. He wants to take over, and he will do so with the aid of Saul's daughter, Michal, who loves him—we're never told he loves her—and Saul's son, Jonathan. He's the roguish leader of a gang of malcontents. He's a political opportunist who usurps Israel's throne, and, in order to do so, actually becomes a Philistine vassal for a while. David will take help from anywhere he can get it. But he's also a king granted a royal eternal covenant by God, indeed, adopted by God. And he's an adulterer who arranges the death of his adulterous partner's husband. He's a parent who allows one of his children to rape another and does nothing about it, and he's a parent who watches yet another son engage in a civil war against him. This is a son David actually loves, Absalom. Finally, he's an old man, bedridden, unable to rule, who cannot find warmth.

These roles and more contribute, in fact, to the scholarly quest of David, so we must raise the question, is David a real person? It would be lovely if archaeological investigation around Jerusalem from the period circa 1000 B.C.E.—Before the Common Era—when we normally date David, showed the great city of Jerusalem, but it doesn't. It would be lovely if we had external sources—archaeological, inscriptional, epigraphic—attesting to David's evidence, but we don't. Some biblical scholars say no David ever existed; he's much like King Arthur, the stuff of legends, inventions passed down from parent to child, glorified here, ambivalent here, always developed, always ongoing. If there is a real King David, and frankly I want there to be—I want there to be somebody who is this rich—there is no way we're ever going to get back to him. There is no way we can penetrate back behind the legends. All we can do at this point, until archaeology discovers something new, is look at the story.

One final point on archaeology. Some archaeologists have claimed to have discovered an inscription on a potshard entitled or read "House of David"—"*Bet David.*" By this, they attest, because the potsherd seems to date from the right time period, "Aha, we have evidence of King David, House of David." The problem is the date of the shard is not entirely clear, and the meaning of the inscription itself is also not entirely clear. Archaeology is sometimes as much a discipline of believing rather than actually scientifically proving. If one wants to believe this is testimony to David, by all means, but the proof is not yet finally in.

We also have a problem with the historicity of David, at least of some of his stories, when we look to the Bible itself. One of the best-known stories, we've already mentioned it, is the death of Goliath, the Philistine giant, the Philistine hero. The problem is when we look at the book of Second Samuel, Chapter 21, verse 19, we also find a reference to the death of Goliath, except this death is attributed to David's soldier, one Elhanan. Did David kill Goliath? I suspect not. It's part of the stuff of legendary development that major stories accrue to heroes. Here is a major story of the death of a particular figure. The person who killed him, this Elhanan, is not well-known. "Ah," said the later legendary developers, "we'll give that one to David, too." We actually find similar stories in United States history. Did George Washington do everything we actually think he did? Actually, no. Sometimes some of those things were done by his generals. Did the pilgrims coming over on the Mayflower do everything we attribute to them? No, in fact, they didn't. Much is the stuff of later legendary development. And so, I fear, it is with David.

We can even see the development of David's legends when we look to later sources in the Bible. Not only are the records in the books of Samuel material of legend, but the legend continues. When we look, for example, at the books of Chronicles, which are basically post-exilic, much later replays of the Deuteronomic history—First and Second Samuel, First and Second Kings—we do find references to David, but when we go to First Chronicles, Chapter 20, we find that First Chronicles will tell us the story of Second Samuel, Chapter 11, about the siege of the Ammonites at Rabbah and the defeat of the Ammonite king. Left out is what happens in between. That's the story of David and Bathsheba. The Chronicler simply bypasses it. Here David's reputation will not be sullied at all. Indeed, whitewashing political peccadilloes is not a modern invention. The Chronicler does it before the Common Era.

It's also, I think, to be expected that David's story would be developed by southern scribes, those people down in Judah, in Jerusalem, who believe that their city Jerusalem, their kingdom Judah, is there by divine right, and they believe it in part because of this royal grant which they claim David to have received. As we'll see later when we get to the prophetic text, people like Isaiah and Jeremiah have a very difficult time convincing the population of Judah and Jerusalem that their kingdoms actually are in danger. They are convinced God will protect them because God is under contract. David is therefore very, very important for people in the south.

Where does this idea come from? In Second Samuel, Chapter 7, spoken to David by the court prophet Nathan, we find God's words: "When your days are complete and you lie with your fathers, I will raise up your seed, your posterity. I will make his throne secure forever. I will be a father to him, and he will be a son to me. When he errs I will chastise him with the rod of people and the lashes of men, but my steadfast love, my *hesed*, my deep abiding love, I will not remove from him. Your house and your kingship shall be secure before me forever, and your throne will be established permanently." Not only do we find this from the pen of the Deuteronomic historian, we also find it in the psalms. In Psalm 89, the poet Ethan the Ezrahite exults that God has promised, "I have made a covenant with my chosen one. I have sworn to my servant David, I will establish your descendants forever and build you a throne for all generations." You can see with material like this why David is so important to Israelite history.

Now let's look closely at one of these stories of David. Although David is exceptionally important, although he has a royal grant, although he is God's beloved, that does not make him a perfect person. Consistent with the way the ancient Hebrews and Israelites told their stories, their heroes are shown, pardon the cliché, warts and all. That's what, in fact, makes them human. That's I think in part what makes them so compelling as literary figures. Our test case here is David and Bathsheba. As we go on you might think to yourselves, "Do I still like David? Do I want him to win? Does he somehow retain my affection? What do I want to happen to him?"

One other point. There is no way we can look at this story without bringing to bear on it our own cultural concerns. I have difficulty looking at some of these biblical stories without thinking about movies. I can't think about King David without thinking about Gregory Peck, and Bathsheba will always be Susan Hayward. But the movies always add on to the text material that the text itself does not say. If you know these films, if you know the stories from popular culture, see if you can bracket them from your mind and just follow along in the text.

Second Samuel, Chapter 11. Here is the opening verse. "In the spring of the year, the time when kings go out to battle, David sent Joab and his officers and all Israel with him and they ravaged the Ammonites." So far, so good. "But David remained in Jerusalem." Already the narrator is cueing us in that something has gone wrong. David is not doing what he is supposed to do. If this is the time when all kings go to battle and David is a king, he should not be home. He should be out at the front; that's where kings belong. David's deficiencies are beginning to show. And not merely has he removed himself from battle, he's sent his soldiers out there. People will die on his behalf. The least he could do is put in an appearance in the field, and he will not do that.

I suspect that this failure right in the first verse simply foreshadows the increasing failures. First David fails on the political front. He fails to become the general he is, to be the king that he is and lead his troops. We'll see subsequent failures in his monarchy simply as we go along in the story, which continues, "It happened late one afternoon when David rose from his couch and was walking about on the roof of the king's house that he saw from the roof a woman bathing, and the woman was very beautiful." This is David, that skilled musician, that man of valor, that warrior sensible of speech and handsome in appearance, whom the Lord favors. This is David our hero who's taking a nap late one afternoon, rising from his couch while his troops are in the field. What sort of warrior is this?

And what of this woman he sees, this luscious Bathsheba in her bath? Bathsheba really doesn't mean "bath." "Bath" is really the Hebrew *bat*—"daughter of," "daughter of Sheba." Interpreters frequently question Bathsheba's complicity in her relationship with David. Does she know he's there? If you see the movie, Susan Hayward knows exactly what she's doing, but Bathsheba the character, I don't know. Does she know that the king hasn't gone to the front? Does she know that he normally walks on his roof at this time of day? Is her bath time a convenience? Had she planned to be seen? Does she know he sees her? Whatever we answer to any of these questions, all of which are legitimate, whatever our answers will be, those answers will influence how we interpret the rest of the story and how we interpret Bathsheba, because once again the woman's motives are never given.

Now, David's relationship with Bathsheba is no simple spur-of-the-moment lust. He's got to plan this out; it's premeditated. Next verse: "David sent for messengers and inquired and said, 'Isn't this Bathsheba, the wife of Uriah the Hittite?'" That's one translation. Another one reads, "It was reported, 'This is Bathsheba the wife of Uriah the Hittite.'" The ambiguity is telling. Does David actually know who she is, or does he have to find out? If he does know, how long has he had his eye on her? Readers familiar with the David story to this point might recollect his other relationships with women because David has been around the block a time or two. For example, he marries the very, very clever Abigail after being, I think, complicit in causing the death of Abigail's husband. A woman's marital state will not stand in David's way if she can provide him something that he wants or something that he needs. Indeed, by marrying Abigail— the story is in First Samuel, Chapter 25— David is able to consolidate his base with the Calebite tribes. So marrying Abigail functions in terms of political opportunity. But here with Bathsheba there is no political opportunity. This is simply lust.

In terms of political opportunity, one could also note how David can manipulate women throughout his life. Michal, Saul's daughter, loves David. It's not clear David ever loves her, but he uses her as a pawn, and, finally, after years of being used by David, Michal finally turns against him. We find this in Second Samuel 6. This is David bringing the ark of the Lord to Jerusalem. "As the ark came into the city of David, Michal, daughter of Saul"—the narrator wants to tell us exactly who she is—"looked out the window [like Sisera's mother, the woman in the window] and saw King David leaping and dancing before the Lord, and she despised him in her heart." So she comes to David, and she berates him for uncovering himself before the eyes of maids and servants, as she puts it, as any vulgar fellow might uncover himself. David retorts to her, "It was the Lord who made me king over your father Saul."

Then we're told Michal, the daughter of Saul, had no child until the day of her death. This is narrative artistry. Did she have no child because God condemned her to barrenness because of her berating of God's beloved

David, or did she have no child because David refused again to come into her bed? If that's the case, why? Because he hated her or because he was afraid that if she had a child that child would also be Saul's heir and that child eventually would raise up an army against David? It's narrative artistry all the way through. In fact, whether David can actually love or not, I think, remains an open question. We know people love David, but it's not clear David loves anyone.

The only time David actually seems to show love is his public lament over Jonathan's dead body. He says, "I am distressed for you, my brother Jonathan. Greatly beloved were you to me. Your love was wonderful, passing the love of women." But it's easy for David to say that then. Jonathan is dead; Saul is dead. David knows his throne is secure. Indeed, he even orders that this song be taught to the people of Judah, but does he actually love Jonathan or is this simply political opportunism—Jonathan's love was passing the love of women; Jonathan is dead? I see David as opportunist. You all can make up your own minds.

Moving back to the story of Bathsheba, David sent messengers to get her. Here is the line, "She came to him; he lay with her. Now she was purifying herself after her period." All this great romance: wine, flower, champagne, a bath—nothing. She came to him; he lay with her—boom. This verse is loaded with questions. Did David abuse his power? If somebody sends soldiers to your house, the king's messengers, and says, "The king wants to see you," it's very difficult to say no. This is a royal summons. Is this a rape? Had Bathsheba any choice? The king wants you. What do are you going to do— say no? Did David recognize by his actions that he's committing adultery? We might look to something like, oh, Deuteronomy, Chapter 22, which says, "Both the man and the woman who in town commit adultery should be put to death." Does he care that he's making Bathsheba an adulteress?

In turn, what about Bathsheba? Could she have said no? Could she have said, "I will come tomorrow"? Was she expecting the invitation, thinking, "Finally I've gotten what I wanted. I've trapped him, and he's risen to my bait"? What of the notice that she came to him, not that they took her? Is this simply an expression, or is there willingness involved? And what about the statement she was purifying herself? It's true, according to the Levitical

277

law codes, after a woman is done with her menstrual cycle, she is supposed to bathe, ritual immersion, and that puts her back in a state of purity, which means she can then have sexual intercourse without incurring being in a state of impurity. Are we told this to be told that Bathsheba is faithful to the laws of God? Or are we being told this to let us know, on the more biological level, here is a woman who was not pregnant, and therefore we know that when Bathsheba conceives, the child is not her husband Uriah's; the child is King David's?

Well, the great romance of Hollywood legend is simply one verse: "He lay with her; she returned to her house." But then events move very quickly. The next verse: "The woman conceived, and she sent to David and she told him, 'I am pregnant.'" My question is, what does she want David to do? It's clearly David's child—he admits that—but what should he do? Does she want him to pray to God that she miscarry so the evidence will be wiped away? Does she want him to procure for her an abortion? Might he know someone who can do this? Does she want him to recall her husband from the front to cover up the adultery—get Uriah home and into her bed quickly? Does she want David to kill her husband and marry her himself so that she could give birth to a child who might at some point be the royal heir? All we know is she tells him she is pregnant, and then he needs to do something.

Questions continue to abound. From coveting his neighbor's wife to adultery, David will next turn to murder. The king recalls Bathsheba's husband from the front. His name is Uriah. He is identified as a Hittite; therefore, he is not an Israelite. He's a mercenary. He's a soldier for hire working on behalf of King David. David recalls Uriah, and, after meeting with him, encourages him, "Go down to your house and wash your feet." This is not simply an invitation to clean up. This is an invitation to connubiality because "feet" in biblical Hebrew, *reglayim*, is a euphemism for genitals. David is simply saying, go home and sleep with your wife. You're back from the front—take leave. Uriah actually knows what David is asking, and he the Hittite, the non-Israelite, responds finally with fidelity.

He says to David, "The ark and Israel and Judah remain in booths. They are in tents in the encampment. Shall I then go to my house to eat and to drink and to lie with my wife?" He knows exactly what David wants, but he goes on, "As you live and your soul lives, I shall not do such a thing." There's loyalty. The next night he gets Uriah drunk, hoping to send him home, and Uriah grabs a blanket and sleeps with the soldiers at the door of the king's house; he still demurs. Finally, David, knowing he's not going to get Uriah home, sends him back with a sealed letter to Joab the general, saying, "Place Uriah in the forefront of the hardest fighting and then draw back from him so that he may be struck down and die." Now the plot is very clear here. We know what David wants ultimately to happen.

But why exactly did David want Uriah to go home? Most of the time when people think about this the answer seems obvious: Go home so Uriah can sleep with his wife and thereby everyone can pass off the baby as Uriah's. David is not going to tell anybody. Bathsheba is not going to tell anybody. And Uriah will never know the difference. That's possible, but there are other possibilities as well. I think we tend not to think about them because we want David to be the good guy, and that's the most benign of all chances.

Might he have wanted Uriah to discover that Bathsheba was pregnant and kill her? That solves David's problem. Might he have wanted Uriah to find Bathsheba pregnant and agree to divorce her? Again, it solves David's problem. Might he have wanted Uriah to kill Bathsheba in a fit of jealousy? And again, David's problem is resolved. Or might he have wanted Uriah to sleep with Bathsheba and thereby violate the conventions of holy war because, as we've seen, soldiers in holy war must keep themselves pure; they are not allowed to have intercourse with women? What happens if they do? The idea would be God would strike them dead because they've violated a divine command, or, if their fellow soldiers found out about it, their fellow soldiers would have to remove that impurity from the camp, and the fellow soldiers would thereby kill him. Again, David is off; he is free. I don't know what his motives are. Some of them are more difficult to believe than others.

And how indeed is Uriah to be assessed here? In the movies Uriah is usually pretty awful, and there are some novels about David and Bathsheba in which Uriah is an abusive wife-beater and David is simply the kind, gentle man who comes to the rescue and provides Bathsheba the love and the tenderness that she had never known. But that's not what we have in the Bible. That makes the story easier, but the Bible doesn't let us off the hook that easily.

Do his fidelity and his innocence make David's decadence even more monstrous? Here the Hittite is the faithful one. David, God's beloved, the Israelite king, is not. Or should we conclude that he has no relationship with his wife whatsoever? Certainly he could have gone home and at least said, "Hello, Bathsheba. How are you?" Nothing required that he sleep with her.

Why does he avoid her? Or is he so in love with her that he knew he could not resist the temptation, because he knew the minute he set foot in that door he would grab his beloved wife and kiss her and, before you know it, the conventions of holy war would be violated? Or does he respect Israel's Torah so much that he, a Hittite, is faithful to what God wants when God's beloved is not? Does he finally realize, after David keeps saying, "Go home, go home, go home," that his fate is sealed? Does he realize what David has done? Because adultery can never stay hidden. The news is going to get out. What exactly does Uriah know? When he is handed the sealed letter signing his death warrant, does he actually know that he is bringing that warrant to the commander and that he will die, and he dies bravely, accepting his fate, because what other choice did he have? Again, the text does not tell us, and this is what makes it so rich.

I can picture people in the ancient world listening to this text and debating it. It may be that the way we answer these questions tells us more about ourselves and our values than the text itself. The text raises the questions; the answers are ours to provide.

Well, Bathsheba, after a time of mourning, marries David and bears him a son. But then we're told, "The thing David had done had displeased the Lord." We've already seen David mourning in public grief for Saul and Jonathan. Here again I question the sincerity of that public grief because I question David's sincerity about Bathsheba all the way through. She mourns. What about him? And by the way, as long as we're here, what about Bathsheba's mourning? Does she do it because it's the socially polite thing to do—if she didn't mourn her husband people would talk? Or does she do it because she really loved him and now she knows her fate is doomed? Or did she do it because she thought, "Good riddance, and I've now got what I wanted—I'm going to marry the king and have his child"?

As for David, what do we do with him? He's gone from voyeurism to adultery to possible rape to murder and then cover-up, and this is the man who has a royal grant. Where is God going to come in? The news of the adultery gets out. God speaks to David through the prophet Nathan, the same one who gave him the royal grant, and Nathan says to him, "You have struck down Uriah the Hittite with a sword, and you have taken his wife to be your wife." What offends God here is less the adultery than the murder. "You have struck down Uriah. Therefore the sword will never again depart from your house. I will take your wives from before your eyes and give them to your neighbor." It turns out that neighbor is David's son, Absalom.

Nathan goes on, "He shall lie with your wives in the sight of this very sun. For what you did in secret, this I will do before all Israel." During the civil war, David's son Absalom, who revolts against him, takes David's concubines up to the roof of the palace and sleeps with them in the sight of all of Israel. Adultery is never private. It involves messengers, Nathan knows, and coworkers and confidants, and it even affects one's children because this adultery will lead to disasters in David's house: the rape of his daughter by his son, the murder of that son by another son, and defeat all around. David doesn't admit his sin regarding Bathsheba, and Nathan tells him that at least this particular sin has been passed over in God's purview. We have Psalm 51, which is entitled, "A Psalm of David when the prophet Nathan came to him after he had gone into Bathsheba."

Despite this repenting, Nathan tells him, "The child that is born to you shall die." And, as we know, older sons do not inherit. David and Bathsheba do have a second child, who, with the machinations of his mother, Bathsheba—who discovers how to work the harem to her advantage—and the prophet Nathan, is put on the throne. This is Solomon. So this is the end of her story, at least. Bathsheba makes her own fate, and Solomon will become the ideal and quite typical Near Eastern king and so fulfill the pro- and the anti-monarchical predictions made back when by the prophet Samuel. What happened to David regarding a woman will ultimately happen to Solomon, because, we're told in First Kings, "Solomon had 300 wives and 700 concubines, and they led his heart astray after idols." We'll see this in the next lecture.

From King Solomon to Preclassical Prophecy
(1 Kings 3–2 Kings 17)
Lecture 17

> According to the biblical tradition, Solomon was a spectacular king. …
> His court becomes a center of wisdom and learning. Solomon is so wise
> that the biblical tradition attributes to him wisdom literature.

The biblical prophet (*Nabi*; plural: *Nevi'im*) is known less for predicting the future than for communicating divine will, usually through poetry, and often in debate with kings and priests. Prophecy thus can be separated neither from politics nor from the concern for social justice. Although Abraham, Aaron, Moses, and Miriam are all called "prophets," biblical scholarship traditionally speaks of the formal role of the prophet as beginning with the monarchy and gradually ending with the rise of the theocratic state. Let's begin with Solomon to establish a picture of the type of king against which the prophets inveighed.

Solomon becomes an ideal, and quite typical, Near Eastern king; thus, he fulfills both the pro- and anti-monarchical views expressed by Samuel. On the positive side Solomon solidifies David's political basis and geographical holdings, builds the Jerusalem Temple, establishes enormous treasury reserves, and develops a positive international reputation, as witnessed by the Queen of Sheba's embassy (1 Kings 10). His court becomes known as a center of learning, such that much of Israelite wisdom literature (the Song of Songs, Proverbs, Ecclesiastes) is attributed to him.

Click Art.

The golden age of ancient Israel began with King Solomon.

Thus, 1 Kings 4:29: "God gave Solomon wisdom and understanding beyond measure, and largeness of mind like the sand on the seashore."

However, on the negative side Solomon's rule is marked by *corvées* (the extrication of unpaid labor from the population). He creates an overextended economy marked by the importation of luxury items, consequently has a heavily taxed peasantry; the "golden age" of Solomon was likely golden only for the elite. Solomon also disobeys Deut. 17:14–20 concerning not only the build-up of capital, but also: "he must not acquire many wives for himself, or else his heart will turn away." "Solomon has three-hundred wives and seven-hundred concubines," who "lead his heart astray" after idols (1 Kings 11:1–8).

Click Art

The temple of Solomon.

The inflated government, in conflict with the Yahwistic premise of social egalitarianism, could not survive and we see the end of a centralized government. Under Solomon's heir, Rehoboam, the northern tribes secede. David's kingdom will remain divided—Israel in the North; Judah in the South—for the next two hundred years. Israel, lacking the Davidic grant and always in a precarious situation with leaders, develops a strong counter to the power of the king: the prophet.

Let's look at divine/human communication. The Urim and Thummim, interpreted by the priests, were likely forms of lots. The King James Version of 1 Sam. 28:8 reads, "Divine for me by a familiar." The Hebrew reads *ob*, the Hittite/Akkadian cognate to which is "hole in the ground." Necromancy, consulting the dead, involves pouring wine or oil into a hole in the ground, although, because of a translation error, it has been misunderstood. Astrology is indicated in Isa. 47:13: "those who 'divide' [the meaning of the Hebrew here is uncertain] the heavens, who gaze at the stars, who at the new moons predict what will befall you." Hepatoscopy, the reading of liver omens, is the best-attested Near Eastern divinatory practice. Archaeologists have located clay livers from Hazor. The technique is noted in Ezek. 21:21: "The King of Babylon stands at the parting of the way, at the head of the two ways to use divination. He shakes the arrows, he consults the teraphim, he looks at the liver."

The division of functions. One theory argues that the office of prophet in its uniquely Hebrew sense was born when the office of judge—with its theological and gubernatorial elements—evolved into two distinct branches: prophets and kings.

An alternative, and complementary, view relates prophesy to ecstatic possession. Etymology of the Hebrew *nabi* has no clear ancient Near Eastern cognates. Its closest linguistic relation, the same root with different vowels, means "to rave like one insane" (cf. 1 Sam. 18:10, on Saul who "raved"). Prophetic ecstasy (literally, "to stand outside, or be beside, oneself") involves possession and, sometimes, an accompanying message.

Ecstatic prophecy is particularly, and problematically, associated with King Saul. Saul meets a band of prophets "coming down from the high place with harp, tambourine, lyre, and flute before them, prophesying." He is told: "The spirit of the Lord will come mightily upon you, and you shall prophecy with them and be turned into another man" (1 Sam. 10:6–7). The account ends: "Therefore it became a proverb, 'Is Saul also among the prophets?'" Saul sends messengers to take David, but "When they saw the company of prophets prophesying, and Samuel standing as head over them, the Spirit of God came over the messengers … and they also prophesied." Saul's next two groups are similarly affected. Finally, Saul goes himself, "and he too stripped off his clothes, and he too prophesied before Samuel, and lay naked all that day and all that night. Hence it is said: 'Is Saul also among the prophets?'" (1 Sam. 19:24).

Ecstatic prophecy, unlike classical (literary) prophecy, is widely attested cross-culturally. For example, the Egyptian "Travels of Wen-Amon" notes that "while he was making offering to his gods, the god seized one of his youths and made him possessed." Num. 24:16 introduces Balaam by saying that the spirit of God possessed him and by describing his position: "falling down but having his eyes uncovered."

This type of prophecy can be and was artificially induced. From a shrine in Anatolia dating to the 5th millennium B.C.E., archaeologists have recovered an opium pipe. In Ugarit, wine was used; in South America, psylocibin, toad skins, and so on; and at Delphi, noxious fumes.

Next we see the shift from ecstatic to pre-classical prophesy. The "sons of the prophets" who travel in bands (1 Sam. 10:5) and prophesy with one voice (1 Kings 22:12) may have served as the transition group. These prophetic bands may be directed by a teacher (cf. 1 Sam. 19–20, in which the leader is Samuel). Elijah's band apparently preserved the traditions of their teacher. The prophetic guilds may have worn external signs of office, such as shaved heads; cf. 2 Kings 2:23–25: "Some small boys came out of the city and jeered at [Elisha], saying: 'go up, you baldhead. Go up, you baldhead.' And he turned around, and when he saw them he cursed them in the name of the Lord. And two she-bears came out of the wood and tore up forty-two of the boys." Separation from the group: When an individual prophesies apart from the group, pre-classical prophesy formally begins. This is the case with Micaiah, the son of Imlah, of whom Ahab, the king of Israel, states: "I hate him, for he never prophecies good concerning me, but evil," (1 Kings 22).

Elijah, the major pre-classical prophet, is cast as a new Moses. Like Moses and Joshua, he parts water (the Jordan, in 2 Kings 2:7). Like Moses, he experiences a theophany at Horeb (1 Kings 19:8ff.). Elijah builds an altar with twelve stones (1Kings 18:30); Moses constructs an altar flanked by twelve pillars (Exod. 24:4). Elijah performs a sacrifice, the altar is consumed by fire, and the people bow (1 Kings 18:38ff.); Moses offers a sacrifice after consecrating his altar, the fire consumes the offering, and the people bow (Lev. 9:24). Like Moses, Elijah has no tomb. He is carried to heaven in a fiery chariot (hence the spiritual; see 2 Kings 2:11). In later legend, Elijah associated with Enoch, who also never "dies." The prophet Malachi, the last of the canon's classical prophets, predicts his return "before the great and terrible 'day of the Lord' comes" (Mal. 4:5 [3:23]).

Elijah's task is to prevent the people from succumbing to Baalism, sponsored by King Ahab of Israel and, especially, by his Sidonian wife, Jezebel. The predominant Canaanite deity is Baal, often accompanied by his consort(s) Anath, Ashtoreth/Ishtar/Astarte. Against their worship not only Elijah but also the classical prophets Amos and Hosea struggle, as we shall see in the next lecture. ■

Suggested Reading

Commentaries in series listed in the bibliography.

Michael D. Coogan (ed.), *The Oxford History of the Biblical World.*

Questions to Consider

1. What is the most effective way of overcoming temptations to syncretism: incorporation of competing language (the psalms), prophetic polemic, political persecution, or other?

2. In what way is madness culturally constructed? Is according a prophetic role to one who "raves" a helpful means of giving people who behave in nontraditional ways a place in society?

From King Solomon to Preclassical Prophecy
(1 Kings 3–2 Kings 17)
Lecture 17—Transcript

At the end of our last lecture we met David's heir—Bathsheba's son—King Solomon, and that begins, at least according to the biblical description, the golden age of ancient Israel, fulfilling some of the pro-monarchical comments already found in First Samuel. We find that King Solomon builds a gorgeous court and constructs a magnificent temple. It would be nice if we actually had some archaeological evidence of that temple; we do not.

But, at least according to the biblical tradition, Solomon was a spectacular king. He establishes enormous treasury reserves. His court becomes a center of wisdom and learning. Many people are familiar with the story of the Queen of Sheba who comes from Africa to Solomon's court because she had heard about his great wisdom. Solomon is so wise that the biblical tradition attributes to him wisdom literature, a genre we will encounter later. Attributed to Solomon, in addition to the love poem, Song of Songs, are also the Proverbs and Ecclesiastes—wonderful wisdom literature. We're told in First Kings, Chapter 4, "God gave Solomon wisdom and understanding beyond measure, the largeness of mind like the sand of the seashore." This is a smart guy.

But there is a downside to the centralized monarchy under King Solomon, and in this sense Solomon also fulfills the anti- monarchical material that we saw voiced by the prophet Samuel. For example, he engages in forced labor, not all that distinct from what the Israelites faced when they were in slavery in Egypt. Solomon creates corvées, laborers forced to work on his temple for him. He has an over-extended economy marked by the importing of luxury items. He's got a very, very heavily taxed peasantry. The golden age of Solomon was golden, I suspect, only for the elite. The vast majority of people were unable to participate in the glories of the kingdom, the wisdom of Solomon, or, in fact, any of the economic benefits.

As we already know, the reign of Solomon will at some point come to an ignominious end, because we're told about Solomon's many, many wives and many, many concubines. In addition to signaling Solomon's apostasy, these various wives lead his heart astray after idols. Why? Because many of them are daughters or sisters or relatives of other ancient Near Eastern kings, and therefore Solomon married these women in order to create political alliances. But it's also the case that, given the over-extended economy and these various international treaties, the center could not hold, and indeed it didn't. After Solomon's reign, his son Rehoboam was unable to retain the throne, and we will return to him in a little bit.

But think right now about the difficulties of a united monarchy, a king who has all power. He's controlling the temple; he built it. He's establishing who the priests will be. He's setting economic and political policy. For governments to stand there needs to be some sort of system of checks and balances, and it may be, given that need, that we can find therein the origins of Israelite prophecy. So it's to Israelite prophecy we will now turn.

In terms of prophecy, we've, in fact, already seen prophets. We've encountered the prophetess Deborah, who's actually a judge in Israel but called a prophetess. We've seen Nathan, David's court prophet who excoriates him for the adultery he commits with Bathsheba and the subsequent murder of Bathsheba's husband, Uriah. And we've seen, of course, Samuel, who epitomizes early prophecy. Indeed, he is the major character in the book that bears his name, First Samuel.

One can already see with this listing of three—Deborah and Nathan and Samuel—that the definition of prophet encompasses a variety of different roles. We have, for example, Deborah the military judge. We have Nathan functioning as the court conscience, and we have Samuel engaged both in priestly activities, engaging in animal sacrifice, for example, as well as in very political activities like anointing kings and, indeed, dispatching kings when he decides they are not good enough.

Today when we think of prophets, at least I typically think about people who predict the far-flung future, folks like Nostradamus or, for more contemporary concerns, Jeanne Dixon or Edgar Cayce. These are people who are interested in what's going to happen five years from now, centuries from now. For the most part the prophets in the Bible are not interested in predicting the far-flung future, in foretelling. As the saying goes, they are much more interested in forthtelling: taking a look at the current climate; how the royal house is functioning; how the economy is going; how the poor, the orphaned, the strangers are being treated; and then speaking to the people who can make a difference—the priests in the cult, the upper classes, the king—and telling them, "Folks, straighten up." The prophets will engage in both political critique, telling kings whether to engage in international treaties or not, and they will engage in cultic critique if they think that the cults are running improperly, as if, for example, people are offering animal sacrifice because they think it's the thing to do without being repentant in their hearts. And they will offer moral critique if they see the ethics of the country going to *she'ol*, their ancient version of hell.

We start with the biblical prophets from the very earliest period—Samuel, Deborah, even farther back. They are all called prophets, but here the term is so vague, like the term "judge," we really can't get a handle on it. When biblical scholars typically talk about prophets, we typically divide them into two categories. We have the pre-classical prophet, epitomized by the prophet Elijah. Pre-classical prophets are known not for writing, so we don't have any written oracles from them, but they are known for engaging in substantial political concerns. Indeed, Elijah is involved with the court of Ahab and Jezebel, and Elijah's successor, Elisha, is actually one of the people who prompts Jehu's very, very bloody coup over against the house represented by Ahab and Jezebel. Those are pre-classical prophets, and we will return to Elijah later in this lecture.

The classical prophets, on the other hand, are those prophets known for their written oracles, prophets who probably had followers who preserved what they said, prophets such as Amos, Josiah, Isaiah, and Jeremiah, and we will turn to them in subsequent lectures.

In terms of these early pre-classical prophets, we can see here perhaps the beginning of true Israelite prophecy, and here is why I want to make a distinction between Moses and Miriam and Deborah and even Samuel, on the one hand, and people like Elijah and Elisha on the other. Prophets ideally in the traditional Israelite sense are there to complain against the system. They are there to provide checks on the system. The problem with classifying someone like Moses or Deborah or even Samuel as a prophet is, in fact, they are the system. They are not engaged in critique; they are engaged in actually telling Israel what to do. They are in charge. By the time we get down to Nathan, we've now got people who are critiquing the system, and, again, Elijah becomes the ideal example of a pre-classical prophet who argues against the king, both for moral reasons as well as for cultic reasons and, indeed, international reasons.

Let's back up a little bit and talk about how prophecy functions in the ancient Near East as a means of conveying information between God and the covenant community and, indeed, the covenant community and God, because both classical prophets and their pre-classical predecessors actually have two jobs when it comes to God. On the one hand, God speaks to them and tells them information that they need to convey to the covenant community, to the kings, to the priests, to the laity, to the elite, to the poor. On the other hand, since the people frequently repent of their crimes—their apostasies—and since God frequently gets very angry at these crimes and apostasies, the prophet is also in the business of mediating back the people's repentance to God. So we might think of prophets as conduits between God and the community. But it's not simply by divine oracle or Holy Spirit that one can get information from God and convey it to the people. There are actually numerous techniques found throughout the ancient Near East, both in the Bible and external biblical sources by which people are able to get information about the divine. Most of these techniques would, in fact, be looked at, at least from current standards, as forms of technology or forms of science. They are learned arts. Priests would study how to figure out what the gods or, indeed, God, wanted.

The process here is known as divination, to determine what the divine has to say, and there are a series of techniques. Let's look at a couple of them because, in fact, we've seen them already. We simply haven't classified them in these terms. One particular divinatory technique we've already seen is called necromancy. Necromancy is the calling up of somebody who is dead to get information about the future. We saw that with King Saul, who sought out a medium, the medium of Endor, to call up the spirit of Samuel. That is actually a form of divination.

The technique we know from ancient Near Eastern sources goes like this. In the ancient Near East early on, during the First Temple Period, there is no sense of dead people living in a glorious heaven. Dead people, at least according to the biblical source, go to a place called *she'ol*. It's non-place; not much happens there. The dead are like shades floating through without much sense of consciousness, but they do have some clue as to what might happen in the future. Now, if you decide you wanted to become a medium or a witch in the ancient world, how would you facilitate your art? You would dig a hole in the ground and into that hole you would pour wine or oil or milk, and that would cause the shades of the dead to come up because, in fact, they are thirsty; nobody is feeding them. That's probably what the witch of Endor did. She dug a hole in the ground, poured something into it, and thereby allowed the shade of Samuel to come up.

We have, however, an interesting translation problem. When the King James Version of the Bible was translating this particular material at the end of First Samuel, the King James translators translated the Hebrew term for "hole in the ground" as "familiar." That's where we get the idea that witches have familiar spirits, often cats or newts or some sort of reptile, some animal that conveys to them what the devil wants. But that's not at all what's happening in the ancient Near East. The problem is they translated "familiar spirit" rather than "hole in the ground." Necromancy is one form of divination.

The priests in ancient Israel had another form called Urim and Thummim. These are actually lots. We might think of dice that they would cast, and, depending upon whether the dice or the lots came up positive or negative, they would be able to determine what God's will was. We actually see this in the inauguration ceremony for King Saul, where the prophet cast lots and first the lot fell on the tribe of Benjamin, and then the lot fell on Saul's family and ultimately on Saul himself. Divination by casting lots or by casting dice was very common.

Astrology, of course, was common. People always looked at the stars, and, if the stars fell into a certain pattern, or if the planets came up in a certain way, one could make predictions. If it was noticed that the planet Mars was on the ascent at a particular time, that, for example, a king died, the next time Mars showed up at exactly the same place astrologers might tell the king, "You better watch out this month; it does not bode well."

My favorite example of ancient Near Eastern divinatory techniques is called hepatoscopy. You actually know what this is because you've heard the term hepatitis. Hepatitis is liver disease. Hepatoscopy is divining by livers. We have from the ancient Near East, both in Israelite territory and beyond, thousands of clay livers with various spots and shapes that priests would consult. They would sacrifice a sheep, and then they would look at the liver, match that particular sheep's liver up with their models, and determine from the connections what the king ought to do, whether the queen would give birth to a son, or whether the nation should go to war. This is called hepatoscopy; it's an ancient science. We have this, in fact, cited in Ezekiel, the prophet Ezekiel, Chapter 21, where Ezekiel describes "the king of Babylon standing at the parting of the ways." He consults his *teraphim* (his family idols); he looks at the liver. Fascinating.

Other forms of divinatory techniques are mentioned in the Bible. I'll give you two more because we will see them when we get to the Joseph saga, which, as you know, we bypassed just slightly. Joseph is in Egypt; his brothers have sold him into slavery. He has risen to a position second in command to Pharaoh, and he needs some way of bringing his brothers to greater consciousness to get them to apologize to him, to repent of their evil deeds. At one point he actually plays a trick on them. He takes his cup and arranges his cup to be put in a sack of grain that his youngest brother, Benjamin, is taking back home. Then he sends out his soldiers to grab Benjamin, and the soldiers find the cup, and they respond, in Genesis 44, verse 5, "Is this not my Lord's cup from which he drinks and by which he divines?" This is probably a form of lecanomancy, the ancient technique of pouring oil onto water and watching the patterns.

Then, finally, and you should expect this, we have interpretation of dreams, particularly associated with Joseph and also associated with Daniel, two of the Jews we find in foreign courts. So we'll come back to dream interpretation later.

Now most of these forms of divination were frowned upon, at least by the official scribes, the writers of the Bible. I suspect that the average person in the ancient Near East—Israelite, Canaanite, Babylonian—would have thought all this stuff was perfectly okay in the same way today that people who would consider themselves faithful and religious and good churchgoers or synagoguegoers might, in fact, consult their horoscopes first thing in the morning. I actually do that myself, but I still consider myself quite religiously faithful. I think biblical figures would have done the same thing.

Now let's move from the question of divination to the question of actual prophecy and where prophecy in its uniquely Israelite sense came about. One explanation, which brings us back to that overextended economy of King Solomon, is that the prophet came about when the office of the judge split into two, one being the king and one being the conscience of the king. Judges are the system, but, by the time we come down to the end of the book of First Samuel, we now have kings, and we wind up with Samuel as that king's conscience. As we move on, we have David as king and Nathan as conscience.

Here the prophet is not so much engaging in divinatory practices, and the prophet is not ruling the country. The prophet is telling the king how to rule both in terms of military function as well as in terms of personal morality. But there is also an alternative view to the separation of the office of the judge, and here we move to etymology, word origins. We've already seen how biblical scholars, when they search for the origins of Yahwism, ask where that tetragrammaton, those four letters, came from. If you look at the letters that spell out the Hebrew word for prophet, the word is *nabi*. There are two possible etymological origins. One is from the Akkadian "to announce," but it's quite vague as to whether this actually works or not. The one that I think probably has the closest meaning is from another Akkadian cognate, meaning, in fact, "to rave like a mad person."

The origin here might be that the prophets in Israel began in terms of ecstatic prophesy, people who were considered possessed by the God and, in that possession, either spoke words that were intelligible, political concerns or moral concerns, or spoke words that were completely unintelligible and then other folks would come along and provide the interpretation. That is, in fact, what happens at the Greek shrine of Delphi, the Delphic oracle. The priestess would sit on a little tripod, and noxious fumes would come up, and she would simply babble. The Greek word *prophetes,* whence we get the English prophet, is actually the man who would interpret her unintelligible utterings.

We do have forms of ecstatic prophecy already in the Bible, and, in fact, we find them most commonly associated with King Saul, so let's go back to Saul for a minute. In First Samuel, Chapter 10, Saul has just been secretly anointed by Samuel, and Samuel says to him, "You're going to meet a band of prophets," and this is what happens. The band of prophets "is coming down from the high places with harps and tambourines and lyres and flutes," a lot of musical instruments, and they are "prophesying." We are not told what their prophecies are. We do not even know if these prophecies have content. They simply may be singing or making unintelligible sounds to the rhythm of the music.

Then we're told—in fact, Saul is told—"the spirit of the Lord," the *ruakh* that we already saw back in Genesis, Chapter 1, the spirit of God that hovers over the deep, the *ruakh*, "the spirit of the Lord will come upon you and you shall prophesy with them," says Samuel to Saul, "and you will be turned into another man." In other words, your own personality will become submerged, and a different person will arise. This is exactly what happens. Saul begins prophesying with this band of prophets—no content here but prophecy, and therefore the account ends. It became, in fact, a proverb: "Is Saul also among the prophets?" This is very positive. It's a sign that God approves of Saul's anointing.

When we get to First Samuel 19, we actually find the same saying, "Is Saul among the prophets?" but here in a very negative way. Saul has by now decided that David is his enemy, and Saul is right because David wants the throne. Saul at one point sends messengers to try to capture David. This is what happens to the messengers: "When they saw the company of prophets prophesying and Samuel standing as head over them, the spirit of God [here, *ruakh elohim*] overtook them and they also prophesied." Now, if you're engaging in this type of ecstatic prophecy you are in no position to be able to capture somebody who is about to usurp the throne.

Saul's messengers can't do what he wants, so Saul appropriately sends another band of messengers. They hook up with the prophets; they start prophesying. Things are not working out too well. A third group goes, and then finally Saul himself goes, and this is how the Bible describes him, speaking of Saul: "He too stripped naked of his clothes, and he too prophesied before Samuel and lay naked all that night and all that day; hence it is said, 'Is Saul also among the prophets?'" It's the same statement, but these are two very different contexts within which that statement is placed. That is, in fact, very, very common in oral traditions, oral cultures. People may well remember a particular phrase but not remember the content that gave rise to that phrase to begin with. For those of you familiar with the New Testament, we have Jesus quoted as saying, "Take up your palette and walk," but Matthew, Mark, and Luke give one particular context for that and the Gospel of John another. But, as you know, that's a very different lecture series.

In terms of ecstatic prophecy, the following example, I think, epitomizes the problem with King Saul. First Samuel 18:10 describes Saul as "one who raved within his house" or "engaged in frenzy within his house." This is why David is called upon to play the harp for him, to play the lyre, "to soothe his spirit." The Hebrew term for "raving" here is *vaet nabe,* which has the root *nabi*, the root for the Hebrew word "prophet." So instead of translating, "Saul raved within his house," we could even say, "Saul prophesied within his house." But this is ecstatic prophecy; Saul is uncontrolled.

We have examples of ecstatic prophecy elsewhere in the Bible as well as through the ancient Near East. The Egyptian "Travels of Wen-Amon," a very well-known and multiply-copied tale, talks about God seizing youths and causing them to prophesy. Among non-Hebrews in the biblical text, if we go back to the Book of Numbers, we find a spectacular prophet. He is not a Hebrew; he's a prophet for hire. His name is Balaam, and the King of Moab actually hires him to curse the Israelites because prophets have connections with the divine. Balaam, however, is possessed by God, and, instead of cursing the Israelite community in the wilderness, he winds up blessing them. The King of Moab complains, "I didn't hire you for this," and Balaam says, "Well, I'm sorry. I can only say the words that God puts into my mouth." Indeed, the irony of ironies here is that Balaam's prophecy is now part of Jewish liturgy. For those of you in the Jewish tradition you might know the song, "*Matovu Ohalekha Ya'akov.*" This is "How Goodly Are Your Tents, O Jacob, Your Encampments, O Israel." That's Balaam's blessing, possessed by the God.

Ecstatic prophecy could be accomplished not only by divine possession, it could also be accomplished by technology. From a shrine in Anatolia dating to the fifth millennium, B.C.E., archaeologists have recovered opium pipes, and I don't think those priests were smoking just because they enjoyed it. I think they used their opium haze in order to divine, to get the words of the gods. In Ugarit, wine was used, and in South and Central America, psilocybin, mushrooms, and toad skins. It was ecstatic prophecy at Delphi, as we've already seen, and perhaps even through transfer mutilation. When Elijah fights the prophets of Baal on Mt. Carmel, we are told that the prophets of Baal "cried aloud and cut themselves after their custom with swords and lances until the blood gushed out." They are beside themselves. They are, in fact, in ecstasy. If you think about the root of ecstasy, it simply means "ecstasis," "to stand outside yourself." That's ecstatic prophecy.

Where are we when it comes to biblical prophecy? I suspect that both explanations—the separation of the role of judge into king and prophet and also ecstatic prophesy—I suspect they are already combined in Samuel, whom we've seen is not only the conscience of the king and not only a political functionary but also the head of a band of prophets. Prophetic bands continued in Israel. We have a very good example of them, not only with the prophet Elijah but also with Elisha, who, along with many other prophets, follows Elijah in his jobs, in his travels. It's even been suggested that the bands of prophets had particular *sigla* such as bald heads.

That may explain Second Kings, Chapter 2, where we are told, "some small boys came out of the city, and they jeered at the prophet Elisha, saying, 'Go up, you baldhead! Go up, you baldhead!" and "go up" then more or less meant what the English equivalent means now. Elisha "turned around and when he saw them he cursed them in the name of the Lord, and two she-bears came out of the woods and tore up 42 of the boys." This is quite nasty, right? Prophets can do miracles, particularly the pre-classical prophet. Is the bald head a sign, a shaven head a sign of prophecy? It could be. It might also be that Elisha was simply bald.

In terms of pre-classical prophets and their formal means, kings hired prophets. Indeed, they hired bands of prophets, so the office of court prophet became quite popular. That's Nathan's job, for example. But eventually the court prophet would separate from the band and give the king oracles that the king did not want to hear. Epitomizing this is a court prophet from the court of King Ahab, Jezebel's husband. His name is Micaiah ben Imlah. At one point King Ahab complains about him so much, he says, "I hate him, for he never prophesies good concerning me but only evil." If the prophet says bad things are going to happen to the king, that's probably a legitimate prophet.

Thus we come to Elijah. Elijah, epitomizing the pre-classical prophet, is cast in the role of Moses. For example, Moses has a theophany, a revelation of God on Mt. Sinai; Elijah has a revelation of God on Mt. Horab, the "E" source's name for Sinai. Elijah performs a sacrifice on Mt. Carmel; the entire altar is consumed with fire. The people see this miracle, and they bow down and worship God. Moses does exactly the same thing in Leviticus. He offers a sacrifice and thereby consecrates his altar. The fire consumes the offering, and the people bow down. In the Hebrew you can see the words being repeated. Like Moses, Elijah has no tomb. Moses, as you know, is buried in secret. For Elijah a chariot comes down from heaven, a fiery chariot, and takes him back up, and that produces the legends that Elijah will at some point come back. In our discussion of canon very early in the series, we saw how the Christian canon puts the prophet Malachi at the end, predicting the coming of Elijah.

In terms of Elijah himself, what does he do? What is his role? His task is not easy. He goes up primarily against the king of the north, King Ahab, and his wife Jezebel. Jezebel you probably think of as someone who's like a prostitute or at least a woman whose morals are suspect. Actually, Jezebel does have her problems: she lies, she steals, she cheats, she engages in libel, she apostasizes, she murders, but she's actually quite faithful to her husband, Ahab. I mean, the one thing she doesn't do is engage in some sort of sexual crime. The reason she gets this reputation is because, right before her death, we find in Second Kings, Chapter 9, "she painted her eyes and adorned her hair, and she stood looking down from the window." This is a woman who knows enough to put on makeup right before she dies. I give her credit for that.

Elijah is not only dealing with Ahab's political crimes, but he's also dealing with Jezebel's sponsorship of her own gods. Jezebel is from Sidon; she worships one of the Baals. So Elijah has to explain to the people, Baal-worship is evil, it's apostatizing, you should only worship the one God. But for the people to whom Elijah is giving these oracles, this did not make much sense. They could not much more conceive of agriculture without Baal than they could conceive of agriculture without rain because they are living in a Canaanite environment and Baal is the nature god. So Elijah has to explain why Baal is simply a false god.

He is thereby depicted as contrasting the powers of YHWH and Baal. In his contest with the priests of Baal on Mt. Carmel, he has the priest on Mt. Carmel set up one sacrifice, he sets up another, and he says to the priest on Mt. Carmel, "Have your god Baal send fire down and consume the sacrifice." Then you can picture him just kind of sitting there, tapping his foot, flipping his fingers, and waiting, and he begins about noontime to taunt the priests of Baal. He says, "Where is your God? Is he on a journey? Is he meditating? Has he gone aside?" "Gone aside" in Hebrew means, "Has he gone to the bathroom?" "Perhaps he's asleep and you have to wake him up."

This is taunting the Baal-worshipers, and ultimately what we see with Elijah is that his God finally sends down fire from heaven and consumes that sacrifice. Throughout the rest of Elijah's career, he will not only combat Baal-worship, he will also establish the model by which future prophets, both pre-classical and classical, find their voice and establish the means by which they can convince the covenant community that their voice is the one that needs to be heeded.

The Prophets and the Fall of the North
(1 Kings 16–2 Kings 17, Amos, Hosea)
Lecture 18

The theophany that Elijah experiences is an anti-Baal polemic because Baal is a nature god manifested through rain, manifested through storms and in thunder. ... Following all these natural signs comes a stillness, and it's in that stillness that God speaks to Elijah. There is the difference between the God of Israel and Baal.

E lijah contrasts the powers of YHWH and Baal. The Canaanite nature god cannot provide food, but in the midst of famine, YHWH's prophet is miraculously fed, and he can miraculously feed others, as he does for the widow of Zarephath. On Mt. Horeb, Elijah witnesses wind, earthquake, then fire, but YHWH comes in the silence: He is neither in, nor controlled by, nature (1 Kings 19:1–18). Yearly, Mot (death) overcomes Baal, but Anath revives him with appropriate rituals. Elijah raises a dead boy, while the "dying/rising god" cannot resurrect himself.

In addition to calling rulers to account, pre-classical prophets also sanction political events. Elijah's successor, Elisha, arranges the coup that deposes Ahab and places Jehu on the throne. The prophetess Huldah legitimates the Book of Deuteronomy. Prophetic signs can solidify political symbols. By the separation of Solomon's kingdom, with Solomon's son Rehoboam continuing the Davidic line in Judea in the South and Jereboam I ruling in Israel, the North (1 Kings 11:26ff.) receives prophetic warrant. The prophet Ahijah states that Solomon had to be punished: "Because he has forsaken me, and worshiped Ashtoreth the goddess of the Sidonians, Chemosh the god of Moab ... and has not walked in my ways, doing what is right in my sight ... as David his father did" (1 Kgs.12:33). The prophet sanctions the split by symbolizing it: "Ahijah laid hold of the new garment that was on him, and tore it into twelve pieces."

The twelve "minor prophets" are collected together after the major latter prophets (Isaiah, Jeremiah, and Ezekiel). This collection is also called "The Book of the Twelve." The minor prophets are: Hosea, Joel, Amos, Obadiah, Jonah, Micah, Nahum, Habakkuk, Zephaniah, Haggai, Zechariah, and Malachi. The order is roughly chronological, from earliest to latest. The Book of the Twelve equals the length of each major prophetic scroll.

Prophetic rhetoric, arresting expressions and evocations of Israel's history, these devices continue the covenant practice of self-criticism. Amos opens with a series of pronouncements against Israel's neighbors: Judah, Edom, Moab, Ammon, and so on. The nations listed first are condemned for their treatment of outsiders (usually Israel and Judah). Israel and Judah are then condemned for internal social oppression. Israel's crime is more heinous in that the people reject God's blessings. Amos 2:10–11 invokes the liberation

from Egypt and the early days of Canaan. Amos adopts the rhetorical forms of cultic proclamation but announces the opposite of what was expected: "Woe to you who desire the day of the Lord! Why would you have the day of the Lord? It is darkness and not light." (5:18ff.).

Amos, one of the earliest prophets.

Click Art.

Devices associated with the wisdom tradition (Proverbs, Ecclesiastes, Job): (1) Rhetorical questions and images from nature: "Do two walk together unless they have made an appointment? Does a lion roar in the forest when he has no prey?" (Amos 3:3–4). (2) Comparisons: "Thus says the Lord: 'As the shepherd rescues from the mouth of the lion two legs, or a piece of an ear, so shall the people of Israel who dwell in Samaria be rescued, with the corner of a couch and part of a bed'" (Amos 3:11–12). (3) Striking characterizations excoriated the upper class: "Hear this word, you cows of Bashan ... who oppress the poor, who crush the needy, who say to their husbands: 'Bring that we may drink ... '" (Amos 4:1ff.). Of particular concern to the prophets was religious complacency, people who observe the rituals while ignoring the poor in their midst.

Amos, although from Judah, proclaimed his message in the cultic shrines of Israel during the reign of Jereboam II (787–747), a time of economic prosperity. He identifies himself (1:1) as "among the shepherds of Tekoa." With only two exceptions, the *Tanakh* uses *ro'eh* for shepherd; Amos uses *noqed*. Comparative philology and Ugaritic cognates indicate that the *noqed* is a shepherd who cares for temple flocks destined for sacrifice. Amos divorces himself from such connections: "I am no prophet, nor one of the sons of the prophets ... [i.e., a member of a prophetic guild], but I am a herder and a dresser of sycamore trees" (7:14). The line may suggest that Amos is a seasonal or migrant worker.

Hosea's initial activity coincides with the last year of Jereboam II (747 B.C.E.) and the Syro-Ephraimite war (Hos. 5:8–14, cf. 2 Kings 15:27–30). In 734–732, Syria and Ephraim/Israel united against Assyria, but Assyria prevailed, and Israel was subjugated by the Assyrian king Tiglath-Pilesar III. Hos. 12:12f. describes "Jacob" as "Fleeing to the land of Aram; there Israel did service for a wife, and for a wife he herded sheep." Jacob's desire is transformed into an unproductive Syrian alliance. Hosea adapts traditions of Israel's past. Hos. 2:1ff. offers an allegory of Israel's covenantal history. Reformation appears to be beyond both the ability and the will of priesthood, court, and people; only destruction will make renewal possible. The allegory evokes the Baal cult: "In that day, says the Lord, you will call me 'my husband' and no longer will you call me 'my Baal'" (2:16–17).

Let's look at the fall of the North. Hos. 5:14 accurately observes, "I will carry off and none shall return." In 725–724, Israel violated its treaty with Assyria and turned to Egypt for protection. Sargon II of Assyria then began a siege that culminated in 722 when Samaria fell and Sargon deported about five percent of the population (see 2 Kings 17). The Assyrian conquest is confirmed by external documentation. An inscription from Sargon II concerning the conquering of Samaria includes the statement: "I led away as booty 27,290 inhabitants of it." Sargon II's inscription goes on: "with the tribes of Tamud, Ibadidi, Marsimanu, and Halapa, the Arabs who live far away, in the desert ... I deported their survivors and settled them in Samaria." They "feared the Lord, but also served their own gods, after the manner of the nations from among whom they had been carried away ... So they do to this day" (2 Kgs. 17:29–41). ■

Suggested Reading

Major commentaries in the series listed in the bibliography.

Questions to Consider

1. Have either political or religious rhetoric changed much over the past two-and-a-half millennia?

2. What elements need to be in place for a culture to survive geographical displacement?

3. In the shared system of governance among kings, priests, and prophets, how is balance maintained?

The Prophets and the Fall of the North
(1 Kings 16–2 Kings 17, Amos, Hosea)
Lecture 18—Transcript

In our discussion of the prophet Elijah and, indeed, of pre-classical prophets in general, we've noticed that often the Deuteronomic historian, the editor of First and Second Samuel and First and Second Kings, will sometimes use earlier materials such as the Moses tradition in order to develop models by which he can convey what these pre-classical prophets are doing. We've noticed that Elijah experiences a theophany on Mt. Horab much as Moses experiences a theophany on Mt. Sinai. But the theophanies themselves are different. Moses receives a law; Elijah, in fact, receives much of a prophetic commission. The theophany that Elijah experiences is, in fact, an anti-Baal polemic because Baal is a nature god manifested through rain, manifested through storms and in thunder.

On Mt. Horab, Elijah experiences an enormous storm, winds coming to rend the mountains and shatter the rocks before him, but then, we're told, "but the Lord was not in the wind." Then after the wind there is an earthquake, but the Lord is not in the earthquake, and after the earthquake there is a fire, but the Lord is not in the fire. The Lord is not in any of these manifestations associated with Baal. Following all these natural signs comes a stillness, such as you would find after a storm, and it's in that stillness that God speaks to Elijah. There is the difference between the God of Israel and Baal.

What does the God of Israel do? The God of Israel says to Elijah, "Hey, go back and preach my religion, my cult. Tell Ahab he's doing the wrong thing. Tell Jezebel she is engaging in apostasy. Let my people hear what they need to hear." So Elijah, commissioned in this anti-Baal theophany, goes back to engage in political concerns because those pre-classical prophets are heavily involved in what the government does. Following the theophany, Elijah actually does return, and what does he do? He is told by God,"Return on your way to the wilderness of Damascus, and when you arrive you shall anoint Hazael over Aram—Damascus, Syria—and you shall also anoint Jehu, son of Nimshi, over Israel [and that's in place of Ahab, who's now on the throne]."

So what God is suggesting is that Elijah produce a military coup. "You shall also," God tells Elijah, "anoint Elisha as a prophet in your place." How bloody does all this become? God continues, "Whoever escapes from the sword of Hazael, Jehu shall kill, and whoever escapes from the sword of Jehu, Elisha shall kill." So not only are pre-classical prophets engaged in giving political advice, they are themselves functionaries within creating the coup.

Elijah's successor, Elisha, actually does arrange this coup. Ahab is deposed. Jehu is placed on the throne. That's what pre-classical prophets do. Indeed, the division of Solomon's kingdom itself into Israel in the north and Judah in the south is arranged, if not facilitated, by a pre-classical prophet named Ahijah. Speaking for God, he announces that Solomon must be punished, as Ahijah puts it, in God's words, "because he has forsaken me and worshipped Ashtoreth, the goddess of the Sidonians and Chemosh, the god of Moab, and he has not walked in my ways doing what is right in my sight as his father, David, did." Ahijah actually sanctions this split by taking a new garment and ripping it into 12 pieces, symbolizing those 12 separate tribes prior to David's and then Solomon's unification of the kingdom. The country will be split apart.

The Deuteronomic historian confirms Ahijah's view by explaining to us that Solomon's heir, Rehoboam, is an unfit ruler. We've already seen that Solomon's kingdom is over-extended. The people are heavily taxed, and they want relief from those economic burdens that the throne is imposing upon them. So a group of envoys primarily from the north goes to Rehoboam, and they say, "We need some relief." Rehoboam has two groups of advisors: one group, an older group that served his father, the wise King Solomon, and a younger group, men with whom he was raised in the palace. We might think about the "J" source's description of those sons of God who abused their position. I think they might be referring to Rehoboam's advisors.

The older advisors say to Rehoboam, "Listen to the people, be nice to them, and they will love you." Rehoboam listens to his younger advisors, who actually tell him to tighten the ropes on them. Rehoboam listens to those younger men, and he says, "Well, my little finger is thicker than my father's loins. I'm more vigorous than he. I'm going to be stricter than he. I will put increasing burdens on you. Don't ask me for mercy. Don't ask me for favors. I am simply not going to give them." And the kingdom's split.

Indeed, Ahijah engages in aiding this split by facilitating the coup staged by Jereboam, and he's the one who will rule in the north. Jereboam is apparently one of the foremen on Solomon's building projects, so he's actually known in the capital, and he has some support from the Egyptian Pharaoh—his name is Shishak. The kingdom's split. Rehoboam, part of the Davidic line, stays in the south, ruling from Jerusalem. Jereboam takes the ten northern tribes with him and establishes his capital in the former Shechem, now called Samaria. What we will have throughout the rest of the Deuteronomic history, up to the end of Second Kings, is two parallel tracks of history: one from the southern kingdom, one from the northern kingdom. It's quite likely that the Deuteronomic historian is actually using court records to bolster his own particular take on what's happening with the government.

As the kingdom's split—and we have the northern kingdom not under Davidic rule but under kings who arise by coup and who are deposed by coup—we begin to find the origins of classical or writing prophecy. The earliest prophets we have include Amos and Hosea, and these are two prophets who prophesy up in the northern kingdom against the shrines in the north, places like Dan—you'll remember the shrine of Dan from the end of the Book of Judges, where Micah's Levite was dragged by the Danites up to that shrine at Dan—as well as places like Beth-El, and you will remember Beth-El from Jacob's dream of those ladders. Those shrines still continue, and that's where we locate Amos, our first classical prophet, and then Hosea.

In order to set the scene for Amos and Hosea, we'll begin with a brief—very brief—overview of the corpus called the "Minor Prophets." There were two groups of prophetic texts, one the major prophets—Isaiah, Jeremiah, and Ezekiel—and then the minor prophets, 12 of them. Why are they separated? It just depends upon the length of the scroll. Isaiah, Jeremiah, and Ezekiel are very, very long; they take up a scroll a piece. If you look at the 12 minor prophets, they will fit nicely onto one papyrus scroll. There are 12 of them. That's handy—it's easy to remember. There are 12 tribes. The Book of the Twelve will include Hosea, Joel, Amos, Obadiah, Jonah, Micah—You notice I have to check with my notes here because I can't remember them, either—

Nahum, Habakkuk, Zephaniah, Haggai, Zechariah, and Malachi. Obviously we won't do them all; we'll hit the highlights.

I want to start with Amos and Hosea because their rhetoric is so exquisite—it's almost palpable; you can feel it—and because, when one looks at them in the context of their historical setting, one can see their involvement with the political climate internationally as well as the moral climate internally to the northern kingdom. Let's look, then, at their rhetorical strategies. Why do people actually bother to write down their materials in the first place? Which, if we think about it, is really quite extraordinary. The canonizers of this text wrote down the words of people criticizing the very establishment that the canonizers themselves represented. This is a covenant community that is very, very much interested in self-critique, and those words of the prophets will continue to echo through the generations. They are indeed still being read in churches and synagogues.

We'll begin with the prophet Amos, who opens with a series of pronouncements against outsiders. He says, "For three transgressions, O Edom, and for four, because you oppress the nations, I will not give you reprieve." "For three transgressions and for four, Moab"; "for three transgressions and for four, Syria." Now picture Amos doing this out loud. I suspect the people in the north would be with him all the way because he's complaining about the traditional enemies: Edom, Moab, Syria. The people are entirely with him. So it may well have come as a shock when Amos then explains to them, "Thus says the Lord, for three transgressions of Israel and for four, I will not give reprieve. I will not revoke punishment." Why? Because "they sell the righteous for silver. They sell the needy for a pair of sandals." It's that concrete imagery that will really grab. "They trample the heads of the poor into the dust of the earth, and they push the afflicted out of the way." That's the power of his rhetoric, and he's got you right there.

Amos does not use some of those key cultic terms we've seen before such as *berit* (covenant) or even *Torah*. Nevertheless, he does anchor his pronouncements in the covenant community's history. For example—this is Amos, Chapter 3, verse 1— "Hear this word that the Lord has spoken against you, O people of Israel, against the family which I brought out of Egypt." So just as we find in the law codes that Egyptian experience, freedom from slavery, becomes the model by which morality is ensured, it also becomes the paradigm, the template by which the prophets express their own concerns about the covenant community's responsibilities, although, as Amos points out, the community was rescued by God. The community doesn't heed that rescue and thereby, in effect, enslaves other people. They repeat history, but here they are in the role of Pharaoh rather than in the role of the oppressed.

How else does Amos get his views across? He actually uses a technique we know from divining, to go back to that earlier version of technical prophecy. Part of divining is to look out and see something and in that thing that you see get a message, as if today you would go outside and you would see a bird sitting where you had not seen a bird before and you take it as a positive omen—or a negative omen if it's on your windshield. Amos can do exactly the same thing.

Here is an example—and the reason this is so compelling is not only because he uses perfectly normal objects, but he enhances his view of something that's perfectly normal with puns. The problem here is we miss the puns in English translation: "Thus the Lord God showed me and behold a basket of summer fruit [something that anybody could find], and he said, 'Amos, what do you see?' and I said, 'I see a basket of summer fruit.'" The Hebrew for "summer fruit" is *kayitz*. And "the Lord said to me, the end [*kaytz*] shall come upon my people Israel." From *kayitz*, summer fruits, to *kaytz,* the people would have heard the harshness even of those expressions, those hard "K" sounds, and they would remember every time they picked up a basket of summer fruits.

Amos also plays upon the people's expectations only to reverse them. All cultures have rhetorical expectations. If somebody begins "The Star-Spangled Banner," we pretty much know how it's going to end, right? If somebody begins a cultic liturgy, a creed, for example, or a familiar prayer in church or synagogue, we know how it's going to end. The people in ancient Israel knew the same. For example, in cultic settings they would talk about the Day of the Lord, something to expect when God's righteousness would become fully manifest, and they would say, "The Day of the Lord, the Day of the Lord." Amos picks up on it, "The Day of the Lord, the Day of the Lord," but then he goes on to say, "It is darkness and not light," totally changing their expectations of what they might have expected.

He also invokes material that sounds very much like the curses we find at the end of Deuteronomy. We might think back here to those suzerainty-vassal treaties that end with a series of blessings if you do what the suzerain wants and end with a series of curses if you disobey the suzerain's commands. "I withheld the rain from you. I smite you with blight and mildew. I sent among you a pestilence after the manner of Egypt." It sounds like the end of Deuteronomy; it's actually Amos, Chapter 4. I think the people would have recognized this particular litany of curses as stemming directly from those suzerainty-vassal treaties. They would have recognized the covenant connections even in the words.

In addition to cultic language and treaty language, Amos also invokes rhetoric from schools of wisdom. We'll experience wisdom later. Well, we've already experienced wisdom, but we'll experience wisdom literature later when we get to books such as Proverbs and Job. The wisdom school itself had a particular form of rhetoric. They would, for example, ask rhetorical questions. For example, "Do two walk together unless they've got an appointment? Does a lion roar in the forest when he has no prey? Does a young lion cry out from its den if it has caught nothing?" My students frequently add, "If a tree falls in the forest and no one is there, can you hear the sound?" Amos does not say that.

But these rhetorical questions go on. "Is a trumpet blown in the city and the people are not afraid?" That's getting a little bit closer. "Does disaster befall a city unless the Lord has done it?" So we go from simple wisdom literature, conventional questions, to the idea of national disaster. Amos is able to take this wisdom literature and use it for his own use. Indeed, sometimes those rhetorical questions will actually be answered by the prophet. "Does a young lion cry out from its den unless it has a prey?" A few verses later Amos will give this incredibly striking image, "Thus says the Lord, as the shepherd rescues from the mouth of the lion two legs or the piece of an ear, so shall the people of Israel who dwell in Samaria [the northern capital] be rescued with a corner of a couch and part of a bed." This is so palpable you can envision it—you can even see it.

Wisdom literature will also develop, by stepping-stone construction, a pattern, one building upon the next building upon the next. Amos will do exactly the same thing. As he speaks of the Day of the Lord and explains, "It is darkness and not light," he goes on, "It is as if someone fled from a lion and was met by a bear"—you can't win in this type of wisdom literature— "or went into a house and rested his hand against the wall and was bit by a scorpion." For Israel's crimes it seems as if there is no redemption.

Enacting this particular metaphorical force, Amos will engage a rhetorical trope that we find with other prophets subsequently, categorizing the people of Israel—and for the southern prophets, the people of Judah—as unfaithful, adulterous wives, as women who are unconcerned with morality. In fact, many biblical scholars these days look at the prophets as engaging in misogynistic, anti-woman rhetoric, but this is, in fact, part of their culture; it's patriarchal culture.

This is Amos excoriating the upper class: "Hear this, you cows of Bashan, who oppress the poor, who crush the needy, who say to their husbands, 'Bring, that we may have a drink.'" "The time has surely come upon you," Amos says, "when they shall take you away with hooks, even the last of you with fishhooks." From ladies mincing as they go, saying, "Bring me a drink," to fishhooks stuck into flesh—this is why Amos's words still carry across the centuries.

Amos had a particular concern with reviving the cult. He was infuriated when members of the upper class would go to the cult and offer sacrifices at those shrines and then continue to oppress the poor. I think contemporary religious leaders and clergy have exactly the same problem. Folks who go to church on Sunday oppress the poor on Monday. Individuals who go to the synagogue on Shabbos on Saturday morning the next week engage in standard business practices. This is endemic to any sort of religion.

Amos brings this idea directly into the people. He says, speaking for God, "Come to Bethel and transgress. Bring your sacrifices every morning, your tithes every three days. For so you love to do, O people of Israel." You can hear the dripping sarcasm here. His most well-known oracles reinforce this point. Speaking for God, Amos says, "I hate, I despise your feasts. I take no delight in your solemn assemblies. Take away from me the noise of your songs. To the melody of your harps I will not listen." Then he goes on in a couplet that has been cited by liberation theologians and American politicians and civil rights workers: "Let justice roll down like waters and righteousness like an ever-flowing stream." That's what he wants.

The prophet Hosea will say the same thing in a much simpler way, "I desire mercy, not sacrifice." Now, when the prophets here complain against the cult, they are not actually saying, in fact, get rid of the cult. This type of hyperbole is a standard form of ancient rhetoric, both Near Eastern in general and Hebrew rhetoric in particular. What the prophets will do is say, "I want this instead of that," but what they are really doing is saying, "This is more important than that."

These diverse rhetorical techniques as well as their marvelously effective employment— and I hope you've been able to hear this—raise questions about Amos's own identity. I mean, who is this guy that he would have come up with such amazingly diverse and powerful sayings from the wisdom tradition, from the cult—"baskets of summer fruit"—that even a peasant could see? We know Amos is actually from Judah, the southern kingdom, and he goes up north to issue his oracles. This is as if somebody, say, from Dallas or Atlanta would go to Boston or Bangor to give particular views. It's amazing that people in the north would have even listened to him. His setting is during the reign of Jereboam II. You'll remember Jereboam I as the man who split away from Solomon's heir.

The time is 787 through 747. It's actually a time in the north of enormous economic prosperity. The north, or at least the upper class, is doing extremely well, but in a good many economies, when the elite is doing extremely well, they may be doing so because the poor are contributing everything. So what we've got is a substantially bifurcated economy. Typically, classical prophets tell us something about their background. Hosea gives us more details than, in fact, we may actually want about his marital life, his children. Amos actually tells us very little. Although it is conventional for prophets to identify themselves by means of their family background, to explain who their father is, no father is listed for Amos. That's actually a break in the convention, and it has caused people to wonder if Amos's father was so unimportant his name did not bear mentioning. Did he even know who his father was?

In a case like this we might pose that Amos is not from the upper classes but actually may be a peasant or from the shepherd group who recognizes injustice and somehow feels compelled to protest against it. Amos identifies himself right at the beginning of his book as "among the shepherds of Tekoa." The word he uses for shepherd, *noqed*, is not actually the standard word that we find for shepherds elsewhere, for example, "David is the good shepherd." A *noqed* is a shepherd who cares for temple flocks destined for sacrifice. Because of that, some scholars have suggested that Amos actually was involved with a cult, that he may have originally been a priest and then separated from it when he noticed those abuses. It's possible.

Others have suggested that Amos was part of a band of prophets, like those guilds we saw in discussion of the pre-classical prophets. Whether he was or he wasn't, he wants to make clear to people who listen to him that he is not associated with the priesthood now and he is not associated at all with prophets. This is what he says: "I am not a prophet nor one of the sons of the prophets. I am a herder and dresser of sycamore trees." Sycamore trees grow sycamore figs; they are the food of the poor people. In case you were wondering, to dress them actually means to puncture them, which is how they become fertile and how they grow.

Amos, in terms of his oracles, never explicitly states that the people will repent. It's not clear whether he expects them to or not. There is a happy ending in Amos, Chapter 9, verses 11-15, a promise that, "In that day I will raise up the booth of David that has fallen. I will restore the house of the fortunes of my people Israel. I will plant them upon their land, and they shall never again be plucked up." But many scholars think this is from a later hand. The prophecies of Amos and Hosea spoken in the north were eventually edited or readapted by scribes down in the south so that, when the northern kingdom fell to Assyria in 722, some of the refugees clearly brought with them the literary traditions of the north, the prophet Amos and the prophet Hosea. By the very reference here to the booth of David, that brings us back to that royal grant covenant with the south. This sounds very much like a southern editor rather than Amos himself.

The north is destroyed in 722. Amos's prophecies about the Day of the Lord being darkness and not light seem to have come true. This particular fall is actually witnessed by the prophet Hosea, whose initial activity coincides with the last years of the reign of Jereboam II, around 747 B.C.E., and, on the international horizon for Hosea, what is called the Syro-Ephraimite war. Amos knows about the empire of Assyria on the horizon, but for Amos the major problems are internal to the cult, to economic oppression internally.

Hosea becomes much more involved in external concerns, and here we find a classical prophet in the mold of those pre-classical prophets like Elijah and Elisha giving the king and the people advice about treaties, politics, and international alliances. For example, in 734–732 B.C.E., the kingdoms of Syria and Israel—Israel called here Ephraim, think about that Elohist (E) source— Syria and Ephraim unite against Assyria. So we have Assyria and Syria—please do not confuse them. Assyria is the major empire in the Middle East, and the Assyrian war machine is making its way, country through country, town through town, attacking and bringing additional peoples into its empire. Syria and Israel are afraid that they are going to be next, and they are right.

It turns out that Assyria was able to prevail against those combined forces, and under the leadership of the Assyrian emperor, Tiglath-Pilesar III—we just don't have names like that these days— Tiglath-Pilesar III subjugates the northern kingdom so that the kingdom of Israel becomes an Assyrian vassal. Hosea actually describes this in Chapter 12, describing Jacob as fleeing to the land of Aram—that's Syria. "There Israel did service for a wife, and for a wife he herded sheep." This is Hosea's complaint against the alliance between Israel and Syria, here using the ancient traditions of Jacob going to Laban to find a wife, Rachel and Leah.

But here this is not a good sign; the ancient tradition becomes a negative example. Hosea says, "Look, your ancestor Jacob went into service and you've done exactly the same thing. Jacob should never have worked for Laban. He was tricked, and you've been tricked, too." Hosea's concerns are archly political. He advises that Jereboam II stay out of that alliance with Syria because, in his view, God will provide everything that's needed. Here again you can find that suzerainty-vassal model, which says, "God alone should be your ruler. Don't have any other alliances with any other nations." We can even hear here that anti-monarchical source in First Samuel, "Don't be like the other nations," because it means treaties and bringing foreign gods into your temple and your shrines.

Hosea is counseling isolationism. But that's not what he got. It may actually have been the case that Hosea's counsel would not have worked. Assyria, given its strength—and we know about Assyrian strength from numerous extracanonical materials; the Assyrians kept great records, and we have parts of their archives as well as *stelae*, inscriptions on stone pillars explaining how they conquered various places, including the north of Israel—Assyria would have conquered Israel anyway. It simply came a little bit sooner, probably because of that Syro-Ephraimite alliance.

In 725 and 724, the Assyrian emperor, Shalmaneser V, sent members of Israel's upper class into exile. In the ancient world, conquering empires would take the elite of a community, the elite of a kingdom—the king, the royal court, the priests, and often the artisans—and ship them somewhere else. They are in the business of population movement. Then they would ship other people in. The idea was here that, if you removed the leaders from your land and stuck them somewhere else, they would not be able sufficiently to regroup and get back home. Even if they did get back home, other people would be there. It's an absolutely brilliant strategy. If your empire lasts long enough and that first generation of exiles dies out, your empire will probably remain. Hosea, Chapter 5, verse 14, notices this initial exile. "I, even I, will rend and go astray. I will carry off and none shall return." Hosea apparently continued to prophesy until the actual fall of the northern kingdom, the conquering of the capital, Samaria, in 722.

At the time that Israel is captured there is no hope. Hosea gives us a sense that perhaps there might be. He describes his initial relationship with his wife as commanded by God, God telling him, "Hosea, go take a wife of harlotry"—He does. He marries a woman named Gomer—"and have children in harlotry." That's his view of Israel making foreign alliances. But ultimately God says, "My relationship with Israel, now committing adultery with these foreign nations, will eventually be reconciled." Hosea puts it this way, "I will allure her and bring her into the wilderness again and speak tenderly to her, and there she shall answer as in the days of her youth, as in the time when she came out of Egypt." He goes on, evoking images from the Baal cult, "In that day, says the Lord, you will call me 'my husband,' [*adoni*] and no longer will you call me 'my Baal, my Lord.'"

But that's not what happens. In 722 the kingdom is destroyed. The 10 tribes of the north are exiled. The remaining literature and some refugees from the north flee to the south and create new legends and give the south additional material by which it will establish its own identity. And that's what we'll see in the next lecture.

The Southern Kingdom
(Isaiah, Deuteronomy, 2 Kings 18–23)
Lecture 19

The combination of the people moved in by the Assyrians and the indigenous population remaining in the land comprise a new group of people who become known as Samaritans.

The Northern Kingdom fell, but both its memory and its reconfiguration continued to affect the identity of Judah. The resettled peoples in the North intermarried with remaining Israelites. They came to be called "Samaritans" from Israel's capital, Samaria, and they will become the enemies of the people in the South. The "10 tribes" are lost to history but preserved in legends. The people of the South yearn for the reconstitution of all the tribes, and from this, certain legends develop: They are the Native Americans; they are the British (from *Berit* [covenant] and *ish* [man]—a false etymology); they were relocated to China, India, or Afghanistan; or they were reintegrated into the covenant community in the Messianic age.

Israel, compared to Judah, has a less visible theological system. With the emphasis on only the Mosaic covenant, Israel perhaps believed that with expulsion, the suzerain was no longer protecting the vassal. The people may have lacked a strong clergy. They lacked a viable "canon." Distinctions between the exile of the Israelites and the exile of the Judeans by Nebuchadnezzar. Assyria fractured ethnic groups in exile; the Babylonians established exiled groups in self-governing neighborhoods. Assyria was not conquered until the Babylonian campaigns of 612, over a century after Samaria fell; Babylonian captivity lasted forty-eight years.

Scholars argue that the biblical book entitled "Isaiah" is a composite representing at least three prophetic voices addressing different historical settings. First Isaiah, chapters 1–24, 28–39. The "first Isaiah" flourished during the second half of the 8th century. The first Isaiah had at least two children, each with a symbolic name (cf. Hosea's children): She'ar-Jashub (7:3), "a remnant will return," and Maher-Shalal-Hash-Baz (8:1–4), "The

Spoil speeds, the prey hastens." His "call" (Isa. 6) occurs "in the year King Uzziah died" (742), after a reign of forty years. His prophetic "school" (cf. 8:16–17) continued into the post-exilic period.

Along with the various rhetorical forms and images associated with Amos and Hosea (woe oracles, the adulterous wife, personification of the rich as indolent women), Isaiah develops the parable (cf. 2 Sam. 12:1–12). Most famous of these is the "parable of the vineyard" (5:1–7), in which God is the planter and Judah the vineyard that fails. For Isaiah, the golden age is not the wilderness period (as it was for Hosea), but Davidic Jerusalem, and it is Jerusalem he seeks to save. Isaiah, seeking Judean political neutrality, counsels against involvement in the Syro-Ephraimite War (7:1–16;

Isaiah, the first major prophet from the Southern Kingdom.

see 2 Kings 20) through the oracle of Immanuel: "Behold a young woman has conceived and shall bear a son, and shall call his name Immanuel. This child shall eat curds and honey when he knows how to refuse the evil and choose the good."

References to a "virgin" birth derive from the Septuagint, which renders the Hebrew "young woman" as *parthenos*. Isaiah 9 and 11 describe an ideal king; the imagery develops into messianic desiderata. Judean royal theology also contributes to messianic speculation.

Like Amos and, especially, Hosea, it is not clear whether Isaiah expects the people to repent. "Go and say to this people: 'Hear and hear, but do not understand; see and see, but do not perceive … ' until the cities lie waste, without inhabitants" (6:9–13). Rather than prophesying total destruction, Isaiah promulgates a "remnant theology," as his son's name, She'ar-Jashub (and see 10:20–23), suggests.

King Hezekiah (c. 704), likely prompted by Isaiah, instituted a series of religious and political reforms (2 Kings 18). Among these reforms was the symbolic end to vassalage by stopping sacrifices to the Assyrian emperor. Domestically, cultic reforms included the razing of "high places" and "sacred poles" and the removal from the Temple of Nehushtan the bronze serpent that Moses had made for apotropaic cures (18:4). Public policy reforms included the Jerusalem water conduit (Hezekiah's tunnel, the Siloam tunnel, a 1,700-foot excavation through solid rock).

The reforms ended with King Hezekiah's death. His successor, Manasseh, returned Judah to vassal status (2 Kings 21). Manasseh also reintroduced apostasy: rebuilding the high places and erecting sacred poles, constructing altars to Baal, and so on.

Josiah, Manasseh's grandson, attempted a second reform based on the laws of Deuteronomy (2 Kings 22–23). Deuteronomy is ostensibly Moses's last will and testament, only discovered during Josiah's Temple renovations (22:8–10). The prophetess Huldah, when visited by a consortium of priests, (indirectly) proclaims the book to be authentic (22:14–20). Deuteronomy abolishes previously legitimate altars (Deut. 12:1–31; 12:5–6). It disenfranchises the Levites, who had presided over the local shrines. It centralizes the cult in Jerusalem (the Samaritan Pentateuch locates the centralization in Samaria, on Mt. Gerizim). Of particular concern are monarchical interests: the divine legitimation of the king. He is exhorted (17:18) to "write for himself in a book a copy of this law." The LXX translates "copy" as *Deuteronomion*, "Second law."

Deuteronomy's notable contributions to biblical law include: (1) Promoting the education of children by inculcation, cf. 6:7: "You shall teach them [the Laws] diligently to your children, and you shall talk of them when you sit in your house, and when you walk by the way, and when you lie down, and when you rise up. And you shall bind them for a sign upon your hand, and they shall be for frontlets between your eyes; and you shall write them upon the doorposts of your house, and upon your gates." (2) The sign and frontlets are *Tefillin* or phylacteries, two small square leather boxes containing scriptural passages worn on the forehead and left arm. And (3) The doorpost/gate reference is to the *Mezuzah* (Hebrew for "doorpost"), a case containing Deut. 6:4–9 (the "Shema"); 11:13–21, and El Shaddai.

The hopes created by the Deuteronomic reform were dashed when Josiah, having reneged on his participation in the Syrian-Egyptian alliance, is then killed by Pharaoh Neco at Megiddo. The failure of the reform and the rise of Babylon set the stage for the prophecies of Jeremiah and for the Babylonian exile, the topics of the next lecture. ∎

Suggested Reading

Commentaries in series listed in the bibliography.

Michael D. Coogan, (ed.), *The Oxford History of the Biblical World.*

Questions to Consider

1. What are the benefits, and the dangers, of interpreting prophetic oracles outside their original historical situations?

2. How does the international scene affect Judean policies, both political and religious?

3. How and to what extent does Deuteronomy respond to the prophetic calls for social justice?

The Southern Kingdom
(Isaiah, Deuteronomy, 2 Kings 18–23)
Lecture 19—Transcript

When the northern kingdom falls to Assyria in 722, all that remains of the covenant community is the southern kingdom. There is still a Davidic king on the throne in Jerusalem, there is still a sense of this eternal covenant, and, although the northern kingdom is gone, its influences remain on the south, indeed, on biblical literature and even on contemporary legendary development.

In terms of history, the combination of the people moved in by the Assyrians and the indigenous population remaining in the land comprise a new group of people who become known as Samaritans. The irony is, as history goes on, the Samaritans in the north become the enemies of the people in the south. Even when you get up into New Testament times, you will find materials such as the parable of the Good Samaritan, and that itself suggests the ongoing enmity between these two population groups.

In terms of legendary development, people in the south continued to yearn for the reconstitution of those 12 tribes, and eventually past the biblical period we have developing legends both of the ingathering of the exiles and the messianic age and also these stories of 10 lost tribes who today frequently show up in pages of things like *The National Enquirer*. There are, in fact, legends of the 10 lost tribes. Some of them are quite early, some of them more recent. My favorite happens to be that the 10 lost tribes somehow found their way to the Western Hemisphere and are now Native Americans. That model actually comes about from some Cherokee inscriptions found in Tennessee, my home, which, if read backwards, look sort of like Paleo-Hebrew. I don't think that's actually the case. Others have suggested that the Israelites exiled by Assyria moved to Afghanistan. That's actually possible because Assyria did have territorial holdings in that area. Others have suggested northern India, China, and there is one Jewish legend that suggests that God moved them to some mystical place beyond some mystical river waiting for the Messiah to come and at that point reconstitute the tribes.

Although the northern tribes are lost to history, indeed, their very existence and the literature that they produced had ongoing value for people in the south. Refugees from the north would bring their material down, and the northern literature, their history, and their etiology wound up bolstering the self-identity of the southern kingdom. This becomes extremely important when the south itself faces Assyrian onslaught, and finally in the sixth century when the south is facing the new empire on the block, the Babylonians.

If we look at reasons why the north fell, and I think the south itself would have considered that, we might be able to get some sense on why the south was able to preserve its ethnic identity when it, too, was taken into exile. For example, the south had the strong concern for the royal grant, the Davidic covenant. In the south the Davidic king is taken into exile, but when Babylonian exile ends, a Davidic king is still present. It helps to have a particular figurehead or politician around whom the community can rally. Because the northern government was based on a series of military coups, there was no national leader and no natural leader, indeed, for the people in the north in exile to follow.

The people in the north may have lacked a strong clergy. The people in the south, particularly when they went into Babylonian exile, not only were able to bring temple functionaries, but they were able to gather clerical support in exile. This is the beginning of the "P" code, which we've already seen in our discussion of source criticism in the documentary hypothesis. It may also have been that the people in the north lacked a canon, a literature that could bind people like the American Constitution or the Declaration of Independence binds us today. People in the south decided it was imperative that they compile their history. The Deuteronomic historian is beginning. The priestly writers are beginning. The "J" material, even the "E" material brought down from the north, provide a repository for the exiles from the southern kingdom, the exilic community in Babylon, to establish their self-identity.

Indeed, the conditions of the exile itself differed. The Assyrians split up communities, but the Babylonians, when they put a community in exile, allowed that community to remain together, as if it were in some sort of golden ghetto. With communities remaining together, they can retain their identity much easier. Moreover, the Assyrian exile lasted much longer than the Babylonian exile. Assyrian exile lasted well over 100 years. There was nobody left from that initial generation to go home and rebuild. The Babylonian exile lasted under 50 years so that, indeed, there were people in Babylon who may well have retained vague memories of living in Jerusalem and at least passed on those memories to their children. The time is close enough to keep that hope of return alive.

The southern kingdom also knew what it was like to face threat. Thus we come to how people in the south with prophets like Isaiah and, as we'll see later, Jeremiah, and with law codes like the Book of Deuteronomy, were able to preserve their identity—religious, political, ethnic—despite incursions first by Assyria, indeed, sieges by Assyria, and later, when the Assyrian empire is conquered by Babylon, still retain their ethos, their self-identity, who they are as a covenant community.

So let's begin now by looking at exactly what the southern kingdom did, because they, too, knew about Assyria. They knew about the fall of the north, and Sennacherib, the Assyrian emperor, also had his sights on the southern kingdom. Things were not easy for them back then. We'll begin with the first prophet, the first major prophet from the southern kingdom. This is the prophet Isaiah, the first of the major prophets as opposed to the minor prophets we discussed in the last lecture. The prophet Isaiah has a corpus in the canon that goes for 66 chapters. It's enormous. Biblical scholars, as is their wont, came to the conclusion that Isaiah did not write all of this material. In the same way that biblical scholars questioned whether Moses wrote the Pentateuch and came to the conclusion that the Pentateuch is actually comprised of a series of different sources ultimately compiled by a single editor, so, too, with the prophet Isaiah.

Today biblical scholars are wont to divide up Isaiah's prophecy into at least three different time periods with three different styles of writing and three different authors. The first Isaiah, who is my major concern in discussing the early southern kingdom, is represented primarily by Chapters 1 through 24. Then we skip a couple of chapters, and then 28 through 39. This prophet flourished during the second half of the eighth century, in other words, the 700s. This particular prophet had at least two children, both with symbolic names, and we've already seen the function of names. One was named She'ar-Jashub, "a remnant will return." That already gives us a sense on Isaiah's view of what will happen. Yes, part of the south will, in fact, fall; the Davidic royal grant will not fully hold. But God's promises cannot simply be revoked *in toto*. Part of the kingdom, a remnant, will return. Isaiah knew that.

Isaiah also had another child whose name in Hebrew was the somewhat awkward, Maher-Shalal-Hash-Baz, similarly awkward in English: "the spoil speeds, the prey hastens," or, as the new English Bible reads, "speedy, spoiling, prompt, plundering." This is a difficult name to give to a child, but it also suggests what Isaiah saw upon the horizon. The Assyrian empire would come; there would be some collapse of the southern kingdom. By having children with these two names, Isaiah was able to demonstrate, whenever these children showed up in public, yes, capture would occur. Yes, disaster will strike part of the kingdom, but, nevertheless, "a remnant will return."

We get a sense of Isaiah from his call-narrative, that generic conventional form that explains how God calls upon, commissions, a particular prophet. Isaiah's is a magnificent view of the heavenly throne, and, indeed, from Isaiah 6, that call-narrative, other prophets will build. Ezekiel has a similar call-narrative, and we'll see this throne vision again when we get to the prophet Daniel. Here is how it starts. Isaiah tells us that he receives his call in the year that King Uzziah died. This is actually 743 B.C.E., and it is an important time because Uzziah had been on the throne for about 40 years. So here we have a major time of transition. What now will happen to the political situation? We also know that Assyria is on the horizon. They are already at the borders of the north, and they are moving inexorably toward Israel and then Judah.

What else does Isaiah tell us? He tells us in his throne vision that God is looking for somebody to help. God is sitting on a throne, a magnificent throne, his train trailing in the temple. That is still his house. Jerusalem needs to be preserved. He says, "Who will help?" and Isaiah says, in effect, "Not me," because, as is typical, prophets do not want their commission. It's a dangerous job. Isaiah says, "I am not worthy. I have sinful lips," but God arranges for a seraph, one of the seraphim—these heavenly beings—

to touch his lips with a coal from the altar (that's from that temple altar where the sacrifice is offered), and Isaiah's lips are thereby purified. God can then say, "Who will go?" and Isaiah says, "*Hineni*, here I am. Send me." That's Isaiah's commission. And what does he tell us? He tells us that the people, in fact, need to repent—standard prophetic rhetoric—but the way he conveys it is to manipulate those prophetic forms in a new and arresting way by pulling on the earlier tradition and developing it. For example, we already have the formulation of the parable, the short story which is meant to convey a particular meaning. We've had one example of this in the Book of Judges where Abimelech, the false judge's brother, Jotham, tells a parable to the people of Israel explaining how all the trees looked for a leader and eventually they settled on the bramble bush—the false judge.

We've also had a parable told to King David by the prophet Nathan, the parable of the ewe lamb, which explains how a very rich man, when a traveler came to visit him, instead of taking a lamb from his own flock, went to a poor man who had only one little ewe lamb whom he fed by hand, whom he took at his table and fed and treated even like a daughter. The rich man slaughtered the poor man's ewe lamb, and Nathan says to David, "And what should be done with such a terrible thing?" David says, "Well, obviously the rich man should be killed," and Nathan looks at him and says, "You are that man because you took Bathsheba and slaughtered Uriah."

So the parable form is already well-known. Isaiah gives us a magnificent example, which becomes a standard trope: Israel as the vineyard. One of the reasons this parable works is because Isaiah forces the covenant community in the south to provide its own response to the parable, just as Nathan forces David's hand.

God plants a vineyard, takes care of it, puts up a watchtower, and makes sure everything is perfect, but the vineyard does not yield for God. It produces wild things, weeds. What now is the vineyard owner God to do? Isaiah ends this parable by saying, "And now, inhabitants of Jerusalem, people of Judah, judge between me and my vineyard. What more was there for me to do for my vineyard?" God through Isaiah gives his own answer, "I will remove its hedge, and it shall be devoured. I will break down its walls, and it shall be trampled upon." Through the parable, Isaiah is able to predict what will happen to the covenant community. Indeed, it's immediately after this parable that Isaiah gives us his call, telling us that Isaiah will be the voice of God to explain the covenant community's fate. It's a staggering and fantastic sense of organization.

Isaiah, like most prophets, is involved not only with morality and repentance, Isaiah is also heavily, heavily invested in political concerns. Like Hosea, he advises political neutrality, and he counsels King Ahaz, from whom, by the way, we actually have archaeological seals remaining—it's attestation of this king—not to get involved in the Syro-Ephraimite alliance. When the kings of Israel and Syria noticed that the Assyrian empire was on the horizon, they formed an alliance. We saw this with Hosea. Isaiah says, "Don't get involved. It will not help." He also tells Ahaz, "Don't get involved with Assyria, either," because Ahaz is very worried. If he doesn't sign on to the Israelite alliance, they might attack him (and, indeed, they did). Should he go to Assyria for protection? Should he engage in that alliance? What should he do?

He eventually goes to Assyria against Isaiah's wishes and makes an alliance, at which point Israel under Ahaz becomes a vassal state. In order to explain why this is not a good thing, why Ahaz should never have even considered Assyrian connections, let alone connections with Israel and Syria, Isaiah tells an oracle set in the king's throne room. This is Chapter 7, right after that call. This oracle remains, surprisingly enough, one of the foundation statements of early Christianity and contemporary Christianity. This is Isaiah talking to Ahaz. He said, "Look, the Lord himself will give you a sign regarding these various alliances. Behold, this young woman has conceived and she'll bear a son, and she'll call his name Immanuel [which means "God with us"], and this child shall eat curds and honey. And when he knows how to refuse the evil and choose the good, the land before whose kings you are in dread will fall. There is no reason therefore for you to engage in political alliance." This child is likely the future king Hezekiah who takes the throne in 715.

What happens here is that, when the Hebrew of Isaiah is translated into Greek, "that young woman," the Hebrew *alma,* is translated as *parthenos*, which means "virgin," and this then becomes, for the evangelist Matthew in the New Testament, a sign of the birth of the Messiah. Matthew actually quotes the Greek version of Isaiah, Chapter 7, verse 14: "Behold, a virgin will conceive and bear a son, and you will call his name Immanuel." But Isaiah writing in the 700s is not going to predict something that's going to happen 700 years later. He's giving a very specific oracle to a king at a very, very specific time.

Isaiah's predictions about an ideal government—and he had great hopes for Hezekiah—will ultimately find their way into messianic predictions. But that's not actually what happened to the kingdom of Israel. Isaiah, I think, did not expect Judah to survive even though Judah had that royal grant, because after he is commissioned he tells us that God told him to prophesy but with the result being that the people would not hear and the people would not understand: "Go and say to this people, hear and hear but do not understand, see and see but do not perceive until the cities lie waste without inhabitants." So the call convention is inverted. Most prophets are called to bring the people to repentance; Isaiah is called here to seal their doom. Rather than prophesying total destruction, Isaiah, as you know, has this view of remnant theology: "a remnant shall return." He speaks of a shoot from the stump of Jessie—that's David's father—returning. The royal grant is there but in a transformed way.

Isaiah becomes very influential during the reign of King Hezekiah and, indeed, prompts Hezekiah to engage in a series of reforms both international and internal. Since there was a transition in the Assyrian government at the time, it makes good sense for Hezekiah to do that. Internationally, he attempts to throw off Assyrian vassalage. Of course Assyria doesn't like this and begins a siege of the kingdom of Judah. Internally, he begins a reform of the temple. We can see this in Second Kings, Chapter 18. He goes into the temple and removes, for example, a bronze serpent that tradition says dates all the way back to the time of Moses but had become an idol for the people.

Regarding public policy, he constructs a water conduit. We actually have archaeological remains of this water conduit, including the inscription. It's a six-line inscription written at the time when the two teams of diggers actually met. One thinks of the transcontinental railroad. This became exceptionally important during the Assyrian siege of Jerusalem because it allowed Jerusalem to have free-flowing water inside. He razes some of the high places, those external shrines, pulls down sacred poles, and tries to wipe out Baalism, which is still strong in the area. Unfortunately what happened is that his successor, King Manasseh, returned the kingdom of Judah to vassal status. He had little choice in the matter. But he also returned the kingdom of Judah to various forms of pagan encroachment. He rebuilt the high places. He erected those special poles. He also apparently sacrificed one of his children. That old view of human sacrifice, that Canaanite view, comes back around. Isaiah offers oracles of hope, oracles of renewal, but ultimately the southern kingdom would fall.

Before it fell, however, there was yet one more reform, and that's a reform that occurs under King Josiah. Now, whether you think Josiah was prompted by simply a coincidental political happenstance or whether Josiah is an exceptionally manipulative, politically astute king, I leave up to you. Here is the story. King Josiah, needing to reform the country once again, engages in renovations of the temple building, and in the process he happens to discover a scroll. The scroll winds up being, in fact, the Book of Deuteronomy. Those scholars who think this is actually a true account suggest that the Book of Deuteronomy had been composed in the north, brought down by refugees to the south, and at that time secreted in the temple, ultimately to be found 100 years later or so by Josiah. What does Josiah do? He implements the concerns of Deuteronomy. He first makes sure that the text is legitimate. He consults a local prophetess—her name is Huldah—and then he decides, "Yes, I will put this new law into place." What does Deuteronomy allow him to do? It allows him to centralize the government. For example, he pulls down, destroys, all of those external shrines. We might think of shrines like the one at Shiloh where Samuel and Eli were functionaries, or, in the northern kingdom, Dan and Bethel.

What this does is it disenfranchises the Levites who were out serving at all those shrines, but, for Josiah's benefit, it centralizes the cult in Jerusalem. This is extremely helpful if you happen to be the leader in Jerusalem because now the temple becomes the only place where you can offer sacrifices, and that means increasing monies coming in as well as the need for pilgrimage to Jerusalem, and thereby Josiah will have a much more economic base. The text itself regarding the centralization of the cult is actually quite vague. The Samaritans, those people up in the north, have their own version of the

Book of Deuteronomy. Whereas Deuteronomy suggests to the people in the south the cult should be centralized in Jerusalem, the Samaritan Pentateuch suggests that that cult should be centralized in Samaria on Mt. Gerizim. One has to be a little careful about what this original text says.

It also asserts that kingship is okay—here against some of that anti-monarchical material we had in First Samuel—but what the king is exhorted to do is avoid all those sins that Solomon had committed. The king is not to multiply wives. The king is not to overextend the economy. The king is not to engage in excessive trade in horses, which is, in fact, what Solomon did, and we have the legend of Solomon's stables. And the king is exhorted, in Deuteronomy, Chapter 17, "to write for himself in a book a copy of this law." The Septuagint translates "copy"—more colloquially, "repetition"—as *Deuteronomion*, a "second law," but it really means "a copy." That's where the name "Deuteronomy" comes from. The king, so says this book, "shall keep this law with him, and he shall read in it all the days of his life, that he may learn to fear the Lord his God by keeping all the words of this law and these statutes and doing them."

Deuteronomy, as we've seen, has some very notable materials in terms of how to deal with the poor and the oppressed, how to celebrate Sabbath, and why to celebrate Sabbath. A good much of Deuteronomy also finds its way into both Christian and Jewish liturgical formulation. Deuteronomy, for example, is exceptionally interested in inculcating knowledge to children. This is, as we'll see later, a connection with wisdom literature. This is Deuteronomy 6:7: "You shall teach them [meaning the laws] diligently to your children, and you shall talk of them when you sit in your house and when you walk by the way and when you lie down and when you rise up." Deuteronomy goes on to say, "You shall bind them for a sign upon your hand and they shall be for frontlets between your eyes." In contemporary—indeed, in ancient—Jewish practice, we have examples of *tefillin*, phylacteries from the Dead Sea areas, ancient, before-Jesus materials. Phylacteries are straps with little boxes connected to them that religious Jews today still put on their head for frontlets between their eyes and wrap seven times around their arm and over their hand for the sign upon their arm. These are, in effect, praying tools.

The text goes on, "You shall bind them for a sign upon your hand, and you shall write them upon the doorposts of your house and upon your gates." Well, the word for "doorpost" or "gate" is *mezuzah*, and this explains why Jewish families even today have little scrolls and little holders attached to the doors of their house. It's simply commanded in Deuteronomy, and it is followed up today. Deuteronomy also has that very famous line, "Hear, O Israel, the Lord is our God, the Lord is one," or "the Lord alone." Deuteronomy, therefore, provides us an example of how an ancient text winds up providing the means for the covenant community to identify itself even in Babylon—can you picture?—with these signs, these praying tools, these positioning of laws on your gates and on your houses. You become self-identified. It is an example as well of how the covenant community can prevail across the centuries.

The hopes created by Isaiah with his view of the remnant returning, and, indeed, created by the Deuteronomic reform, are dashed. Political circumstances become increasingly difficult. Assyria is on the rise. Josiah the king decides that he will make an alliance with Egypt for protection but then ultimately pulls out of the alliance. Egypt then takes reins against Josiah. The pharaoh whose name is Pharaoh Neco—finally we have a pharaoh with a name—goes to battle against King Josiah. They meet at the Megiddo Pass, which is, by the way, in Greek, "Harmageddo"—Armageddon. It's a place where disasters happen. They meet at the Megiddo Pass; King Josiah is killed. The reform is dashed. Josiah's heir brings back the community into apostasy.

That leads us to the time of Jeremiah, and what will Jeremiah build on? Jeremiah, to a great extent, will build on the prophet Isaiah, and what we will wind up seeing is a sense of a remnant perhaps returning but also a continuing hopelessness. Where are we then with the literature of the southern kingdom? We have all of that material from the north brought down south. We have the "E" writer telling us patriarchal stories. We have the prophecies of Amos and Hosea edited by people in the south. We have the prophecies of that first Isaiah, the remnant returning. The second Isaiah, by the way, prophesies during the time of the Babylonian exile. There is yet a third Isaiah, the last 10 chapters of the book, the prophecies from the time of the return from exile. They are all simply put together in one particular school.

We have other people who are prophesying at this time, such as Habakkuk and Micah. I think the best way of summing up what's happening in the south is to give you a statement from Second Kings regarding the abuses of King Manasseh, because this is where the Deuteronomic history will end and how the Deuteronomic historian explains why the southern kingdom fell. Here is how it goes: "Judah had done abominable things." So this is the word of the Lord, the God of Israel: "I am bringing such evil upon Jerusalem and Judah, I shall wipe out Jerusalem as one would wipe a dish, wiping it and turning it upside down. They shall become a spoil and a prey." You can hear Isaiah's child in the background, "the spoil speeds, the prey hastens." "They shall become a spoil and a prey to their enemies." But, as Isaiah would put it, "a remnant will return."

Babylonian Exile
(2 Kgs. 24–25, Jeremiah, Isaiah 40–55, Ezekiel)
Lecture 20

> I often think that we should take pity on those poor prophets who had
> to speak to the covenant community in the southern kingdom of Judah.
> Their kings and their people were convinced that there was no way the
> country would ever fall. They had the promises to David.

The siege of Judah: "In the 14th year of King Hezekiah, Sennacherib King of Assyria came up against the fortified cities of Judah and took them" (2 Kings 18:13). Recognizing the disaster of the Kingdom of Israel, the South had to respond. To prevent catastrophe, King Hezekiah pays enormous tribute, including stripping the gold from the Temple, but the siege prevails. Herodotus (*Hist.* II.131) attests that the Assyrians suffered a defeat on the borders of Egypt because their equipment was ruined by some ravenous field mice, a notice some scholars connect with the Judean situation. Sennacherib's own version implies that after a successful attack on Jerusalem, Hezekiah agreed to increased tribute, which he would send directly to Nineveh. The Deuteronomic historian attributes the lifting of the siege to divine intervention: "And that night the angel of the Lord went forth and slew 185,000 men in the camp of the Assyrians" (2 Kings 19:34; cf. Isa. 36–39). Judean theologians concluded that the royal grant protected Jerusalem (Isa. 10:24ff.).

Babylon defeats the Egyptian-Assyrian coalition at the Battle of Carchemish in 605 (see Jer. 46:2; 2 Kings 24). Judah is now under Babylonian control. Jehoiakim, King of Judah, rebels after a three-year submission but dies (in 598) before Babylon retaliates. Jehoiakim's son, Jehoiachin (Jeconiah), surrenders to Nebuchadnezzar (Nebuchadrezzar) in 597 (see Jer. 21:2; 2 Kings 24; this surrender is attested in Babylonian records). Probably between 3,000 and 10,000 people are then deported.

We see the end of the Judean monarchy when Mattaniah (probably another son of Josiah) is made king and renamed Zedekiah to symbolize his vassal status (1 Chr. 3). Zedekiah seeks an alliance with Egypt (Jer. 17; 1 Kings 25; Ezek. 17). In retaliation, Nebuchadnezzar destroys Jerusalem, forces a second deportation, takes the Temple valuables to Babylon, and executes Zedekiah. Gedaliah, a friend to Jeremiah (Jer. 39–40), is appointed governor but assassinated by a member of the royal family.

Given this dismal situation, Jeremiah reflects an intense spiritual struggle. His oracles are juxtaposed with events in his life such that his personal tragedies mirror the nation's doom. His "temple sermon" provokes a judicial hearing. His prophesying put his life in danger: Manasseh probably executed prophets (2 Kgs. 21:1b), and King Jehoiakim certainly did (2 Kgs. 26:20–33; Jer. 2:20). His solution to Judah's failings is a "new covenant" (31:31ff.), in which YHWH "Will put my law within them, and I will write it upon their hearts ..."

After Gedaliah's murder, Jeremiah and his scribe, Baruch, are taken by Judean refugees to Egypt. The Book of Lamentations, although traditionally attributed to him, manifests his sorrow but not his themes or style. From Jeremiah's exile develops the legend that the ark, last seen when Solomon placed it in the Holy of Holies (1 Kings 8), was brought to Egypt. Second Maccabees 2:4ff. suggests that Jeremiah hid the ark on Mt. Nebo and proclaimed, "The place shall be unknown until God gathers his people together again and shows his mercy."

Ezekiel proclaimed both invective and hope to the Babylonian exiles c. 593–563. Probably part of the first deportation of 597, Ezekiel found an exilic community confident that rescue was imminent and the Temple, inviolable. These Judeans linked their position with that of Abraham: "The word of the Lord came to me, 'Son of man, the inhabitants of the waste places ... keep saying, 'Abraham was only one man, yet he got possession of the land; but we are many; the land is surely given to us to possess'" (33:24). Ezekiel insists that this view is incorrect; the people are not yet deserving of redemption. His message is less one of consolation than of justification. The people's apostasy caused YHWH to bring about the exile. Redemption will follow repentance (36:24): "I will take you from the nations, and gather you from all the countries, and bring you into your own land." But this will occur only "after many days … in the later years" (38:8–16).

Earlier prophets and the Deuteronomic history spoke of sin as a corporate problem, and its results could be inherited (e.g., the sins of Manasseh precipitate the exile). Ezekiel stresses individual responsibility: "The son shall not suffer for the iniquity of the father, nor shall the father suffer for the iniquity of the son; the righteousness of the righteous shall be upon himself, and the wickedness of the wicked shall be on himself" (18:20).

Ezekiel's prophecy is enhanced by highly symbolic terminology (wheels within wheels [the "chariot vision"]; the valley of the dry bones). He also engages in symbolic actions (Ezekiel is commanded not to mourn the death of his wife, to remain in particular positions for extremely long periods of time). Perhaps the intensity, if not complete oddity, of his pronouncements and visions is best seen in the context of exilic trauma. His visions foreshadow changes in prophetic language as prophets find increasing resistance to their proclamations: after exile, what more could be threatened?

The Second Isaiah offers a message of consolation. YHWH, not Marduk, controls history. Because exile was predicted, prophecy of restoration is also credible: "A voice cries, 'In the wilderness prepare the way of the Lord; make straight in the desert a highway for our God'" (40:3). The return of the exiles will be a new Exodus (Isa. 43). Babylonian gods will go into captivity as Babylon is destroyed (Isa. 46–48).

YHWH's universal sovereignty and suffering servant. Isa. 44:5 anticipates universal recognition of God and the covenant community: "This one will say, 'I am the Lord's'; another will call himself by the name of Jacob." The "suffering servant" motif extends the *diaspora* promise: "I will give you as a light to the nations, that my salvation will reach to the end of the earth …" (49:1–6; cf. 42:1–4; 51:4ff.). Isaiah's image of Abraham reverses that in Ezekiel. Isa. 51:2–3 reads: "Look to Abraham your father and to Sarah who bore you; for when he was but one I called him, and I blessed him and made him many."

YHWH appoints Cyrus of Persia ("God's anointed," Heb: *Messiah*) to defeat Babylon (Isa. 44:24–45:13). In 539 B.C.E., the Babylonian king Nabonidus flees, and the Persian army takes Babylon peacefully. Cyrus will, in 538, sponsor an edict to permit those in exile to return home. This practice is confirmed by the Cyrus Cylinder, dated to 528 B.C.E. ■

Suggested Reading

Commentaries in series listed in the bibliography.

Michael D. Coogan, (ed.), *The Oxford History of the Biblical World.*

Questions to Consider

1. Are references to other nations in a universal monotheism indicative of inclusion, co-optation, colonialism, or all three?

2. How does one distinguish between a theology of hope and a theology of self-deception?

3. How does "religion" (defined as you will) in a *diaspora* or in exile differ from religion in the homeland?

Babylonian Exile
(2 Kings 24–25, Jeremiah, Isaiah 40–55, Ezekiel)
Lecture 20—Transcript

I often think that we should take pity on those poor prophets who had to speak to the covenant community in the southern kingdom of Judah. Their kings and their people were convinced that there was no way the country would ever fall. They had the promises to David, the Davidic royal grant. They knew that God would protect Jerusalem because Jerusalem, David's city, was God's own city. It was where God's temple was located. It was where the train of God's cloak stayed, as we saw in Isaiah's call vision. Indeed, people in the south even had history on their side.

Pity poor Jeremiah, for example, who had to deal not only with all these conventions of royal grants and theology but also with history such as the following: According to the Deuteronomic historian, in the fourteenth year of King Hezekiah, Sennacherib of Assyria came up against the fortified cities of Judah and actually took them. One would think at this point people in Jerusalem would begin to panic. Recognizing that disaster was on the horizon, King Hezekiah actually did take some action. He paid a bribe to the Assyrians. This typically works in the Near East, and it seemed to work a little bit at that time; Sennacherib actually withdrew. But then Hezekiah revolts against Assyria, and this is what happens. The Assyrian campaign actually comes back, and it's ready to take Jerusalem.

Now, given the highly stylized nature of the Deuteronomic history, it's not exactly clear what happened. But this is what we find out in Second Kings, Chapter 18 and 19. There was a siege. The people were convinced they were going to die. Then suddenly, at the last moment, "That night the angel of the Lord went forth and slew 185,000 men in the camp of the Assyrians, and when the morning dawned, there they were all dead." Contemporary political analysts have a difficult time ascribing military victory to angelic intervention.

There have been some other suggestions as to what did happen to this actual historical siege of Jerusalem. Herodotus is often cited here, his book of

Histories. I don't think this actually had any bearing whatsoever, but since biblical studies textbooks tend to cite it, I'll share it with you. According to Herodotus, the Assyrians had suffered a defeat on the borders of Egypt about this time, because their equipment was ruined by some ravenous field mice that had a taste for the leather. Therefore, the Assyrians needed to withdraw their troops on the borders of Judah in order to bolster their campaigns in other areas. It's a lovely story, but I don't think it helps us with the biblical tradition. Sennacherib in his archives provides us his own version. He implies here that the attack on Jerusalem was actually successful, at which point Hezekiah agreed to increase tribute yet again, which he promised that he would send directly to Ninevah, the Assyrian capital.

It's not exactly clear what happened, but we know what the effects are. The people in Judah are convinced nothing will ever happen to their kingdom, and this is the context in which we look at a prophet like Jeremiah on the eve of the attack against Judah by Babylon, trying to convince the kings, trying to convince the people, that, in fact, God might not protect Jerusalem, might not protect Judah. So let's look at Jeremiah and the fall of the northern kingdom to see how he expressed his views, what the political circumstances were, and how, in fact, the people once taken into exile did manage to preserve their identity through the priestly writers, through the second Isaiah, through the prophet Ezekiel.

In order to understand Jeremiah we need to understand his setting in life. You will recall that's the technical term, *Sitz in Leben.* He begins at about the time of Josiah's reform, which we discussed in the last lecture, when the Book of Deuteronomy was discovered during temple renovations. His call likely came in 627 B.C.E.—this is the thirteenth year of the reign of Josiah. Already political events on the horizon do not bode well, but at least Jeremiah at the beginning of his life could take some heart that the reforms would work. Alas, Josiah, as you know, is defeated by the Egyptians, by Pharaoh Neco at a battle set at the Megiddo Pass. The reforms are for nothing. The kingdom sinks back into apostasy. Jeremiah simply cannot fathom how this is happening. Moreover, Jeremiah had in his mind the Deuteronomic ideal that people who behave appropriately will be rewarded by God and people who sin will be punished by God. But then he notices that King Josiah, one of the good kings, dies in battle, and the reforms end. Where is God here?

Meanwhile, on the international horizon, an Egyptian-Assyrian coalition is designed to prevent Babylon from succeeding in its drive to conquer the entire Mesopotamian area, but that Egyptian-Assyrian coalition comes up against Babylon at the battle of Carchemish in 605, and they lose. Judah, which had previously been in vassalage to Assyria, becomes a vassal state of the Babylonian empire, and this is the context—official context—for Jeremiah's preaching. Things were not going well, and Jeremiah knew it. He knew that the government of Judah was unstable, and, as he watched the Babylonian empire deal with puppet kings, the situation went from bad to worse.

Under Babylonian control, Jehoiakim, King of Judah, rules for three years of submission, and then stupidly he rebels. He dies, in fact, before Babylon is able to take any stand against this rebellion. Jehoiakim's son, Jehoiachin, also named Jeconiah—there were two different names given for him—then surrenders to the Babylonian ruler. This is King Nebuchadnezzar, also pronounced "Nebuchadrezzar," and we have both spellings from antiquity. Jehoiakim's son, Jeconiah, surrenders in 597, and at this stage Babylon engages in what other ancient Near Eastern empires do. They begin to deport upper-class members and royal members and priestly members of the capital city. Babylon deports between 3,000 and 10,000 people from Jerusalem, including the king. They are taken into exile, where they remain in Babylon. We're going to leave them there for just a little bit.

Meanwhile, back in Judah, Mattaniah, who is probably related to Josiah, perhaps one of his sons or grandsons, assumes the throne under Babylonian protection. Babylonians rename him Zedekiah simply to symbolize his vassal status. But Zedekiah, established by Babylon, in yet another remarkably politically stupid move, seeks an alliance with Egypt and rebels against Babylon. In retaliation, in the year 587, King Nebuchadnezzar re-enters Judah, re-enters Jerusalem, and, at this point, burns down the temple constructed by Solomon, burns down God's house, the setting of Isaiah's call vision. He burns down the place that everybody in Judah and Jerusalem consider to be inviolate. He destroys the city, forces a second deportation, takes the valuables left from the temple's destruction into Babylon, and executes Zedekiah.

Gedaliah, who is actually a friend of Jeremiah—and we see him referred to in Jeremiah, Chapters 39 and 40—is appointed governor, but he's soon assassinated by a member of the Davidic royal family, one of the few who are left in Jerusalem. Given this incredibly dismal situation, one can understand why the Book of Lamentations is often attributed to Jeremiah. He did not write it, but, as you can hear even in the name Lamentations, this is a text that somehow bears his stamp.

That Jeremiah took all of these international events seriously is confirmed by his own call-narrative, and thus we go back to that convention of the prophetic commission. We learn in Chapter 1 that he is from the town of Anathoth, which is a little over two miles northeast of Jerusalem. He's from an area that would be affected by any sort of political policy because events in Jerusalem—the news, indeed, the attacks—would certainly trickle out to the suburbs. He's also intimately familiar with events regarding the cult. It's often suggested that Jeremiah is a descendant of one Abiathar who served as high priest under King David, but Abiathar was subsequently deposed by Solomon in favor of another priest whose name is Zadok. Abiathar was actually banished to Anathoth, Jeremiah's village, because he was involved in a coup, a failed coup, against King Solomon. He attempted to put Solomon's brother, Adonijah, on the throne. If Jeremiah is connected to this priestly family, one can understand Jeremiah's intense concern about the temple cult as well as the royal family. There are specific connections to Jerusalem here.

The call narrative also tells us that Jeremiah's father, Hilkiah, was a priest and therefore Jeremiah must have known about those old priestly traditions, no doubt, including the idea of the Davidic royal grant, because the priests and their scribes would have passed on that tradition from Second Samuel 7. Given this Judahite theology, given the historical events, given the fact that the temple was there in Jerusalem and it looked like it would stay there forever, how is Jeremiah ever going to communicate to the people that something might, in fact, go wrong? He tries to tell the people that the kingdom will fall. He lets them know, in fact, that at some point God will come back and help them but at this point the best they can do is hold on to their traditions. This despair comes out in his sense of what will happen to the people because he believes the covenant has actually fallen.

He predicts, therefore, an ideal future covenant, no longer one established in written literature but one established by the heart. This is Jeremiah's view of the new covenant, which we've actually already mentioned in our discussion of where the term "New Testament" comes from. As he states in Chapter 31—YHWH, speaking through Jeremiah—"I will put my law within them, and I will write it upon their hearts. No longer shall each person teach a neighbor and a relative, saying 'know the Lord.'" We might hear in the background, hear Deuteronomy: "Teach this diligently to your children when you walk by the way, when you sit down, and when you rise up." Jeremiah knows that the Deuteronomic reform did not work. Teaching, public presentation, no longer works. The covenant will be written on the heart: "No longer shall each person teach a neighbor and a relative, saying 'know the Lord,' for they shall all know me from the least of them to the greatest."

Jeremiah engages in a series of his own lamentations describing his heartbreak at the deportations and the fall of Jerusalem. His scribe, whose name is Baruch—from whom, by the way, we actually have a seal left; it's now in a private collection, so it's difficult for archaeologists to get a really, really close look on it, but it does, perhaps, perhaps, seem to be Baruch's actual seal—Jeremiah and his faithful Baruch continue to issue oracles. They are condemned by the kings. They are condemned by the priests. Apparently no one in Judah or Jerusalem likes them. That's part of the job of the prophet. No one likes them; they give bad news. But everybody needs a prophet.

What finally happens? In 582 Gedaliah is murdered. As you know, this prompts the third exile. People in Jerusalem who were still left needed to get away to avoid the Babylonian ongoing destruction. A group of them actually take Jeremiah and Baruch with them to Egypt, which is here remaining a place of safety. We've seen throughout this military history that Egypt goes from being in alliance with the people to being their enemy. At this point Egypt is against Babylon. It's part of that old view, the enemy of my enemy is my friend.

Egypt, at least at this point, is on Judah's side. Jeremiah goes to Egypt, where apparently Baruch actually compiled some of Jeremiah's oracles, and here is where the Book of Jeremiah comes from. It's also Jeremiah's being brought to Egypt that begins part of the legend of the lost ark. I mention this because of the movie, *Raiders of the Lost Ark*. So there becomes, even in contemporary American thought, this idea that the ark is important. The ark had been in the temple in Jerusalem. The temple in Jerusalem is burnt down by Nebuchadnezzar. Where is the ark? From Jeremiah's exile develops the legend that the holy ark was last seen, by the way, when Solomon put it in the Holy of Holies. Nobody has mentioned it since (First Kings, Chapter 8). That Jeremiah and his companions brought it down to Egypt is possible.

First Kings 14 mentions a raid against Jerusalem by the Pharaoh Shishak, and we saw him as part of Jereboam's support when the united kingdom separated. According to First Kings 14:26, "In the fifth year of Rehoboam, Shishak king of Egypt came up against Jerusalem. He took away the treasures of the house of the Lord [that's the temple] and the treasures of the house of the king." Then the Deuteronomic historian adds, "He took away everything." Could Pharaoh Shishak have brought the ark with him to Egypt at that time?

From the Old Testament Apocrypha, the deuterocanonical collection, we have a text called Second Maccabees. Second Maccabees, Chapter 2, suggests that Jeremiah hid the ark on Mt. Nebo and proclaimed, "This place shall be unknown until God gathers his people together and shows his mercy." For Jews in the Second Temple Period under Hellenistic rule, the ark remained a mystery, and they wanted it back. I think what Second Maccabees is doing here is connecting the ark, say, with Moses and with Elijah, hidden but ultimately to return in a new form when God's true rule breaks in.

The most likely scenario is that it was either burned down by Nebuchadnezzar, or, if Nebuchadnezzar did despoil the temple prior to the full destruction of Jerusalem, that Nebuchadnezzar brought it with him to Babylon. We will see reference in the Book of Daniel to some of those temple treasures, but I think Daniel was not actually recording history. I think that material is more legend than fact.

Jeremiah, Chapter 3, suggests that the ark remains in the communal memory of the people even if it's not there. It's not in physical space, but it's around.

Jeremiah suggests, "When you have multiplied and increased in the land in those days, says the Lord, they shall no longer say, 'the ark of the covenant of the Lord,'" as if somehow that's a refrain that Jeremiah here has repeated, like a litany, "the ark of the covenant of the Lord." Jeremiah goes on, "It shall not come to mind or be remembered or missed, and nor shall another one be made." In Jeremiah's view—and this is associated with this idea of the new covenant—you don't need an ark because Jerusalem itself will be the Lord's throne. The nations will gather in Jerusalem. The exiles from the northern kingdom, the 10 lost tribes, will return, and the people, as Jeremiah puts it, "will no longer stubbornly follow their own will." These are glorious predictions of a future to come that we obviously haven't had yet.

Jeremiah's text, by the way, is just as mysterious as his fate. We're not exactly sure what happened to him after he went to Egypt. Part of our problem is that we have two quite different versions of the Book of Jeremiah. We have the Hebrew, or Masoretic, text, which is actually quite long, and we have the Greek, or Septuagintal, text, which is much more compact. Complicating this even more, the Dead Sea Scrolls have both traditions represented among their remains. There are two editions, therefore, of the Book of Jeremiah. Could it be that Jeremiah's scribe Baruch prepared one in diaspora, in Egypt, perhaps the longer one, and a shorter one retained by people in Judah? Could it be that Baruch prepared two different versions for two different liturgical settings or two different groups of readers? We simply do not know.

As the refugees in Egypt bring Jeremiah and Baruch with them in order to have a prophetic voice to keep their community intact, so the Judahites deported to Babylon have their own prophets, and that prophetic voice helps in allowing people from the southern kingdom to retain their identity, whereas people in the north were unable to do so. The notable prophets who exist in exile are first Ezekiel and then second Isaiah.

So let's look first at Ezekiel. Ezekiel proclaimed both a message of hope, an incredible, in fact, possibly pornographic, invective to the people in exile from about 593 to about 563. Ezekiel may have been part of that forced deportation in 597, and when he arrived in Babylon he found a people still confident. The initial people taken into exile thought, "Oh, this is not going to last very long. This is just a minor blip in history. Of course the covenant with David will be preserved. Of course God has loyalty to Judah and Jerusalem. We're here to be punished, yes, we probably deserve it, but it's not going to last all that long." Ezekiel finds a people with an enormous amount of hope, and it's his job to say, "Hunker down people, we're going to be here for a quite a while. Your punishment is not at an end yet."

These Judeans link their position with Abraham. This is Ezekiel citing them: "The word of the Lord came to me, son of man" [which is how God refers to Ezekiel. Here it simply means, "you human being."]. "Son of man, the inhabitants of the waste places [that's Babylon] keep saying, 'Abraham was only one man, yet he got possession of the land, and we are many. The land is surely given to us to possess.'" In other words, we're going to get it back. Ezekiel insists this is incorrect; the people are not deserving of redemption yet. His message, then, is one less of consolation than it is of justification, that God is still in control. Nothing has gone wrong. The people deserve their fate. It is their apostasy that forced YHWH to put them into exile. Redemption will follow, but it requires repentance. This is Ezekiel 36: "I will take you from the nations and gather you from all the countries [and we might think of those exiles in Egypt] and bring you into your own land," but, as Chapter 38 goes on, "after many days in the later years."

Ezekiel, in order to convince the people that they need to repent, changes one of the views promulgated by Deuteronomy. Deuteronomy, and indeed much of the earlier religious thought of the community, suggested that sin was a corporate problem. Deuteronomy speaks in the plural, "If you sin you will be punished." What Ezekiel wants to do is emphasize the idea of individual personal responsibility. He cites the proverb, "The parents have eaten sour grapes, and the children's teeth are set on edge." We suffer for what our parents do—that's Ezekiel 18. But, according to Ezekiel, "The son shall not suffer for the iniquity of the father, nor the father suffer for the iniquity of the son. The righteousness of the righteous shall be upon himself, and the wickedness of the wicked shall be upon himself." Every individual creates his or her own fate. If something goes wrong for one of us, it's because we deserved it and not because there is some sense of inherited guilt.

Obviously this is still going to cause a problem when it comes to questions of the theodicy because, if an individual is still behaving and the individual suffers—and of course we think of Job here—Ezekiel's system doesn't work. But at least here the people unburdened or without the justification of corporate guilt have to take on more personal responsibility.

To this point, Ezekiel's message fits very, very well within the biblical prophetic tradition, but there are parts of his oracles that are strange, peculiar, aberrant, bizarre. Ezekiel's prophecy, for example, is enhanced by exceptionally rich symbolic imagery. He begins his call vision with a description of a divine chariot of wheels within wheels of four living creatures, each with four faces and four wings. This is the beginning of what's known in Judaism as *merkabah*, "mysticism." This is the vision of God's chariot, God's throne. People are still trying to figure out what exactly Ezekiel saw. He also has the very well-known vision of the valley of the dry bones in Chapter 37. "Suddenly there was a noise," Ezekiel says, "a rattling, and the bones came together, bone to its bone, and I looked. There were sinews on them, and then flesh had come upon them, and then skin had covered them." This is incredibly graphic. It's his view of how the covenant community, like a corpse, will ultimately regain sinew, regain flesh, and literally pull itself back together. It's as if he is struggling to find the language to express what he's seeing, and, even when it comes to his description of God, language somehow fails him. He describes God in his call vision, Chapter 1, as "the appearance of the likeness of the glory of God." He simply can't get close linguistically.

He also engages in highly symbolic action. Jeremiah had done the same thing. For example, Jeremiah, in order to describe the yoke of the Babylonian exile, the Babylonian kingdom, actually put a regular yoke around his own shoulders, which a local priest broke off of him because local priests didn't like Jeremiah. Ezekiel is, for example, commanded not to mourn the death of his wife (Chapter 24). He remains lying on his left side for 390 days and then on his right for another 40 days to symbolize time in exile. He is commanded to eat food cooked over human dung, and connected with these bizarre actions are his invectives against Judah and also Israel. They are highly stylized, but they are also highly sexual, even misogynistic. Some people have called them pornographic.

He describes the kingdom of Israel and the kingdom of Judah as women, as adulterous women. We've already seen that with Hosea. But he also describes how God will rape them in the streets and display them naked before the people after whom they have gone in search of love affairs. The allegory in Chapter 23 of the sisters, Aholah, meaning "her tent"—that's Samaria—and Aholibah, meaning "my tent is in her"—that's Jerusalem—is so difficult that I will not read it to you. Chapter 23, if you can bear it. Perhaps the intensity if not the complete oddity of these visions represent for Ezekiel the trauma of exile. The people hadn't expected it; they still can't come to terms with it. It may be that the only way Ezekiel can grab their attention is through such shocking pronouncements. As prophecy goes on, as we move from Amos and Hosea through the first Isaiah to the time of the Babylonian exile, people will become used to prophetic rhetoric. If you get used to rhetoric it's much easier to ignore it. Through shock Ezekiel is at least able to gain the attention of the people.

His visions and his rhetoric foreshadow visions and rhetoric yet to come, that of apocalyptic literature, which really comes to the fore after the exile is done in the Second Temple Period, beginning, in fact, with some proto-apocalyptic material in the third Isaiah. This actually brings us to the second Isaiah, Ezekiel's younger contemporary during the Babylonian exile. By the time Isaiah is prophesying, the people have come to believe Ezekiel's message, "The end of exile has not come" and the message is now not one of perseverance per se but one of consolation, that God really does love this people, that God will retain the covenant, and that God will redeem these people. Because the exile was predicted, the second Isaiah said, "therefore restoration is also likely."

As the second Isaiah puts it in Chapter 40, "A voice cries in the wilderness, 'Prepare the way of the Lord. Make straight in the desert a highway for our God.'" In other words, build that highway out there because we're going back home. This is the statement, by the way, at the beginning of the Gospel tradition where John the Baptist is called "a voice in the wilderness," and you can see here punctuation problems. For the second Isaiah, it's "Go out into the wilderness and build a highway." For the Gospel of Mark, it's "a voice in the wilderness crying." This is simply Christian adaptation of prophecy, perfectly normal for first-century Jewish or Christian writers.

Evoking past tradition, the second Isaiah presents the return of the exiles, as in return of the exiles in Babylon, as, in fact, a new Exodus, the coming out of Egypt again, and he demonstrates here and elsewhere how Israel's own history serves as the model here for Israel's redemption. We might think back to those prophets of the north for whom Israel's own history served as a sign of their ultimate demise. History is usable material. You can use it to console; you can use it to complain. Finally, Isaiah also asserts that the Babylonian gods will go into captivity as Babylon is destroyed—that's Chapters 46 through 48. This is an alternative version of that peripatetic journey of the ark. Just as the ark went into exile—into Philistine territory—and came back, so ultimately the Babylonian gods will go into exile, but they will not return.

Isaiah's words of comfort would have also received support on the international front because, by the year 550, Persia is the empire on the rise, and King Cyrus of Persia looks like he's fated to take over. He had consolidated his empire, and he is encroaching on Babylon. Isaiah, Chapter 44, verse 5, anticipates the universal recognition of God, perhaps facilitated by the Persian conquering of everyone. This is Isaiah 44: "One nation will say, 'I am the Lord's as another will call himself by the name of Jacob." The Gentile nations will all stream to YHWH. They stay Gentiles. They don't become Jews, they are not circumcised, and they don't keep the dietary laws in this view, but they begin to worship the one true God. This motif extends into the *diaspora* promise that we saw already back with Abraham, who was guaranteed, "You will be a blessing to the nations."

This is Isaiah: "I will give you as a light to the nations that my salvation will reach to the ends of the earth." This is symbolized by Isaiah's vision of the suffering servant: beaten now, despised now, but ultimately showing God's own glory. For Isaiah, the suffering servant is primarily the nation of Judah, the Jews, the kingdom of Israel, which eventually will carry God's message throughout the empire. This message of consolation and vindication so different from Ezekiel even uses some of Ezekiel's own imagery because the second Isaiah, too, will go back to Abraham but here using Abraham as the model for God's blessing.

Second Isaiah's words are themselves vindicated by King Cyrus of Persia. Isaiah proclaims that Cyrus of Persia has been appointed the Lord's anointed. The Hebrew is *mashiah*, "Messiah." The Greek translation would be "Christ." He is appointed Lord's anointed to defeat Babylon, and that's exactly what happens. In 539 B.C.E., the Babylonian King Nabonidus flees his capital, and Persia comes in quite peacefully and takes over. In 538 King Cyrus of Persia promulgates an edict permitting the Jews in exile in Babylon to return home. We have something, an archaeological remain called the Cyrus Cylinder, in which this practice of returning the exiles back home is actually recorded.

The Jews go back home, and they have with them the literature of the exile. They bring as well the priestly material, the "P" code, and, through the priestly material and then third Isaiah and all of these traditions combined, when they return home they still have their own identity, but the problem is that what they find when they go back is not quite what they had anticipated.

Restoration and Theocracy
(Isaiah 56–55, Ezra–Nehemiah, Haggai, Zechariah, Malachi, Ruth, Jonah)
Lecture 21

> When King Cyrus of Persia promulgated his edict in 538 B.C.E.,
> permitting the Jews in exile in Babylon to return home, great excitement
> no doubt occurred. … with enormous hope people left and returned
> home. Unfortunately, things were not as they had hoped they would be.
> The destruction that Nebuchadnezzar had brought when he destroyed
> Jerusalem had not been repaired. The city was in ruins. Moreover, the
> people who had not been taken into exile resented the return of those
> from Babylon.

The Cyrus Cylinder (cf. Isa. 44:28; 45:1; 47ff; Ezra 1:2–4; 2 Chron.
36:23: Ezra 6:3–5) states: "I returned to [these] sacred cities on the
other side of the Tigris, the sanctuaries of which have been ruins for a
long time, the images which [used] to live therein, and established for them
permanent sanctuaries. I gathered all their inhabitants and returned their
habitations." Under Persian rule, the Judeans are encouraged to rebuild their
Temple with funds provided from the royal treasury. Cyrus allows the return
of Temple vessels plundered by Babylon (2 Kings 24:13). Persia's tactics
were politically expedient: toleration of a subject nation's cultural practices
and limited autonomous governance. Both fostered stability and provided
a bulwark against the growing Greek threat. The Jewish military colony at
Elephantine notes that Cambyses (529–522) did not damage their temple
despite destroying "all the temples of the gods of the Egyptians."

Darius I (522–486) divides the empire into twenty satrapies; Judah belongs
to Avar Nahal, "beyond the river." Persia offered satrapies substantial
autonomy, developed an efficient means of communication, and facilitated
the flourishing of commerce. The satraps (first the Davidide Zerubbabel,
then the courtier Nehemiah) were chosen with regard to local concerns.

For many, the Jerusalem anticipated by the Second Isaiah was a severe disappointment. "Zion has become a wilderness, Jerusalem a desolation; O holy and beautiful house where our fathers praised you have been burned by fire, and all our pleasant places have become ruins" (Isa. 64:10–12). Second Isaiah's universalism ("light to the nations") transforms into siege mentality: "I have trodden the wine press alone ... I trod them with my anger and trampled them in my wrath" (Isa. 63:3). Haggai deplores the languishing of the cult and the poor condition of the Temple: "Who is left among you who saw this house in its former glory? How do you see it now? Is it not in your sight as nothing?" (2:3). The Temple's rebuilding did not, contrary to expectations, usher in an age of prosperity. Hag. 1:6ff. and Zech. 6:8–9 reveal a people who are starving, freezing, and poor. Many questioned the value of serving YHWH. As Malachi opens, "'I have loved you,' says the Lord; but you say, 'How have you loved us?'"

Contributing to the disappointment was the failed restoration government. Haggai exhorts the priest (Joshua) and the governor (Zerubbabel) to take courage and work. Ezra and Zechariah attest to their collaboration. Zerubbabel disappears from history and leaves no heir. Persian authorities may have removed or even executed him; the Davidic line is lost here. Levites sought to regain power wrested from them under Deuteronomic reform. Aaronides still worked to consolidate the power accorded them by the P source/the Babylonian Judean establishment.

The struggle for power was ultimately won by the Aaronide priests. The legitimacy of the priesthood was established in the symbolic rites of investiture (comparable to a royal coronation) involving Joshua (Zech. 3:1–9). Priestly rule is epitomized in the authority accorded Ezra by his own community and by the Persian government. For Malachi, the task of religious and moral instruction passes from the prophets, whose authority rested on revelation, to those entrusted with a hereditary commission, the priests.

By the Persian period, classical prophecy was on the verge of collapse (Ps. 74:9; Lam. 2:9; Zech. 13:2–5): "I will remove from the land the prophets. ... And if anyone again appears as a prophet, his father and mother who bore him will say to him, 'You shall not live, for you speak lies in the name of the Lord … '" The movement's demise followed the exile: What more could prophets threaten, after exile, the destruction of the Temple, Persian rule, and famine? Prophetic promises, such as those of the Second Isaiah, failed. Sin prospered, and righteousness was ineffectual (Mal. 3:14; Eccl. 9:13–15). Malachi was unable to take for granted even the most basic element of Israelite theology: God's love for the community.

Jonah preaching to the Ninevites.

A contributing factor was the demise of the monarchy. Government was in the hands of priests and their Persian sponsors. Whom was the prophet to condemn? The priests were themselves associated with divine sanction, and the Persians did not care. The post-exilic period needed unity, which prophetic argument threatened to undermine; without the countering force of the throne, prophetic critique would create political imbalance.

Genealogy and ethnic identity become increasingly important as Judea recognizes itself to be part of an empire. Ezra legislates that Judean men divorce their foreign

Boaz and Ruth.

wives; genealogy becomes increasingly important (cf. 1, 2 Chron.). Likely written to combat this ethnocentrism are the novellas of Ruth and Jonah. The novellas offer positive views of gentiles but implicitly warn against assimilation. Ruth, continually identified as "Ruth the Moabite," seduces Boaz on the threshing floor, a scene reminiscent of Genesis 19. Ruth the Moabite becomes David's great-grandmother. Jonah—attempting to escape the divine command to preach to Nineveh—is first tossed overboard, then swallowed by a great fish, and ultimately left to the burning sun while the Assyrians repent. ■

Suggested Reading

Commentaries in series listed in the bibliography.

Michael D. Coogan, (ed.), *The Oxford History of the Biblical World.*

Kenneth M. Craig, *The Poetics of Jonah: Art in the Service of Ideology,* 2nd ed.

Questions to Consider

1. How are moral values promulgated in circumstances of despair?

2. What adaptations do cultures make when they become part of an external empire?

3. What prompted the post-exilic stress on genealogy and the concern for assimilation?

4. How might Ruth be compared to Abraham? What are the implications of her Moabite ancestry?

5. Is Jonah a comedy or a tragedy?

Restoration and Theocracy
(Isaiah 56–55, Ezra–Nehemiah, Haggai, Zechariah, Malachi, Ruth, Jonah)
Lecture 21—Transcript

When King Cyrus of Persia promulgated his edict in 538 B.C.E., permitting the Jews in exile in Babylon to return home, great excitement no doubt occurred. The people in Babylon had been bolstered in part by their memories of what they had left behind. The next generation had heard stories from their parents about the glories of the temple, the glories of Judea, and, indeed, they had been bolstered as well by the prophecies of second Isaiah, saying, "Go build a highway in the wilderness. Head home. God's glory is about to break through. You will be a blessing to all nations." With enormous hope people left, they followed Cyrus of Persia, and they returned home.

Unfortunately, things were not as they had hoped they would be. The destruction that Nebuchadnezzar had brought when he destroyed Jerusalem had not been repaired. The city was in ruins. The infrastructure was completely destroyed. Moreover, the people who had not been taken into exile resented the return of those from Babylon. So we have the community at odds with each other, a land in destruction, and very little hope. That's where we begin with the discussion of the immediate post-exilic period. How is this community going to put itself back together? Where is the leadership to come from? Is the Davidic king going to last? What will the priests do? What will happen to the people who were left? Who will take over?

In order to get a handle on what's going on during this period, we have to look at a variety of different types of literature. We have, for example, from the prophetic corpus the third Isaiah. The first Isaiah we've already met preaching during the reign of King Hezekiah; the second Isaiah providing hope and consolation to people during exile; and the third Isaiah reflecting upon the shattered dreams of the people who had returned. We also have information from the prophets Haggai, Zechariah, and Malachi, who are exhorting the people first to rebuild the temple and then, subsequently— particularly with Malachi—exhorting the priests to function properly. The cult needed to be revived, and people needed to renew their trust in it. That becomes the job ultimately of the prophetic school to bolster the priesthood.

We also have historical material from Ezra and Nehemiah, Persian envoys entrusted by the government with developing the economy, the stable political system, and, indeed, solidifying the priesthood of the exilic community. Finally we have a couple of short stories or novellas, if you will.

Part of the problem of the post-exilic period was the new sense of self-definition for the people. This is the time when they are changing from being an ethnic group, Judeans, to being a combination of both an ethnos and a religion. We're now finding a time when people no longer simply affiliate with the group, as would a stranger or a resident alien. This is a time when people can actually convert to Judaism. So we have here questions about how the Judean population becoming Jews will relate to Gentiles. The two books in question are Ruth and Jonah.

Let's start out with a basic history of the early Persian period. An artifact from the sixth century B.C.E. from Persia, the Cyrus Cylinder, which we mentioned in the last lecture, provides information on Persian policies. This is what the cylinder states: "I returned to these sacred cities on the other side of the Tigris [which includes the area of Judea], the sanctuaries of which have been in ruins for a long time [and one has to deal with strained syntax here], the images which used to live therein, and established them permanent sanctuaries. I gathered all their inhabitants and returned their habitation." In other words, not only for Jews but also for several of the other population groups that the Babylonians had taken into exile, Cyrus said, "Go back home." This was exceptionally astute on the part of the Persian empire. By encouraging exiles to return home, and indeed rebuild their temple, Cyrus was able to develop a new infrastructure, and the people leading that new government had their loyalties to Cyrus of Persia. Thereby he had allies in all these new kingdoms that he had, in effect, inherited from the Babylonian empire.

Persia's tactics were sufficiently politically expedient that we have evidence of them from other places throughout the ancient Near East. You might recall the community at Elephantine in Egypt, the Jewish military colony that had the god Yahu and Mrs. Yahu. Among their documents we have some information on Persian policies in the late sixth century, talking about the King Cambyses, a successor of Cyrus of Persia, who began his rule about 529. The Elephantine papyri note that when the Persians came in they did not damage the Jewish temple down there, although the Persians destroyed all the temples of the gods of the Egyptians. The idea was to keep here the loyalty of the Jewish military colony and avoid having the Egyptians, bolstered by their own priests, engage in some sort of revolution against Persia.

In Judah's case Cyrus had a secondary goal here. The new empire on the horizon is Greece, and it often helps to have someone on the shores of the Mediterranean protecting your initial investments. That's what the Jews, to some extent, were able to do for the Persian empire. So here we are, under the rule of Persia beginning with Cyrus and continuing on with people like Darius I, who ruled from about 522 for about 30 or 40 years after. The empire winds up getting divided into various satrapies; Persia now has Judea firmly in its hand. The Persians offered their various satrapies a fair amount of autonomy. They didn't need to have complete control over everything as long as they knew that the government was not likely to revolt. The Persian empire sponsored, and the Jews were able to take advantage of, new efficient means of communication which facilitated commerce. They also had, at least the Jews also had, their own king.

Returning from Babylon we find a king, or at least a ruler, whose name is Zerubbabel, and you can hear simply in his name that Babylonian echo. This is a community and a kingship that has to some extent assimilated with Babylon. The priests and the prophets of the immediately returning exilic community had enormous hope for Zerubbabel. Although they didn't have the government they used to have, although this was no longer the glories of Judea, there was enough there that at least part of the population, particularly those who had returned from exile, could get a sense that perhaps the community might be able to rebuild and at some point reestablish the glories that they had originally had.

We'll leave Zerubbabel for a minute and talk briefly about the disappointed hopes of some of the others, because, while the upper classes were able, for the most part, to exult in the relative freedom they had with Persia, some of the exiles didn't have that much authority, and a good many of the people who had been left in the land had even less. Third Isaiah attests to the disappointment of the return and indeed gives us a hopeful vision that, when redemption comes, it will not be brought about through Persian rule. It will not be brought about so much by human endeavor. It will be brought about by divine fiat, by the heavenly hosts entering into history, God straightening up the mess that Nebuchadnezzar had originally caused. This is Isaiah 64 describing what he thought of Judea when he returned: "Zion has become a wilderness, Jerusalem a desolation. Our holy and beautiful house where our fathers praised you has been burned with fire, and all our pleasant places have become ruin." I suspect that's what a good many people who returned from exile thought.

Second Isaiah's universalism, this vision of being a light to the nations, has become less a universal mandate. Now it's more of a siege mentality. There is isolationism coming in with the third Isaiah. As part of his despair, speaking God's word, third Isaiah says, "I have trodden the winepress alone. I trod them with my anger and trampled them with my wrath." There's no hopeful means of communicating with Gentiles from this particular viewpoint. For this situation, the divine promise of redemption remains, but it's not anything that people can do themselves. Isaiah explains, again speaking for God, "I am about to create new heavens and a new earth. The former things shall not be remembered or come to mind, but be glad and rejoice forever in what I am creating. For I am about to create Jerusalem as a joy and its people as a delight." And it remains wishful thinking.

Haggai, too, another prophet who would return from Babylon, finds conditions in post-exilic Judea absolutely deplorable. He laments the languishing of the cult, the very poor condition of the temple. There had been some early renovations about 538 when the first group of exiles returned, but not much had been done. Haggai's disappointment is exacerbated because the Persian government had promised help in rebuilding the temple, but the exilic population who had returned did not take advantage of that help. Cyrus had promised the funds. Who was using it?

By the time of 520, close to 20 years after Cyrus had promulgated his edict of return, the temple was still in ruins, and this is when Haggai begins to write. As he puts it to the people who had come back with him, "Who was left among you who saw this house in its former glory? How do you see it now—is it not in your eyes as nothing?" Which, in fact, it was. So under Haggai's urging and subsequently under the prophet Zechariah's urging, and under the combined efforts of the governor Zerubbabel, that Davidic descendant, as well as a high priest whose name is Joshua, the temple renovations began, and the basic structure was finally completed about the year 515. The same general information that we get from Haggai and Zechariah is confirmed in the Book of Ezra, Chapter 5.

But the temple's rebuilding did not, contrary to Haggai's hopes and Zechariah's hopes, lead to a glorious view of redemption. I suspect some of these people who were involved in the renovation would have thought, "Once we get this temple built God will retake his seat in the throne of the temple. Everything will be right in heaven and on earth." But that's wishful thinking, and it's not quite what happened.

Zechariah, whose oracles, at least in Chapters 1 through 8, were promulgated between, say, 520 and 518, continues to reveal a people despondent. This is his vision of what will be, but not yet of what was: "Thus says the Lord of hosts, 'Old men and old women shall again sit in the streets of Jerusalem, each with a staff in hand because of their great age. And the streets of the city shall be filled with boys and girls playing in those streets.'" That's the vision of the peaceful community, like a heaven on earth, where people are settled underneath their own vines and fig trees. It's actually the prophet Micah, but this is the ideal, and they simply didn't have it in the post-exilic period.

Indeed, the more the prophets made promises, the less the people could trust them. There was not much left that the prophets could say. Could they threaten exile unless the temple was built? As my daughter would have said, "Been there; done that." What else could they possibly do? By the time we get to the prophet Malachi, who comes at some point after Haggai and Zechariah, but his oracles are, in fact, difficult to date—probably some time in the first half of the fifth century—the people had begun to question even the most basic elements of Judean theology. They wondered why they should continue to serve God. This is the way Malachi opens, "I have loved you, says the Lord, but you say, 'How have you loved us?'" which, given their situation, is not an illegitimate question. Where is the glory? Where is the redemption we had been promised?

God laments in Malachi, "A son honors his father and servants their master. If, then, I am a father, where is the honor due me? If I am a master, where is the respect due me?" From Malachi's perspective, God was not being honored either as a parent or as a master. The people were lacking in hope and therefore lacking in any sort of religious response that Malachi considered legitimate. Indeed, not even the priests were doing what they were supposed to do, and Malachi's invective goes particularly against the priesthood rather than the people. We can hear echoes even here of Amos's complaints about the cult hundreds of years before.

The priests are particularly important here because, in the absence of a Davidic king, with the collapse to some extent of the royal grant theology, it's the priests who were supposed to pick up the pieces. If the priests don't do their job, the community is not going to last. If the temple is rebuilt but there are no caring officiants, it's nothing. So Malachi winds up saying, "Oh, that someone among you would just shut the doors so that you would not kindle fire on my altar in vain." For Malachi, the priests are just going through the motions—what's the point?

Contributing to the disappointment was the ultimate failure of the restoration government because the government, no matter what it could do, still remained under Persian control. This was no independent Davidic monarchy. Haggai spoke directly to the people who had some sort of ability to engage in restructuring the temple and restructuring the government. He addresses Zerubbabel, the Davidic descendant and Persian-appointed governor, and Joshua the high priest in strong exhortation. This is Haggai: "'Take now courage, Zerubbabel,' says the Lord. 'Take courage, Joshua the high priest. Take courage, indeed, all you people of the land and work, for I am with you,' says the Lord of Hosts. 'According to the promise that I made with you when you came out of Egypt, my spirit abides among you. Do not fear.'"

There is exhortation, and at the beginning there is high hope that perhaps this government will indeed succeed. Zechariah, for example, has a vision of the high priest Joshua standing before the angel of the Lord. We might think of Isaiah's call vision here, where priests and prophets are brought to the heavenly throne room. Here is Joshua, the high priest, standing before the angel and the accuser. This is like a prosecuting attorney. The Hebrew was *ha-satan;* hence we get "satan." We'll return to him when we get to the Book of Job. Here he is simply an accuser. He stands on the high priest's right hand to accuse him, and God the Lord says to *ha-satan*, the accuser, "The Lord rebuke you, *ha-satan.* Is not this man a brand plucked from the fire [something to be redeemed and restored]?"

Zechariah goes on, "Joshua was dressed with filthy clothes as he stood before the angel." Priests are supposed to wear white garments. There is a sense of investiture in how they dress and how they present themselves. "The angel said to those who were standing before him, 'Take off his filthy clothes,' and to the high priest the angel said, 'I will clothe you with festive apparel'" (Zechariah 3).

Zechariah also prophesies about Zerubbabel, "This is the word of the Lord to Zerubbabel: 'Not by might nor by power but by my spirit,' says the Lord of hosts. What are you, great mountain? Before Zerubbabel you shall become a plain." Now, if Zerubbabel is good enough to turn a mountain into a plain, that's high hope. We didn't even get a molehill out of him. Even Ezra attests the collaboration: "Then Zerubbabel and Joshua set out to rebuild the temple, the house of God in Jerusalem, and with them were priests helping." That's Ezra 5.

But Zerubbabel disappears from history. After references in Haggai and Zechariah and Ezra, we do not know what happened to him. I have my suspicions that the Persian government, recognizing the hope that some of the priests and prophets had put in him, simply decided he was too much of a liability and perhaps got him out of the way. Perhaps he simply faded off, not having accomplished very much and without descendants to continue the Davidic line. After Zerubbabel there is no firm Davidic line that historians can trace down. At this point the Davidic heirs pass into legend. Although the New Testament attributes to Jesus descent from King David, the genealogies we have in the Gospels of Luke and Matthew do not agree even past the time of King David. So the Davidic line is, at least as far as we can tell, lost. Hope for that royal grant, that promise, passes into messianic speculation. It's no longer there for politics.

Not only is the government in disarray, so is the priesthood. We've already seen struggles between the Levites and the government when King Josiah closed down all the high places and centralized the cult. Deuteronomy thereby limited the power of the Levites. But some of this limitation also had to form a means of coalescing. When the temple is destroyed by Nebuchadnezzar, not only is the government taken into exile but so are many of the priests, and it's during the time of the exile that the Aaronide priests, the priests who traced their descent from Moses' brother Aaron, begin to take over the cultic symbols and develop the laws. This is the time during the exile, and immediately after that the "P" code is written—the priests responsible for Genesis, Chapter 1—we've already seen that.

What these Aaronides needed to do in order to establish their authority—because there were other rival groups of priests, for example, the Zadokite priests whom Ezekiel sponsored—the Aaronides, in the process of editing the Pentateuch, actually rewrote their own history. When in doubt, as it were, send Moses back up the mountain and get a new law. We can actually trace this out through a bit of source criticism. They needed to figure out a way to establish their own authority. Here is how they did it. They noticed that, in "J" and in "E," Aaron, Moses' brother, is appointed to be high priest but the major thing he does is construct the golden calf. His reputation is not that good. Even in Deuteronomy all he does basically is construct the golden calf and then die.

What do the Aaronides do? They come back in, and they create at least three scenes whereby God invests the Aaronide priests, Aaron and his sons, with authority. In Exodus 29 the "P" code writers come in and provide us the ordination ceremony of Aaron and his sons. In Exodus 40, Aaron and his sons get the blessing of a perpetual priesthood throughout their generations. It is as if the Davidic royal grant established for the monarchy is now given to the priests and the priests would function as God's cultic representatives in perpetuity. Finally, in Leviticus 8, continuing into Leviticus 9, we have

Aaron's coronation—and it really is a coronation—and then he offers a sacrifice and delivers a priestly blessing.

"P" also revamps polity, the idea that people would go to the temple and offer sacrifices, into a much more regularized system. Now people have to go and offer sacrifices. The only place they can do it, as we know from Josiah, is in Jerusalem, and who's going to function? The priests, the Aaronide descendants. So since the cult now becomes much more formalized, one needs a formal clergy through inheritance, through descent, in order to facilitate the cult. This was absolutely brilliant on the Aaronides' part.

Sometimes my students fuss about this and call it evil or Machiavellian, but it may have been that, through this Aaronide gesture, that's the only way the covenant community would have survived. The monarchy was no longer functional. The prophets had nothing left to tell the people. They had threatened and promised all they possibly could. It would be the priests who would be able to keep the people together by providing them a written record. We have Ezra's reading of the Pentateuch to the people and providing them laws and providing them a cult and holding onto those religious traditions. It's the priests who wind up saving the covenant community, ironically enough, and their influence remains so strong that the culture becomes a theocracy, and the priesthood comes to dominate Judean civilization all the way down to the second century, when we begin to find another monarchy coming in.

Priestly rule, I suspect, would be epitomized by the prophet Ezra. He is both priest and prophet, and his legitimacy is established not only by the other priests who will defer to him but also by the Persian government itself. The Persians seemed to like priestly rule. It was safer than having kingly rule. Ezra himself apparently returned from Babylon during the second or even a third wave of returnees under King Artaxerxes in the middle of the fifth century, so we're now down several decades from the time of Haggai and Zechariah. And, as you know, he brought with him an early version of the Pentateuch, as we've described before, the Book of the Law of Moses, which he read to the congregation, and that's described in Nehemiah, Chapter 8.

For Malachi the priests needed to do their job. They weren't really doing it. The idea of the prophetic voice was in shambles. We come now during the post-exilic period to what might be considered the end of prophecy, and, as we'll see in a lecture or two, prophecy will eventually die out, and we find in place of prophecy both wisdom literature and apocalyptic visions. We can see the end of prophecy already in Zechariah—this is Chapter 13—"I will remove from the land the prophets, and if anyone again appears as a prophet, his father and mother who bore him will say to him, 'You shall not live, for you speak lies in the name of the Lord.'" You can't trust a prophet these days, in the post-exilic period.

Why did prophets die out? In part because there wasn't anything left to threaten and, I suspect, in part because of the demise of the monarchy. As we saw in our discussion earlier of the origins of prophecy, the prophet begins work when the office of judge splits, and then we have the prophet serving as the conscience of the monarchy. But if you no longer have a monarchy, in fact, you no longer need a prophet. At this point in the post-exilic period the important thing is not to provide invective against the ruling class. You need somebody who is going to support the ruling class because they are sufficiently fragile. Prophets no longer had a specific audience. They could rail against the priests as Malachi did, but the population doesn't get much out of it except despising the priests, which is not what you want if you want to build a society.

Haggai and Malachi could not do very much. When Ezra takes over as both priest and prophet, we find fewer prophetic oracles, the type of poetry that we saw with Isaiah or Amos or Hosea. What we find now is the priest-prophet combination legislating morality, indeed, legislating whom one could marry and how. One of the distresses that Ezra found when he returned is that people who were left in the land, as well as some of the earlier returnees, had married local women and not all Judean—now Jewish—women. They had married women from Samaria, perhaps Persian women, or others who had come into the territory. Ezra discovers that the children of these women were no longer even speaking the language of the Jews. They didn't know Jewish tradition. They didn't know anything about the Exodus or Sinai. They were, in fact, from Ezra's perspective, pagans, and Ezra takes the drastic move of insisting that the Jews divorce their foreign wives, push away those foreign wives and those foreign children.

We begin to see in the post-exilic period not only in Ezra but continuing on through the Chronicler—First and Second Chronicles—a concern for genealogy, a concern for passing on the lineage, the tradition, both in terms of inculcation—that's Deuteronomy, teaching your children—but now also in terms of ethnic identity. It becomes biological. This is the negative view of the Gentiles, but it's not the only view that we have in this particular period. We also have the books of Jonah and Ruth, difficult to date, but I agree with those scholars who want to put these books in the post-exilic period functioning as counterarguments to this idea of putting away your foreign wives. The epitome of the counterargument is the Book of Ruth. It's an absolutely fascinating story.

Here is the basic storyline, and you can hear in it, both the idea that Gentile women can be even better to, say, an Israelite mother than seven sons, but also still a little bit of an ambivalence. Yes, the Gentile women might actually be fine, but they still make us a little bit nervous. The story of the Book of Ruth starts out with a woman named Naomi, her husband, and her two sons leaving Israel, leaving the town of Bethlehem, because there is a famine. Bethlehem is not only the city of David, but the word "Bethlehem" itself actually means "House of Bread." So here we have "House of Bread" and famine—something is obviously wrong. They settle in the land of Moab, and Moab, as you know, is one of the perpetual enemies of Israel. We've already talked about the Moabites as descended from the incestuous relationship between Lott and his daughters.

They settle in Moab, the sons marry local women, and finally all the men in the family die. Naomi, the mother-in-law, decides she wants to return to Bethlehem—the famine is over—so she announces this to her daughters-in-law. Her daughters-in-law say, "We want to go with you." One daughter-in-law is named Orpah; the other is named Ruth. Naomi says, "There is no point. I'm not going to give you any more sons to marry. I have no hope in my own life. I'm a bitter old woman. Go back to your mother's house." In fact, she says, "Find a new husband. Establish your own life." After much tears, Orpah finally kisses Naomi and turns, but Ruth cleaves to Naomi. In fact, the word used here is *davaq*. It's the same word that we find in Genesis 2 when Adam says, "A man shall leave his father and mother and cleave to his wife." That's as close as Ruth gets to Naomi. So, as Adam says, "We will become one flesh," that's Ruth's view, and she says to her mother-in-law— these are famous lines—"Whither thou goest, I will go, and your home will be my home, and your God will be my God." Naomi, who has nothing left to say, basically allows Ruth to come after her.

When they arrive in Bethlehem the women find lodging, and Ruth goes to glean in the fields of an older relative. It turns out the older relative, whose name is Boaz, is available, and after a few brief comments passed back and forth between Boaz and Ruth, Boaz actually likes Ruth. He's heard how she is taking care of her mother-in-law. Ruth says to Boaz at one point, "May I continue to find favor in your eyes, my lord, for you have comforted me and spoken kindly," etc. Naomi gets the idea, "Well, Boaz is a relative; perhaps he might redeem us," the idea being, in the sense of lever- relationships, that a woman who is widowed without a child would marry ideally a brother-in-law but sometimes a near kinsman and that near kinsman, a brother-in-law, would have a child with the widow, and that child would inherit the dead husband's property and name. Naomi actually says to Ruth when she gets this idea in her head, "Take a bath, put on your best clothes, put on some perfume, go down to the threshing floor late at night, and wait until the man Boaz's heart is heavy with wine. Mark where he lies down. Go lie down next to him. Uncover his feet [which, as you know, is a euphemism for genitals], and he'll tell you what to do." I would call this a seduction scene. You've got to give Naomi some credit here. And Ruth agrees.

She goes down to the threshing floor at midnight, Boaz wakes up, notices his feet are uncovered, looks at Ruth, and says, "Who are you?" which is a good question. Ruth responds to him, "Spread your cloak over me, my lord, because you are next of kin." They have a brief conversation. Boaz gets Ruth out of the way before anybody notices her. As he said, "Let it not be said that a woman has come to the threshing floor." Through this relationship, Boaz, in the very next chapter—and it's only a four-chapter book—announces to the closer relative that he, Boaz, will redeem Ruth, will marry Ruth, and ultimately Boaz and Ruth become married. Ruth gives birth to a son, and through that line we eventually get King David.

What is this book saying? That a Gentile woman—indeed, descended from the Moabites—becomes great-grandmother of the greatest hero in Israel. Why, therefore, put away your foreign wives? If this Moabite woman can do so much for her mother-in-law, how much more could some of these foreign wives during Ezra and Nehemiah's time do? Similarly with the Book of Jonah we also have a little bit of a problem. Jonah, as you know, is the one successful prophet. He preaches to the Ninevites, and they, in fact, convert. Jonah is actually identified as a prophet in the Deuteronomic history. He lived prior to the time of the fall of Ninevah. If Jonah hadn't prophesied and they hadn't converted, Ninevah would have been destroyed, and, if we add up the dates, the northern kingdom would never have been destroyed either. There is an ambivalence here. The Gentiles can be good. They can repent. But they also may wipe you out, so we need to be a little bit more careful than we might have thought originally.

Wisdom Literature
(Song of Songs, Proverbs, Ecclesiastes, Job)
Lecture 22

When we look at the wisdom tradition, we find an amazing influence by and indeed respect for the international community, the international wisdom community. We've already seen this earlier in discussions of Solomon's court, where people from the nations would come to experience the wisdom that he himself promulgated and the wisdom of the other people he brought into his court.

The international implications of empire, while manifested in the xenophobia of Ezra and Nehemiah and the irresistible universalism of YHWH according to Ruth and Jonah, take on a third form: "wisdom," a tradition well established in the Near East. Biblical wisdom is partially epitomized by the books ascribed to Solomon: Song of Songs (Song of Solomon, Canticles), Proverbs, and Ecclesiastes.

Song of Songs (Song of Solomon, Canticles) is actually less a text of "wisdom" teaching than a celebration of the joys of love, emotional as well as physical. Its literary parallels are less Proverbs and Ecclesiastes than Egyptian love poetry. The song's overt sensuality complements the earthiness of Genesis and Judges, as does its powerful woman's voice. Under Hellenistic influence, the song became regarded as a spiritual allegory of the love between Israel and God or the Church and the Christ. Some interpreters propose that parts may be parody (e.g., "Your hair is like a flock of goats streaming down Mt. Gilead" [4:1]). Current multicultural readings call attention to the fact that the Hebrew can bear either of two translations of "I am black and/but beautiful."

Proverbs, a cross-cultural form for promoting proper attitudes and behaviors, receives divine sanction by Lady Wisdom herself (1–9). The proverbs encourage (male) readers to cleave to Lady Wisdom and avoid the paths of Strange (foreign, adulterous) Woman (Dame Folly). Wisdom as a character is increasingly developed in the Old Testament Apocrypha/Deuterocanonical writings (e.g., Wisdom of Solomon). She finds herself contributing to the *Shekinah*, the feminine manifestation of the divine, in Judaism, and the *Logos*, the pre-existent form of the incarnate Christ, depicted in the Prologue of the Gospel of John.

Ecclesiastes (Qoheleth, "leader of the assembly") negotiates life in a world of ennui. Tradition suggests that the Song of Songs is the product of Solomon's youth; Proverbs, of his adult prime; and Ecclesiastes, of his age. The text combines a pessimistic view of life ("Vanity of vanities ... all is vanity" [12:8]; "there is nothing new under the sun" [1:9]) with utilitarian advice following from it (eat, drink, and be merry [cf. 9:7]; rejoice in your youth [cf. 11:9]). Everything has its season (3:1–8); risk taking is advisable ("Cast your bread upon the waters" [11:1]); fear God (12:13, perhaps from the hand of a later editor).

Robert Gordis states, "There is not, nor can there be, universal agreement on such major issues as the structure, the unity, and the basic meaning of the book, or even on such relatively minor questions as its style, date, and origin." Perhaps the book offers less a solution to the problem of suffering than an opportunity for readers to engage the question. Various appropriations include Goethe's *Faust*; MacLeish's *J.B.*; H. G. Wells's *The Undying Fire*; and Heinlein's *Job, A Comedy*.

The traditional interpretation, premised on the prose frame, views Job as an ideal figure who continually engages in pious action; accepts the loss of his property and the death of his children with faithful resignation; refuses to follow his wife's advice, "Curse God and die"; repents of any possible doubt; and submits before divine majesty. A variant view makes Job an existentialist "everyman" demanding meaning from a chaotic world. Appropriately, this Job is not Jewish or Israelite (he descends from Esau). This is the Job of G. K. Chesterton: "The *Iliad* is great because all life is a battle; the *Odyssey* is great because all life is a journey; the Book of Job is great because all life is a riddle." Some see the book as a satire depicting a hypocritical protagonist who confirms the Satan's accusations (pious when rewarded; argumentative when his life is destroyed; pious again when the opportunity of restoration is presented) and a tyrannical, unstable God who demands worship as a form of extortion. Perhaps Job is a realist who is sure only of his righteousness but recognizes that the world lacks justice. This is the Job who tells God: "I know you can do all things …" but, so knowing, pities humanity: "I mourn in dust and ashes" (42:2–3). There may be mutually exclusive Jobs: one from the prologue and one from the poem, with the epilogue fitting both.

The prosaic Job remains faithful, "Then Job arose, and rent his robe, and shaved his head, and fell on the ground, and worshiped. And he said, 'Naked came I from my mother's womb, and naked I shall return. The Lord gave, and the Lord has taken away; blessed be the name of the Lord.' In all this, Job did not sin, or charge God with wrong" (1:20). The poetic Job bewails his fate, curses the Deity (e.g., 16:11), curses his birth, and longs for his death (from the opening line).

How are we to understand God, who permits Job's suffering, then condemns Job's friends for defending traditional theology in insisting on a correlation between faith and fate? Eliphaz appeals to mystical visions (4, 15) and describes suffering as a

Job and his friends.

Doré Bible Illustrations, Courtesy of Dover Pictorial Archive Series.

form of discipline and a mark of divine love (5). Eliphaz also echoes the Deuteronomic view that "the sins of the fathers are visited upon the sons" (22) and bolsters it with appeal to the corporate community's mutual responsibility. Bildad, invoking traditional wisdom (8), and Zophar, appealing to esoteric wisdom (11), recapitulate Eliphaz's arguments. Elihu adds that suffering serves to deter sin (33, 36), such as pride. Does God favor Job because he speaks from experience rather than theory? Or is the Deity simply arbitrary?

Even further complicating interpretation are the whirlwind speeches (38:1–40:5; 40:6–41:34). Does the whirlwind indicate that God is unknowable, yet operating purposefully? "Where were you when I laid the foundations of the earth, tell me, if you have understanding. Who determined its measurements, surely you know" (38:4). Might the point be less what is said but the theophany itself, that the divine is not indifferent (42:5: "I have heard of you by the hearing of the ear, but now my eye sees you")? Or is it all just sound and fury?

Job 13:15 yields three mutually exclusive translations: KJV: "Though he slay me, yet I will trust him"; RSV: "Behold he will slay me, I have no hope"; and Anchor Bible: "He may slay me, I'll not quaver." Job 19:25 traditionally reads, "For I know that my redeemer lives …" but the translation is uncertain. ■

Suggested Reading

Marcia Falk, *Love Lyrics from the Bible, The Song of Songs: A New Translation and Interpretation.*

Roland E. Murphy, *The Tree of Life: An Exploration of Biblical Wisdom Literature.*

Questions to Consider

1. Why would ancient Israel canonize pessimistic wisdom, such as Ecclesiastes and Job?

2. Is the God of Job the God of the *Akedah*? Of Jephthah? Of Saul?

3. How does the scribe, responsible for wisdom, relate to king, priest, and prophet?

Wisdom Literature
(Song of Songs, Proverbs, Ecclesiastes, Job)
Lecture 22—Transcript

We've seen in the post-exilic period a certain ambivalence regarding the Gentile nations. On the one hand we have Ezra and Nehemiah insisting that Jewish men divorce their foreign wives, and on the other we have books like Ruth and Jonah suggesting that Gentiles might actually repent and contribute enormously to the ongoing life of the covenant community. The ambivalence shows up in particular in the prophetic tradition and then in the priestly tradition.

But when we look at the wisdom tradition to which we are turning in this lecture, we find an amazing influence by and indeed respect for the international community, the international wisdom community. We've already seen this earlier in discussions of Solomon's court, where people from the nations would come to experience the wisdom that he himself promulgated and the wisdom of the other people he brought into his court. That's why the Queen of Sheba came to visit him.

Wisdom literature itself is an international phenomenon. We have, from the fourth millennium B.C.E., from the kingdom of Sumer, a theodicy, a document that describes why bad things happen to good people, why the wicked prosper, why the innocent suffer. The question is as old as humankind, I suspect. From Babylon itself there is a text called the "Babylonian Theodicy." This question is not unique to Israel, and, indeed, when we go over to Greece we find Cynics making aphorisms, questions, and couplets trying to describe why the world is the way it is. Why does sometimes nature aid us and why does sometimes nature kill us?

Various genres can raise the question and, indeed, provide some answers to this issue of theodicy. Scientific treatises might tell us why nature functions the way it does. New discoveries in neurology or psychiatry might explain why some people are good and some people are sociopathic. Poetry can explain or at least explore some of these questions that we simply cannot answer fully by rational means, and it's a combination of poetry and the wisdom literature as genre within which the Bible, especially, raises some of these questions.

Biblical contributions to wisdom literature take a variety of forms. We have the relatively upbeat Book of Proverbs, which is primarily instruction to young men on how to get along in life: what to do, what not to do, whom to follow, whom not to follow. We also have the somewhat depressing book of Ecclesiastes, also called Qoheleth, for whom the world is just set. "There is nothing new under the sun," as he puts it, and he provides basic information like, "Eat, drink, and be merry, because that's just the way the world is." With it we also have the Book of Job, and on that we will concentrate in this lecture.

But first I want to give a little bit of a foretaste of some of this other wisdom literature that the Bible has. I also want to bring in one other text that I don't really have an opportunity to discuss. I'm stuck with only 24 lectures; I need at least 48 to cover this text. That's a text called the Song of Solomon. It's not really wisdom literature, it's love poetry, but it is attributed to King Solomon, and therefore I feel more or less legitimate that I can slide it into the wisdom school. So let's just stop for just a bit and take a look at this wonderful text.

It's a collection of poems, independent poems spoken first by a woman, then a man, back and forth and back and forth. They rejoice in the joys of each other's body. They rejoice in the idea of physical love, and, indeed, it's not even clear that they are married. Tradition suggests that the man is Solomon and the woman perhaps a member of his court. Later legend suggests the woman might actually be the Queen of Sheba. This text is, in fact, at home in the Bible. We often think of biblical literature as holy and, indeed, holier than the rest of us. It's to be up there on a pedestal somewhere, and we can revere it but we can't really wrestle with it. Song of Songs is there to be enjoyed. Its overt sensuality compliments the earthiness that we found in some of the stories in Genesis and certainly in Judges, if we think of Ehud and Deborah. Its powerful woman's voice recollects the Song of Hannah, the Song of Deborah, Ruth, and Miriam crossing the sea.

The Song is clearly erotic. We can see it right at the beginning: "Let him kiss me with the kisses of his mouth, for your love is better than wine." The poem gets increasingly passionate and indeed increasingly graphic. Lest there are people here under 18 listening to this tape, I will not read aloud for you Chapter 5, verses 4 to 5, but I encourage you on your own to take a look. Under Hellenistic influence, after 333, when Alexander the Great came through and Jews suddenly found themselves part of the Greek empire, and later on as people began to speculate about this text, the idea that this was love poetry didn't settle quite so well. In the Jewish tradition, by the first century of the Common Era, certainly by the beginning of the second century, this text is looked at as an allegory of the love between God and Israel. In the church, similarly, it becomes an allegory of the love for Christ and the church. That doesn't keep it from being love poetry, but it makes it a little bit safer to be recited in churches and synagogues.

Indeed, today some scholars have gone over this poetry and thought that perhaps it's not just erotic love poetry. Some even consider it to be comedy. There is this wonderful line in Chapter 4 where the man is describing his ladylove. He says, "Your hair is like a flock of goats streaming down Mt. Gilead." The problem is, if you actually watch goats going down a mountain, they tend to go one by one by one. This woman's hair is not overly thick if this is, in fact, a line of parody rather than a line of compliment. Others, particularly feminist scholars, have seen this text as a man's fantasy because the woman is so in love that she actually risks censure by people in the community. She actually puts her own life at risk by being able to follow her man and hoping to do so.

Finally, the Song gives rise to controversy in translation. We've already seen some difficulties in translation regarding text criticism where the Greek and the Hebrew disagree, for example. Here the Hebrew was abundantly clear; the issue is how to translate it. It's part of the opening chapter which had until the past two or three decades frequently been read, "I am black but beautiful," with the idea being that this woman has been out in the sun, she's been darkened by the sun, and the standard of beauty in antiquity, at least for this poem, is that one be fair skinned. I think about *Gone with the Wind* with southern belles walking outside with umbrellas lest they get a single freckle.

Given concerns today for inclusive language and multiculturalism, it's becoming increasingly common in scholarship as well as in formal productions of the Bible to translate, "I am black and beautiful," as if those terms are not mutually exclusive. The Hebrew can bear either translation. How you translate this becomes up to you. But recognize that translation carries more than simply historical meaning. Translation very much can affect the reader, and one can notice the negative effects that that earlier translation had on a good many people who read this text.

Moving on to our actual example of wisdom literature, we start with Proverbs. We've already had some hints of the type of techniques wisdom literature has—for example, enumerations. We've heard this in the prophets: "For three transgressions and for four" or examples from the natural world: "Does a lion roar unless it has found a prey?" Indeed, rhetorical questions, and that's the type of form we find in Proverbs. But Proverbs actually goes on beyond this type of secular protocol and beyond simple exhortations to people on how to behave.

The unique biblical contribution to wisdom literature that Proverbs provides is a concern not only that "the fear of the Lord is the beginning of wisdom," in other words, if you don't have faith, wisdom is for naught—that's already in Chapter 1—but also a focus on a figure called Sophia in Greek, *Hochma* in Hebrew, or in English typically referred to as "Lady Wisdom." We have in Proverbs a father exhorting his son, "Get wisdom. Get insight," but this wisdom is personified as female. "Do not forsake her; she will keep you. Love her, and she will guard you. Prize her highly; she will exalt you. She will honor you if you embrace her." It's as if wisdom, hypostatically, is standing there right in front of him. "She will place on your head a fair garland." This is how to win the race—you go for wisdom. "And she will bestow on you a beautiful crown." This is how you become royal—you gain wisdom.

Proverbs thus encourages its male readers to cleave to Lady Wisdom. She's better than any possible real woman could be. She's totally faithful. She's the wife behind the successful man, as it were. She's the ideal lover, the ideal spouse, and, like the woman in the Song of Songs, she actually pursues her man—here not for physical delights but for metaphorical ones. This is

Lady Wisdom's description: "Wisdom has built her house. She has hewn her seven pillars." So if you've heard about the seven pillars of wisdom, it comes from the Book of Proverbs. "She has slaughtered her animals. She has mixed her wine. She has also set out her table [because wisdom is a banquet at which anyone can feast]. She has sent out her servant girl. She calls from the highest places in town [public announcement]. You that are simple, turn in here. To those without sense, she says, 'Come eat my bread and drink the wine I have mixed.'" Her call is irresistible. If you want to succeed, if you want to love God, if you want to know what God wants from you, follow Lady Wisdom.

But be careful because Lady Wisdom has a counterpart who is often referred to as "the strange woman" or "the foreign woman" or sometimes simply "Dame Folly," often conveyed in this text as an adulterous wife, and her path leads not to life but to death. If you listen to the words of Dame Folly and follow her, you will go in the opposite direction from which Lady Wisdom would lead you. This is Dame Folly—she too calls out, says the Book of Wisdom: "You who are simple, turn in here. And to you without sense she says, 'Stolen water is sweet, and bread eaten in secret is pleasant.' But they do not know," says the author, "that the dead are there with Dame Folly and that her guests are in the depths of Sheol." They are in hell.

So here the young man in Judean civilization, Israelite civilization, has a choice. Do you follow Lady Wisdom, or do you follow her counterpart? This is what my children would refer to as a no-brainer. Of course you go with Lady Wisdom; but watch out, because graphically Proverbs will describe the negative results if you don't follow Wisdom but if you follow Dame Folly.

This idea of the hypostatic wisdom, wisdom personified as a woman, develops in the Old Testament Apocrypha, the deuterocanonical materials such as the wisdom of Jesus ben Sirach, also called Ecclesiasticus, and the wisdom of Solomon. The figure of wisdom becomes so developed that she becomes almost like a goddess. The tradition eventually develops in Judaism to the idea of the *Shekinah*, the feminine presence of God, and it actually underlies the description of the Logos. The term is a masculine term, but the Logos in early Christianity, the Logos who in the Gospel of John was with God at the beginning of time, has as characteristics the descriptions of Lady

Wisdom from the earlier material. So wisdom speculation will continue on in both church and synagogue.

The next wisdom text we can look at is the Book of Ecclesiastes, also known as Qoheleth. If we think of Song of Songs as a text written by Solomon in his youth and Proverbs as a text written during middle age, Ecclesiastes is typically ascribed to Solomon at the end of his life when he's dealt with everything that can be. He's seen all that there is. He's been through his 300 wives and his 700 concubines, and he's done his international relations, and there is nothing left to amuse him. There is nothing left much at all. This is a text of ennui. I don't think Solomon wrote it, but I can understand the ascription.

This text contains an exceptionally pessimistic view of life—not that life is terrible but there is just not that much new to appreciate. "Vanity of vanities. All is vanity," a phrase you are probably familiar with, comes from Chapter 12 of Ecclesiastes. Another translation is, "Everything is futility. There is no point." Chapter 1, verse 9, does, in fact, suggest "There is nothing new under the sun." So, with a world like that, what does one do simply to get up the next morning? There are some hints here: "Eat, drink and be merry," which is a summary of Chapter 9, verse 7. "Rejoice in your youth." If you've got energy and you've got strength, enjoy it because indeed it's sort of downhill from there. I don't really think so, but that is what the text suggests. The text also suggests that, "Everything has a season," and one can either look at that in a pessimistic way—Oh, it's winter again—or one can look at it in a helpful way: To everything there is a season, a time to be born, a time to die; the world can function in an appropriate and, indeed, ordered way.

So unlike the Book of Job, as we'll see, where the world is chaotic and that causes obvious distress for Job, here in Ecclesiastes perhaps the problem is the world's too ordered. The nice thing about the biblical canon is we can read one text next to the other, so if one particular worldview becomes too much for us there is an alternative there. As I mentioned very early on in this series, this Bible does not always give us answers. It raises questions, and it provides us different resources once we can find those answers.

For people interested in economics, this particular text of Ecclesiastes provides us some business advice. You've probably heard the expression, "Cast your bread upon the waters." What that actually means is send out your grain overseas in hope of a profitable return. It's not simply giving breadcrumbs to ducks. It's a good economic view. Some commentators suggest that Ecclesiastes was edited by a more upbeat, more optimistic final redactor because there are various spots in this book that suggest that things are really okay in the end and God loves us, which is probably true. Whether that happy material is also from the original author who himself, or even herself, simply couldn't make up his mind/her mind as to how the world functions, or whether it comes from someone else, it allows us to read Ecclesiastes either as simply a document of pessimism or as a document of world knowledge coupled with both experience and a little bit of hope. One might say, "Been there; done that," but one might also say, "You know, the world progressed the way it should have progressed and, indeed, eat, drink, and be merry because it is a pretty good world after all." How you read this text is actually up to you, and that's basically the advice for Job. How you read it is up to you.

Biblical scholar Robert Gordis, who has written some excellent material on Job, said the following, "There is not nor can there be universal agreement on such major issues as the structure, the unity, and the basic meaning of the book or even on such relatively minor questions as its style, its date, and its origin." Job is simply out there as a mystery both in terms of origin and in terms of interpretation. Sometimes I think that this book less offers a solution to the problem of suffering, to the question of theodicy, than an opportunity for readers to engage the question.

If one thinks about the Bible as a text that is simply up there giving us God's word, then Job does not function well for us. Job, rather, gives us permission to question everything else that's in that text, to go back to the Book of Deuteronomy, which says, "The good prosper and the wicked suffer," and say, "Well, maybe not." I can raise questions to this. I can question my life in the world. I can question the justice of God. Indeed, numerous authors in various cultures and times have raised precisely these questions influenced by the Book of Job, from Goethe's *Faust*; which has a Joban background, to Archibald MacLeish's *JB*. H. G. Wells raised the question in *The Undying*

Fire; Heinlein more recently wrote a book called *Job, A Comedy.* Plays, poems, operas, novels—people are still wrestling with Job, and I suspect they are never going to find an answer that will suit everyone.

Job's character poses us the first problem because the character, in fact, differs as we move from the prose or, in fact, prosaic opening to the poem in the middle and then to the prose conclusion, the prose epilogue. The traditional interpretation of Job is premised on the prose frame, and it views Job as an ideal figure who engages in pious action. He is religious, he's good, he loves God, and he accepts the loss first of his property and then the death of all of his children with a faithful resignation. His wife says to him, "Curse God and die." The Hebrew, by the way, actually says, "Bless God," but that's simply a euphemism. We know what she is saying.

This is a Job who has no doubt, and he submits himself before divine majesty. He's the moral exemplar. A variant view of this makes Job an everyman, an everyman who desires meaning from life. It's this existential quest. This is a Job who is not specifically Jewish; he's anyone. Indeed, we find out at the beginning that Job is from the land of Uz, and Uz, as we know from Genesis, is one of the descendants of Esau. Job may well be an Edomite. He's not a Jew; he can be everyone. This is the Job of G. K. Chesterton, who said about the book, "The *Iliad* is great because all of life is a battle. The *Odyssey* is great because all of life is a journey. And the Book of Job is great because all of life is a riddle." He doesn't, however, provide us an answer to this.

In this sense Job might be a mirror of our own lives: We can't make sense of it, but we simply struggle through, muddle through, and do the best we can. I am attracted to, although I am not convinced by, the argument that Job is a satire depicting a hypocritical or at least practical protagonist who confirms the Satan's accusations at the beginning. This is a text, perhaps, that says, "Well, you know what? God is sort of arbitrary, but if you behave yourself for the most part, you will succeed, and if you are wicked at the end God will punish you." This is a Job who finally says, "Well, God's is the only game in town, and I'm going to play it." It's a Job who realizes that God's power is much more than anything he can bear. He is simply going to submit because that's all, in fact, he can do—cynical, satirical, and depressing.

Or perhaps Job is simply a realist. He is sure of his righteousness. He knows he hasn't done anything wrong, but he also recognizes that the world lacks justice. This is perhaps the Job who tells God at the end, "I know you can do all things" but then so knowing, in fact, winds up pitying humankind. This depends upon how you want to read the line, "I mourn in dust and ashes." Is Job repenting from what he does not know about God's greatness, or is Job mourning because he recognizes that humankind has to deal with a God who is not on call, with a God who permits evil to exist in the world, with a God who will sometimes respond positively and sometimes negatively? This is the God of Cain and Abel. We never know when God will act positively or when God will cause us to suffer. These may be several mutually exclusively Jobs: one from the prologue, one from the poetry, one from the epilogue. They are all a possibility.

Let's go back to the prosaic Job at the beginning. Job has just been bereft of everything, and, in total equanimity, totally sanguine, Job responds, "Naked came I from my mother's womb and naked I shall return. The Lord gave; the Lord has taken away. Blessed be the name of the Lord," and the narrator adds, "In all this Job did not sin or charge God with wrong." On the other hand, as soon as we get to the poem, Job curses his fate, argues against God, assaults God, curses his birth, and longs for his death, and that's in the opening couple of verses. The first line of the poetry reads as follows, after this: after Job's entire household/family has been killed, Job's body has been besieged with boils, and he's sitting on a dung heap. You can't get any lower than this. The poem says, "Why did I not die at birth, come forth from the womb and expire? Why were there knees to receive me or breasts for me to suck? Now I would simply lie down and be quiet. I would be asleep and then I would be at rest." This is a man who not only longs for death but wishes he had never been born in the first place. This is not, "Naked came I from my mother's womb." This is a guy who is suffering, and the emotion that he feels is palpable. For the Job of the poem, death would be a comfort, and it would remove him from the tortures that God places upon him.

Worse, contributing to Job's anguish are his three so-called friends. They are called friends at the beginning. By the time we get toward the end of the poem they are simply called men. They are ostensibly there to comfort and console him (that's Chapter 2), and what they wind up doing is giving him the old tried and true answers to the question of theodicy. They explain to him, "Well, you know, Job, how we're supposed to understand God." I'll give you those in a minute, but notice at the end that, after the friends, after three rounds of discussion, give Job the tried and true answers, God winds up condemning the friends and blessing Job. So I'm still worrying about what to do with God.

Eliphaz, the first friend, appeals to mystical visions and describes suffering as a form of discipline and a mark of divine love, so he says, for example, "Happy is the one whom God reproves. Therefore, do not despise the discipline of the Almighty." That's Chapter 5, Verse 17. Discipline is one thing. Having your entire family killed and being reduced to an itchy, scratchy boil-filled person sitting on a dung heap is a little bit more than simple discipline. Job's not going to buy that one. He's hardly in a position to be happy based on God's reproof.

Eliphaz also echoes the Deuteronomic view that punishment comes from evil, and so he condemns Job. If Job is suffering, therefore Job must have done something wrong. He says, "Is it for your piety that God reproves you and enters into judgment with you? Is not your wickedness great? There is no end to your inequities." You know, with friends like this. . . But Job knows he's been righteous, so he simply can't respond, "Oh yes, I've been wicked. I'm sorry." Eliphaz concludes that Job should repent. He says, "If you return to the Almighty, you will be restored. If you remove the unrighteousness from your tents." But from what could Job possibly repent? He hasn't—at least as far as he knows and we as readers know—done anything wrong.

Bildad, the second friend, evokes traditional wisdom. He says, and good old rhetorical questions here, "Does God pervert justice? Does the Almighty pervert the right?" The problem with rhetorical questions is that you don't always get the answer you might have thought, and although Job does not answer directly to these questions, one can imagine what he's thinking: "Yes, justice here has been perverted. Yes, the right has been perverted." Bildad also continues, "How then can a mortal be righteous before God? How can one born of women be pure?" It's not normally in the Bible the anthropological view that we are simply wallowing in sin. That's not the way the Old Testament, the *Tanakh*, looks at humankind.

But even if one looks at human beings as somehow flawed, and indeed we are—that's why we have things like the Torah to keep us on the right path and means of atonement in case we mess up—it is one thing to say, "Well, we're all not particularly righteous." It's something else for Job to look at his own situation. Indeed, if one looks at Bildad's question from Job's perspective, Job might just as well say to Bildad, "Well, how come you're not here on the dung heap with me? If everyone lacks righteousness, why am I suffering and why are you doing quite well?"

Zophar, the third friend, appeals to esoteric wisdom. "Can you find the deep things of God? Can you find out the limits of the Almighty? It is higher than the height of heaven. What can you do? It is deeper than the pit of Sheol. What can you know?" In other words, "Job, God has a rationale here. God's wisdom so surpasses anything that humans can know that there is a reason for your suffering. Hold tight—eventually you'll know what that reason is." But this does Job little good. It's fine to be told there is a rationale to the universe and God has infinite wisdom, but that's not going to help Job, given his present circumstances. I also wonder if this particular friend Zophar actually knows all those mysteries himself. It sounds good, but does he really grasp the mysteries of the universe?

There is a fourth friend, this young man, Elihu, who some people think was added on by a later editor. He, for the most part, repeats what the other friends have said, but he doesn't begin the same way. We're told that the three friends had come to Job to comfort and console. Not Elihu. He's identified as a young man who is very angry not only at Job but at the three friends. He is angry at Job because Job has justified himself rather than God. Job is saying, "God, I am in the right; you're in the wrong," and Elihu says, "No, no, no. We simply can't have that. That's not good religion." He's also angry at the friends "because they had found no answer though they had declared Job to be in the wrong." He wants those friends to provide an answer that's going to convince Job that God is right and that Job has somehow sinned and that Job has misjudged God.

Elihu recaps the arguments made by the friends: God is just, God chastises with pain and punishment, and Job's situation is clearly that he has sinned. Elihu goes on for several chapters doing this (the enthusiasm of youth). He also adds that suffering serves to deter sin such as pride. And that may well be part of Job's problem. He is a somewhat prideful man. But on the other hand, we haven't been told he did anything wrong yet. Ultimately all these views are rejected. The Lord says to Eliphaz the Temanite, "My wrath is kindled against you and against your two friends, for you have not spoken of me what is right as my servant Job has." But Job has been the one who has been kvetching and complaining all the way through. Eliphaz is told to offer a sacrifice and to have Job pray for him and his fellows, which Job is happy to do once he's off the dung heap.

Then I wonder, why does God finally favor Job? Because he speaks from experience, perhaps, rather than from theory? Or is God simply arbitrary? Or do we have to separate the poetry from the prose? Are they simply two different stories that don't sit well together? Complicating all of this are God's speeches to Job from the whirlwind. We've seen theophanies before— Elijah hearing the stillness, that still small voice on Mt. Horab, and Moses getting the law on Mt. Sinai—but we have not seen theophanies like this. Job asks for an ordered court. He says, "Would he plead against me with his great power?" No, says Job, "He would put strength in me. There the righteous would dispute with him." In other words, Job is asking for an orderly response. He wants a court of justice. He gets a whirlwind. Does the whirlwind indicate God's unknowability? "Were you there when I laid the foundations of the earth?" asks God. "Tell me, if you have any understanding, who determined its measurement? Surely you know?" Or is there an order to existence we fail to recognize, just as beasts in nature can eat their young but there is an order and indeed a beauty there? Might the point be less what is said than the fact that God responds at all, that there is a response?

If we think we've got a handle on this text, Job 13, verse 15, gives us four different ways of viewing it. The King James Version says, "Though he slay me, yet I will trust him." The Revised Standard Version, "Behold, he will slay me; I have no hope." The Anchor Bible, "He may slay me; I'll not quaver." The Revised English Bible, "If he wishes to slay me, I have nothing to lose." From the poetry to the prose there are no easy answers.

The easiest figure that we can grasp in this text happens to be the Satan, the accuser, and in the next lecture we'll begin with the Satan, the accuser, to find out how he affects Israelite theology. Then we'll move on to tales of Jews in the Diaspora.

Life in the Diaspora
(Genesis 30, 37–50; Esther; Daniel 1–6)
Lecture 23

The Babylonian exile gave rise to the *diaspora*, the "dispersion" of the Judeans now known as "Jews" to places outside their homeland.

The least controversial figure in Job is *ha-satan*, "the accuser." In Zechariah, as in Job, *the* Satan ("the accuser") is the heavenly prosecuting agent whose task is to weed out evil and hypocrisy. Isa. 14:12–15 contributes to the mythic development: "How you are fallen from heaven, O day star, son of Dawn ... You who said in your heart, 'I will ascend to heaven above the stars of God ... I will make myself like the most high ...' But you are brought down to Sheol, to the depths of the pit." Ugaritic texts speak of Shahar, god of Dawn, and his son Helal, Morning Star. Isaiah identifies the Babylonian king with Canaanite gods. "Day star" or "light bringer" is, in Latin, Lucifer. The "tales of the diaspora" present as heroes figures representing the wisdom tradition: Daniel and Mordecai. It is to the Books of Daniel and Esther, and to a discussion of Jewish life outside Israel, we next turn.

The Book of Esther may well have taken shape during the Persian period. However, even if King Ahasueros is to be associated with Xerxes I, there is no external record of his having a Jewish queen or prime minister. Esther exists in Hebrew as well as two Greek versions. The LXX version (the Deuterocanonical text [Old Testament Apocrypha]) has six major additions that give the story an overt religious component: the mention of God over fifty times, an explicit distaste for intermarriage (cf. Ezra and Nehemiah), concern for dietary regulations, and so on. Compounding the difficulties of determining an "original" story is the absence of Esther from Qumran.

In a variant of the convention, the Book of Esther offers rival wives (Sarah and Hagar, Rachel and Leah, Hannah and Peninnah), but the rivalry is presented through behavioral differences rather than through personal conflict: Esther only appears, can only appear, after Vashti is dismissed. Vashti refuses the king's order to appear at his banquet. Vashti refuses to leave her own banquet to attend the king (her rationale—disgust at being an object of display for drunken men, involvement with her own party, mean-spiritedness—is never explained). Vashti's refusal prompts a law that "all women will give honor to their husbands, high and low alike" (1:20). Vashti's refusal results in a law mandating her banishment, i.e., Ahasueros writes into law the confirmation of her refusal.

Ahasueros is less malevolent than inept: He holds a banquet for "all his officials and ministers, the army of Persia and Media and the nobles and governors of the provinces," the entire infrastructure of the empire, for six months. He is almost always drinking or drunk. He chooses a bride not for political alliance but on the basis of a "beauty" contest in which each candidate spends a year marinating in myrrh, followed by one night with the king. From this contest, he decides to marry Esther, even though he knows nothing of her background. "Esther did not reveal her people or kindred, for Mordecai had charged her not to tell" (2:10). Yet Mordecai insists such silence will not, ultimately, help (Est. 4:13). The danger to the Jews comes first from Haman, the prime minister, whose hatred of Mordecai, Esther's uncle or cousin, extends to all Jews, then from those people in the empire who are willing to carry out the genocidal decree. The enmity between Haman and Mordecai may even have been predicted: Mordecai is a Benjaminite, as was Saul (Est. 2:5; 1 Sam. 9:1; each is explicitly identified as the "son of Kish"). Haman is an Agagite (Est. 9:24), and Saul's sparing of Agag and his taking of booty contribute to his tragedy (1 Sam. 15). Esther does save her people. She, unlike Vashti, comes unbidden to the king. Further, she invites her husband to a banquet in which she manages to place Haman in a compromising position. He is then hanged on the gallows he erected for Mordecai. The book consequently suggests that diaspora communities need to be aware that they may suddenly find themselves no longer welcome in the land they have made their home (one recollects the Exodus), and that even if the authorities wish to protect them, the local population may not.

By king's command and Esther's instruction, "The Jews struck down all their enemies with the sword, slaughtering and destroying them, and did as they

Esther accuses Haman.

pleased to those who hated them. In the citadel city of Susa the Jews killed and destroyed five-hundred people" (9:5–6). "The other Jews who were in the king's provinces also gathered to defend their lives, and gained relief from their enemies, and killed seventy-five thousand of those who hated them; but they laid no hands on the plunder" (9:16). Although the desire to strike back at enemies and to rid the world of anti-Semitism is understandable, is holy war commendable (booty was not taken)? Better is the way that the Book of Esther insists one celebrate the holiday of Purim—the date picked by Haman for the slaughter of the Jews, then hailed as a time of redemption: with "feasting and gladness [and] sending gifts of food to one another and to the poor" (9:22) and with "peace and security" (9:30).

The earliest reference to a Daniel (Dan'el) is that of a Ugaritic king who lived in the 14th century B.C.E. Ezek. 14:14 associates "Danel" with Noah and Job: three (gentile?) individuals known for wisdom. According to Ezek. 28:3, "Danel" knows secrets. Dan. 1:1 dates the story to the "third year of the reign of King Jehoiakim" or 606 B.C.E. (2 Chr. 36:5–7). Jehoiakim's son, Jehoiachin, ruled when Jerusalem was captured in 587. Nebuchadnezzar reigned from 605 to 552 B.C.E. but did not invade Judah until after 605. Such chronological problems are typical of folktales. The accounts of Daniel and the other Jewish youths taken into captivity reflect a time in which the imperial rule is ignorant and dangerous, rather than malevolent, and in which diaspora Jews live in peace, if not with a complete sense of security (contrasting Dan. 7–12, as we see in the next lecture). Consequently, the tales are most often regarded as products of the Persian (538–333 B.C.E.) or early Hellenistic (333–168 B.C.E.) periods. Dan. 2.4b–7.28 is written in Aramaic, the common language of the Near East from the Babylonian exile until the incursion of Hellenism; Dan. 1, 8–12 are in Hebrew, which had become a liturgical language in the Second Temple period.

Complicating the linguistic history are the Septuagint and Old Greek versions, which contain additions to the Daniel cycle: the Book of Susanna, the Prayer of Azariah and the Song of the Three, and Bel and the Dragon (all three appear in the Old Testament Apocrypha). Still more books in the corpus were found among documents discovered in 1948 at Qumran, the so-called "Dead Sea Scrolls." One, the Prayer of Nabonidus (4QprNab), may be an earlier version of Daniel 4. Daniel raises many questions of special concern to those Jews living under foreign rule: Should we eat non-kosher food? Should idols be worshipped? Should one cease to pray to God according to royal decree?

Joseph is sold by his brothers into Egyptian slavery; Moses is born in Egypt and compelled by God to return; Daniel is taken into Babylonian captivity; Esther is brought to court as part of a beauty pageant. The Jews find themselves in foreign courts not of their own volition, but on arriving, they make the best of their circumstances: Joseph gains charge of Egypt (Gen. 41:37–45); Moses bests Pharaoh; Esther becomes queen and Mordecai, the prime minister (Est. 8:1–2); Daniel is "made ruler" (2:48). All four cases present matters of the utmost seriousness: Joseph saves Egypt and his family from famine; Moses saves his people from death and slavery; Daniel's own life is continually threatened; and Esther saves her people from genocide. Variations in the role of God also inform these stories: Joseph receives divine aid in all that he does, and he makes explicit that his ability to interpret dreams comes from God (Gen. 40:8; 41:16). Moses receives divine aid but must be prompted. Daniel, like Joseph, succeeds in service to the ruler through his God-given ability to interpret dreams, as well as to tell the content of them before the interpretation (Dan. 2:19–23). The Book of Esther does not mention the Deity.

The additions to Esther feature highly symbolic dreams that give cosmic import to the story. As the Book of Daniel continues, the hero is no longer the interpreter of dreams but one in need of interpretation of his own visions. The changes mark a shift from folktale to apocalyptic literature, the subject of the final lecture. ■

Suggested Reading

Danna Nolan Fewell, *Circle of Sovereignty: A Story of Stories in Daniel 1–6.*

Michael Fox, *Character and Ideology in the Book of Esther.*

W. Lee Humphries, *Joseph and His Family: A Literary Study.*

James L. Kugel, *In Potiphar's House: The Interpretive Life of Biblical Texts.*

Lawrence Wills, *The Jew in the Court of the Foreign King: Ancient Jewish Court Legends* (Minneapolis, MN: Fortress Press, 1990).

Questions to Consider

1. Can one distinguish between a historical event presented in folktale style and a folktale that purports to describe a historical event?

2. What circumstances, if any, might warrant the violence described in the Book of Esther?

3. Why were Esther and Daniel the only Hebrew narratives expanded in the LXX?

4. What is the theology of Esther?

Life in the Diaspora
(Genesis 30, 37–50; Esther; Daniel 1–6)
Lecture 23—Transcript

From Proverbs to Ecclesiastes to Job, we've already seen the international concerns of wisdom literature. Since the questions these texts raise, from how to live the good life, to what's the point of living at all, to where is the justice in the world, are international questions, they are certainly not unique to the covenant community. These international concerns also influence much else of the covenant community's literature, its interpretation, and even its setting. In terms of interpretation, we'll begin this talk with just a brief comment or two about the development of the legend of Satan. We've already seen the accuser in Zechariah. We've met him in Job. But it's from international connections moving even from Hebrew into Latin that Satan comes to be the figure we know and worry about today.

Then we'll move on to some of the "court tales," questions about Jews in courts of foreign kings, with a focus on Esther, and then a look at Daniel to talk about how Israel dealt with its role as part of a global world, part of the Persian empire, later part of the Greek empire. This is not a community that exists in a vacuum.

So we'll start here with Satan. In Zechariah and in Job, Satan is simply *ha,* "the," *satan,* "the accuser." If you remember the old Perry Mason movies, this is Hamilton Berger, the person who doesn't often win but always brings a case against somebody who is typically innocent. Here *ha-satan* in Zechariah will bring a case against the high priest Joshua. In Job, the case is against Job, the righteous. Developing the imagery of Satan requires flitting through various parts of the Bible. When we look at the prophet Isaiah, we find in Chapter 14 the following: "How you are fallen from heaven, O day star, son of dawn . . . You who said in your heart, 'I will ascend to heaven above the stars of God . . . I will make myself like the Most High . . .' But you are brought down to Sheol, to the depths of the pit."

Ugaritic texts speak of Shahar, the god of dawn, and his son, Helal, the morning star. What Isaiah is actually talking about are Babylonian kings and

Canaanite gods. These are political statements talking about the fall of those nations who have oppressed the covenant community. When this text is translated into Latin, we begin to see the development of satanic speculation. If we take the term "day star," which can also be read as "light bringer," and we bring that into Latin, we get "Lucifer," and that's where we start finding the development of Satan materials.

By the early Hellenistic periods, second to third centuries of B.C.E., after the time of Alexander the Great, as Israel comes in contact with Greek thought and Greek gods, the idea of evil gods then starts to influence the covenant community's view of its own theology, and satanic concerns begin to develop. We don't find them in the Old Testament materials, but we do find them well played out in the New.

As we move to other examples of international literature, translation, and concern, we find ourselves addressing the question, what is life like in the Diaspora, where people might not speak our language, where they are no longer speaking Hebrew but perhaps Persian or Greek? Where Hebrews, Jews, come into contact with people who don't share their values, indeed, don't even understand their values? We're talking here about something called the Diaspora. The term actually comes from a Greek word meaning "dispersion."

From the time of the Babylonian exile we find pockets of Jews living outside the land of Israel, in Babylon, but not Babylon only—in the Persian kingdom, in the Egyptian kingdom, later on in Greece, moving off to Rome, and in North Africa. How are these people to survive amid the alien culture? This might be considered the reverse of the question Ruth poses. Ruth is the Gentile who comes into Jewish territory. When we meet figures like Esther and Daniel, here we have Jews who are existing in Gentile territory. How much of their ethnic identity do they preserve? To what extent can they acculturate or assimilate? These are the questions Jews had to raise as they themselves found themselves either in the Diaspora or as Israel became heavily influenced first by Persian culture and then certainly by Greek.

Larry Wills wrote a monograph several years ago entitled *The Jew in the Court of the Foreign King*. This may well be a convention because the idea of a Jew in a foreign court actually applies through various texts in the Bible: Joseph in Pharaoh's court, Moses raised in Pharaoh's court, and then these latter tales of the Diaspora, Esther and Daniel.

So we'll start with a look at the Book of Esther, which I think is a terrific book, and see what advice this text gives us. Now, I warn you about Esther, because its canonical status has always been controversial. The Hebrew version of Esther never mentions the name of God. The early Jews debated whether it should be included in the canon or not. Martin Luther from the Protestant Reformation despised this book. Other people have loved it. It has caused enormous hope. It's also caused quite a good deal of tragedy.

Here is the Book of Esther. It's set in the Persian court, first line: "In the days of Ahasuerus," the same Ahasuerus who ruled over 127 provinces from India to Kush or Ethiopia. If you even think of the term "Ahasuerus," which is difficult for me to say and, in fact, difficult for most, it sounds sort of silly, and I think in Hebrew it's supposed to because at least the beginning of this text is not merely comedy; it's, in fact, farce. We don't know who this Ahasuerus is. He is typically associated with the Persian King Xerxes I who ruled from 485 to 464 B.C.E., but when we look at the details in the Book of Esther and then look to Persian records, which are, in fact, quite good, we find no confirmation of anything in this book. There is no external record of Xerxes having a Jewish queen or a Jewish prime minister. There is no evidence of a grand vizier named Haman who wanted to sponsor genocide. The easiest way and probably the most appropriate way of approaching the Book of Esther is to approach it as a book of fiction, which, through its storytelling, provides information to the people who read it. You might think of this as a very, very big parable.

Esther may have been composed during the Persian period. It's certainly set in the Persian court. But it actually may be a product of the Greek age as well. The text is exceptionally stylized, but the style itself fits both the earlier material, such as the Joseph material, as well as later materials, such as, for example, Hellenistic romances. In terms of the text, again we have a problem because the Book of Esther exists in different versions. There is the Hebrew text, the Mazoretic text—this is the one that never mentions the name of God—but the Greek translation of Esther, the text that's found in the

Septuagint, has a substantial number of major additions to it, and the Greek text actually Judeafies the book. The Greek version of Esther mentions God over 50 times. It displays, in the spirit of Ezra and Nehemiah, a distaste for intermarriage. The Hebrew Esther marries the Persian king; nobody raises a fuss. In the Greek, everybody—Esther, Mordecai—they all raise a fuss. Intermarriage is bad.

The Greek text has an enormous concern for dietary regulations, keeping kosher. You will recall those laws from Leviticus. The Hebrew never mentions it. The Greek has a good many dreams, which are highly symbolic. Much as Joseph interprets dreams and Daniel interprets dreams, that's part of this Jewish tradition. The Book of Esther leaves that material out. So whether the Greek is the original and the Hebrew is derivative, or whether the Hebrew was original and the Greek derivative, or whether actually a third text, called the Alpha Text, which is not in anybody's canon—either in the Old Testament Apocrypha, the Greek text, or the Hebrew canon—whether the Alpha Text is the first one or the third, we simply don't know. The textual tradition of the Book of Esther is, in a word, confused. Making it even more confused, there is no copy of the Book of Esther found among the Dead Sea Scrolls, so we don't even know what its canonical status was, let alone what early records of this text suggested, how it read.

In terms of the book itself, it's completely artificial. It pulls upon motifs that we've already seen, drawing upon literary conventions. If we didn't have the Book of Esther, we probably could have written it based on material we already had. It begins, for example, not only with a foreign court, which we can see from Daniel or even the Joseph saga, it begins with a type scene of two wives in competition. We've seen that with Sarah and Hagar, with Hannah and Peninnah, and with Rachel and Leah. Here we have it with Esther and the first queen, whose name is Vashti.

But circumstances here are not quite the same as they were before. In earlier examples of this convention, the two wives duke it out over who's going to have a child, whether there is a barren wife or a fertile wife, or who will have the love of the husband, but they exist together, the two wives, in enmity. In this particular case, the first wife Vashti is off the scene before Esther ever arrives. Indeed, Vashti's dismissal from the court is what causes Esther to be invited into the court in the first place.

When we think of this particular text and how the convention plays out, here we move into farce. Ahasuerus basically throws parties. He spends most of the book either drinking or drunk. The first chapter is set out with an enormous banquet that he's thrown for all of his principles, his advisors, his captains, and his governors. Midway through the banquet he orders his queen, Vashti, to appear before him and his lords. Vashti, meanwhile, is hosting a banquet of her own for some other ladies in a different part of the palace, and she sends word back, "I refuse to come." Why she refuses we're never told, and scholars have, in fact, speculated about this as they do frequently when we have a fictional character. Clearly there must be some sort of motive. Does she despise her husband? That's easy enough to do. Does she find disgust at being asked to be an object of display before a group of drunken men? Is she involved with her own duties and doesn't want to give up her job as hostess? Is it simply mean-spiritedness, or is it, as one Jewish *midrash* says in expansion on this story, that she was suffering from an outbreak of pimples at the time and was simply too embarrassed to show up? The king says to her, "Appear in your royal crown." Another *midrash* reads, "She was asked to appear only in her royal crown and out of modesty refused to come."

Whatever her rationale, she incites the king's fury. Of course, she's a wife— she should have obeyed him. So the king, who is, I will continue to remind you, not bright, proceeds to consult his sages. What do you do if your wife disobeys you? He consults his sages, who knew the laws, for this was the king's procedure toward all who were versed in law and custom. He's a by-the-books kind of guy. We might here contrast him with Israelite law, where the laws are sane, where they tell you what to do, but they certainly don't legislate what to do if your wife doesn't show up when you call her. The king's advisors are very much concerned with this, however.

They note, "This very day the noble ladies of Persia and Media who have heard of the queen's behavior will tell against the king's officials, and there will be no end of contempt and wrath." So they come up with a new law. They advise the king to promulgate a law throughout his extensive empire, "that all women will give honor to their husbands high and low alike." So the king therefore passes a law that every man be the master of his own house. This is somewhat difficult to legislate, and I think here we can see part of the farcical aspect of this. The king of the Persian empire is now involved in minute domestic disputations. Ahasuerus, also advised by his eunuchs, who help him out here, decides to banish Queen Vashti, which may well have been exactly what Vashti wanted. She refuses to come to the court. He says, "Fine, I'll make a law you can't come to the court."

Now the king has a problem. He needs a queen. How is he going to get a queen? Now, if I were a king in antiquity and I needed a queen, I would go to my nearest rival and marry that rival's daughter or sister because, in antiquity, indeed, as we've seen through the monarchy up through the Middle Ages to contemporary times, monarchs marry other monarchs. They are good for economic alliances. They are good for political alliances. They prevent war. Not this king. He, on the advice of his ministers and other advisors, decides he's going to hold a beauty contest and he's going to pick the winner. How does this contest work? He sends messengers out to the entire empire, "Find me all the virgins you can." This is Persia—there are a fair number of virgins—and they are all brought to the palace, where they are entrusted to the care of one of the king's eunuchs, and they spend the next year marinating in myrrh and precious oils. Then each one, subsequently, night after night, one by one, visits the king in the evening and then in the morning goes to a second harem.

When I read this story when I was a child, I used to think they played canasta. I don't think that's actually what they were doing. But then the king has to decide which of these women he will accept, and he winds up accepting Esther, good girl that she is, who goes into the king taking only what the king's eunuch advised her. She's a girl who knows how to take advice. That's how Esther gets to be queen. This is clearly farce.

Part of the fiction is also taken up with Esther's uncle or cousin—the textual tradition differs on this. His name is Mordecai, and he is a bit of a problem here. He is a Benjaminite, as was King Saul, by the way, and Mordecai is related to a man named Kish, and, as you will recall from our introduction of Saul, Saul's father's name is Kish. So there is a connection here with that earlier Deuteronomic history. Mordecai at one point refuses to bow down to the king's prime minister—his name is Haman or Hamen, and he is an Agagite. The problem here is that it was Saul's sparing of Agag that led to his dismissal by Samuel. You might recall that wonderful line about "Samuel hewed the body of Agag to pieces."

So what we have in the Book of Esther is a replay of that ancient enmity between the Hebrews and the Agagites, between Saul and his enemy, but here Mordecai, Saul's descendant, will make good what his ancestor lost. Mordecai has obtained Haman's enmity because he has not bowed down. Haman decides he wants to commit genocide against the Hebrew people because he finds out Mordecai is a Jew, and he decides all Jews have to go. Haman, however, and, in fact, no one else, knows that Esther is Jewish because, when Esther was taken into the Persian court, Mordecai had told her, "Do not reveal your people or your nation." So she is a Jew in secret there in the Persian court.

How are things going to play out? As soon as the edict promulgating the death of the Jews is made, and it's made by casting *purim*, which means "lots" or "dice," Haman gets the king's signet ring. He also gives the king a nice bribe of silver and says to the king, "I want to get rid of this people who have their own laws and don't obey you." Well, it's true they have their own laws, but, as we've seen with laws and covenants, Jews who exist in foreign countries, who live there, have to obey the laws of the state. The king never even asks, "Well, what people is this?" He simply says, "Fine, do as you will."

Mordecai goes into mourning. He rends his clothes. Esther hears about it through palace intrigue, and she sends word to her cousin, "What's wrong?" Mordecai tells her what's happened and says, "You need to plead with your husband to rescue us," and Esther says, "Well, wait. The Persians have a law"—because that's what they do in Persia—"The Persians have a law that says you cannot go to visit the king if you've not been invited, on pain of death. Unless the king extends to you his golden scepter, you die. He's going to kill me." Mordecai says to her, "Look, perhaps it is precisely for such a time as this that you were put into the harem." He doesn't evoke God here, but one can read in some sort of divine or at least providential impulse.

Mordecai also goes on to say, "Do not think your role as queen will save you. You will die if you don't do something, and then help will come from some other place"—God, perhaps, or somewhere else? Mordecai doesn't say.

So Esther gets herself together. She dresses up nicely, and she goes to the royal court, and, thank heaven, Ahasuerus extends his golden scepter to her. He says, "What do you want, O queen? I will give you whatever you want, even up to half of my kingdom," which is a very stupid thing for a king to promise. We can see here the irony. Vashti is dismissed from the court for refusing to come; Esther comes unbidden. In fact, Esther winds up doing everything that Vashti doesn't and in doing so slightly transgresses the law— not too bad but just a little bit, takes it into her own hands.

What does she do? She invites the king to a banquet, here again the reverse of Vashti, who refuses to come, and she says, "Come to my banquet, and have your minister Haman come as well." This is not quite what the king was expecting, but he's quick on the uptake, and he's always happy to party, so he, in fact, goes with her, and they have a banquet. Then they have another banquet, and Esther is setting her plot. Finally, finally, at the last banquet, when they are drinking and the king is happy, and the king says, "What can I give to you, Esther, even if it's up to half of my kingdom?" Esther responds, "Well, listen, if we were simply sold as slaves this would be okay, but my people have been sold to death, I and my people. Find me some way of protection. Stop this law." Ahasuerus says, "Who would have done such a thing?" and Esther looks at Haman and says, "The wicked Haman." The scene is nicely set.

This being a farcical text and somewhat contrived, at this point Ahasuerus leaves the room, ostensibly because he's upset. This gives Haman time to throw himself on the dining couch where Queen Esther is lying to plead for his life, and, of course, at this opportune moment Ahasuerus walks back in, sees Haman having thrown himself on his wife, and says, "Will you ravish my wife as well?" He thinks there is a rape in progress. He decides at this point to kill Haman, and, at this point as well, Esther keeps her mouth shut. Haman actually gets condemned for doing something he didn't do, attacking Esther, rather than condemned for something he did do, sponsoring genocide. Haman is hanged on the gallows that he had actually erected for Mordecai.

But the dangers of this text continue because the law has been passed that the Jews are to be killed on a certain day. As we know, the laws of the Medes and the Persians say, once the law is made you cannot revoke it. What's going to happen? Esther has to arrange with her cousin Mordecai and the king that a new law be promulgated, giving the Jews in the Persian empire the opportunity to defend themselves, which is actually quite helpful. What then happens? "By the king's command and Esther's instruction, the Jews struck down all their enemies with the sword, slaughtering and destroying them, and did as they pleased to all who hated them. In the citadel of Susa [which is where the Persian kings had their summer palace], the Jews killed and destroyed 500 people" (Ch. 9).

But that's not all, and here we move from farce into what I would regard as tragedy. The other Jews who were living in the king's provinces also gathered to defend their lives and gain release from their enemies and killed 75,000 of those who hated them, but, the text goes on to say, "they laid no hand on the plunder." It is as if these Jews in the Persian empire are engaged in holy war, and, as we've see before with holy war, you can kill people—indeed, you're supposed to kill people—but you're not supposed to take any of the booty. When we think back to that original conflict between King Saul and the Agagites, what was the problem? Saul conquered his enemy but took some of the booty and allowed the king to remain alive. At this point, Mordecai and his fellow Jews wind up slaughtering everybody. There is no one left among the enemy, but the booty is not taken.

This desire to strike back at enemies and to rid the world of anti-Semitism is certainly understandable, and holy war is indeed part and parcel of the way the ancient world functioned. The problem is, this text, the Book of Esther—it is called the *Megillat* Esther, the scroll of Esther—is read every year in synagogues on the Jewish Festival of Purim. Contemporary synagogues are not, these days, always reading the last couple of chapters about the destruction. In 1994, having heard this text read in Israel, a settler who was actually from the United States and moved to Israel the next day went to the mosque at Hebron, opened up with machine-gun fire and massacred over 30 Muslim people at prayer. This is a text that can inspire both hope and incredible hatred.

Better is the way, I think, the Book of Esther insists one actually celebrate the holiday. The holiday is celebrated on the date that Haman picked for the genocide of the Jews, and it's now turned into a celebration of life rather than death. We're told in Chapter 9 that the Jews in the Persian empire celebrated this holiday "with feasting and gladness and sending of gifts of food to one another and to the poor and with peace and security." That's the way the holiday needs to celebrated. That's the way it's traditionally celebrated. But we need to be careful because this is a text of enormous violence, and the farce turns to tragedy. If we continue to look at Esther as a book of farce, perhaps we might not take that ending quite so seriously, and I actually like the idea of not reading it out loud liturgically.

That's Esther and Mordecai, and they certainly survive in the court of the foreign king. Esther remains queen. Mordecai is given Haman's old job, and suddenly we have a Jewish grand vizier in the Persian empire. Ahasuerus certainly could have used it—he is not too bright—but Mordecai is appreciated by all the people, including the king.

And so we leave the Persian Court and move to the Babylonian court, and this brings us to the stories of Daniel. As with the Book of Esther, dating the Book of Daniel is no simple matter. The earliest references to a figure named Daniel or Dan'el—it's a slightly different spelling in the Hebrew— are to a Ugaritic king. There is actually a figure named Dan'el who lived in the fourteenth century B.C.E., the 1300s. The prophet Ezekiel in Chapter 14 associates one Dan'el with Noah and Job, perhaps three Gentiles, from Ezekiel's perspective, who are known for wisdom. Ezekiel tells us even, in Chapter 28, this particular Dan'el knows secrets.

The Book of Daniel itself, Chapter 1, Verse 1, dates the story to the third year of the reign of King Jehoiakim, and we met him when we talked about the Babylonian destruction of the southern kingdom. This would be about 606 B.C.E. Jehoiakim's son, Jehoiachin or Jeconiah, ruled when Jerusalem was captured in 587, and Daniel is in Babylon after the destruction of the temple. Now, I did that very quickly, and you probably didn't catch the dates, but the point is here, the dates of Daniel do not match up with the dates of the Babylonian emperors or the Hebrew—the Judean—empires, or the destruction of the temple. The dating here seems to be contrived.

It's fictional. Daniel, based on his own dating, is in Babylon prior to the time that the temple was destroyed, but the text itself says the temple is already destroyed.

If we look at this, then, as a book of fiction, a book of folktales, then we can get a handle on it. The accounts of Daniel and the other Jewish youths taken into captivity reflect a time when imperial rule is ignorant and dangerous, much like the Book of Esther, rather than malevolent. When we get to the apocalyptic sections of the Book of Daniel, imperial rule becomes malevolent. The question is how to survive in foreign countries where the kings simply do not understand you rather than, for the most part, want to kill you.

The tales of Daniel are most often regarded as products of the Persian period from 538 to 333 or the early Greek period—Alexander the Great comes through in 333—up to about the year 168. Daniel, Chapter 2, Verse 4b until Chapter 7, Verse 28, is written not in Hebrew but in Aramaic, which is actually the common language of the Near East in the time of the Babylonian empire up to the rise of the Greek empire. Daniel, Chapter 1, and the remaining Chapters 8 through 12, happen to be in Hebrew, which, by the Second Temple Period, by, say, about 200 B.C.E., was becoming much more a liturgical language than a spoken language. Aramaic was, as it were, becoming the lingua franca of the period.

Complicating the history of the Book of Daniel, as with the Book of Esther, the Greek text has a different version or, indeed, has additions. You may have heard of the story of Susanna, this lovely young lady who was in the process of taking a bath when some elders came and attempted to attack her. That's an addition to the Book of Daniel. Or the stories of Bel and the dragon or the prayer of Azariah and the song of the three young men. These are all part of the Danielic corpus. They are in the Greek text, and they are in the Old Testament Apocrypha, but they are not in the Hebrew. Indeed, Danielic traditions continue even to the Dead Sea Scrolls, where additional books attributed to Daniel are there.

In terms of the folktales, the major questions are those of assimilation. Daniel raises questions like, should we eat non-kosher food? Absolutely not, the response is. Should idols be worshipped? Absolutely not, the response is, even if the refusal to participate in idol worship causes you to be thrown into a fiery furnace, and that's what happens with Daniel's three friends. Should one cease to pray to God according to royal decree? This is not asking for overt idolatry; it's asking for simply a refraining. One might think of sins of commission versus sins of omission. Should one cease to pray to God according to royal decree? Absolutely not, even if one's fate by doing so is to be thrown into a lion's den—and there is Daniel in the lion's den.

Through all these dangers, there is also a great deal of humor in these folktales. Daniel's enemies in the royal court always receive their just reward. Daniel manifests his interpretative gifts, his ability to interpret dreams, not only the way Joseph does—Pharaoh tells him a dream and Joseph makes the interpretation—but in this case Nebuchadnezzar and the other kings will say to Daniel not only "Interpret my dream for me" but also "Tell me what I dreamt and then interpret my dream," which is a much harder thing to do. Daniel, like Joseph, of course, always gives the credit to God.

And we find in Daniel, Chapter 5, that very famous handwriting on the wall. "MENE, MENE, TEKEL, PARSIN," it says, which basically says, "Evil empires will be divided up and will fall." I think other empires since might note this handwriting on the wall sometimes applies to them, and for the Book of Daniel, which knew about the fall of the Babylonian empire and probably about the fall of the Persian empire, the handwriting on the wall did come true.

As biblical chronology moves from the patriarchs to Persia, this motif of the Jew in the court of the foreign king develops from Joseph to Moses to Mordecai to Daniel, and one can see in this, in fact, literary conventions. They are all in foreign courts not by their own choice, for example. Joseph is sold; Moses is brought there—he didn't ask for it; Daniel is taken into captivity during the Babylonian onslaught; and Esther is brought to the court as part of a beauty pageant and her cousin follows her. But they all succeed. Joseph gains charge over all of Egypt. Moses bests Pharaoh. Esther becomes queen and Mordecai the prime minister. And Daniel, according to Chapter 2, Verse 48 of his book, is made ruler. One can see how these stories would be, at the very least, uplifting to people within a minority group.

All four cases present matters of the utmost seriousness. Joseph saves Egypt and therefore his family from famine. He is there to protect. Moses saves his own people from death and slavery. Daniel saves his own life and by extension the life of every Jew in the Diaspora, and Esther saves her people from genocide. There are also variations on the role of God in all these stories. Joseph receives divine aid all the time. Moses receives divine aid, but he's got to be prompted—God's got to push him through. Daniel, like Joseph, succeeds through the gift of interpretation of dreams. In a major break with the convention, Esther never evokes God. Neither does Mordecai.

As these stories are compared, these tales of Jews in the foreign court, many more insights can be gained both in terms of individual narratives and as a collection, and you might want to pursue that at your leisure. The other thing that we find with these tales is these are tales also of wisdom. Daniel is a figure of wisdom. Mordecai, with his royal advice, is a figure of wisdom. Wisdom is one form that Israelite literature takes in antiquity. But, as we see with continuation of the Book of Daniel, in addition to novels and folktales and wisdom, there is one more genre yet to go. So for our last lecture we'll look at the genre of apocalypticism.

Apocalyptic Literature
(Isaiah 24–27, 56–66; Zechariah 9–14; Daniel 7–12)
Lecture 24

Apocalyptic literature is a combination of a variety of other literatures. From the prophets it takes the idea of the concern to inculcate moral values and that God is active in history. From wisdom literature it takes speculation on the universe. It raises questions of theodicy. From novels it pulls from characters who are put in awkward, difficult, dangerous positions and then somehow they have to come to terms with their existence, often through the help of a divine mediary.

The genre "apocalyptic" (Greek: "revelation," "uncovering") takes its name from the last book of the New Testament: the Book of Revelation or the Apocalypse of St. John. Books are classified as apocalypses based on several features, not all of which appear in every apocalypse. The genre is notoriously hard to define. Apocalyptic materials sometimes are combined with other forms: the Apocalypse of Daniel is tacked onto folk tales.

What does apocalyptic writing do? It raises universal questions concerning the *Urzeit* (the time of creation) and the *Endzeit* (the end of time). It often leaves its symbols unmediated and unexplained; its audience may be familiar with the codes. It is primarily a written, not an oral, genre. It frequently offers a pessimistic view of history. Still, its determinism means that God has established a plan that includes redemption for those who now despair. Popular in apocalyptic literature is a sense of de-evolution. When things get bad enough, then God intervenes. Dualistic thought divides both mundane and supernatural realms into warring camps of good and evil. The cosmic war pits the heavenly hosts, led by the archangel Michael, against the forces of evil, led by such fallen angels as Mastema, Belial, and Satan, or the devil. On earth, the Sons of Light battle the Sons of Darkness (the Qumran War Scroll).

Daniel is an interpreter of dreams; he later becomes the visionary who needs others to interpret his dreams. In one vision, he sees the Son of Man awarded an everlasting dominion and needs an angelic explanation. Sometimes, these visions are unexplained, left to the reader's speculation. The motif of secrecy is part of the apocalyptic genre; it is like reading a mystery novel and not having all the pieces. Apocalyptic frequently gives itself a false or pseudonymous author by backdating its time of authorship.

Most scholars date Daniel's apocalyptic materials to the eve of the Maccabean revolt (2nd century B.C.E.). After Alexander's death (323), his empire was divided among his generals. To Ptolemy in Egypt went the satrapy "Across the River" (Dan. 2:41). In 198, at the Battle of Paneas, the descendants of Seleucis of Syria gain Judea. In about 168, rebellion breaks under the Seleucid Antiochus IV Epiphanes. The Temple is profaned ("abomination or desolation" or "desolating sacrilege," Dan. 8:1–14, 11:30; 1 Macc. 1:54; 2 Macc. 6:2), circumcision and Sabbath observance are forbidden, and Jerusalem becomes a Greek *polis*. The Hasmonean family (Maccabees) rout the Syrians and their supporters and replace the assimilationist families as rulers. Daniel's vision is, ultimately, one of redemption. His apocalypse is eschatological, and we still await its fulfillment.

We are at our own eschaton now that we've reached the end of the course. Given the enormous scope of the Old Testament/*Tanakh*, we are unable to cover many subjects: the court histories of David, the poetry of the Psalms and Lamentations, the development of the worship system, the canonical process, or how the texts were put together,archeological remains, such as the Moabite inscriptions to name a few. There is much in this text still to explore. Now you should have a good sense of how rich the material really is. ∎

Suggested Reading

John J. Collins, *The Apocalyptic Imagination: An Introduction to Jewish Apocalyptic Literature*, 2nd ed.

Jacob Neusner, William Scott Green, and Ernest S. Frerichs (eds.), *Judaisms and Their Messiahs at the Turn of the Christian Era* (Cambridge/New York: Cambridge University Press, 1987).

J. Edward Wright, *The Early History of Heaven.*

Questions to Consider

1. What are the heirs of apocalyptic writing as a literary genre? Who are today's apocalyptic communities, and how should those who are not members regard them?

2. What motivates some modern readers to adopt radically eschatological, apocalyptic worldviews?

Apocalyptic Literature
(Isaiah 24–27, 56–66; Zechariah 9–14; Daniel 7–12)
Lecture 24—Transcript

Biblical wisdom literature seeks to convey information on how to live the good life and to establish at least the question, if not the answers, of the justice of God. Prophetic literature seeks to communicate divine will to human beings and to mediate back to God humans' concerns. The tales of the Jew in the court of the foreign king that we just visited in the last lecture seek to provide advice to people on how to live in the world even when the world is not responding appropriately. But there are times when answers are not forthcoming and, indeed, when the world seems to be caving in on people, as if that genocide that the Book of Esther suggested might happen would really come, as if we were really dealing with history and not simply with folktale or farce.

The difficulties in negotiating the world when bad things continue to happen and when it appears to the people that there is no way that they on their own can provide any sort of rectification—when all these bad things continue, a new genre proceeds to develop in biblical literature. We find it both in Old Testament and in New Testament materials, and this is known as apocalyptic.

The term "apocalyptic" comes from a Greek word meaning "uncovering" or "revelation." You might have heard of the New Testament book, the Book of Revelation—no "s" on the end, by the way. It's also called the Apocalypse of John. Apocalyptic literature is a combination of a variety of other literatures we've already seen. From the prophets it takes the idea of the concern to inculcate moral values and that God is active in history. From wisdom literature it takes speculation on the universe. It raises questions of theodicy. From novels it pulls from characters who are put in awkward, difficult, dangerous positions and then somehow they have to come to terms with their existence, often through the help of a divine mediary. Apocalyptic is, in effect, a combination of the breakdown of prophecy with a little bit of wisdom thrown in and then with influences from Persian thought and then Greek thought.

Let's take a look, then, at some of the influences on the development of apocalyptic, and then we'll look at the Bible's one full-blown—and here "full-blown" is actually a technical term in biblical literature—apocalypse, the last several chapters of the Book of Daniel. In terms of the origins here, it's actually very difficult to define early apocalyptic. People have described apocalyptic much as folks have described pornography—in the sense of, "Well, I can't really describe it but I know it when I see it." Therefore, some earlier texts that many consider to be apocalyptic others will look at as proto-apocalyptic, or moving toward apocalyptic. These would include materials such as the prophet Zechariah, Chapters 9 through 14, where we begin to find unmediated visions, visions not explained fully; symbols; odd angels suddenly showing up and providing information; and mysterious beings flying through the heavens.

Others have looked at the last piece of information that we get from the prophet Isaiah, fourth Isaiah, if you will, Chapters 24–27, where we start getting information about resurrection of the dead, which, as you know, we've not seen much of before. We might want to consider this proto-apocalyptic.

We also have the problem of apocalyptic materials showing up in literature that is not in itself apocalyptic. Sometimes apocalyptic literature is tacked on to other materials. For example, the apocalypse of Daniel is tacked on to those folktales. When we go to the New Testament, the apocalyptic material in the Book of Revelation is actually tacked on to seven letters, so you have an epistolary opening and then you have an apocalypse. And we actually find this non-canonical literature of the early Roman period (the first century Common Era), texts like the Apocalypse of Baruch, Second Baruch, or Fourth Ezra, or even the Apocalypse of Abraham. They begin with letters or folktales, and then suddenly these apocalyptic visions take over.

What does apocalyptic do? Well, it raises questions of universalistic import. Whereas the prophets are interested in the covenant community's history, apocalyptic, like wisdom literature, is interested in all history. It frequently uses a motif referred to in German as *Urzeit, Endzeit*. In other words it takes the ur-time, that original time, the Garden of Eden, and then looks at the *Endzeit*, that end time when the covenant community will finally be redeemed, when there will be a general resurrection of the dead, when the wicked will finally be punished and the good rewarded. It matches up the two as if we started in the Garden of Eden and sometime, when history comes to its *telos*—when it comes to its goal—we will regain that Garden of Eden. Apocalyptic is therefore interested in universal history, not just in terms of Israelite history.

We can see some of that cosmogonic opening even at the beginning of Daniel. Daniel 7 talks about the four winds of heaven stirring up the great sea, evoking here that image from Genesis, Chapter 1, about the spirit of God hovering over the deep. It's an *Urzeit*, or first-time, image coming back up, the wind in the sea recollecting the first chapter of Genesis. And the beasts Daniel describes give us another example of apocalyptic imagery. When the prophets use allegory or metaphor, they tell us what they mean. Amos's basket of summer fruit clearly signifies the end time coming—we know that. Apocalyptic literature often leaves its symbols unmediated, unexplained, because apocalyptic is less literature for the public than it is literature for an in-house community, a group of people who already know the codes, already know the symbols.

Here is an example of an image that is not fully described in the Book of Daniel. "After the four winds of heaven stir up the great sea," Daniel tells us, "he sees four beasts coming out from the sea." The beasts—the lion, the bear, this four-winged leopard, and some sort of creature with great iron teeth and 10 horns—actually represent empires such that the lion is Babylon, the bear is the kingdom of the Medes, Persia is the leopard, and this odd beast with its teeth and its horns, that's the empire of Greece—Alexander the Great and those who succeeded him. But Daniel doesn't spell out in detail what all these visions mean.

Apocalyptic is primarily a written genre rather than an oral genre. People would speculate over the texts themselves, and I suspect that, when the apocalyptic material of the Book of Daniel was first being studied, people would look at it and then teachers would tell students, this refers to this and this refers to that. The benefit of this type of literature is that, because the symbols are not always described, the literature is ever new, so a particular beast does not necessarily have to represent Babylon. Two or three hundred years later it could represent Rome or Germany or Iraq or the United States. With the symbols unmediated, apocalyptic becomes a universal literature not only across space but also across time.

Apocalyptic literature also frequently, somewhat like the Book of Ecclesiastes here, offers a very pessimistic view of history, as if history is going on toward something so totally negative that only an act of God can come in and rectify the situation. This is not upbeat material in the least, but at the same time that it shows this pessimistic view of history, apocalyptic is frequently deterministic. That means that God has everything under control, that history is following out a set plan God has established. God had predetermined things were going to go from bad to worse to worst, but ultimately there will be a redemption, a vindication. That allows people living in a state of hopelessness (either a real state of hopelessness, where they really are being persecuted, or in a perceived state of hopelessness, because there are people who are convinced that the world is bad who are actually living relatively the good life), people who are convinced that they have no power, that things are bad, that ultimately God is in control—the literature, by telling them that everything is predetermined, allows them to have hope. It encourages them in perseverance.

My own sense of this, and it comes from the New Testament expression that hell is a place of "wailing and gnashing of teeth," is that apocalyptic literature is somewhat like going to the dentist's office. You know it's going to hurt, and you're told exactly how much it's going to hurt, but at the end there is redemption. You have peace. There is no longer any pain. And you can begin to smile.

Popular in apocalyptic literature are symbolic overviews of time, therefore, with a sense of de-evolution. Daniel actually presents this model in the folktale rather than in the apocalypse. Chapter 2 of Daniel gives us a dream by Nebuchadnezzar. He dreams of a great statue, its brilliance extraordinary and its appearance exceptionally frightening. The head of the statute is described as being a fine gold, its chest in arms of silver, its middle and thighs of bronze, its legs of iron, and its feet partly of iron and partly of clay. The interpretation of the dream is basically an apocalyptic worldview, where you start out with a golden age, and things go to silver, and then they go to bronze, and then, in effect, they go to pot. That's the way apocalyptic literature describes history. But, when things get really bad, that's when God breaks in.

Apocalyptic, given this very negative view of history, and given the fact that the authors and communities that support this view consider themselves to be oppressed, is, as you might expect, dualistic. There are good guys and there are bad guys, and it's very, very easy to tell the difference between them. Apocalyptic is the sort of literature that will proclaim, "I'm saved and you're not," or "I am predetermined to be rewarded at the end, and you are so wicked there is no way you will ever succeed." This is known as dualism.

Frequently we find in apocalyptic a cosmic war pitting the hosts of heaven, often led by angels like the angel Michael, over against the hosts of hell, often led by the developing Satan figure or other demons named Mastema or Belial, figures, supernatural figures, who fight against God. On earth we find in the Qumran community, the Dead Sea Scrolls, a text describing the war of the Sons of Light against the Sons of Darkness. Daniel has the same thing. There are bad guys and there are good guys, and Daniel tells us that the righteous will be raised to everlasting life and the wicked do not get that benefit. Here is an example from Daniel, "Many shall be purified, cleansed, and refined, but the wicked shall continue to act wickedly. None of the wicked shall understand, but those who are wise shall understand." That's Daniel, Chapter 12.

With all these various visions, many of them unmediated, simply symbols without interpretation, apocalyptic, in order to get its message across, actually needs a little bit of interpretation. We find in the Book of Daniel, in the first part, the folktales, that Daniel is an interpreter of dreams. Nebuchadnezzar has a dream; Daniel tells us what it means. When we get to the apocalyptic section, Daniel himself is the dreamer or the visionary, and he needs heavenly figures like angels to come and explain to him what he has dreamed. Here Daniel is the apocalyptic visionary, and he needs heavenly interpretation.

Daniel, for example, has a vision—it's a very famous vision for both Jewish and Christian traditions—in which he sees one like a son of man coming with the clouds of heaven. "He came to the Ancient of Days [this is the idea of God on the royal throne in heaven, envisioned as an old man, old as time] and was presented to him, and to him was given dominion and glory and kingship, that all peoples and nations and languages should serve him." Daniel goes on to say that "The son of man's dominion is an everlasting dominion that shall not pass away, and his kingship is one that shall not be destroyed." This is quite a vision. Daniel then tells us, "My spirit was troubled within me, and the visions of my head terrified me. So I approached one of the attendants to ask him the truth concerning all of this." Daniel knows what he sees; he simply doesn't know what it meant. Therefore he needs the angel's explanation, which he gets in the latter part of Chapter 7.

At times these visions are not interpreted, and you notice I'm not going to give you the interpretation of that one. Sometimes they are simply left up to speculation. It may be, as these stories are told within covenant communities, that the teller of the tale will know what the answer is. The text simply does not provide us that.

In terms of the secrecy motif, I suspect that that secrecy motif is also part of the literary artistry of apocalyptic. Apocalyptic can't simply be bizarre symbols that no one understands because then why would anybody read it? There has got to be a little bit that we can relate to and then we want more, as if we're reading a mystery novel but we don't have all the pieces. Or we find out about a secret society or a fraternity and we know a little bit about what they do and we want to know more. The apocalyptic literature actually provides us hints that draw us in. For example, in Daniel, Chapter 12, an angel tells Daniel, "You, Daniel, keep the words secret and this book sealed until the end of time," as if here is something we wait for. Indeed, what apocalyptic frequently does is provide itself a false author or a pseudonymous author.

Apocalyptic is frequently written during a time of particular stress, but the author, the narrative author is himself—and it's usually a him—frequently backdated 500 years earlier, 1,000 years earlier. A first-century book from the Common Era, called Fourth Ezra, is actually attributed to Ezra, who lived right after the Babylonian exile. If Daniel is a figure of the Babylonian period, as he is in the folktales, and he's presenting these visions, isn't it amazing that all of his visions takes us down to about the year 168-167 B.C.E. of the time of the Greek period, the reign of Antiochus IV Epiphanes of Syria? It is as if Daniel, looking forward from the Babylonian exile, can predict the rise of Persia and the rise of Greece; the rise of the Seleucid dynasty, the inheritors of Alexander; and ultimately the outrages of Antiochus IV Epiphanes. Here is the way apocalyptic can grab you. It can predict time, and, since it looks like that ancient author got it right from the past, perhaps what that ancient author is saying about contemporary times might also be correct.

The Book of Daniel itself, at least the apocalyptic material, was probably written around 168-167 Before the Common Era. Here is the social situation. The empire of Alexander the Great splits up after his death and gets divided among his generals. Judea passes into the hands of his general Ptolemy, who was basically in charge of Egypt. So if you've ever heard of the Ptolemaic empire, that's where it comes from. There is another general whose name is Seleucis who gets the area around Syria, and he founds the Seleucid dynasty.

Then, like any two kingdoms next to each other, they proceed to fight back and forth and back and forth. In the year 198, at the Battle of Paneas, Judea—or Palestine, if you will—at this time passes from Egyptian to Syrian control, and, other than the fact that the Jews are now paying their taxes to a different empire, nothing much changes. But in the middle of the century a new Seleucid king comes to the throne. His name is Antiochus IV, and he calls himself Epiphanes, which means "God made manifest." At the same time as well, some of the high priests, the elite members of the community in Jerusalem, decide that the covenant community should no longer be removed, distinct, from the other nations of the world, that it should become a Greek polis and take its place among the other empires, other cities, that Alexander the Great had founded.

Innovations began to take place in Jerusalem at that time. We have, from the Books of the Maccabees, information that circumcision was becoming outlawed. Kosher food was becoming difficult to find, if not impossible. Sabbath observance was no longer permitted. Indeed, Maccabees even tells us that, for women who circumcised their babies, the Greek soldiers would come and kill those babies and hang the corpses of the infants around their mothers' necks and force the mothers to walk the parapet at the temple.

This is a time of desperation, and it's that time of desperation that prompts an apocalypse like the Book of Daniel. Daniel even notes that the Greeks had so much come into the country and so taken over the temple that a pig—totally non-kosher, horrible in Jewish eyes—had been sacrificed on God's altar in the temple of Jerusalem. Daniel refers to this as "the abomination of desolation," or "the desolating sacrilege." This is a comment from Daniel 12. He says, "From the time that the regular burnt offering is taken away [because kosher sacrifices by appropriate priests are no longer permitted; indeed, the official high priest has been removed from office and executed] and the abomination of desolation is set up, then the end time must come."

And here is another aspect of apocalyptic literature. Daniel says, "There shall be 1,290 days. Happy are those who persevere and attain the 3,335 days." It's as if, perhaps—in fact, quite likely—another editor, another author, had come in and updated the Book of Daniel. He's gotten history right, up to the abomination of desolation, but Daniel himself does not write or even perhaps live long enough to see the end of the Seleucid outrages, the replacement of these assimilationist Jews by more traditional people, by, in fact, the Hasmonean family, who are also known as Maccabees. But that material, in fact, moves us past what the Old Testament covers and into what's known as the Old Testament Apocrypha.

Daniel ultimately has a vision of universal redemption, at least for the good people. This is Daniel 12:2 through 3: "Many of those who sleep in the dust of the earth to the end shall awake: some to everlasting life and some to shame and everlasting contempt. Those who are wise shall shine like the brightness of the dome, and those who lead many to righteousness like the stars forever and ever." We have similar imagery in Isaiah 24 through 27. Daniel does not record the ultimate vindication of the Jews, the faithful Jews in Jerusalem, but at least he expects, in part of his apocalyptic vision, that vindication, in fact, will come by God and it will have a heavenly focus.

In this sense, Daniel's apocalypse might be considered eschatological, from a Greek term meaning "concerning the end time"—when time itself stops and God actually breaks into history. We've already seen hints of that with the third Isaiah predicting new heavens and a new earth. Eschatological literature is, in fact, one of the major forms that apocalyptic takes, and we can see this type of material continuing through history into the New Testament, into medieval speculation about the end of time, and even into contemporary groups seeing signs—with nuclear war or perhaps the foundation of the state of Israel—that the end-time must be coming.

But the point of apocalyptic literature is not so much to predict the end; it is to give people at a specific time hope, indeed, that God will bring about an end. So to take some of those apocalyptic symbols from antiquity and say that they apply today—it's certainly something one can do, but I think the authors of those ancient apocalypses would have been quite surprised because that's by no means what they intended.

A problem here that I have is that, with all this apocalyptic material with its influence of, say, Persian dualistic thought and Greek speculation of heaven and hell and wisdom's concern for nature and prophecy's concern for the divine word, all of this creates for us an *eschaton* because we're at the end of this course, and there is so much more we can do, and it's so frustrating for me that we simply don't have the opportunity. We're not at the end of biblical studies; there is no way we ever could be. We have only scratched the surface. There is so much more to do.

Among the materials that we've only briefly mentioned, it needs so much more: the court histories of David; his war with Absalom. The court histories of everyone else, for that matter—what happens in the northern kingdom and the southern kingdom? What does happen, say, to Jezebel's daughter, Athalia, who becomes queen down in the south? What were the abuses and benefits of Jehu's dynasty? What about the Elisha story, Elijah's successor who creates great miracles and engages in bloodbaths? What about the promise of the prophet Micah, one who, along with the first Isaiah, notes that there will be a day coming when *lo yisa goy el goy herev*, when nation will not lift up sword against nation and study war no longer?

We miss the beauty of so many prophets because there are too many to cover, and we miss the beauty of all of the Psalms and of Lamentations, each with its own aesthetic value and its striking imagery, each with its heartfelt liturgical application.

We miss the artistry of Jonah, which is one of the best short stories ever written, from pathos to humor, from righteous Gentiles to a Hebrew prophet who doesn't want the people to whom he prophesied to repent.

We missed the post-exilic enmity between the returnees from exile and the kingdom of Samaria. When we talk in the New Testament about the Good Samaritan, it's not just the fall of the northern kingdom that causes that problem, it's ongoing political and social difficulties from the edict of Cyrus on down to the first century, and this is, in fact, recorded in Old Testament material.

We missed the development of the worship system. We know that the priests have organized sacrifice, but of what sort and why? And how do all those laws function? What are the laws of family purity? Why are they there? Did people actually keep them? What do people do with them even today?

We missed to a great extent the change in community self-definition from a tribal organization, which we've seen, but then to a kingdom. What was it like to be a member of the kingdom at the time of Jehu, the northern kingdom? How does this kingdom, this ethnic group, ultimately become a religion? Originally this is a tradition in which one could join as, say, a resident alien, a stranger within the gates, but, ultimately, close to the time probably of the composition of Esther, and certainly by the time of Daniel, this is a community into which one can convert. It's not just an ethnic group; it's also a religion. What prompts that change, and how does that change affect how people would have thought of themselves, as you move from ethnic group to religion?

We missed the canonical process. How finally were these texts put together and at what time? Is it true, as many, perhaps most, Old Testament specialists think, that Ezra really did have an inchoate Pentateuch there that Nehemiah, Chapter 8, records? Or was most of this material put together even in the Greek age? How late is it? Because we don't have any manuscripts earlier than the Dead Sea Scrolls. Could some of this material be Hellenistic—late Hellenistic, even—besides just the Book of Daniel? And who put it together and where? How do we wind up with a standardized text? As you know, the original Hebrew doesn't have any vowels. That's why we have that verse in Job that can be translated in so many different ways. Who finally standardized the texts—put in the vowels, put in the punctuation—and are they correct? How did Jews and Christians decide whether to read from the Greek or whether to read from the Hebrew?

We miss a part that I absolutely love, which are all the ancient Near Eastern parallels to this material, and not just ancient Near Eastern in terms of Sumer, but Egypt and Babylon and Persia and Greece and even some little hints of Rome coming in. We've looked at a little bit of this—you can't really understand what's going on in Genesis 1 without knowing about the Babylon cosmogony—but there is so much more.

The tale of Joseph and Mrs. Potiphar, which we've only mentioned but not gone into detail with, actually has an Egyptian match called "The Tale of the Two Brothers."

We've talked about the relationship between the Mosaic law code and the code of Hammurabi, but we haven't looked at how sacrifice functions in other Near Eastern cultures. We haven't looked at how laws of family purity—who can sleep with whom under what circumstances and at what times—function throughout the rest of the ancient Near East. At the very least this shows us that the Hebrew culture is not anomalous.

What about the Philistines? We've mentioned them, and they've always come off in quite a negative manner. I've often thought that what the Philistines need is some sort of Anti-Defamation League because they are probably not as bad as the Bible portrays them, and from their records, I suspect, if we had enough of them, their views of ancient Israel would be quite as negative as Israel's views of ancient Philistines.

Archaeological remains: the Moabite inscriptions, the Moabite stone in which King Meisha of Moab describes his victory over Israelite kings, or the black obelisk of Shalmaneser III of Assyria, which you can see today, showing, among other figures, King Jehu of the northern kingdom, actually paying him tribute. He's actually a king whose face we can see in an archaeological remain.

The ancient Near Eastern background to wisdom literature—I've mentioned it, but there is so much more there that makes Israelite wisdom richer.

In terms of the stories themselves, some of the tragedies we haven't looked at: the rape of Jacob's daughter, Dinah, and how that affects community self-definition and, indeed, ultimately plays out to describe why Levi and Simeon lose their land, a story which ultimately finds its culmination in the Book of Judith in the Old Testament Apocrypha. The development of biblical material thereby. Midrashim develop stories on Abraham's childhood, on Moses' marriage. The stories of Melchizedek, and we haven't even talked about him. Melchizedek is a wonderful figure who, in Genesis, is a king of a place called Salem, and that becomes Jerusalem, and we find out that Abraham pays tithes to him. But Melchizedek, this mysterious figure, also shows up in the Psalms. He shows up in the Dead Sea Scrolls, and, by the first century, he is a major figure of speculation in both Jewish tradition and even in the New Testament epistle to the Hebrews. We haven't even been able to touch on him.

And finally, messianic speculation. We have all those promises to David of Jerusalem the golden, of the royal grant, of Davidic heirs, promises from the prophets about a wonderful king, a mighty counselor, who will bring about divine redemption. Promises in Daniel to the son of man who, in Daniel, really does represent the corporate community but in later speculation becomes an individual figure who will somehow redeem humankind. How do all those speculations cohere and come together and give us the various messianic portraits and, indeed, job descriptions that we find in Judaism and Christianity?

Obviously, I could go on and on. I won't. I simply want to give you a sense of what else is left both in terms of developing material that we've already looked at and in looking at material we have not even had time to touch.

I can sense that this eschatological moment is approaching, and when I look back *Urzeit* to *Endzeit*, I can find at the beginning of time, or at least at the beginning of our time together, a move from myth to saga to history, from tragedy to comedy to farce. Economic and political pronouncements and beautiful literature and poetry, court intrigue and prophetic morality, heavenly miracles, and sometimes heavenly silence. Questions of theodicy. Answers that satisfy and answers that don't. Destruction and re-building, despair and hope. There is everything in this text to explore.

If I've done my job right, and I hope that I have, at least you've got some sense of how wonderful and how rich this material is. And perhaps some day we'll be able to talk about this in person. I hope you enjoy, and thanks for being with me.

Timeline

Notes: All rounded numbers are approximate. All dates are B.C.E.

1800–1700
(Middle Bronze Age) .... Patriarchs and matriarchs.

1700–1300 .... Israel in Egypt.

1300 .... Exodus from Egypt.

1280 .... Reign of Ramses II (1290–1224).

1250–1200 .... The "conquest."

1200–1000 .... Period of the Judges.

1000–922 .... Davidic monarchy; time of the (hypothetical) "J" writer.

922–722 .... The Divided Kingdom; time of the (hypothetical) "E" writer.

850 .... Elijah, Jezebel, and Ahab.

c. 750 .... Amos.

c. 740 .... Hosea.

724–722 .... Siege of Samaria.

722 .... Assyrian conquest of Israel; dispersal of the ten northern tribes.

715–687 .... Hezekiah rules the Southern Kingdom.

701.. Sennacherib's unsuccessful siege of Jerusalem.

700.. The first Isaiah.

640–609.. Josiah.

622.. Josiah finds the Book of Deuteronomy and implements the Deuteronimic Reforms.

c. 620–597...................................... Jeremiah.

612.. Nineveh (the Assyrian capital) falls to Babylon.

609.. Josiah is killed and the Deuteronomic Reform ends.

597.. First deportation to Babylon.

587.. Nebuchadnezzar destroys Jerusalem; second deportation.

587–539/8 .... Ezekiel; the second Isaiah; the priestly writers edit J and E.

539/8 .... Edict of Cyrus.

522–486.. Darius I; work on rebuilding the Temple begins.

c. 515.. Haggai, Zech. 1–8.

465–424.. Ezra (Ruth? Jonah?); editing of Proverbs.

423.. Nehemiah.

400–300.. Early versions of the Book of Esther and Dan. 1–6.

331... Battle of Issus: Alexander the Great conquers the Persian empire.

323–198.. Judah under Ptolemaic rule.

198... Battle of Paneas: Seleucids gain Palestine.

175–163.. Antiochus IV Epiphanes.

167... Maccabean revolt; Daniel 7–12.

165... Rededication of the Temple.

Glossary

Aaronides: Descendants of Aaron and a subset of the Levites who came to power during and after the Babylonian Exile.

A.D.: *Anno Domini*, in the year of our Lord (see **C.E.**).

Amarna letters: Cache of letters found in el-Amarna in Egypt, dating to the 15th century and testifying to the political turmoil in Palestine involving the Habiru.

Ammonites: Descendants of the son conceived by Lot and his older daughter (see **Moabites**).

Anthropomorphism: Describing the non-human (God, the divine presence, Wisdom) by means of human characteristics.

apocalyptic: From the Greek for "revelation" or "uncovering"; a type of literature, often ascribed to an ancient worthy, with a concern for heavenly secrets, substantial use of symbolism, and frequently an eschatological focus (e.g., Dan. 7–12).

apocrypha: From the Greek for "hidden," a term designating the books written by Jews during Hellenistic and Roman times (c. 200 B.C.E.–100 C.E.), included in the LXX, that became canonical for Catholic and Orthodox Christianity (see **Deutero-Canonical Texts**).

Apodictic Law: Absolute or unconditional law (as in the Decalogue); a characteristic of Israelite law but rare elsewhere in the ancient Near East (see also **Casuistic Law**).

Aramaic: A Semitic language closely related to Hebrew and Syriac (see **Peshitta**); parts of the books of Daniel and Ezra are in Aramaic.

Asherah: The Canaanite mother goddess, as well as the trees or groves dedicated to her.

Atrahasis: Hero of a Babylonian flood myth whose story is preserved on clay tablets dating to the 17th century B.C.E.

Baal: The Canaanite god of thunder and rain and, hence, of fertility; the popularity of his cult motivated both polemic from the prophets and the co-optation of his imagery by the psalmist. When not used as a proper name, the noun means "master" or "husband."

B.C.: Before Christ (see **B.C.E.**).

B.C.E.: Before the Common Era; a non-confessional expression for B.C.

Canaan: The geographical area between the Jordan River and the Mediterranean Sea; in Genesis, God promises it to Abraham and his descendants. The region was later called "Palestine."

canon: From the Greek for "reed, measuring stick, plumb line," the list of books considered inspired or official; the foundation documents of a community.

Casuistic Law: Standard ancient Near Eastern legal formulation that lists prohibitions and consequences for violation.

C.E.: Common Era; a non-confessional expression for A.D.

cherubim (sing. **cherub**): half-human, half-animal creatures, often depicted with wings, who guard the divine throne.

circumcision: The removal of the foreskin; the initiation ritual (for men) into the covenant community and the sign of the covenant.

codex (pl. **codices**): The book form as opposed to a scroll.

corvée: State-mandated forced labor.

Cosmology: A myth describing the ordered origin of the universe.

Cyrus Cylinder: Artifact from 528 B.C.E. reporting the Persian policy of repatriating exilic communities and promoting their cultic practices.

D (Deuteronomic) Source: One of the four (hypothetical) sources contributing to the composition of the Pentateuch; represented in the Book of Deuteronomy and likely composed in the late 7th century B.C.E. (See also **Deuteronomic History**.)

Dead Sea Scrolls: Manuscripts found in 1948 and subsequently on the shores of the Dead Sea (see **Qumran**), including numerous copies of biblical books; extremely helpful for text criticism.

decalogue: Literally "ten words"; a term designating the "ten commandments" (Exod. 20:1–17 [see also Exod. 34]; Deut. 5:6–21).

Deutero-Canonical Texts: The "second part" of the canon of the Old Testament; an alternative designation by Catholic and (Christian) Orthodox churches for the (Old Testament) Apocrypha. (See **Apocrypha**.)

Deutero-Isaiah: The "second Isaiah" who wrote to comfort the exiled community in Babylon (Isa. 40–55).

Deuteronomic History: The Book of Joshua through Second Kings; likely redacted in the early Second Temple period, the narrative displays the Deuteronomic view that righteousness is rewarded and evil, punished.

Deuteronomic Reform: See **Josianic Reform**.

Diaspora: Greek for "dispersion"; from the Babylonian Exile to the present, any place outside of Israel where Jews live.

Divination: Attempts to determine divine will or predict the future through omens, dreams, and the like.

Documentary Hypothesis: Also called the Graf-Wellhausen Hypothesis; the theory that four sources, J, E, D, and P, were combined to create the Pentateuch.

E (Elohist) Source: Hypothetical source marked by the use of "Elohim" for the Deity; likely composed in the Northern Kingdom c. 800.

Edomites: From the Hebrew for "red"; descendants of Esau who settled south of the Dead Sea; one of Israel's enemies.

El: Generic word for a god; sometimes used as a proper name, for example, the head of the Canaanite pantheon.

Elohim: Grammatically the plural of El; when used as a designation of the biblical God, it takes singular verbs.

Enumah Elish: "When on high"; the Babylonian creation myth that shares striking similarities to the Genesis cosmogony (Gen. 1).

Ephraim: A son of Joseph and one of the twelve tribes; a (poetic) name for the Northern Kingdom.

Eponymous Ancestor: Figure who gives his or her name to a group of descendants, e.g., Israel, Moab.

eschatology: Literally, "words concerning the end"; material describing the end of an age or of time and often involving the in-breaking of divine rule.

etiology: A story of origins.

Exegesis: From the Greek for "to lead out," critical interpretation of biblical material.

Form Criticism: Analytical approach to the structure of a pericope that seeks to determine genre, function, and *Sitz im Leben.*

Gemorah (Gemara): Section of the Talmud containing both legal and narrative materials; a commentary on the Mishnah that links it to the *Tanakh.*

***Gilgamesh* Epic**: Ancient Near Eastern epic, preserved on clay tablets from c. 1750 B.C.E., with parallels to the Garden of Eden and Flood stories.

Graf-Wellhausen Hypothesis: See **Documentary Hypothesis**.

Habiru: A group, comprised of various ethnicities, whose presence is attested in Canaan in texts from the second millennium B.C.E. (see **Amarna Letters**); this apparently wandering band may have some connection to the Hebrews.

Hannukah: Hebrew for "dedication"; festival celebrating the rededication of the Jerusalem Temple by the Maccabees after their defeat of Seleucid forces.

Hasidim: "Pious ones" who resisted the assimilationist mandates of Antiochus IV Epiphanes.

Hasmoneans: From Hasmon, the grandfather of Judah Maccabee; another name for the Macabees, usually used in reference to the dynasty they founded.

Hebrew: A Semitic language in which most of the Old Testament/*Tanakh* is written; a Semitic population group descended from Eber (an eponymous ancestor, Gen. 10:24); a designation for the covenant community from the patriarchal period until the Babylonian exile, perhaps derived from the Hebrew "to cross over."

Hellenism: Greek thought and culture brought to the East by the conquests of Alexander the Great.

Henotheism: Belief in one supreme god among many divine beings.

Hermeneutics: Term derived from the Greek god Hermes; biblical interpretation related to Exegesis but often with the connotation of involving the presuppositions and goals of the interpreter.

Hexateuch: The first six scrolls (Genesis–Joshua); a theory that the first part of Israel's story ends with the "conquering" of the Promised Land.

Hittites: Non-Semitic people, centered in the second millennium B.C.E. in Syria and Asia Minor.

Horeb: E's name for Sinai; location of Elijah's theophany.

Hyksos: Asiatic group who ruled Egypt from c. 1710 until being expelled by Pharaoh Ahmose c. 1570; sometimes associated with the stories of Joseph and the Exodus.

J (Yahwist [German: Jahweh]) Source: Hypothetical source beginning with Gen. 2:4b and extending perhaps as far as 2 Sam. 7; marked by anthropomorphic descriptions of God, the use of the name YHWH before the Exodus, the reiteration of the promises of descendants, land, and blessing; usually dated to the Southern Kingdom (Judah) c. 900 B.C.E.

Jehovah: *See* **YHWH**.

Josianic Reform: Sponsored by King Josiah in Judah c. 622 B.C.E. and supported by the discovery of a version of what became the Book of Deuteronomy; its major action was the centralization of the cult in Jerusalem.

Judah: Son of Jacob; tribe of Israel; Southern Kingdom (following the cessation of the northern tribes under Jereboam I).

Judea: Name for and geographical location of the Post-Exilic state; attested in Ezra and Nehemiah; its inhabitants became known as "Jews."

Kenite Hypothesis: Proposal that Yahwism stems from the Kenites—perhaps through the priest of Midian, Jethro, Moses's father-in-law.

Kenites: Midianites who affiliate with Israel in the wilderness and join the settlement of Canaan.

Ketuvim: Hebrew for "writings"; the third division of the *Tanakh*.

Levites: Priestly group descended from Levi; disenfranchised from local shrines by the Josianic Reform. Following the Babylonian exile, those who are not also Aaronides become Temple workers.

LXX: Abbreviation for the Septuagint, the Greek translation of the *Tanakh*; the designation "seventy" comes from the legend that the translation was produced by seventy scribes from Jerusalem.

Maccabees: Jewish family who led the rebellion against Antiochus IV Epiphanes in 167 B.C.E.

Marduk: Patron god of Babylon and hero of the Enumah Elish.

Masoretic Text (MT): The received form of the *Tanakh*; edited and standardized by the Masoretes, Jewish scholars who added "points" (i.e., vowels), c. 7th through 9th centuries C.E.

Megillot (sing. **Megillah**): Hebrew for "scrolls"; traditional designation for the Books of Lamentations, Ecclesiastes, Ruth, Esther, and the Song of Songs.

Merneptah Stele: Egyptian inscription erected by Pharaoh Merneptah (c. 1210) that contains the first extra-biblical reference to Israel.

messiah: Hebrew for "anointed" (Greek: Christos).

Mezuzah: Hebrew for "doorpost" and, hence, for the receptacle affixed thereon that contains passages from Deuteronomy (see Deut. 6:9).

midrash: Jewish stories that expand and/or explain biblical texts.

Mishnah: Collection of Jewish laws codified c. 200; part of the Talmud.

Moabites: Descendants of the son conceived by Lot and his younger daughter (see **Ammonites**); traditional enemies of Israel; Ruth's ethnic origin.

monotheism: Belief that there is only one God.

myth: A story of origins, often featuring divine beings, that expresses a society's self-identity.

Nazirite: An individual consecrated to God, usually for a specific period, whose practices include abstaining from wine and alcohol, avoiding corpses, and eschewing haircuts.

Nevi'im: Hebrew for "Prophets"; the second division of the *Tanakh*.

Noachide Laws: Jewish legend positing that seven laws were given to Noah to provide gentile nations with a moral code.

P (Priestly) Source: Marked by attention to law, Aaron, and genealogies, this (hypothetical) source redacted J, E, and D sometime during or soon after the Babylonian Exile.

Palestine: See **Canaan**; the name derives from the Philistines.

Pentateuch: From the Greek for "five scrolls," the first five biblical books, the Torah.

Pericope: From the Greek for "to cut around," a narrative unit that can be analyzed apart from its literary context (e.g., story, poem, saying).

Peshitta: Syriac translation of the *Tanakh* especially useful for text criticism. Syriac was a dialect of Aramaic that flourished in the early years of the common era, especially among Christians in the eastern part of the Roman empire.

Philistines: Non-Semitic, probably Mediterranean people who settled the coastal areas of Canaan in the early Iron Age (c. 1200); often enemies of Israel (Jdg.–1 Sam.) until the Davidic monarchy.

Pilgrimage Festivals: Three feasts for which it was traditional to visit the Jerusalem Temple: Passover/Feast of Unleavened bread (Hebrew, Pesach), commemorating the Exodus and the winter harvest; Weeks (Hebrew, Shavuoth; Greek, Pentecost), commemorating the giving of the Torah at Sinai fifty days later and the spring harvest; and Booths/Tabernacles (Hebrew: Sukkoth), commemorating the Exodus, the wilderness period, and the fall harvest.

Prophecy ex Eventu: Prophecy after the fact; the attribution of a text to an ancient worthy such that its description of history appears as prophecy rather than as reflection.

Prophets: The second section of the *Tanakh*.

Pseudepigrapha: Literally "false writings"; Jewish texts from Hellenistic and Roman times ascribed to ancient worthies (e.g., 4 Ezra, 2 Baruch).

Ptolemies: Heirs of Alexander the Great's general, the dynasty that governed Egypt and, from 323–198, ruled Judea.

Purim: Persian for "lots"; festival for which the etiology appears in the Book of Esther.

Qoheleth: A derivation from the Hebrew for "to assemble" (Greek: Ecclesiastes, from *Ecclesia*, "assembly"); a title for the book and the author.

Qumran: Area where the Dead Sea Scrolls were found.

Ras Shamra: Northern Syrian location where a cache of Canaanite religious texts, including Baal myths, was discovered in 1929.

redaction criticism: An analysis of concerns of the editor (redactor) of a text as determined by editorial expansion, arrangement, and comment.

Royal Grant: Covenant granted by a suzerain, sometimes as a reward for past service, and in guarantee of future aid and protection; this covenantal formulation, as opposed to the **suzerainty/vassal model**, is associated with Noah, Abraham, and especially David (2 Sam. 7; Pss. 89, 132).

Samaria: Capital of the Northern Kingdom.

Samaritans: The population of the former Northern Kingdom of Israel following the deportation by Assyria of many Israelites and the resettling in Samaria of peoples from elsewhere in the Assyrian empire.

Second Isaiah: See **Deutero-Isaiah**.

Second Temple Period: Judaism from the beginning of Persian rule to the destruction of the Temple by Rome in 70 C.E.

Seleucids: Heirs of Alexander the Great's general, the dynasty that governed Syria and, in 198, obtained Judea from the Ptolemies.

Septuagint: See **LXX**.

Shekinah: The feminine presence of the Divine.

Sheol: The home of the dead, a shadowy place below the earth; early references display no conception of punishment or reward.

***Sh'ma* (*Shema*)**: From the Hebrew for the imperative "Hear!"; the Jewish statement of faith beginning with Deut. 6:4–9.

Sinai: Today called Jebel Musa, the "Mountain of Moses"; J's expression for the traditional site of the giving of the Torah to Moses.

Sitz im Leben: German for "setting in life"; the cultural and historical context of a book or pericope.

Son of Man: A human being (Ezek., Pss.); in Dan. 7:13, the symbol of the covenant community who appears in the heavenly throne room and who is given earthly rule.

Sons of the Prophets: Bands or guilds of prophets, sometimes traveling with a prophetic leader, such as Elijah or Elisha.

Sophia: Greek for "Wisdom"; the personification of Wisdom in female form.

stele: A free-standing pillar with inscriptions.

Suzerainty/Vassal Treaty: Covenant formulation between unequal parties guaranteeing protection on the part of the suzerain and fidelity on the part of the vassal; the form of the Mosaic covenant (see **Royal Grant**).

tabernacle: The wilderness shrine that housed the Ark (see Exod. 25–40).

Talmud: A compendium of Jewish law and lore consisting of the Mishnah and the Gemorah; the Babylonian Talmud was codified c. 700 C.E. and the Palestinian, c. 400 C.E.

Tanakh (Tanak, Tanach): Acronym for "*Torah, Nevi'im, Ketuvim*"; a way of designating the canon used by the synagogue.

targum: An Aramaic translation/paraphrase of a biblical book.

tefillin (Greek: *phylacteries*): Small boxes containing scriptural passages that are worn on the left hand and forehead for worship and kept in place by straps wrapped, respectively, seven times around the left arm and around the head.

tel (*tell*): From the Hebrew/Arabic for "hill," an artificial mound created by the layers of habitation debris.

Tetragrammaton: Expression for the "four letters" (consonants) that stand for the personal name of the Deity (see **YHWH**).

text (textual) criticism (low criticism): Method for determining the original wording of a text.

theodicy: From the Greek for "justice of god," the question of why the wicked prosper and the righteous suffer.

theophany: From the Greek for "god's appearance," a manifestation of the Divine.

Torah: Hebrew for "instruction" or "law"; the first five books of the Bible.

Twelve, Book of the: The collection also known as the "Minor Prophets": Hosea, Joel, Amos, Obadiah, Jonah, Micah, Nahum, Habakkuk, Zephaniah, Haggai, Zechariah, and Malachi.

type scene: A literary convention; manipulation of the conventional elements entertainingly reveals character development; examples include the "ancestress in danger," the "woman at the well," "annunciations," and "rival wives."

Ugarit: Canaanite city in modern Syria; location of a major cache of Canaanite myths.

vulgate: From the Latin for "common," St. Jerome's translation of the Hebrew canon into Latin in 405 C.E.

Wisdom Literature: An international genre addressing questions of theodicy and nature and how to live the good life. Biblical examples are Proverbs, Ecclesiastes (Qoheleth), and Job; the Old Testament Apocrypha/Deuterocanonical collection offers Wisdom of Solomon and the Wisdom of Jesus Ben Sirach (Sirach, Ecclesiasticus).

YHWH: The personal name of God, likely meaning "he will be what he will be"; it is not pronounced in Jewish liturgical settings. English translations usually render this term as "Lord" (the four letters in each facilitate remembering the connection).

Ziggurat (Ziqqurat): Mesopotamian temple in the form of a terraced mountain or pyramid erected to serve as a symbolic bridge between heaven and earth.

Zion: Another name for Jerusalem; the Temple mount.

Bibliography

Essential Reading: The Old Testament/the *Tanakh*.

Note: The Hebrew is to be preferred in all cases. No translation can capture the riches of the original: the puns, the polyvalency, and ambiguity. Should the reader not be fluent in biblical Hebrew (which is not the same as modern Hebrew), several very good translations are available. These include, but are not limited to, the ones listed below.

Everett Fox, *The Five Books of Moses: Genesis, Exodus, Leviticus, Numbers, Deuteronomy: A New Translation with Introductions, Commentary, and Notes* (New York, Schocken Books, 1995): An attempt to preserve the sense of the Hebrew (better when read aloud). See also Fox's *Give us a King! Samuel, Saul, and David: A New Translation of Samuel I and II* (New York: Schocken Books, 1999).

The Jewish Publication Society (JPS) version: *Tanakh: A New Translation of the Holy Scripture According to the Traditional Hebrew Text*.

The King James Version (KJV) or "Authorized Version" is the one with language most familiar to English speakers. The volume was commissioned by King James I of England for use in the Anglican Church. It is, however, often difficult to understand, and its renditions of the Hebrew do not have the advantage of more recent manuscript discoveries, linguistic study, or the witness of the Dead Sea Scrolls. It also occasionally adapts the Hebrew to the Christological concerns of the New Testament.

The New American Bible (NAB): Translation produced by and for Roman Catholics.

The New International Version (NIV): Produced by and for Protestant Evangelicals.

The New Revised Standard Version (NRSV): Substantially the same as the RSV, but gender inclusive (which sometimes skews the connotations of the Hebrew). Several editions with critical notes from interfaith scholarly contributors are available, for example, Gail R. O'Day and David Petersen (gen. eds.), *The Access Bible: New Revised Standard Version, with the Apocryphal/Deuterocanonical Books* (New York: Oxford University Press, 1999).

The Revised Standard Version (RSV): An essentially literal translation but with updated language.

I encourage students to avoid modern paraphrases, such as *Good News for Modern Man* and *Today's English Version* (TEV).

Note: Studies of the Old Testament/*Tanakh* have been produced since the Hellenistic period; written by Jews, Christians, and Unitarians, as well as atheists, agnostics, and members of other traditions; they are found in synagogues and churches, seminary libraries and secular bookstores, in private homes and in museums. The bibliographic items listed after each chapter and below offer only a small representation of the academic study of the Bible. I have attempted to avoid works requiring knowledge of ancient languages, works requiring a nearby divinity school or seminary library (including articles in professional journals), and works with a relatively narrow denominational or confessional focus. I have attempted to include works that present a variety of opinions and approaches and to list primarily recent studies (in almost all cases, the sources listed below have their own bibliographical references to earlier scholarship). I also list several encyclopedias and dictionaries.

Resources:

Achtemeier, Paul J. (gen. ed.), *The HarperCollins Bible Dictionary* (San Francisco: Harper San Francisco, 1996): Dictionary produced in cooperation with the Society of Biblical Literature (a major professional society of biblical scholars).

Aharoni, Yohanan, and Michael Avi-Yonah, *The Macmillan Bible Atlas* (New York: Macmillan, 1977).

Brown, Raymond, Joseph A. Fitzmyer, and Roland E. Murphy (eds.), *The New Jerome Biblical Commentary* (Englewood Cliffs, NJ: Prentice Hall, 1999).

Coogan, Michael D. (ed.), *The Oxford History of the Biblical World* (New York: Oxford University Press, 1998): Articles by leading scholars on the historical and cultural periods in which biblical events took shape.

Farmer, William R. (ed.), *The International Bible Commentary: A Catholic and Ecumenical Commentary for the Twenty-First Century* (Collegeville, MN: Liturgical Press, 1998).

Freedman, D. N., et al., *The Anchor Bible Dictionary*, six vols. (New York: Doubleday, 1992; available on CD-ROM): Signed articles by leading scholars; inclusive bibliographies; a major resource for scholar and lay reader alike.

Hayes, John H. (gen. ed.), *Dictionary of Biblical Interpretation*, 2 vols. (Nashville: Abingdon, 1999): Major scholars and methods.

Knight, Douglas A., and Gene M. Tucker (eds.), *The Hebrew Bible and Its Modern Interpreters* (Philadelphia: Fortress Press, 1985): Excellent collection of essays on the major issues and theories in academic biblical study.

Matthews, Victor H., and Don C. Benjamin, *Old Testament Parallels: Laws and Stories from the Ancient Near East* (New York: Paulist Press, 1991).

Metzger, Bruce M., and Michael D. Coogan (eds.), *The Oxford Companion to the Bible* (New York: Oxford University Press, 1993): Short articles on major figures, events, locations, and other topics in dictionary format.

Newsom, Carol A., and Sharon H. Ringe (eds.), *The Women's Bible Commentary* (Louisville: Westminster/John Knox, 1992): Essays by women academics that combine more traditional approaches with attention to gender roles, women's history, and hermeneutical implications.

Shanks, Herschel (ed.), *Bible Review* (as well its sister publication, *Biblical Archaeology Review*): An often original, sometimes irreverent magazine written by scholars but designed for the general public; the illustrations are superb.

Series (commentaries on individual books, as well as major subject areas):

Anchor Bible (New York: Doubleday).

Anchor Bible Reference Library (New York: Doubleday).

Berit Olam (Collegeville, MN: Liturgical Press).

Feminist Companions, edited by Athalya Brenner (Sheffield: University Press).

Hermeneia (Philadelphia: Fortress Press).

New Interpreter's Bible (Nashville: Abingdon).

The Old Testament Library (Louisville: Westminster/John Knox).

Introductions (a few among many):

Anderson, Bernard, *Understanding the Old Testament*, 4th ed. (Englewood Cliffs: Prentice Hall, 1986).

Flanders, Henry Jackson, Jr., Robert Wilson Crapps, and David Anthony Smith, *People of the Covenant: An Introduction to the Hebrew Bible*, 4th ed. (New York: Oxford University Press, 1996).

Frick, Frank S., *A Journey through the Hebrew Scriptures* (Fort Worth: Harcourt Brace College Publishers, 1995).

Gottwald, Norman K., *The Hebrew Bible: A Socio-Literary Introduction* (Philadelphia: Fortress Press, 1985).

Levenson, Jon D., *Sinai and Zion: An Entry into the Jewish Bible* (Minneapolis: Winston, 1985).

Individual Studies:

Ackerman, Susan, *Warrior, Dancer, Seductress, Queen: Women in Judges and Biblical Israel*, Anchor Bible Reference Library (New York: Doubleday, 1998).

Alter, Robert, *The Art of Biblical Narrative* (New York: Basic Books, 1981): A prize-winning literary critical study that popularized the study of type scenes, traced the impact of themes and even key words throughout different books, and explored the importance of the juxtaposition of stories for mutual interpretation.

Anderson, Gary, Michael Stone, and Johannes Tromp (eds.), *Literature on Adam and Eve: Collected Essays*, Studies in Veteris Testamenti Pseudepigrapa (Leiden and Boston: E. J. Brill, 2000).

Bailey, Lloyd R., *Noah: The Person and the Story in History and Tradition* (Columbia, SC: University of South Carolina Press, 1989).

Bal, Mieke, *Death and Dissymmetry: The Politics of Coherence in the Book of Judges* (Chicago: University of Chicago Press, 1988).

Ballentine, Samuel E., *Prayer in the Hebrew Bible* (Philadelphia: Fortress, 1993).

———, *The Torah's Vision of Worship* (Minneapolis: Fortress, 1999).

435

Barr, James, *The Garden of Eden and the Hope of Immortality* (Philadelphia: Fortress, 1993).

Blenkinsopp, Joseph, *The Pentateuch: An Introduction to the First Five Books of the Bible*, Anchor Bible Reference Library (New York: Doubleday, 1992): A good overview of approaches, with a helpful description of the Documentary Hypothesis.

Brueggemann, Walter, *Theology of the Old Testament: Testimony, Dispute, Advocacy* (Minneapolis: Fortress Press, 1997).

Collins, John J., *The Apocalyptic Imagination: An Introduction to Jewish Apocalyptic Literature*, 2nd ed. (Grand Rapids, MI: William B. Eerdmans, 1998).

Craig, Kenneth M., *The Poetics of Jonah: Art in the Service of Ideology*, 2nd ed. (Macon, GA: Mercer University Press, 1999).

Delaney, Carol Lowery, *Abraham on Trial: The Social Legacy of Biblical Myth* (Princeton, NJ: Princeton University Press, 1998).

Dever, William G., *Recent Archaeological Discoveries and Biblical Research* (Seattle: University of Washington Press, 1990).

Douglas, Mary, *Purity and Danger: An Analysis of Concepts of Pollution and Taboo* (London/Boston: Ark Paperbacks, 1966, 1984).

Dundes, Alan (ed.), *The Flood Myth* (Berkeley: University of California Press, 1988).

———, *Holy Writ as Oral Lit: The Bible as Folklore* (Lanham, MD: Rowan and Littlefield, 1999).

Eilberg-Schwartz, Howard, *The Savage in Judaism: An Anthropology of Israelite Religion and Judaism* (Bloomington: Indiana University Press,

1990): Prize-winning, controversial study of ritual practice and the use of metaphor.

Exum, J. Cheryl, *Fragmented Women: Feminist Subversions of Biblical Narratives* (Sheffield: JSOT Press, 1993).

Falk, Marcia, *Love Lyrics from the Bible, The Song of Sons: A New Translation and Interpretation* (San Francisco: HarperCollins, 1990): Poet and linguist happily meet.

Fewell, Danna Nolan, *Circle of Sovereignty: A Story of Stories in Daniel 1–6* (Sheffield: Almond Press, 1988).

Fox, Michael, *Character and Ideology in the Book of Esther* (Columbia, SC: University of South Carolina Press, 1991).

Friedman, Richard Elliott, *Who Wrote the Bible?* (Englewood Cliffs: Prentice-Hall, 1987). Idiosyncratic but extremely engaging study.

Harrelson, Walter, *The Ten Commandments and Human Rights* (Philadelphia: Fortress Press, 1981): A study by a leading Old Testament scholar of how the Bible has been, and can be, used for purposes of social justice.

Humphries, W. Lee, *Joseph and his Family: A Literary Study* (Columbia, SC: University of South Carolina Press, 1988).

Jobling, David, *First Samuel* (Collegeville, MN: Liturgical Press, 1998).

Kirsch, Jonathan, *Moses: A Life* (New York: Bantam Books, 1998).

Kugel, James L., *In Potiphar's House: The Interpretive Life of Biblical Texts* (San Francisco: HarperCollins, 1990).

———, *Traditions of the Bible: A Guide to the Bible as It Was at the Start of the Common Era* (Cambridge, MA: Harvard University Press, 1998).

Kvam, Kristen, Linda S. Schearing, and Valarie H. Ziegler, *Eve and Adam: Jewish, Christian and Muslim Readings on Genesis and Gender* (Bloomington: Indiana University Press, 1999).

Larsson, Göran, *Bound for Freedom: The Book of Exodus in Jewish and Christian Traditions* (Peabody, MA: Hendrikson, 1999).

Lemche, Niels Peter, *Early Israel: Anthropological and Historical Studies on the Israelite Society before the Monarchy* (Leiden: E.J. Brill, 1985).

Levenson, Jon D., *Death and Resurrection of the Beloved Son: The Transformation of Child Sacrifice in Judaism and Christianity* (New Haven: Yale University Press, 1993).

Matthews, Victor H., Bernard Levinson, and Tikva Frymer-Kensky, *Gender and Law in the Hebrew Bible and the Ancient Near East* (Sheffield: Sheffield Academic Press, 1998).

Mazar, Amihai, *Archaeology of the Land of the Bible: 10,000–586 B.C.E.* (New York: Bantam Doubleday Dell, 1990).

McKenzie, Stephen L., *King David: A Biography* (Oxford and New York: Oxford University Press, 2000).

Meyers, Carol, *Discovering Eve: Ancient Israelite Women in Context* (New York: Oxford University Press, 1988): Prize-winning, innovative study combining sociology, archaeology, and linguistics.

Murphy, Roland E., *The Tree of Life: An Exploration of Biblical Wisdom Literature* (New York: Doubleday, 1990).

Neusner, Jacob, William Scott Green, and Ernest S. Frerichs (eds.), *Judaisms and Their Messiahs at the Turn of the Christian Era* (Cambridge/New York: Cambridge University Press, 1987).

Niditch, Susan, *Ancient Israelite Religion* (New York: Oxford University Press, 1997).

———, *Folklore and the Hebrew Bible* (Philadelphia: Fortress Press, 1993).

———, *War in the Hebrew Bible: A Study in the Ethics of Violence* (New York: Oxford University Press, 1997).

Olyan, Saul, *Rites and Rank: Hierarchy in Biblical Representations of Cult* (Princeton, NJ: Princeton University Press, 2000.

Perdue, Leo, and Clark Gilpin (eds.), *The Voice from the Whirlwind: Interpreting the Book of Job* (Nashville: Abingdon, 1992): Studies addressing historical, literary, and theological issues edited by a professor of biblical studies and a theologian.

Rendtorff, Rolf, *The Covenant Formula: An Exegetical and Theological Investigation*, Margaret Kohl, trans. (Edinburgh: T&T Clark, 1998).

Rogerson, John, and Philip Davies, *The Old Testament World* (Englewood Cliffs, NJ: Prentice-Hall, 1989).

Sawyer, John F. A. (ed.), *Reading Leviticus: A Conversation with Mary Douglas* (Sheffield: Sheffield Academic Press, 1996).

Smith, Mark, *The Early History of God: Yahweh and Other Deities in Ancient Israel* (San Francisco: Harper, 1990).

Spiegel, Shalom, *The Last Trial*, Judah Golden, trans. (New York: Schocken, 1969): Fascinating study of the history of the interpretation of the *Akedah* (Gen. 22).

Steussy, Marti J., *David: Biblical Portraits of Power* (Columbia, SC: University of South Carolina Press, 1999).

Trible, Phyllis, *Texts of Terror: Literary-Feminist Readings of Biblical Narratives* (Philadelphia: Fortress Press, 1984).

Wills, Lawrence, *The Jew in the Court of the Foreign King: Ancient Jewish Court Legends* (Minneapolis, MN: Fortress Press, 1990).

Wright, J. Edward, *The Early History of Heaven* (New York: Oxford University Press, 2000).

Yee, Gail (ed.), *Judges and Method: New Approaches in Biblical Studies* (Minneapolis: Fortress Press, 1995).